A HIEROGLYPHIC VOCABULARY TO THE BOOK OF THE DEAD

E. A. WALLIS BUDGE

DOVER PUBLICATIONS, INC., *New York*

Published in Canada by General Publishing Company, Ltd., 30 Lesmill Road, Don Mills, Toronto, Ontario.

Published in the United Kingdom by Constable and Company, Ltd., 3 The Lanchesters, 162–164 Fulham Palace Road, London W6 9ER.

This Dover edition, first published in 1991, is an unabridged republication of the work originally published in 1911 by Kegan Paul, Trench, Trübner & Co. Ltd., London, under the title *A Hieroglyphic Vocabulary to the Theban Recension of the Book of the Dead with an Index to All the English Equivalents of the Egyptian Words* (Vol. XXXI in the series *Books on Egypt and Chaldæa*). The Kegan Paul edition was itself the revised and expanded second edition of a work that had first appeared in 1897. A number of obvious typographical errors have been tacitly corrected.

Manufactured in the United States of America
Dover Publications, Inc., 31 East 2nd Street, Mineola, N.Y. 11501

Library of Congress Cataloging-in-Publication Data

Budge, E. A. Wallis (Ernest Alfred Wallis), Sir, 1857–1934.
[Hieroglyphic vocabulary to the Theban recension of the Book of the dead with an index to all the English equivalents of the Egyptian words]
A hieroglyphic vocabulary to the Book of the dead / E. A. Wallis Budge.
p. cm.
Reprint. Originally published: A hieroglyphic vocabulary to the Theban recension of the Book of the dead with an index to all the English equivalents of the Egyptian words. New ed., rev. and enl. London : K. Paul, Trench, Trübner, 1911.
Includes index.
ISBN 0-486-26724-5
1. Book of the dead—Concordances. I. Book of the dead. II. Title.
PJ1557.Z8 1991
299′.31—dc20 90-28983
CIP

PREFACE TO THE SECOND EDITION.

THE following pages contain a Hieroglyphic Vocabulary to all the texts of the Chapters of the Theban Recension of the Book of the Dead which is printed in this Series (Vols. XXVIII—XXX),* and also to most of the supplementary Chapters of the Saïte and Graeco-Roman period which are appended thereto. The whole work has been comprehensively revised, and in the case of characters to which the values given in 1897, when the first edition was compiled, are now obsolete, special care has been taken to place them in the order in which they have since been proved to belong. The arrangement of the words and their various forms is usually alphabetical, and it is hoped that the few exceptions to this rule will cause the reader no difficulty. A very considerable number of words and forms have been added to this edition, and it was necessary, for reasons of space, to omit all references.

*Dover's edition of *The Egyptian Book of the Dead* is 0-486-21866-X.

A new feature of this edition of the Vocabulary is the Index to all the English equivalents of Egyptian words printed herein. This was prepared in answer to the requests of many who had used the first edition of the Vocabulary.

For the care which Mr. Adolf Holzhausen has given to the printing of this work my sincere thanks are due.

E. A. WALLIS BUDGE

BRITISH MUSEUM,
February 4th, 1911.

VOCABULARY.

 A.

aatā, ***atitā***	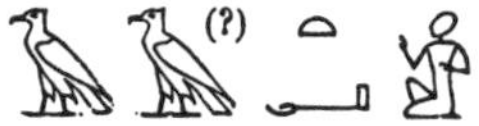	ministrant, celebrant, a kind of priest.
aȧr		to bind, tie together, to put under restraint, to coerce, to persecute, to oppress.
au		to make a gift or offering, to present.
ait	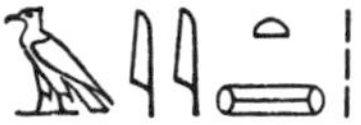	bread-cakes, loaves of any shape offered for funerary oblations.
aut	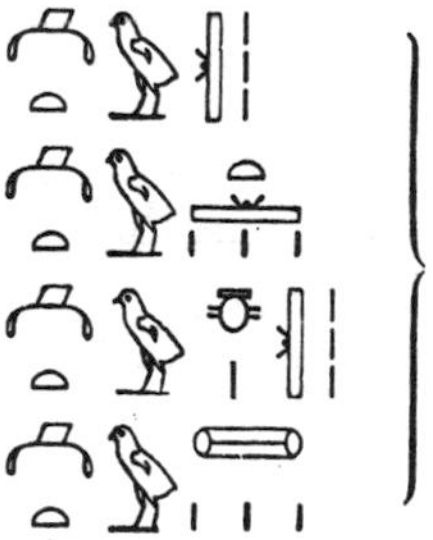	offerings of meat and drink, sacrifices, bread-cakes, etc.
aut		light, radiance.
au		to be long, length, the opposite of  *usekh* breadth,

to extend, be extended, *e. g.* extended (*i. e.*, lavish) hand, length of the back, extended of years, long of strides; compare also .

au — to expand, to dilate (of the heart), hence , joy, gladness, pleasure, delight.

au — fully, exceedingly, to the utmost, to the full extent.

Au-ā — the "god of the extended arm".

au — children, youths, the young, unmarried men, synonym of *sheriu* children.

ausek — stick, staff, sceptre, symbol of high position and dignity.

abit — an insect which brought the deceased into the Hall of

Osiris, identified with the praying mantis. A variant gives *bai* .

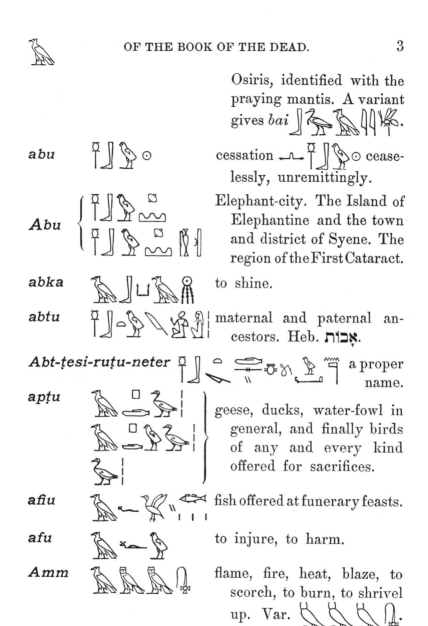

abu  cessation  ceaselessly, unremittingly.

Abu  Elephant-city. The Island of Elephantine and the town and district of Syene. The region of the First Cataract.

abka  to shine.

abtu  maternal and paternal ancestors. Heb. אֲבוֹת.

Abt-ṭesi-ruṭu-neter 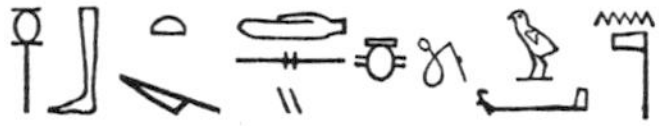 a proper name.

apṭu  geese, ducks, water-fowl in general, and finally birds of any and every kind offered for sacrifices.

afiu  fish offered at funerary feasts.

afu  to injure, to harm.

Amm flame, fire, heat, blaze, to scorch, to burn, to shrivel up. Var. .

Am[m]u the Fire City of the Other World.

amm 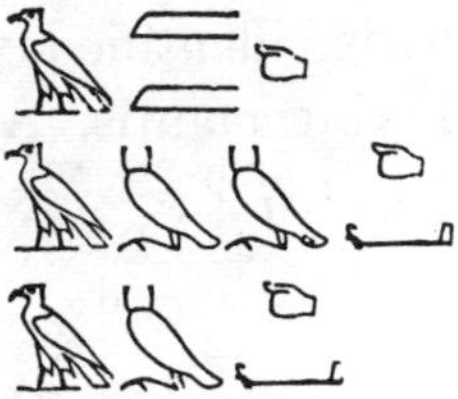 to grasp with the hand, to hold in the fist, to seize, take by violence, snatch at, fist, grasp.

amu 

ames  the name of a sceptre, or staff, associated with Àmsu, or Menu, the god of generation and fertility.

Ani  a scribe and treasurer of holy offerings.

Arthikasathika  a proper name.

ah  to be troubled, injured, suffering.

aha  evil, injury, harm.

Ahat  an ancient goddess, who was identified with Hathor, and appeared in the form of a cow or a woman.

Ahit 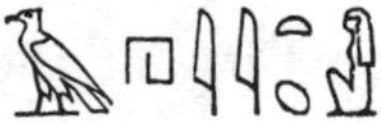 a goddess who supplied the dead with food.

Aḥu		a god who was connected with offerings.
Aḥui (?)		the name of a canal (?).
aḥu	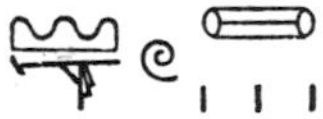	food, bread-cakes, offerings of all kinds.
aḥet		fields, estates, farm, cultivated land.
akh		to bloom, to blossom, flower, bloom.
akhakh		flowers of the sky, *i. e.*, stars.
akhi		reed, water-plant, rushes, marsh flowers.
akhet		the first season of the Egyptian Year.
akhaā		to enter, to penetrate.
akhab		to give to drink.
Akhabiu		a class of divine beings, or gods, who were associated with the Akeru-gods .
akhetu		*i. e.*, , things, objects, food, bread-cakes.
Aseb		the name of a Fire-god in the Other World.

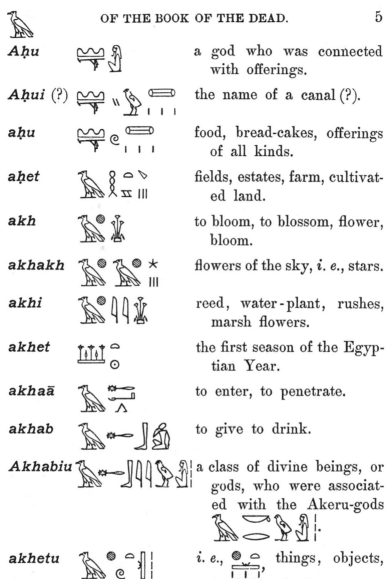

asbiu  sparks of fire, flames, fiery spirits.

Aseb-ḥer-per-em-khetkhet  a god with a face of fire which advanced and retreated alternately.

askh  to cut a crop, to reap.

asta 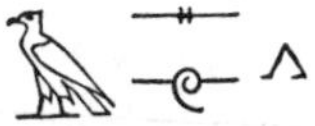 to hasten, to hurry, be swift or rapid.

asta ȧb 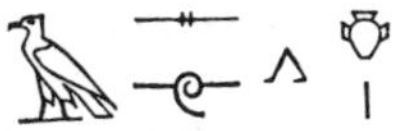 to hurry the heart, to arrive at a hasty judgment.

astu  water in motion, a stream or canal.

Ashu 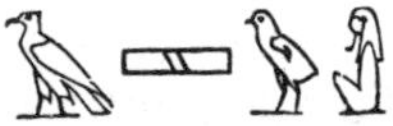 name of a god.

Ashbu 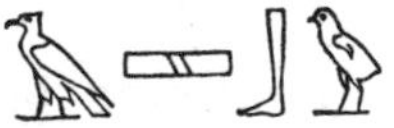 name of the warder of the 5th Ārit.

Asher  name of a city, or temple district, or god.

ashert  roasted flesh of animals, or birds, grilled meat, steaks, joints, etc.

akit  a chamber, or hut, or small house.

Aker  a very ancient name of the Earth-god.

Akeru  The two gods who guarded the western and eastern ends of the tunnel through the earth which the Sun-god passed through nightly. They were the ancestors of the Akhabiu gods, 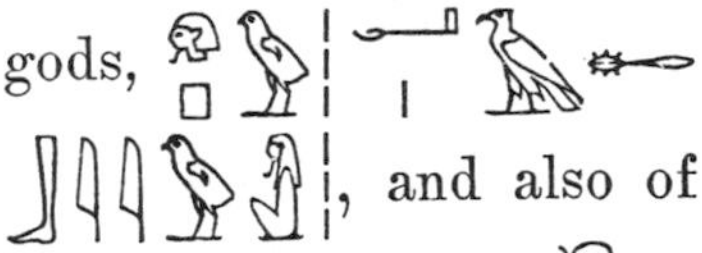, and also of Rā 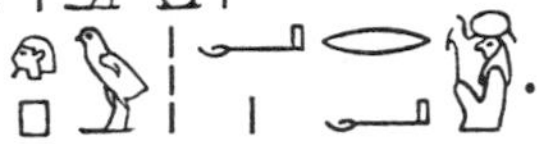.

Akeriu  a group of earth-gods who appeared in the form of serpents.

aqa  *i. e.,*  dirt, filth, what is filthy.

Aqeṭqeṭ  one of a group of seven gods or spirits associated with Osiris.

Aḳab
Aḳb  the great celestial ocean and the god who presided over it, water, flood, celestial Nile.

Akḳbȧ	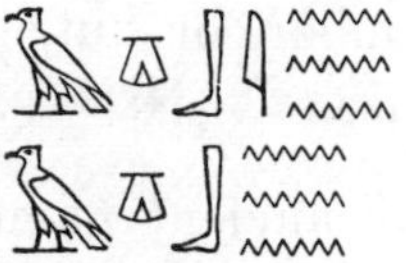	the great celestial ocean and the god who presided over it, water, flood, celestial Nile.
at		injury, assault, attack.
atu		
at		a support of a god, a perch for a bird, etc. The word is also written with a wrong determinative .
at		the vertebrae, back, the middle of something.
at	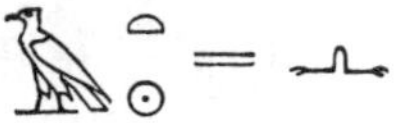	not
at		moment, a period of time, season.
Ati		The ninth nome of Lower Egypt; its capital was Per-Ȧsȧr (Busiris).
atiu		evil beings, fiends, enemies.
atutu		a kind of wood.
atep		a load, a burden, something carried on the head, to carry, to bear, to support.

atef — name of one of the principal crowns of Osiris.

atefu — name of one of the principal crowns of Osiris.

Atef-ur — a proper name.

aṭ — to be wounded, injured.

atȧu — a ceremonial garment with magical properties.

aṭu — crocodile, or water lizard. Plur.

Ȧtes ḥer-mer (?) — a proper name.

aṭet — the vertebrae, back. Also written

Ȧ.

A — The god Thoth. The form is common in the later period.

ȧ — Personal pronoun. I, me, my.

ȧ — O! Hail!

ȧ — praise, acclamation.

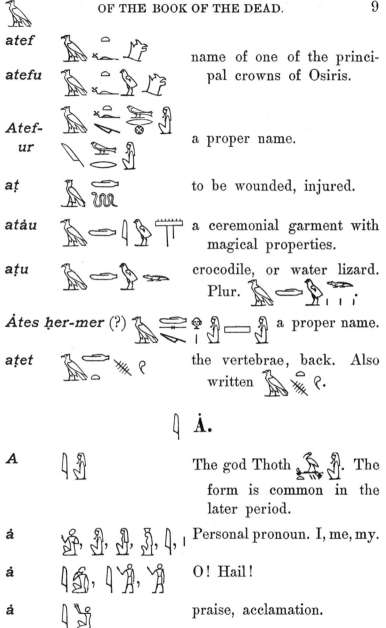

àa  boat.

àa  standard, perch for a sacred bird.

àaa  plants, flowers, growing crops.

àaau  he of the two feathers, plumed one.

àaat  standard, perch for a sacred bird.

àau
àaut  aged one, old age, old man, senior; plur. .

àait  aged gods, divine old men.

àau  to praise, to applaud, to ascribe glory to, to acclaim, to rejoice.

àaiu  praise, praises, acclamations, rejoicings, glorifyings.

ȧaiu 
ȧaut  praise, praises, acclamations, rejoicings, glorifyings.

ȧait 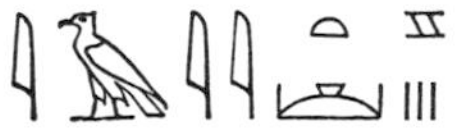 tombs, or funerary domains under the charge of priests, sepulchres.

ȧaiti  the gods who preside over the Ȧats; see Chapter CL.

ȧamḥet  see 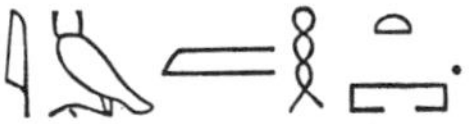.

Ȧaru   a region in the Other World which formed a portion of the abode of the blessed.

ȧarret  eyes (?).

ȧarret 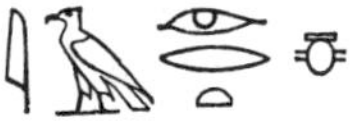 milk.

ȧaret  vine, vineyard.

Ȧaheṭ   a god whose functions are undefined.

ȧakhu  light, splendour, radiance, brilliance, rays, the god of light or splendour.

Ȧakha-bit  the name of a goddess.

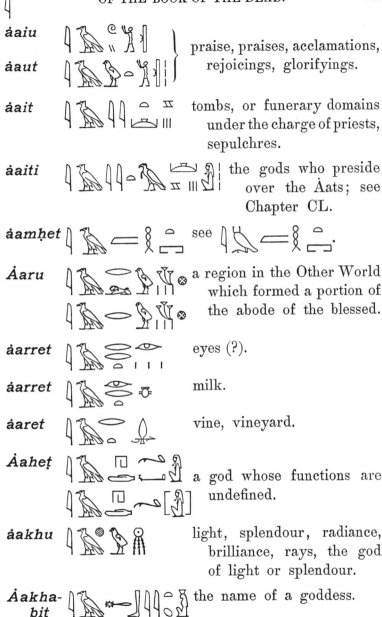

Ȧaku the name of a group of gods or of deified human beings.

ȧakebi, ***ȧakebit*** women who wail and pluck out their hair, professional wailing women or mourners.

ȧakebu groans, lamentations, mourning, wailings. Another form is .

ȧaqet flowers, grass, herbs.

Ȧaqeṭqeṭ "He who revolves", name of a god.

ȧat dignity, rank, grade of honour, position, preferment. Plur. .

ȧaat things possessing a bad or strong smell.

ȧat an article of dress, part of a girdle (?).

ȧat the vertebrae, back.

ȧat to split, to cleave asunder, to break.

ȧat standard, perch, pedestal.

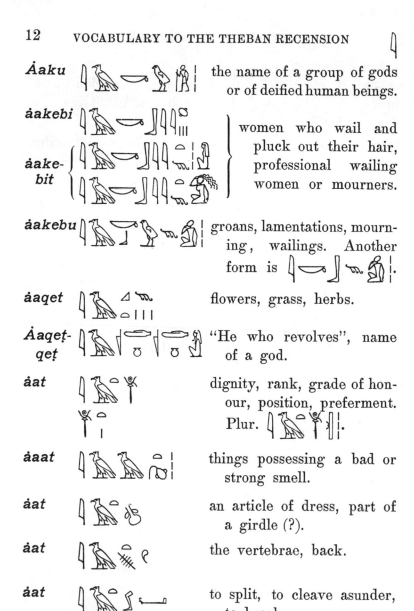

Ȧat ent Ȧp-uat  "Standard of Ȧp-uat", name of the lower deck of the magical boat.

ȧat  domain of a god, tomb of a god, funerary district; plur. . The kingdom of Osiris contained 14 Ȧats :—

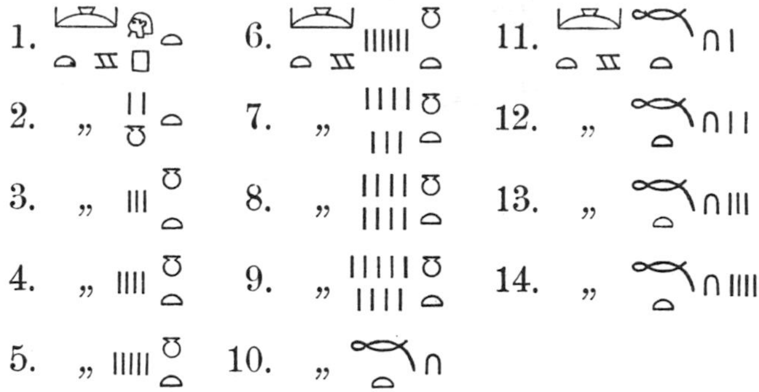

ȧat Ȧmentet  the funerary domain of the West (Ȧmentet).

ȧat khu  the Ȧat of blessed souls.

ȧat en khet 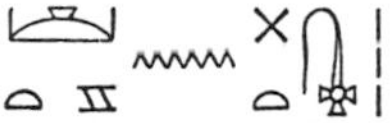 the Ȧat of fire.

ȧati  The two Ȧats, *i. e.*, the Ȧat of Horus and the Ȧat of Set, or the two Ȧats of Osiris.

Ȧat-urt  the god of the Great Ȧat.

Ȧat ent Kher-āḥa The Ȧat of Kher-āḥa, *i. e.*, the ancient Egyptian city which stood near Old Cairo (Fusṭâṭ).

ȧatu praise, praisings, adorations.

ȧati, ***ȧatu*** slaughter houses, chambers of tortures; places where the enemies of Rā and Osiris were punished.

ȧaṭ child, male or female, youth.

ȧaṭeb flood, storm, rush of water.

ȧaṭet net for snaring birds or fish, the net in which the Enemy snared souls.

ȧaṭet rain-storm, dew, moisture.

ȧaṭti oppression, injury, oppressor.

ȧā , , to wash, to cleanse, purify, to wash the heart, *i. e.*, to cleanse the heart by taking vengeance.

ȧāu  a washing, a cleansing.

ȧā 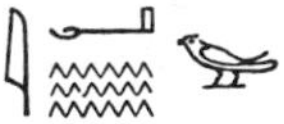 a sinful act.  to sin against the god.

ȧāāu  apes, incarnations of the spirits that praised the rising sun.

ȧāb  to come towards, to meet, to present an offering, one opposite, an offering.

ȧāb, **ȧābet** 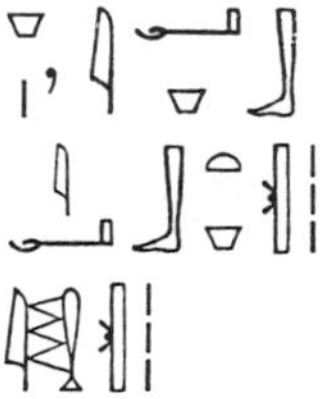 an offering, oblation, ceremonial gift, a vessel of offerings.

ȧāb  an offering of a libation.

ȧānu  praise, adoration, words of glorification ; plur.  .

ȧār, **ȧārt**, **ȧārtu** 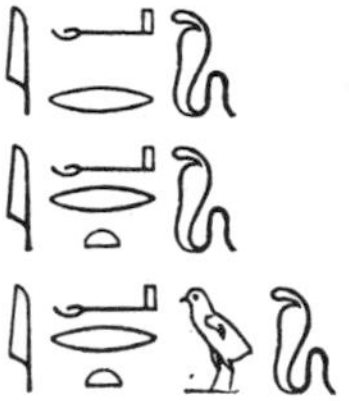 serpent, snake, cobra. The Greek form is οὐραίος, uraeus.

ȧārāt 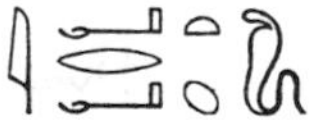 snake goddess ; plur.  .

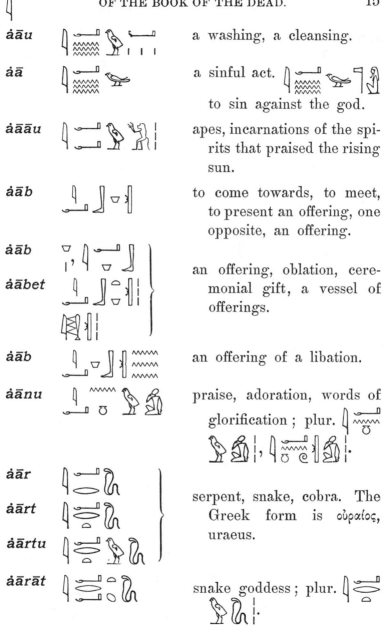

ȧārti — the Two Snake-goddesses, *i. e.*, Isis and Nephthys; the Four Snake-goddesses.

ȧārtu ānkhu — the "living uraei" which lived on the cornice of the shrine of Osiris.

ȧāḥ, ***ȧāḥu*** — the moon.

ȧāḥu — the Moon-god, in later times called Khensu.

ȧātu ent khert — name of a part of the magical boat (Chap. XCIX).

ȧu — praises, rejoicings.

ȧu — old man.

ȧu — used in later times for *er* from, to, into, for, at, in, etc.

ȧu — to be, to exist; I am, thou art, he is, we are, she is; as an auxiliary , etc., and see *passim.*

ȧu — to be shipwrecked,

the shipwrecked man.

ȧu — offence, sin, crime, iniquity, wickedness, defect, breach of the Law.

ȧui
ȧuit
ȧut — evil, harm, injury, defects, deceit, to commit wickedness, or sin.

ȧu — to speak, cry out, utter words.

ȧu — to conceive a child, be pregnant.

ȧua — ox (of the Earth-god Seb).

ȧuai — roof of a building.

ȧuȧu — dogs, jackals.

Ȧuu-ba — a proper name.

ȧuāu  the living body.

ȧuā / **ȧuāu**  flesh and bone, joint of meat, haunch of an animal, carcase.

ȧuā / **ȧuāā** / **ȧuāu** 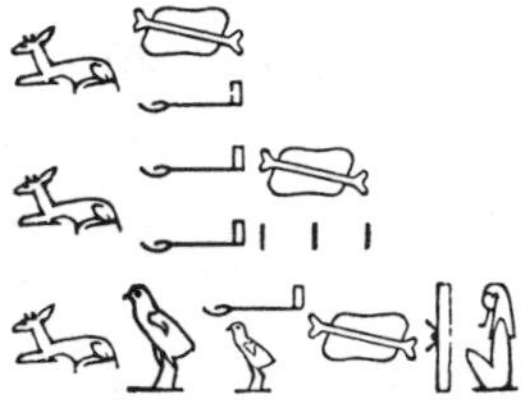 to be flesh and bone of some one, to be the heir, inheritance, the divine Heir.

ȧuāu  heir.

ȧuāt  heirship, inheritance.

ȧuāu  heirs, kinsfolk, people of one's own flesh and blood.

ȧuiu  those who lacerate or cut.

åuur  to conceive, conception, pregnant.

åuurt  a pregnant goddess.

 heir.

åuf  flesh, limbs, members.

Åuf-āankh  a proper name.

åumes  false or deceitful speech, exaggeration in speech, lies.

åun  colour, skin, hair.

åuna  certainly, assuredly.

åunt  a garment, clothed, dressed.

Åuråu-åaqer-sa-ånqrebathi 
 a proper name.

åuhet  to utter words.

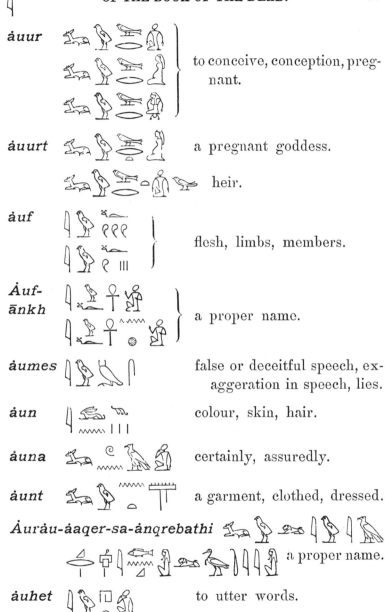

àuheṭ  name of a god or divine being.

àuḥ  to be submerged, sprinkled.  steeped in something.

àukhemu  a group of gods, stars.

àukhemu urṭu  stars which never rest.

àukhemu seku  circumpolar stars which never set.

àukhemu Pen-ḥeseb (?) 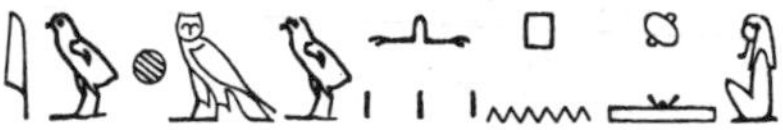 stars of the god Pen-ḥeseb.

àukhekh  night, evening, darkness.

àusu  scales, balance.

Àuḳer

Àuḳert  the name of the Other World of Heliopolis (Ànnu).

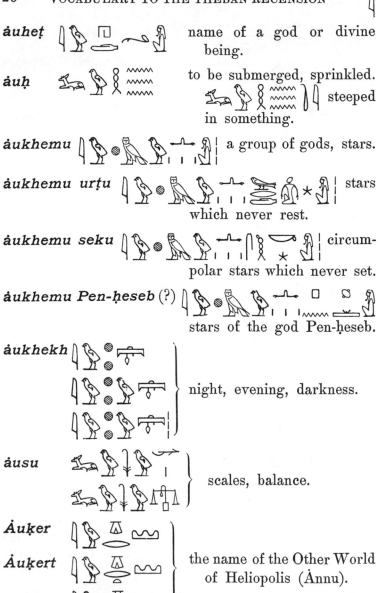

Àuḳeru  the gods of the Heliopolitan Other World.

Àuḳert  the goddess of Àuḳert.

Àuḳert-khentet-àst-s  name of one of the seven sacred cows.

àuṭ  to travel.

àu-t  thou art.

àu-ten 
àu-then  ye are.

àuti  fiends, enemies, foes.

àb  desire, wish.

àb  pegs, stakes.

àb  thirst.

àb  thirsty man.

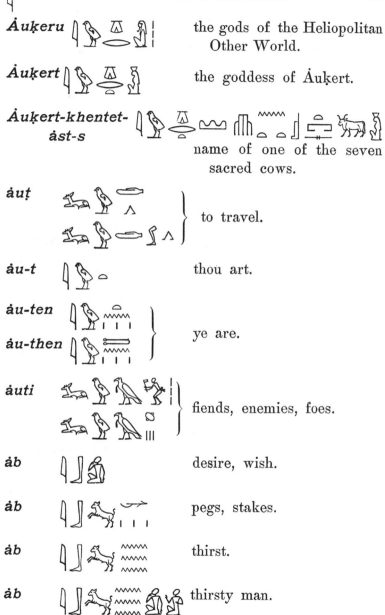

Ȧb = Abtu Elephantine.

ȧb = name of a fish.

ȧb left side.

ȧb cessation.

ȧb the physical heart, will, wish, love, desire; plur.

to judge hastily.

to do as one pleases.

"great of heart", bold, brave, arrogant, boastful.

of joyful heart.

to eat the heart, *i. e.*, to lose the temper, be sorry.

valiant.

be brave.

to fill the heart, to satisfy, be satisfied.

within.

	 with 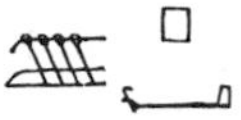	heart's desire.
	 with 	prompting of the heart, desire.
	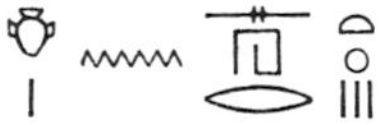	the amulet of the carnelian heart.
ȧba		heart-soul.
ȧbu		drink.
ȧbu		the desired one.
Ȧbu-ur		a proper name.
ȧbu	, or 	to stop, to cease.
		cessation.
ȧbui		left side.
ȧbi		panther or leopard skin.
ȧbit		the praying mantis.
ȧber		a kind of unguent.
ȧbḥu		tooth. Plur.  

àbekh to penetrate, to make a way through.

àbsit hull of a boat.

Àb-ka, ***Abt-ka*** a proper name.

àbku grief, to grieve, to weep.

àbt middle hall, or chamber, of a house.

àbt coffer.

àbt thirst.

àbt left hand side, the east.

àbt, ***àbti*** east wind.

àbt, ***àbti*** eastern country, or region. eastern sky, east of heaven;

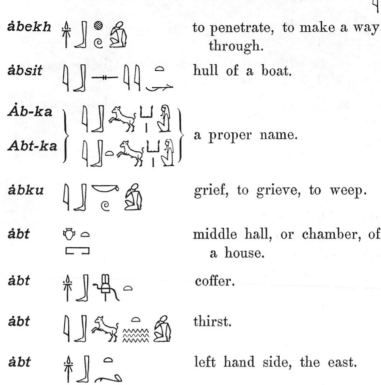

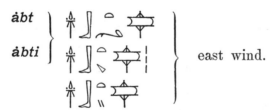

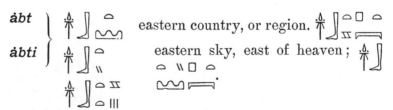

àbti 

àbtet (**àbti**) 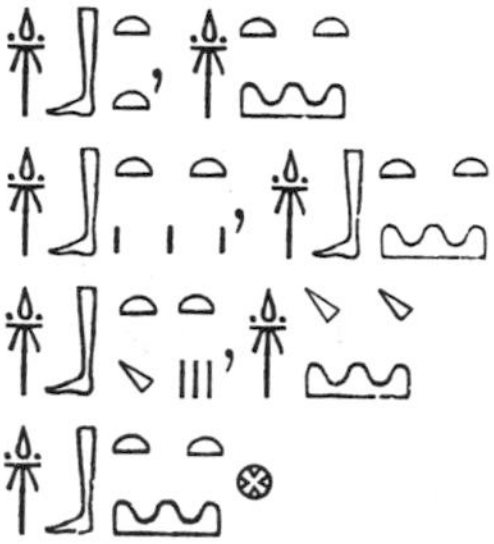 east, eastern country, or region.

àbtet  goddess of the east.

àbtiu  gods of the east, eastern deities.

àbt  net.

àbtu  slaughter, slaughterings.

Àbṭ 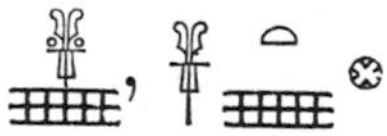 the nome of Abydos.

Àbt 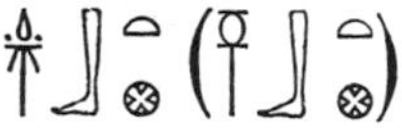 the city of Abydos.

Àbṭu  the city of Abydos.

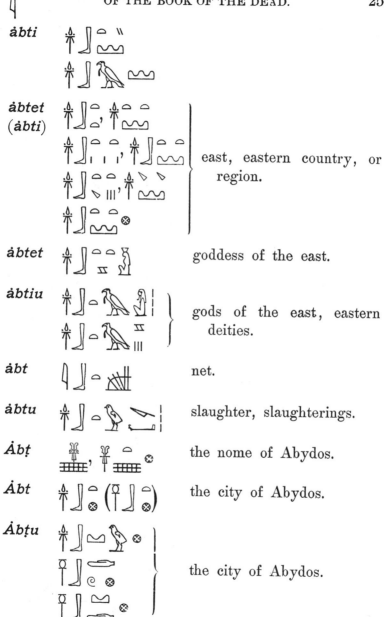

Àbṭu 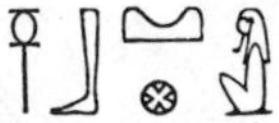 the city god of Abydos.

àbeṭ 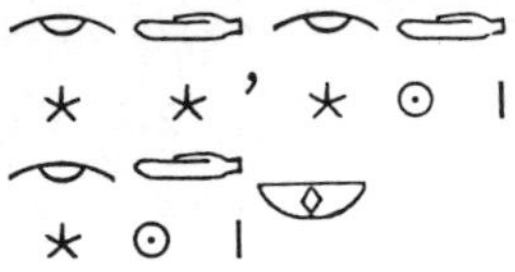 the month of thirty days, plur. 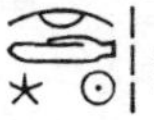; the monthly festival, plur. .

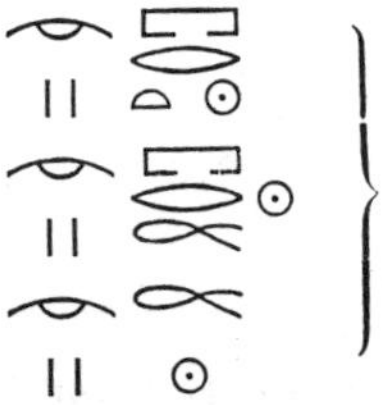 the second month of the season Pert, the last day of the second month of this season.

àbṭ 
àbṭu  a mythological fish which swam before the Boat of Rā; its companion was the *ànt* fish.

àp  to count up, to reckon, to consider, a reckoning, a counting, 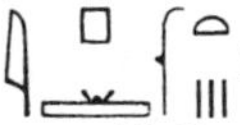 reckoner of years,  counter,  numbered, counted.

àppet 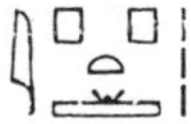 reckoning, account.

àp 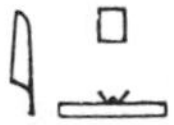 to judge, to be judged, to decree, be decreed, judgment.  great judgment.

ȧp  judge of dooms.

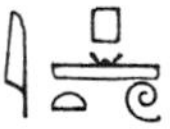 judged. 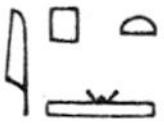 judge.

ȧp, **ȧpu**  to judge, to dispute or argue with someone, to award, be awarded, to bring a message, to announce tidings.  a judge of words or affairs,  *ȧp maāt* righteous judge.

ȧpt  decree, judgment, sentence of doom.

ȧput mitu  sentence of death.

ȧp, ȧpu, ȧpi, ȧpt  to open.  open!   opened.

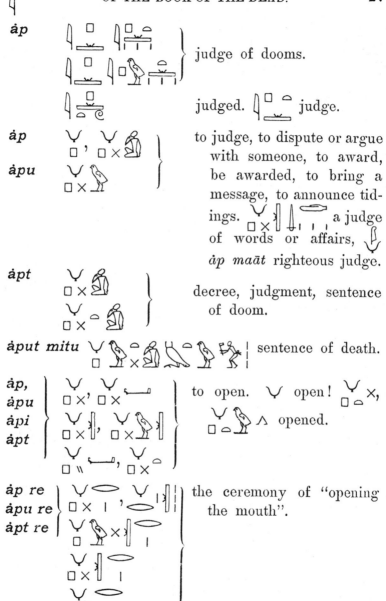

ȧp re, ȧpu re, ȧpt re 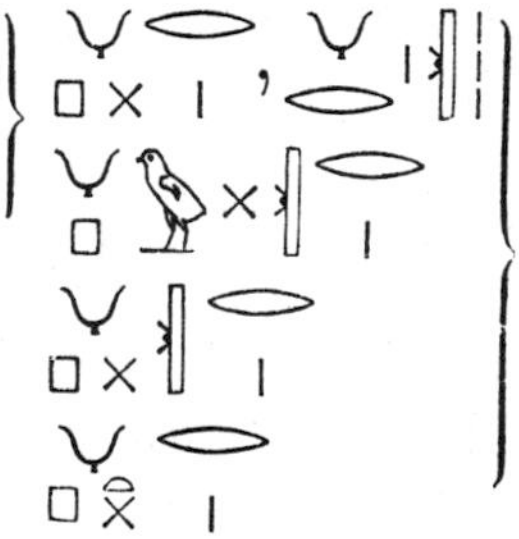 the ceremony of "opening the mouth".

Åp-uat
Åp-uati
Åp-uatu  "Opener of the roads", a name of a wolf-god who was supposed to conduct the deceased over the roads which lead to the Sekhet Åaru, or Elysian Fields. Åp-uat was a companion of the jackal-god Ånpu, with whom he is sometimes confounded.

Åp-uat meḥt sekhem pet 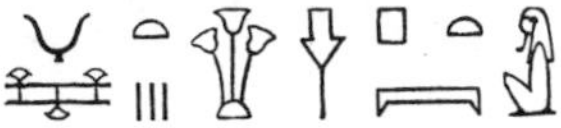 The god Åp-uat of the north as guide to the roads of heaven.

Åp-uat resu sekhem taui  The god Åp-uat of the south as guide to the roads of earth.

Åp-ur  "great opener", name of a god.

åp ḥer  except. 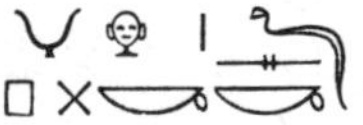 except thyself.

Åpu  A city, the Panopolis of the Greeks, the Akhmîm of the Arabs.

åpu
åpiu  these,  these gods, 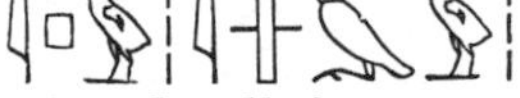 these who dwell in.

àpiu  openers, those who make a way.

àputi  messenger, envoy, ambassador; plur. .

 two envoys.

àppiu  judges.

àpen  (see 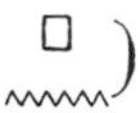) these.   these gods who dwell in.

Àpsi 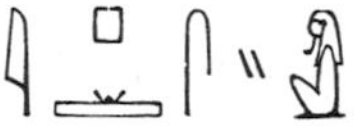 a name or title of a god.

àpt 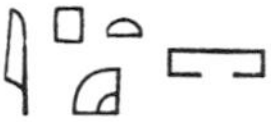 sacred chamber of a temple, private apartments of a house, sacred or profane *ḥarîm.*

àpt 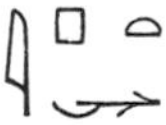 stick, staff, sceptre.

àpt àst 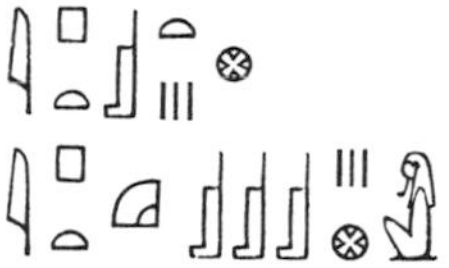 name of a portion of Eastern Thebes, Karnak (?).

àpt  message, envoy.

àpt  messengers.

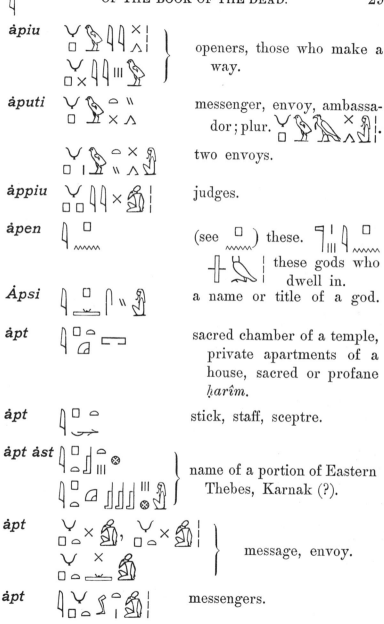

àpt 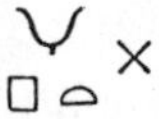 brow, forehead, top of the head (?).

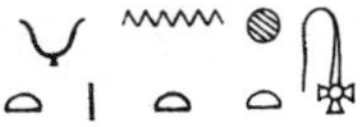 the hottest part of the fire.

 top, surface (?) of the waters.

 brow of the god Qaḥu.

àptu 
àpten  } these.

Àp-shāṭ-taui 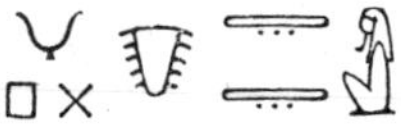 a name of Osiris.

àf, afu  flesh, limbs, members.

àfṭ  to rest, to sit down.

àfṭu 
àfṭet 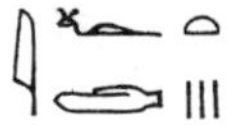 } four.

àfṭi  a kind of cloth or garment.

àm  in, into, inside.

àm (?) 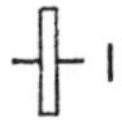 a standard.

àm  a boat.

àm  to arrive in safety.

ȧm 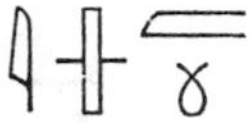 flax, a kind of cloth.

ȧm  not, do not.

ȧm, **ȧmu**  to eat, to consume, swallow up, devour.

ȧmi  eating, eater; plur. 
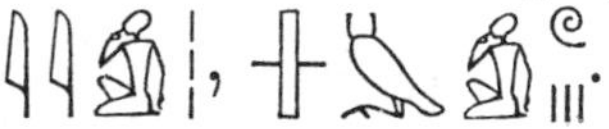.

ȧmti  eater.

ȧm baiu  eater of heart-souls.

ȧm besku  "Eater of Livers", or intestines.

ȧm sāḥu 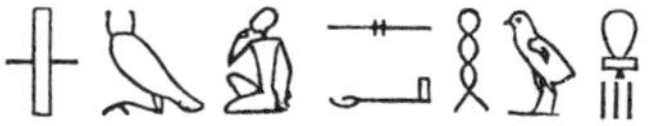 "Eater of mummies".

ȧm snef  "Eater of Blood"; one of the Forty-two Judges in the Hall of Osiris.

ȧm (*un*)  to eat, to consume.

ȧm  bread-cakes, food.

 drink.

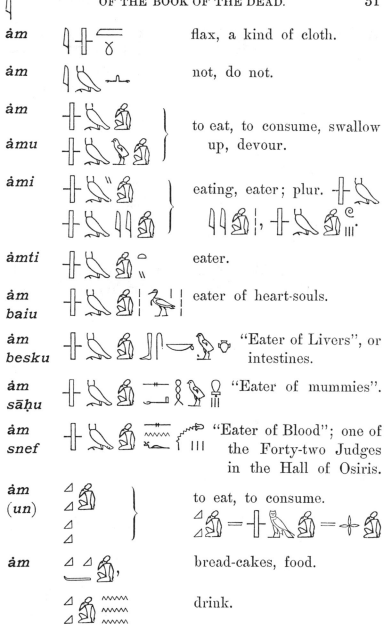

Am-ḥauat-ent-pehui-f  "Eater of the offal of his body"; the name of the doorkeeper of the Third Ārit.

åmt, *åmtu* 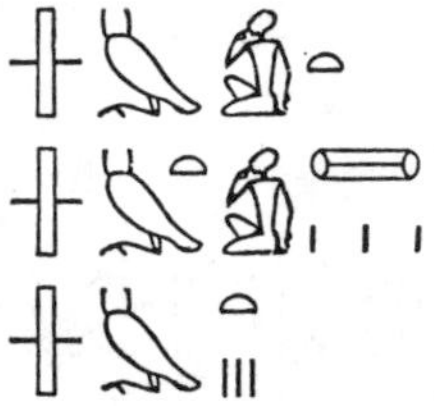 food, something fit or used for food.

åm, *åmt* 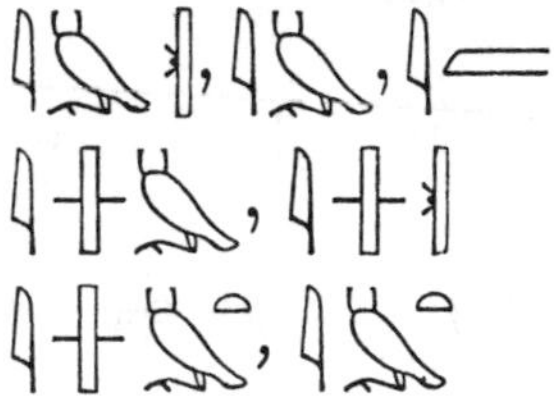 in, among, with, through, upon, by, around, there, therein.  in it (or him),  in it (or her),  by the back of.

åm, *åmt* 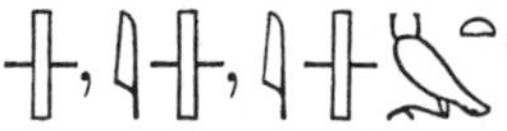 dweller in.

åmi  he who is in, dweller in; plur. ,  those who are in.

ȧm-ā / **ȧm ȧst-ā** 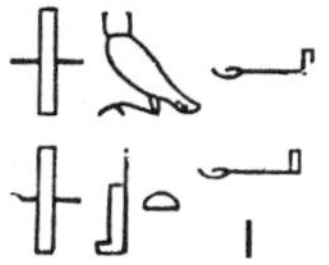 a title of a priest or ministrant.

ȧm-uḥet (?) **neb ta Tchesert**  "he who is in the embalmment chamber, Lord of Ta-tchesert", a title of Anubis, the divine physician and embalmer.

ȧmi-at  one in, or at, the supreme moment.

ȧmi ȧb  he who is in the heart. 

ȧm-ȧten-f 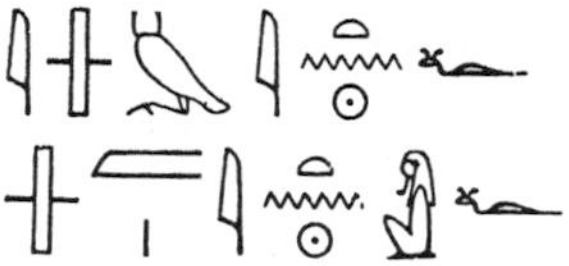 he who is in his disk, *i. e.*, Rā.

ȧmi-uȧa-f  he who is in his Boat, *i. e.*, Rā.

ȧmi mu  he who is in the water, *i. e.*, Sebek.

ȧmi unnut-f  he who is in his hour.

Ȧmi-meḥen-f  / **ȧmi-meḥent-f**  he who is in his Meḥen serpent, *i. e.*, Rā, or Ȧf; plur. .

ȧmi-ḥa-f  he who is in his time, or place.

ȧmi-ḥem-f  he who is in his fiery serpent, *i. e.*, Rā.

ȧmi-khet  he who is in his fiery disk.

ȧm-khet
ȧmi-khet 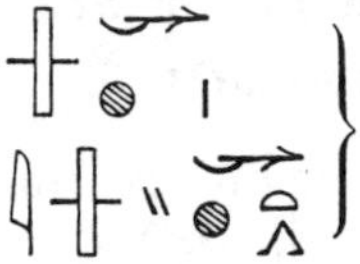 he who is in the following of.

ȧmi-suḥt
ȧm-suḥt  he who is in his egg, *i. e.*, Rā.

ȧmi-mer-nesert (?) 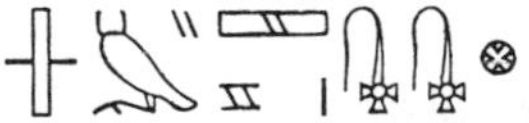 he who is in his fiery Lake, *i. e.*, Rā.

ȧmi-karȧ-f  he who is in his shrine, *i. e.*, Rā or Osiris.

ȧmi-ṭebtu 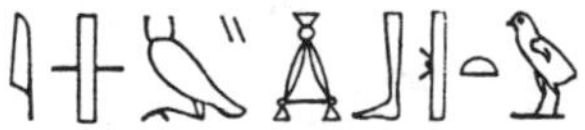 he who is in his coffin, *i. e.*, Osiris.

ȧmi-tchetta  he who dwelleth in eternity.

ȧmiu-ȧat-sen  the gods in their domains.

ȧmiu Ȧbṭu  those in Abydos.

àmiu-Ànu		the gods in Ànu (Heliopolis).
àmiu-àḥ-ur		those in the Great Field.
àmiu-āāui		those in the hands.
àmiu-baḥ		the gods who are in the presence.
àmiu-beḳa		those who are in a weak state.
àmiu em-baḥ		the gods who are in the presence.
àmiu-hru-sen	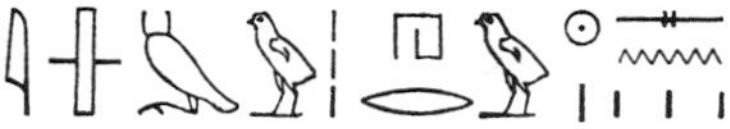	those who are in their days.
àmiu-Nekhen		those who dwell in Nekhen.
àmiu Kher-neter		those who are in the Other World.
àmiu Neṭet		those who dwell in the city of Neṭet.
àmiu khet / **àmiu khet**		those who are in the following of.
àmiu khuti		those who are in the two horizons.

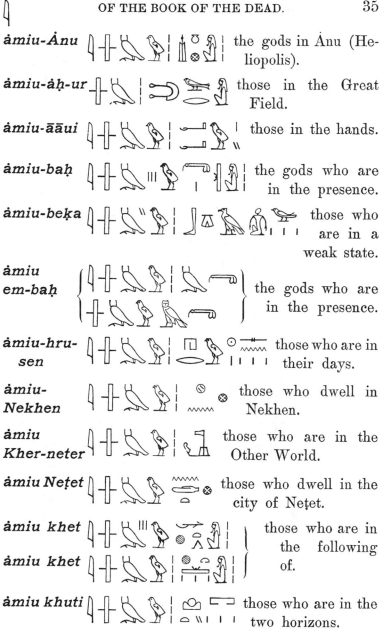

àmiu sāḥu 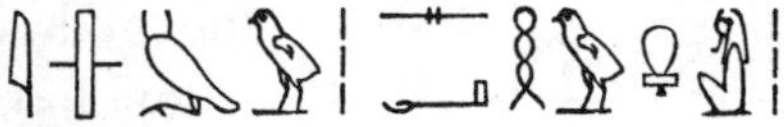 those who are in their mummied forms.

àmiu-sut-sen  those who are in their hair.

àmiu seḥu-sen  those who are in their halls.

àmiu-shems 

àmiu-shemsu  those who are in the following of.

àmiu-karà-sen  those who are in their shrines.

àmiu-ta  those who are in the earth.

àmtu 

àmth 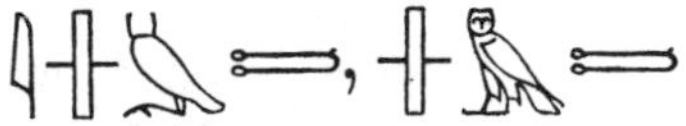

àmith 

àmithu 

among, between;  Chap. CIV. 1,  CIV. 1.

àmt  in .

àm àb 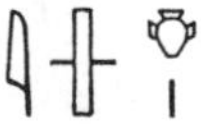 what is in the heart, thought? prayer?

àm khent 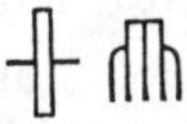 title of a priest.

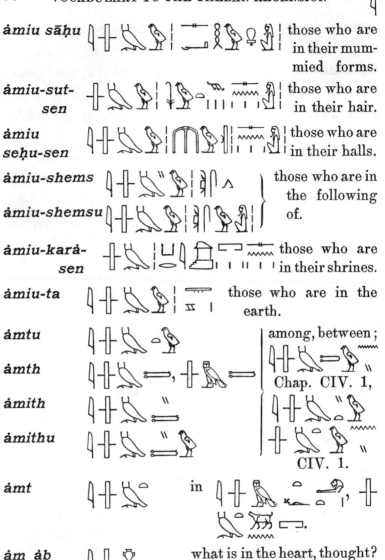

ȧma  tree.

ȧmam  date-palm.

ȧmakh  serf, servant, one who venerates another, or is venerated, a beatified being, .

ȧmakhi  partic. masc.  partic. fem.; plur. , 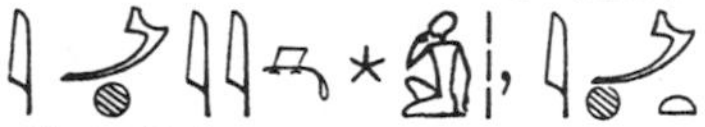 . A late form is .

ȧmu  divine beings.

ȧmu  trees, plants.

ȧmu  flames, fire.

 gods of fire.

ȧmu  colour, pigment.

Ȧm-urt  a proper name.

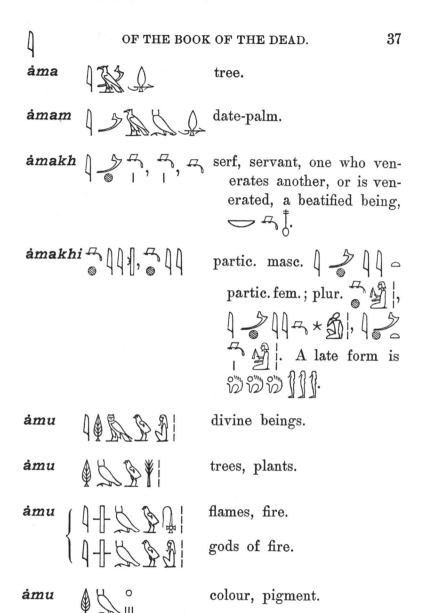

ȧmi 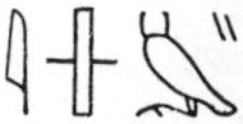 shrine, chamber.

ȧmuhettu 
ȧmihettut 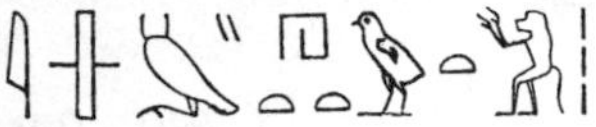 } apes, incarnations of the spirits of the dawn.

ȧmuti  image, figure.

ȧmem  palm-tree.

ȧmem 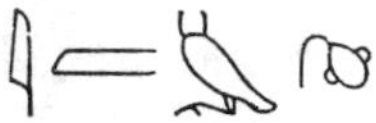 to putrefy.

ȧmem  skin, hide.

ȧmmā 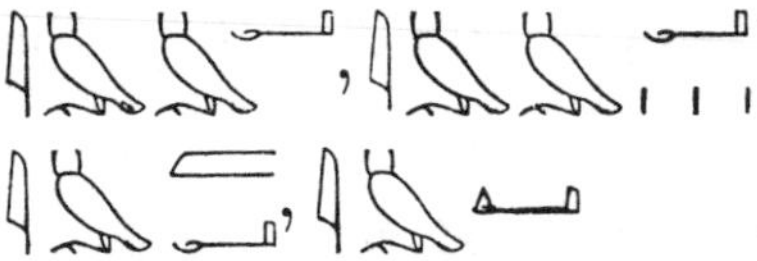 } grant, give, let there be, prithee, 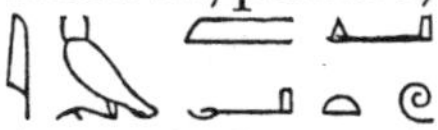 give I pray,  open I pray,  give water and air,   give thy hand,  let me pass,   give (*i. e.*, incline) thy face.

ȧmmu  beams, rays of light, splendour.

ȧmmu  boats.

ȧmmeḥet  a portion of the Other World of Seker.

ȧmm ḳeḥu  those who are in a state of weakness.

Ȧmen 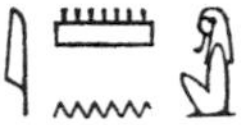 a god of generation and conception, who symbolized the invisible creative forces of Nature.

 "Ȧmen which art in heaven".

 "Ȧmen the prolific Bull".

Ȧmen-nathk-ruthi-Ȧmen 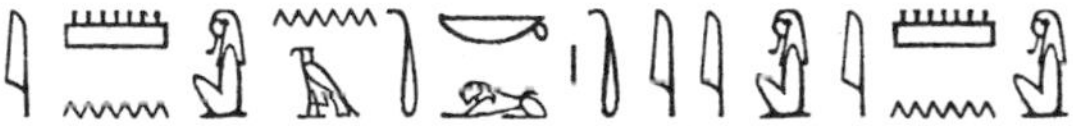 A Sûdânî form of Ȧmen.

Ȧmen-nau-ȧn-ka-entek-Sharu  A Sûdânî form of Ȧmen.

Ȧmen-Rā 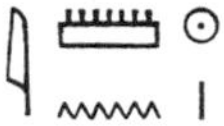 the great god of Thebes, chief element in the triad Ȧmen-Rā, Mut and Khensu.

 "Ȧmen - Rā, Lord of the throne of the Two Lands".

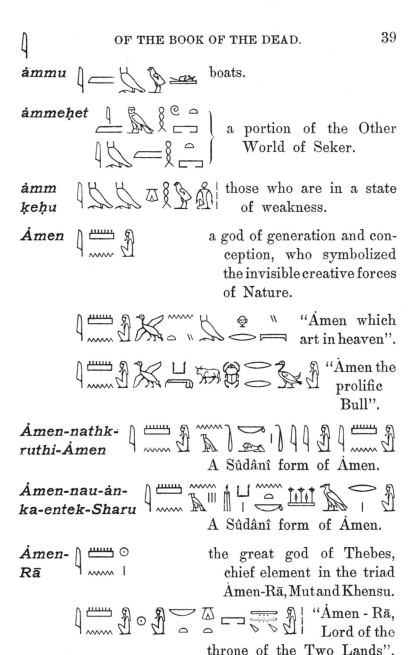

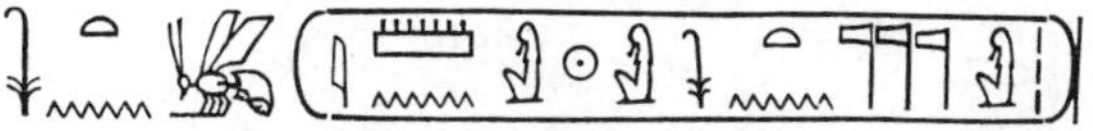 "King of the South and North, Ȧmen-Rā, king of the gods".

Ȧmen-Rā Ḥeru-khuti  Ȧmen-Rā Harmachis.

Ȧmen-ruti  Ȧmen and the two lion-gods Shu and Tefnut.

ȧmen 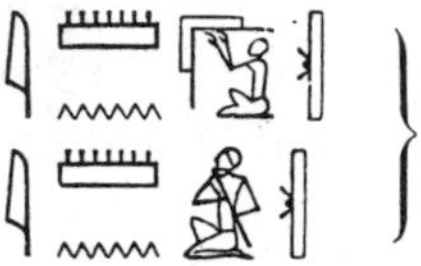 to hide, be hidden, hidden one, something hidden. , 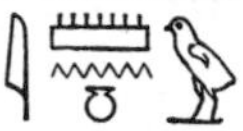  those who hide, 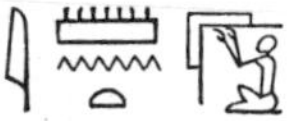 hider, 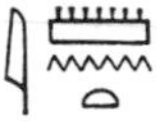  secrecy, in secret,  the hidden gods.

ȧmenu-ā  those whose arms are hidden.

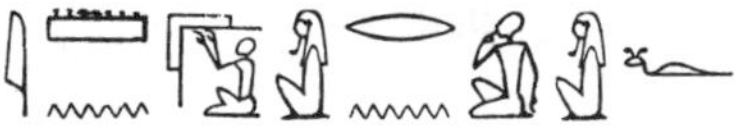 he whose name is hidden.

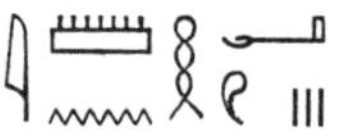 those whose bodies are hidden.

 those whose mysteries are hidden.

ȧmenḥiu 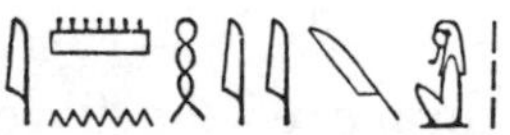 the divine butchers, or gods of slaughter.

Ȧmen-ḥetep 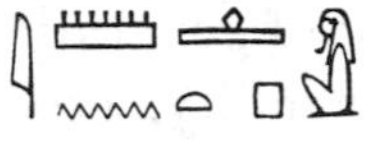 a proper name.

Ȧment, *Amenti*, *Ȧmentet*  the "hidden" place, or land, the West, the abode of departed spirits, the name of the first division of the Other World. A late form of the name is .

 the "beautiful Ȧmentet".

Ament 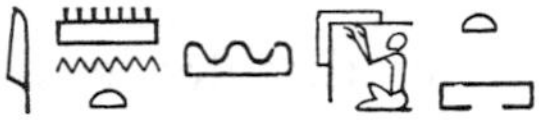 hidden place; plur. .

ȧmentiu  divine beings who live in Ȧmenti, or the West;  Ȧmenti deified, 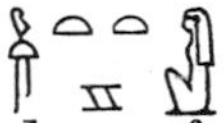 the goddess of the West, or Ȧmenti.

ȧmenti 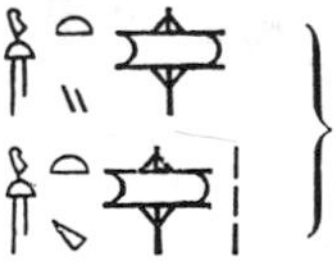 the west wind.

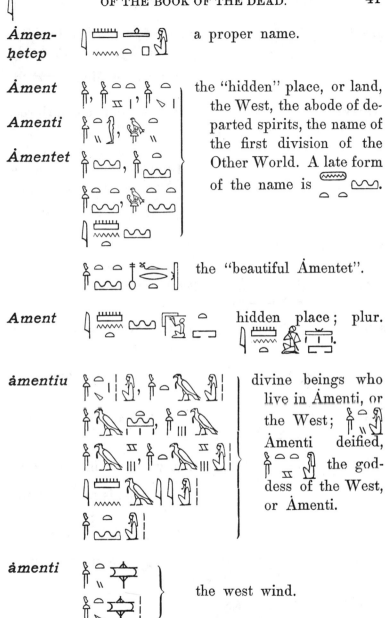

ȧmsi — a god of generation, fertility, fecundity, etc. Probably a form of Menu.

Ȧmseth — one of the four sons of Horus. The reading appears to be a mistake made by the Egyptians in reading *Ȧmseth* instead of *Ȧḳesth*. See Ḳesthȧ.

ȧmt — chamber, house, abode.

ȧmt — possessions, goods of a house.

ȧmt — the title-deeds of a house or property.

ȧmt — tree (?), or tent, camp.

ȧmt — light, radiance, splendour.

ȧmt — that which is in. what is in the waters. , etc.

Ȧmt-ṭehen-f — a proper name.

ȧmtiu — . . . .

ȧn 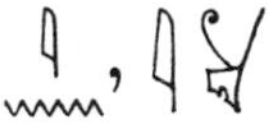 a mark of emphasis or interrogation, used sometimes as a preposition, behold! lo! cf. 

ȧn ḳert  lo moreover.

ȧn (*n*) 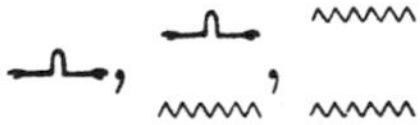 no, not, mark of the negative. 
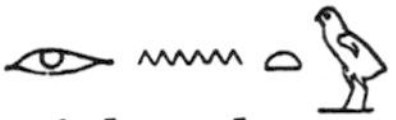 most certainly there cannot be done.  I am not.

ȧn ȧs 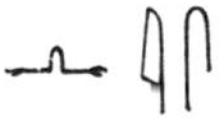 except, unless.

ȧn ȧbu  ceaselessly.

ȧn urṭ  unresting.

ȧn petrȧ  unobserved.

ȧn maa 

ȧn maa-n-tu  } unseen, invisible.

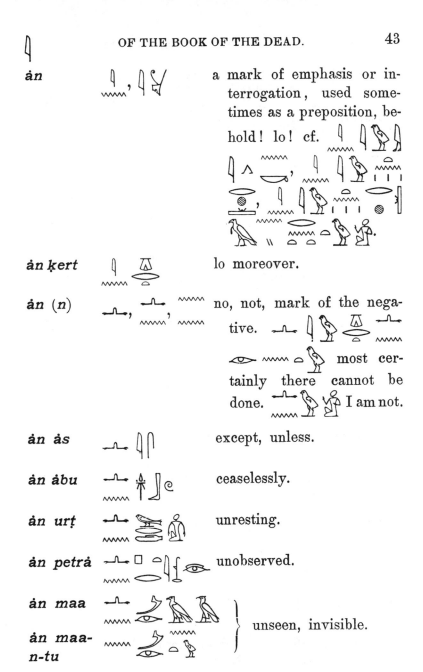

ȧn maa-n-tu 
ȧn maatu
} unseen, invisible.

ȧn mu 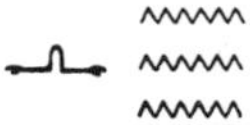 waterless.

ȧn meḥ 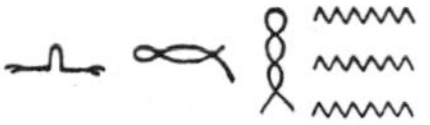
ȧn meḥ-f 
} undipped (?), unwashed (?). Also 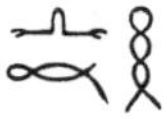 .

ȧn nifu  airless.

ȧn netchnetchet  not to be discussed or gainsaid.

ȧn rekh 
ȧn rekhtu 
} unknown.

ȧn kheper  never was.

ȧn sep 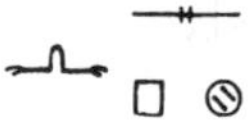 at no time.

ȧn smȧ 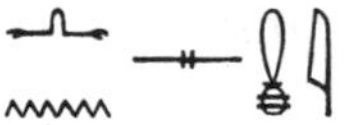 untold.

ȧn sek 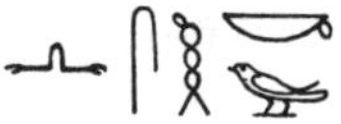 indestructible,

ȧn seṭ  unsplit.

ȧn shenārtu  unturnable.

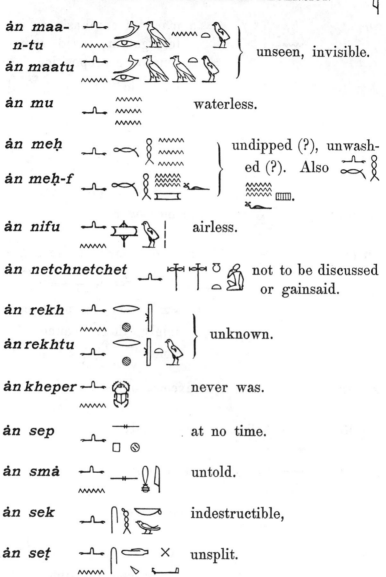

Ȧn ȧruṭ-f
Ȧn ȧarruṭ-f — the place where nothing grows.

Ȧn-erṭā-nef-bes-f-khenti-heh-f — name of one of the Seven Spirits with Osiris.

Ȧn-ḥeri-ertisa — name of a god.

ȧn
ȧnu — to bring, to bear, to carry. to bring, bringing, brought, those who bring; something brought.

ȧnu — what is brought in, gifts, increase.

ȧntu — offerings; peace-offerings.

Ȧniu — name of a god.

Ȧn — name of a god.

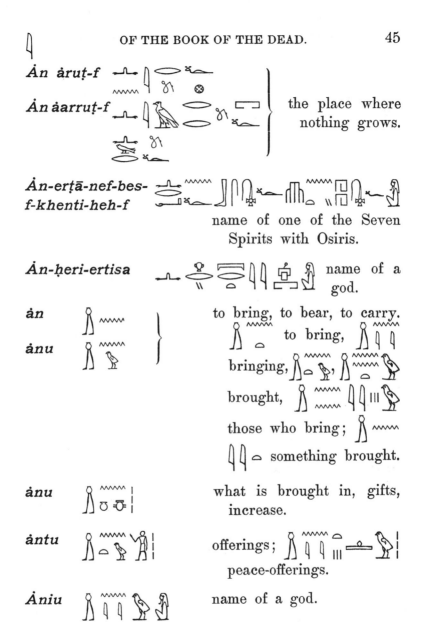

Ȧn-{ṭes / ṭemt} a proper name.

ȧnit a dwelling, chamber, house.

ȧnuk I.

Ȧnu On, Heliopolis.

ȧnnu skin.

ȧnnuit skin, hair, plumage.

Ȧn-ȧtef-f "Bringer of his father", a proper name.

Ȧn ā-f "Bringer of his arm"; the name of one of the Forty-two Judges in the Hall of Osiris.

Ȧn-urt-emkhet-uas name of the mast in the magical boat (Chap. XCIX).

ȧnb to dance, to rejoice.

ȧneb wall; plur.

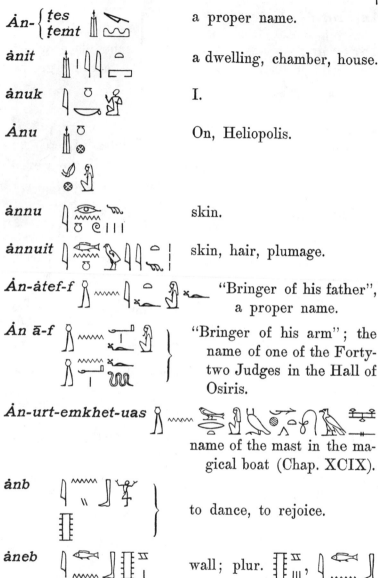

ȧneb  mason.

ȧnep  region, estate, ground.

Ȧnp 

Ȧnpu 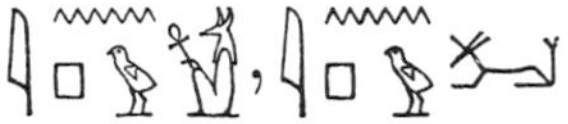

The god Anubis, son of Set and Nephthys, a jackal-god who embalmed the dead, and guided the souls of the blessed to the Other World. Titles: , .

Ȧn-mut-f  "The pillar of his mother", title of a ministrant or priest.

ȧnem 

 skin, hide.

ȧnemsit  a kind of garment.

ȧnenit 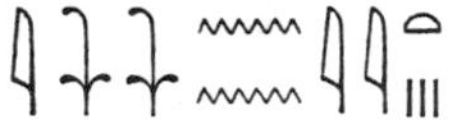 a proper name?

Ȧn-ruṭ-f  the god of the place where nothing grows.

Ȧnreruṭ-f  the place where nothing grows.

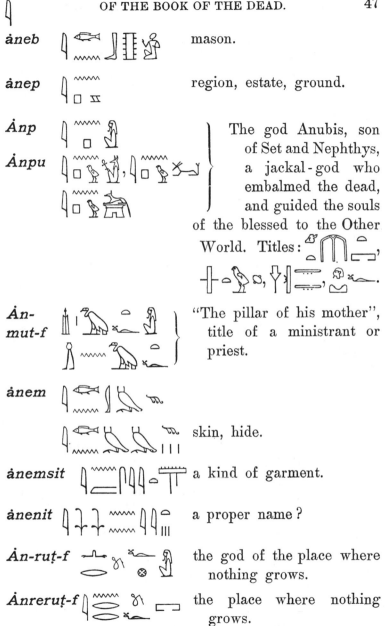

ȧner  stone.

 "Stone of Maāt", a proper name.

ȧner 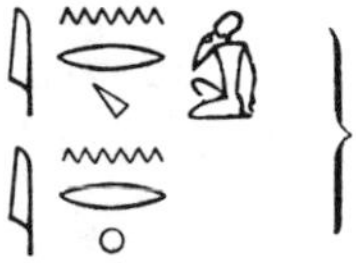 a proper name.

ȧnhetet  ape.

ȧnḥui  the two eye-brows.

ȧnḥu-tu  surrounded.

Ȧn-ḥer  "Bearer of the sky"; an ancient god of Upper Egypt who is often associated with .

Ȧn-ḥer  name of the warder of the Sixth Ārit.

Ȧn-ḥetep  one of the Forty-two gods in the Hall of Osiris.

ȧnes, **ȧnsi** 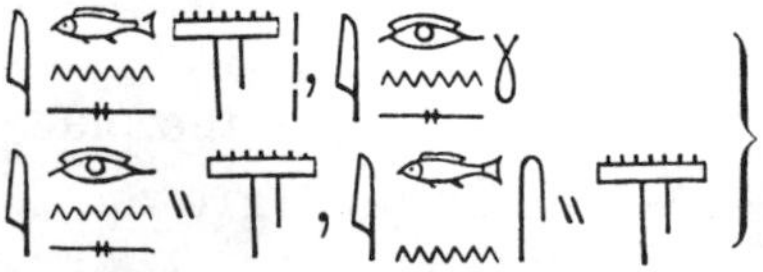 name of a ceremonial garment.

ȧnset 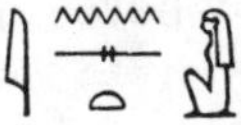 a goddess (?).

àneq		to bind, tie on, to fasten.
ànqet		to embrace, to surround.
ànqet		name of a tool, or instrument, "clincher", rope (?).
ànt	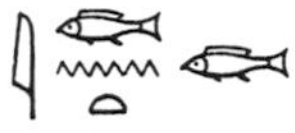	name of a mythological fish which swam before the boat of Rā.
ànt	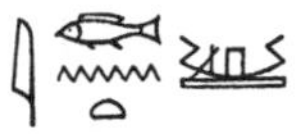	name of a solar boat.
ànt		a valley, especially a funerary valley.
àntet, ànti	 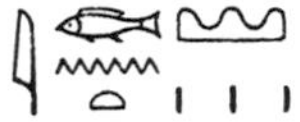	
ànti		pillars, columns.
Ànti	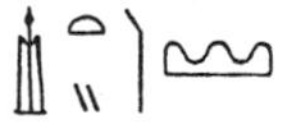	the hill-folk who lived in the Eastern Desert of Ta-sti 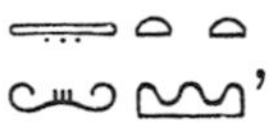, or Nubia.
ànti		a hindrance, obstruction.
àntiu		those who have nothing, the destitute, those who are not, or do not exist.
àntet		to go back.

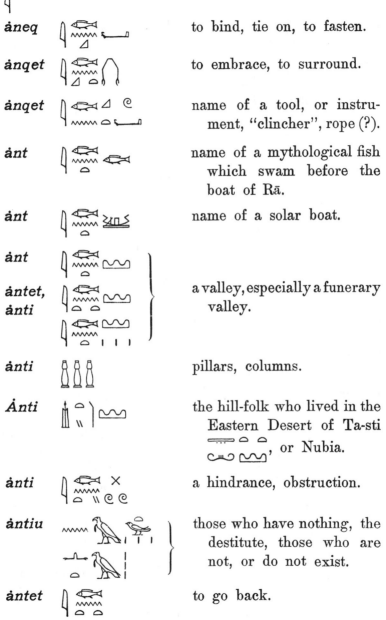

ȧntet — cord, fetter, chain.

Ȧn-ṭebu — the name of a god.

ȧnetch — to incline, to bow.

ȧnetch ḥer — to incline the head to a suppliant, to turn the face towards.

ȧr — to tie together.

ȧr — if, now.

ȧr sa — if after, now as for.

ȧr ḳert — if moreover, however.

ȧr, ***ȧru***, ***ȧrit*** — to do, to make, to create, to form, to fashion; , doing, making, creator; , made, wrought, made; make ye; things done.

àrit  to work the heart, to think.

 to make or prepare a path or road.

 to prepare food.

 to celebrate the Haker festival.

 to keep festivals.

 to make protection, to perform ceremonies for the protection of some one.

 to work for successful results, to strive for peace.

 to perform a transformation.

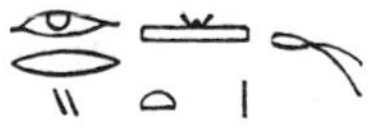 to make, or write, or recite, a book.

 to do into writing, to make a copy, to write.

àriu 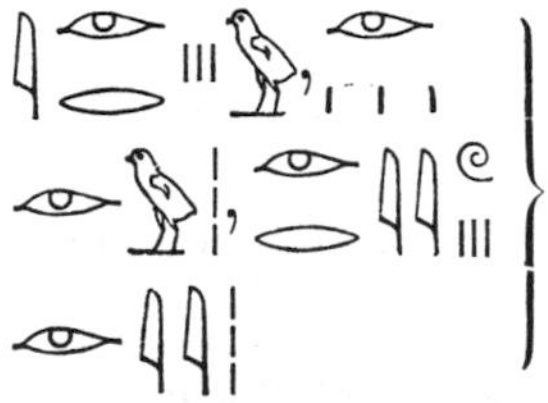 doers, makers, workers.

àriu  workmen; fem. .

ȧrit  work, something done.

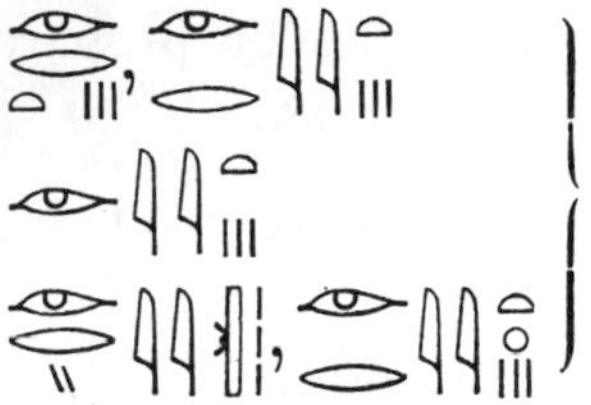 actions, deeds, labours, works, things done or to be done.

ȧr, ȧri 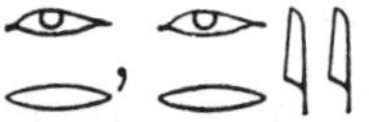 used as an auxiliary verb, see *passim*. "Maker of

ȧri-Maāt 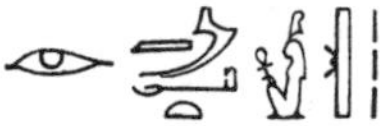 truth, or righteousness", a title of Osiris, Hathor, and other gods.

Ȧri-em-ȧb-f  the name of one of the Forty-two Judges in

Ȧri-en-ȧb-f 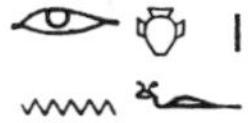 the Hall of Osiris.

Ȧri-nef-tchesef  name of a plank or peg in the magical boat.

Ȧri-entuten-em-meska-en-Mer-ur uṭebtu-en-Suti

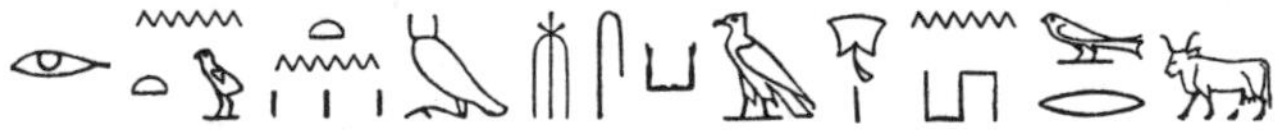

 name of the leather bands in the magical boat.

Ȧri-ḥetch-f  a proper name.

Ȧrisi  a proper name.

ȧru 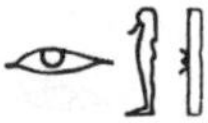 form, attribute, figure, image; plur. .

àri belonging to: their name; their seat; their bull (var.); their length.

àri a person in charge of, or belonging to, or attendant upon something, watcher, porter, guardian.

guardian of my flesh.

guardian, or guardians, of the sky.

keeping watch about, or around.

keepers of my mouth.

watching the limbs.

keeping guard over the neck.

belonging to the leathers.

guarding the earth.

åri āa porter, doorkeeper, guardian ; plur.

porter of the door of Åmentet.

åriu ārrtu warders of the Ārits.

åri mākhait warder of the Scales.

åri ḥemit warder of the oar, *i. e.*, steersman.

åri ḥenbiu warder of the cultivated lands.

åru khut guardians of light, *i. e.*, beings of light.

åri såpu keepers of the records, or books of doom.

åri sebkhet-f keeper of his pylon.

ȧri qeb en meru en khet  keeper of the Bend of the Lake of Fire.

ȧrārti 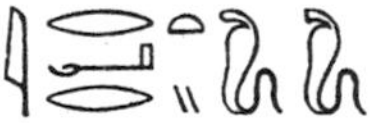 two uraei.

Ȧruhut  a proper name.

ȧrp 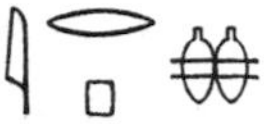 wine.

ȧrpu  ... Chap. CLXIX. 1.

ȧref  an emphatic particle.

ȧrmā  with.

ȧrek  a particle.

ȧrt 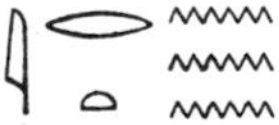 to flow, what flows.

ȧrt 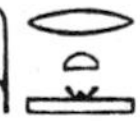 Chapter LB. 1.

ȧrtet 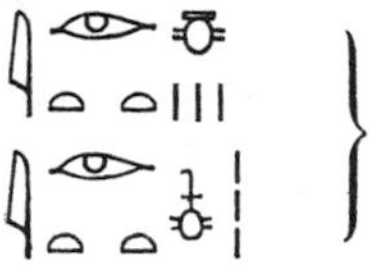 milk.

_ȧh_  calamity.

ȧhabu  joy, gladness, cries of joy.

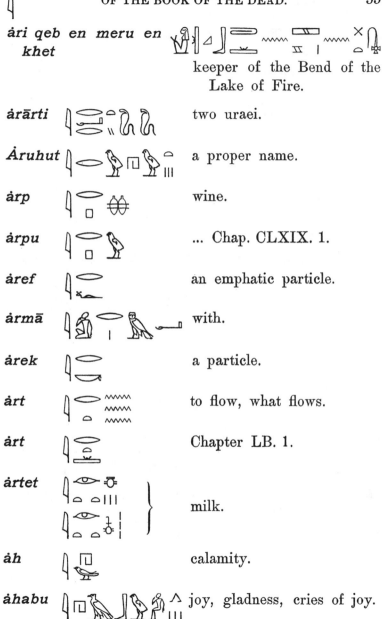

ȧhen a kind of wood.

ȧhehi rejoicings, cries of joy.

Ȧḥ the Moon-god.

ȧḥ ... Book of Breathings II. 22.

ȧḥ collar, embrace, to ward off.

ȧḥ, ȧḥu ox; plur. oxen.

ȧḥai a sistrum bearer.

ȧḥāu members.

ȧḥi
ȧḥu the name of one of the Forty-two Judges in the Hall of Osiris; a proper name.

ȧḥu fields (?), measuring cords.

ȧḥu wooden tools or instruments.

ȧḥui the two *ȧḥui* gods.

Àḥibit  name of a god.

àḥunnu  youth, child.

àḥemu (?)  ... Chap. XCII. 13.

àḥti  throat.

Aḥti  a name of Osiris.

Àkh  O!, would that,  O tell me.

àkhabu  grain.

àkhib  to speak.

àkhemu urṭu 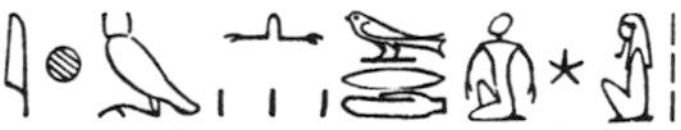 a class of stars.

àkhekhu 

àkhekhui 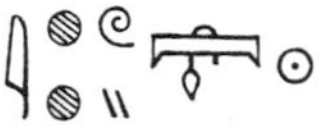 darkness, night.

Àkhsesef 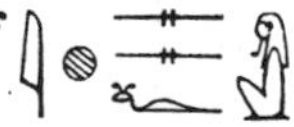 a proper name.

Às  a proper name.

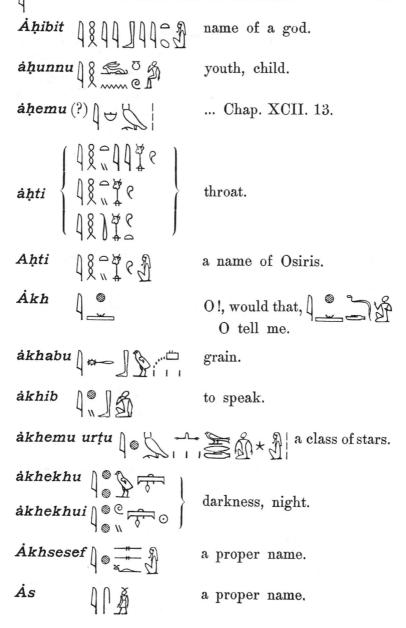

ȧs — behold, to wit, namely, .

ȧsu — intestines.

ȧsu — winds.

ȧsu (?) — ... Chap. CXXVII B. 17.

ȧsi, ȧsu — , tomb, sepulchre.

ȧsu — recompense or in return for, in place of.

ȧs — to pass forward, to advance.

ȧsu
ȧsi — to decay, to rot, destruction. decay, incorruptible.

Åsår 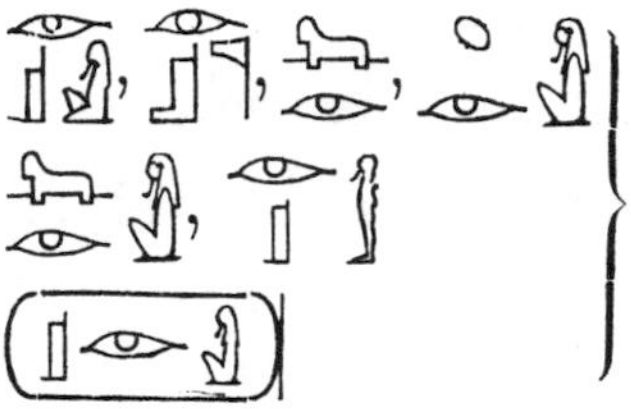 the god Osiris, son of Seb and Nut, husband of Isis, and father of Horus. The deceased is usually identified with Osiris and is called by his name.

Åsår Ånpu 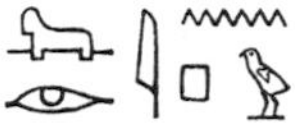 Osiris-Anubis.

Åsår ānkhti  Osiris the Living One.

Åsår Unnefer  Osiris Un-Nefer.

Åsår Utetti  Osiris the begetter.

Åsår-ba-erpi  Osiris, soul of the divine Image.

Åsår-bati-erpit 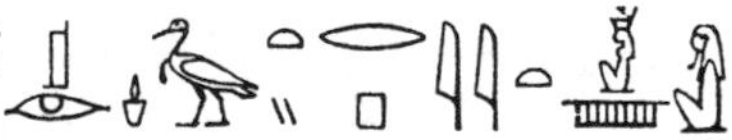 Osiris, twin soul of the divine image.

Åsår Ptaḥ neb ānkh  Osiris-Ptaḥ, Lord of Life.

Åsår-em-pesuru 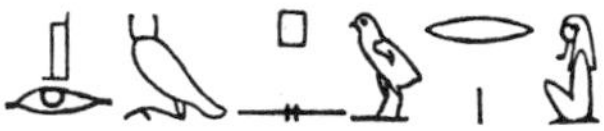 Osiris in Pesuru.

Åsår em pesṭ ent nut-f 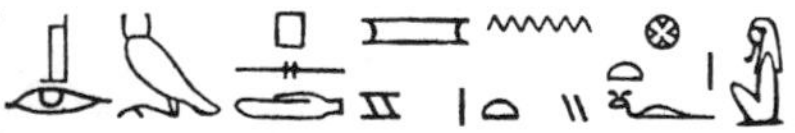

Åsår em Seḥnen 

Ȧsȧr em Ṭenit 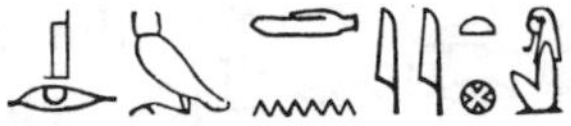

Ȧsȧr nub ḥeḥ 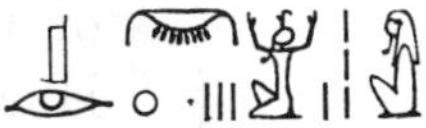 Osiris, gold of eternity.

Ȧsȧr neb ānkh  Osiris, Lord of Life.

Ȧsȧr neb er tcher  Osiris, Lord to the boundary, *i. e.*, of All.

Ȧsȧr Netchesti 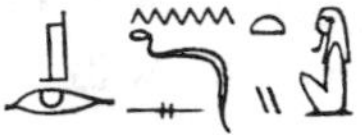 Osiris the Less.

Ȧsȧr Ḥenti  Osiris of the two crocodiles.

Ȧsȧr Ḥeru  Osiris-Horus.

Ȧsȧr Ḥeru-khuti Tem  Osiris-Harmachis.

Ȧsȧr ḥer ȧb semt  Osiris in the funerary mountain.

Ȧsȧr ḥer shāu-f  Osiris on his sand.

Ȧsȧr khent Ȧbṭu  Osiris, President of Abydos.

Ȧsȧr khenti Ȧmenti  Osiris, President of Amenti, or the Other World.

Asàr khenti Àmentiu  Osiris, President of those who dwell in the Other World.

Àsàr khent Un 

Àsàr khenti 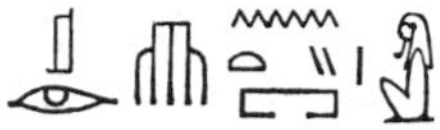

Àsàr khenti Nefer (?) 

Àsàr khenti nut-f 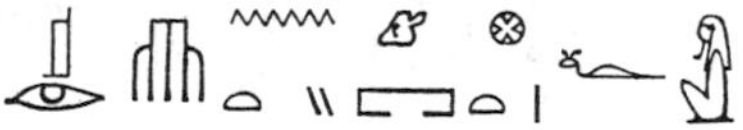

Àsàr khenti nestu 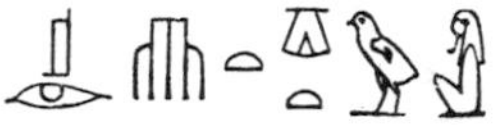

Àsàr khenti Ru-stau 

Àsàr khenti seḥ ḥemt 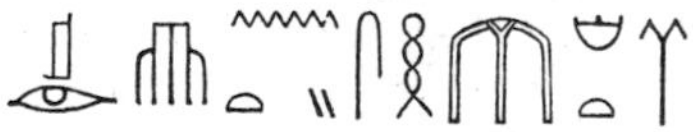

Àsàr sa Nut 

Àsàr saa 

Àsàr Sab (or *Ḳeb*?) 

Àsàr Saḥ 

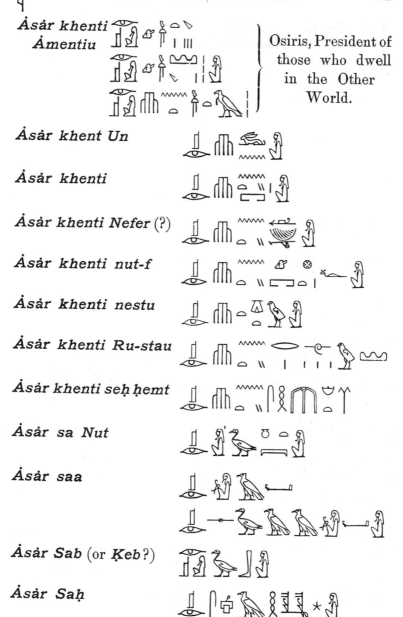

Ȧsȧr Sekri 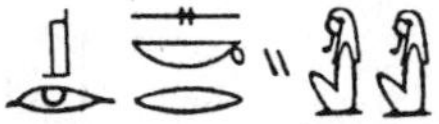

Ȧsȧr Taiti 

Ȧsȧr tua 

Ȧsȧr Ṭem ur 

Ȧsȧr Teḳaiti 

Ȧsȧrtiu  beings like unto Osiris.

ȧsi  who?, what?

ȧsp  grief (?), misery, wretchedness.

ȧsfet, *ȧsfeti*  faults, sins, evil deeds, sinners, evil ones.

ȧsfetiu  evil fiends, sinners.

ȧsentu  cords, ropes.

ȧser  tamarisk (?),  plants, herbs, grass.

Ȧsert  name of a city.

åsha  linen, some kind of woven stuff.

Åses 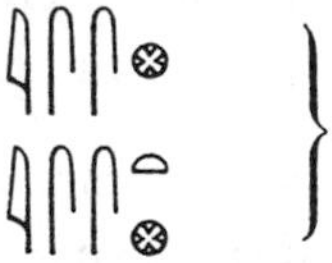
Åsest
a city in the seventh Åat.

åses  to rope in, to bind.

åsstu  a rope.   those whose heads are tied.

åsk  behold, lo!

åst, åstu 
åsth
behold.

Åst  the goddess Isis.

åst 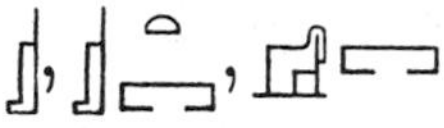 seat, place, habitation, abode, shrine; plur. 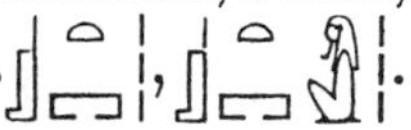.

åst åb 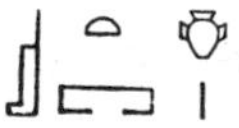 place of the heart, heart's chosen place.

åst āāui 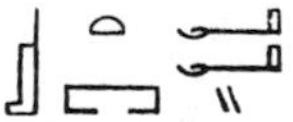 place of the two hands.

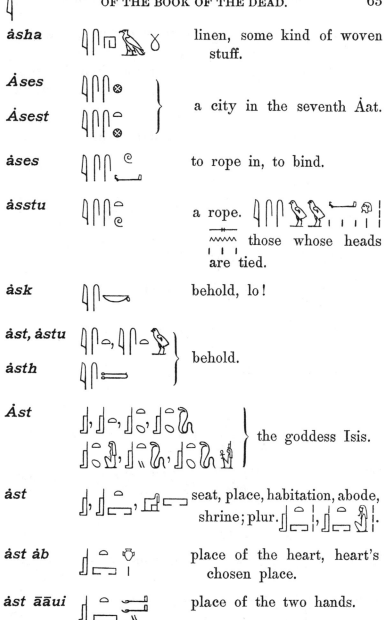

àst urt  great place, *i. e.*, the sky.

àst utchat 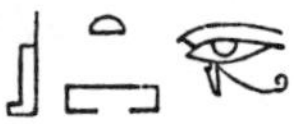 seat of the Utchat, resting place of the Eye of Rā.

àst maāt  the place where the Law is administered.

àst ḥert 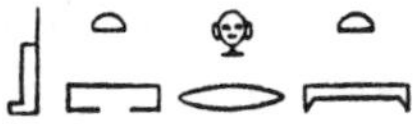 heaven.

àst ḥeḥ 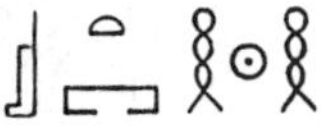 everlasting abode.

àst Ḥeqet 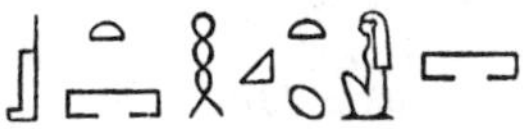 shrine of Ḥeqet.

àst ḥetep 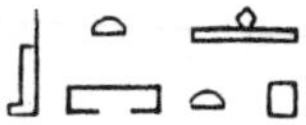 place of repose.

àst ḥetep àb 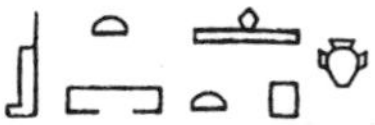 seat of rest of the heart.

àst shetau en Ḥeru  the secret abodes of Horus.

àst qebḥ  place of cool water, bath.

àst taa  place of fire in the Other World.

àst tchesert 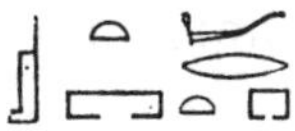 shrine, sanctuary, holy place.

àsṭ  to tremble, make to shake.

Àsṭenu 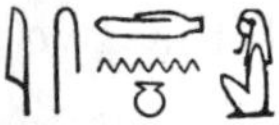 name of a god.

åsteḥ (?) 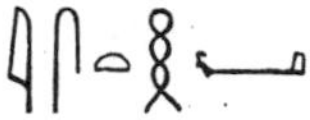
åstheḥt (?) 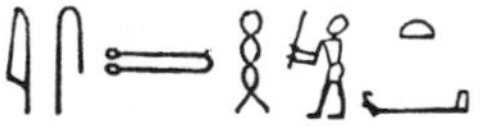 } to beat down.

Åsṭes 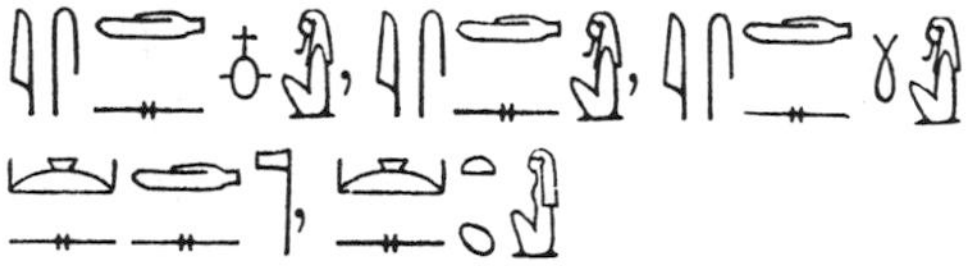 } name of a god.

Åstcheṭet  name of a district.

åshāt 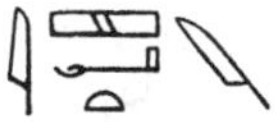 knife, slaughter.

åshep  light, radiance.

åshpit  chamber, hut, house.

åsheset 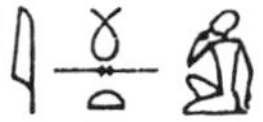 see åqeset.

åshesh 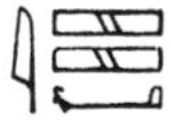 to be carried away.

åshet 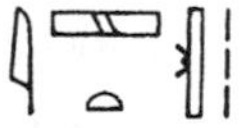 subsistence, oppression, oppressor (?).

åshta 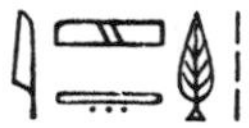 tree.

åsheṭ  } persea tree, trees, plants.

åk  injury.

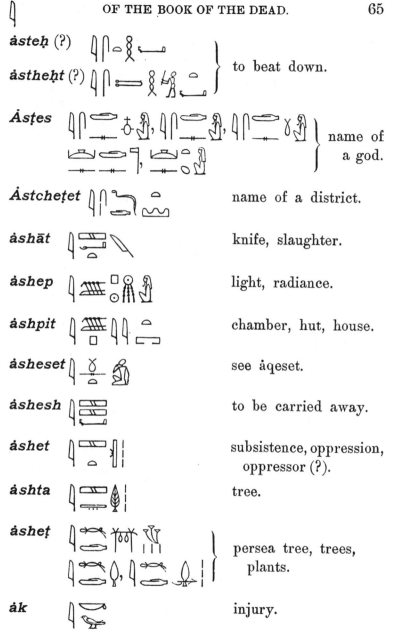

ȧkebu hair.

ȧkeb, ȧkebu ,
ȧkebet lamentation, wailing, weeping.

ȧkebit wailers, mourners.

Ȧkeniu a proper name.

Ȧkentaukha-kheru the porter of the Sixth Ārit.

Ȧkenti a proper name.

Ȧksi a city of the Ninth Ȧat.

Ȧqen name of a god.

Ȧqeh name of a god.

ȧqer perfect, strong, complete, skilful; plur. , a skilful scribe.

Ȧqrit a goddess.

Ȧqert-khenti-ḥet-set the name of one of the Seven Cows.

ȧqḥu to enter.

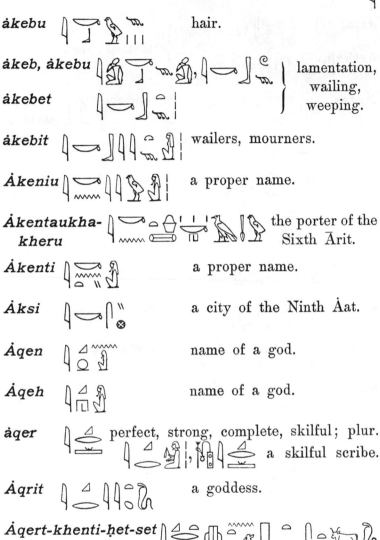

àqeset 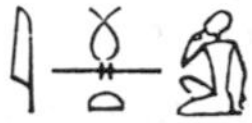 who, what, where, .

àqet 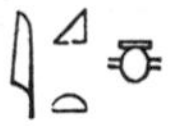 wine, beer.

àqeṭu  builders, masons, architects.

àqeṭs  bad, wicked, evil.

Àḳau  name of a god.

àḳap 
àḳep  } rain-storm, tempest.

Àḳeru 
Àḳeriu  } gods of the Other World.

Àḳert 
Àḳertet  } the name of the Other World of Heliopolis.

Àḳert-khent-Àset-s 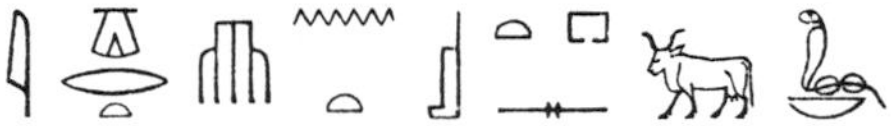 the name of one of the Seven Cows.

àḳeḳit 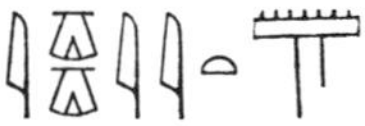 a kind of garment, robe.

àt  father.

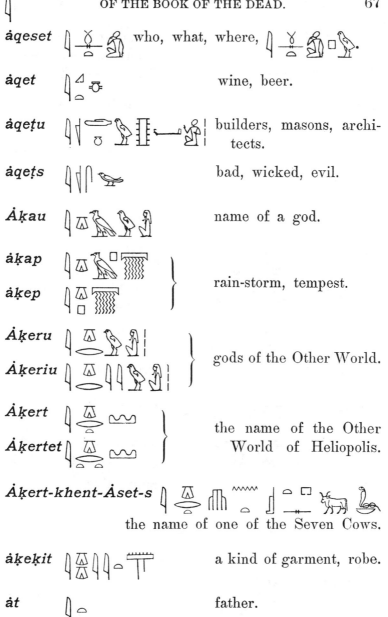

ȧt (for ***ȧnt***), ***ȧti*** (for ***ȧnti***), ***ȧtet*** — negation, no, none, not, cannot, without, impotence, plur. things which are not, evil beings; without, destitute, abjects.

ȧti āḳhem unquenchable.

ȧti uteb immutable.

ȧti men painless.

ȧti maa invisible, not seeing, blind.

ȧtu rekh unknown.

ȧtu ḳhesef irresistible.

ȧtu ȧsi incorruptible.

ȧti sek undecaying.

ȧti shes impassable.

ȧt emanation.

Ȧtaru-ȧm-tcher-qemtu-renu-par-sheta a proper name.

àteb territory, region.

àtef father; dual , ; plur. , , father gods , , Father Osiris , Father Kheperà .

Àtem see under Tem, Temu.

àten the solar disk.

the god of the solar disk.

the two-horned disk.

àtennu appellations.

àter

àtru river, canal, water-flood, stream; plur. .

àtert one half of the sky, or world.

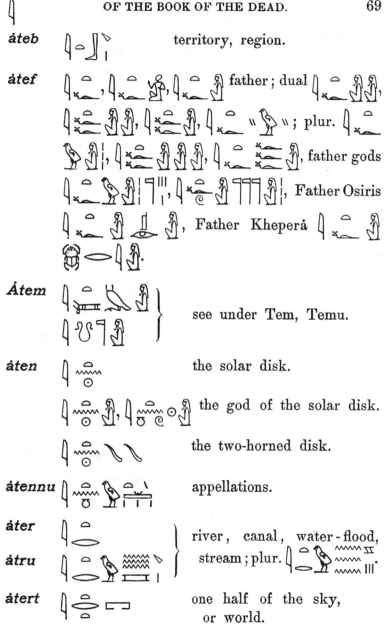

ȧtert meḥt 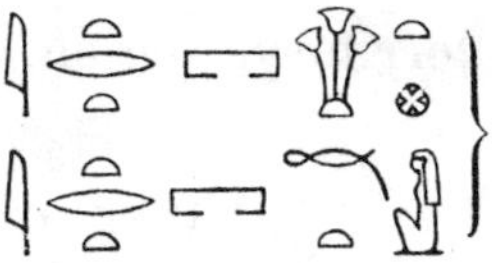 the northern half of the sky.

ȧtert shemā 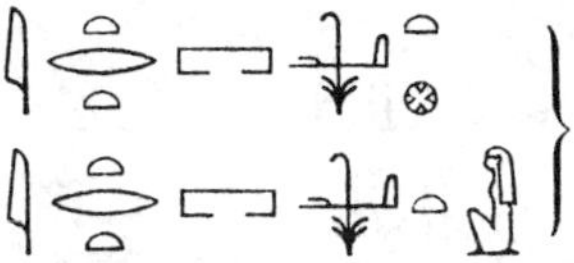 the southern half of the sky.

ȧterti

ȧturti 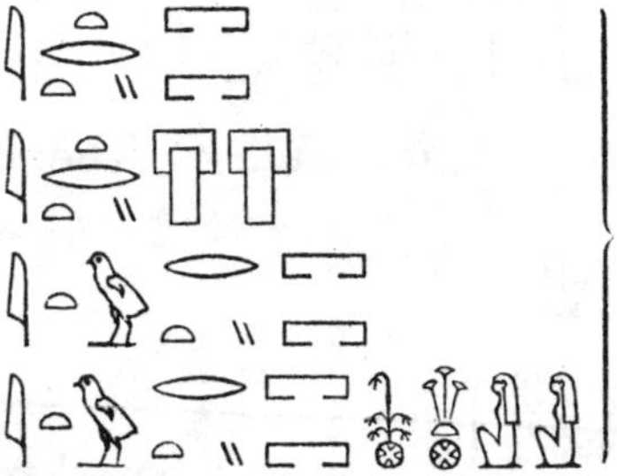 the two halves of the sky.

Ȧthabu  name of a city.

ȧtḥu 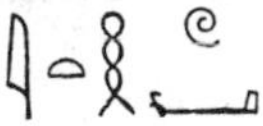 to drag, pull, draw.

Ȧtektaukehaqkheru 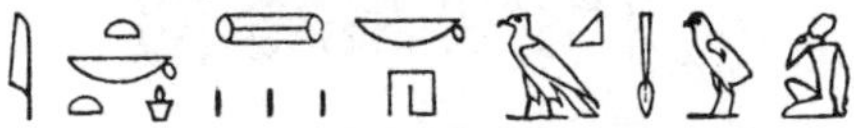 a proper name.

ȧṭ  oppression, oppressed one.

ȧṭ  to be deaf.

Ȧṭu  a city of the Eleventh Ȧat.

ȧṭu  children.

ȧṭeb  region, domain; plur. 

ȧṭmȧ 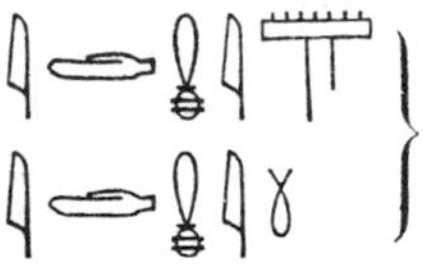 a kind of cloth, a ceremonial garment.

ȧṭen 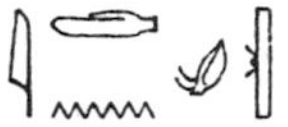 deputy, vicar, chief?

ȧṭent  division, a separation.

ȧṭerit  misfortunes, calamities.

ȧṭḥu  papyrus swamps, the Delta generally.

ȧṭeṭiu  those who injure.

ȧthi (**ȧti**)  prince, sovereign, king.

ȧthen 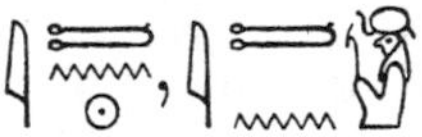 the solar disk, the god of the solar disk.

ȧtheth 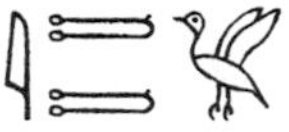 to hover, to alight.

ȧtcha  robber, man of violence, violence.

Ā.

ā   hand, arm, paw of an animal; dual [hieroglyphs], [hieroglyphs], [hieroglyphs]; plur. [hieroglyphs], power [hieroglyphs]; [hieroglyphs] at once, straightway, immediately, [hieroglyphs] ancestor (see ṭep ā); [hieroglyphs] "Eater of the Arm", name of a god, [hieroglyphs] a flight, [hieroglyphs] action of battle, [hieroglyphs] place of yesterday, [hieroglyphs] before.

Āāiu, etc.   [hieroglyphs] the name of the posts of the magic net (Chapter XCIX).

ā, āa   [hieroglyphs] house, dwelling.

āa   [hieroglyphs] to advance, journey onwards.

āa   [hieroglyphs] door, gate; plur. [hieroglyphs]

āatu   [hieroglyphs] [hieroglyphs]; the two leaves of a door [hieroglyphs].

 gods of the doors.

 the two doors of the sky.

 the two doors of truth.

 the two doors of the sky.

 the two doors of Ta-qebḥ.

āa / **āat** 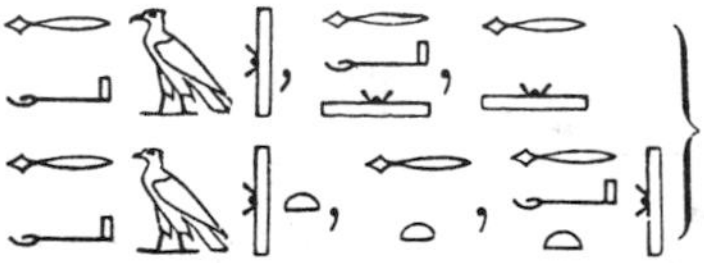 great, large, mighty, to be great;  great one,  great god,  great goddess; plur.  , .

āaui / **āaāa**  twice great.

āati 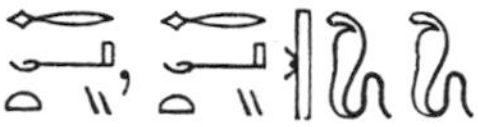 two great goddesses.

āa-ȧb  great of heart, *i. e.*, proud, arrogant.

 great forms, *i. e.*, possessing many forms.

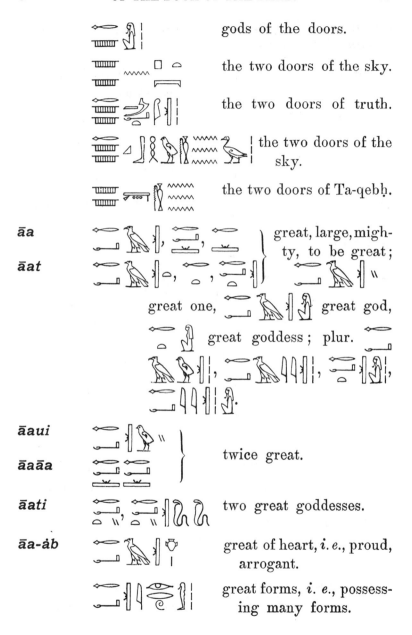

āat ur sep sen		most exceedingly great.
āa baiu		great of souls, *i. e.*, most valorous.
āa mertu	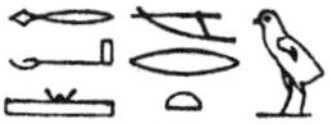	greatly beloved.
āa neruȧ		greatly victorious.
āa rennu		possessing many names.
āa khāu		possessing many crowns.
āa kheperu	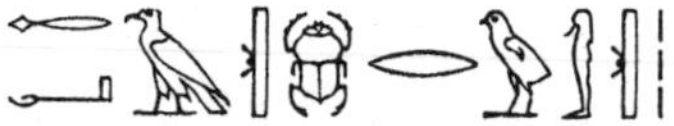	of many transformations.
āa senṭ		he who is greatly feared.
āa sekhemu	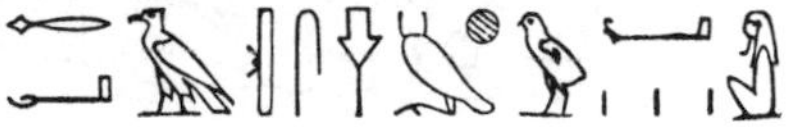	great one of powers.
āa sheps		most holy.
āa shefshefit		most terrible, or awful one.
Āa-kheru		"mighty of speech", the warder of the Seventh Ārit.
Āat-em-khut		"great one in the horizon", a proper name.

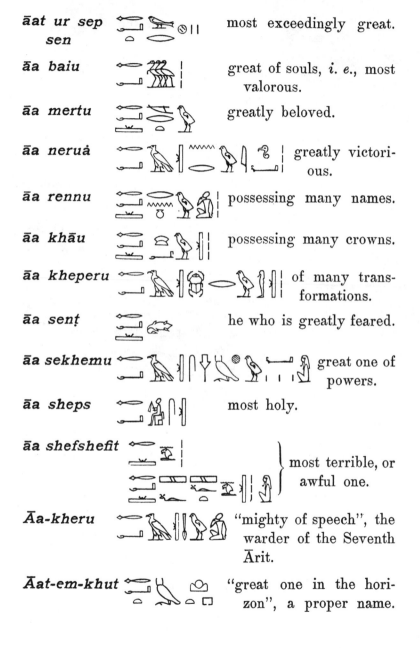

āā  to eat ?

āā 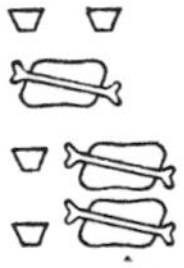 heir, inheritance, heritage, to inherit.

āat 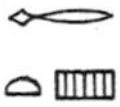 stone amulet, plur. 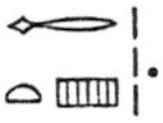.

āt, āāt 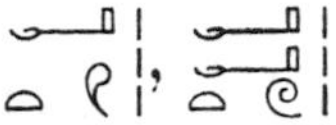 members, limbs, body.

āātu-pu-ent Kher-neter  name of the oar-rests in the magic boat (Chap. CXIX).

Āaṭi  the name of one of the Forty-two Judges in the Hall of Osiris.

āu, āāu  ass.

āān, ***āānā***, ***āānāu***  ape, monkey.

āu, ***āut***  animals, quadrupeds.

āu  sins, offences (vol. II, 148, 4).

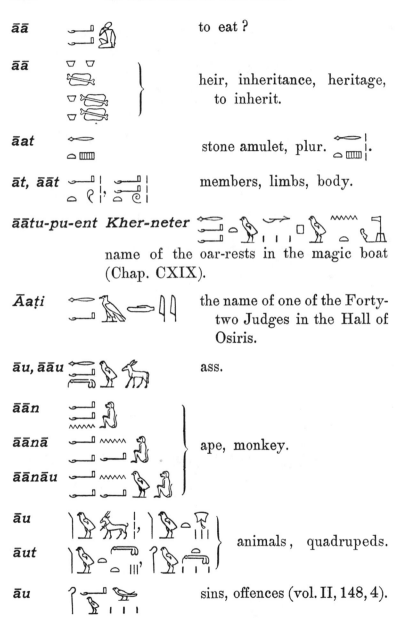

āua
āuau — to be strong, to act violently, to plunder, to rob, to oppress, vanquish, etc. , violence, wrong, evil act, evil doer, robber; ill treated, oppressed; (Chap. XVII, Nebseni, l. 25).

āuai — violence.

āun, **āunu** — , to be strong, violent, fierce.

āun-ȧb (?) — to be of a fierce disposition, violence.

āuq — pool, marsh, watery ground.

āb — , with , opposite, before, in front of, thus; , , , , , .

āba (*uba*) — opposition.

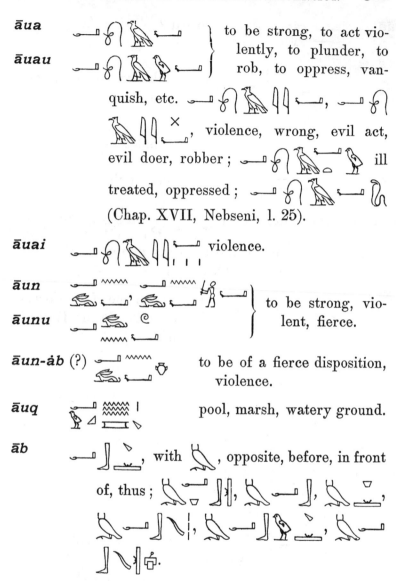

āb  altar, table of offerings.

āb 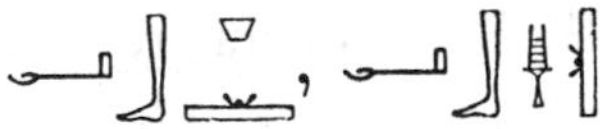 to present offerings, to offer up a sacrifice.

ābuaa  to bring before, to present.

āab, **āabet, ābet** 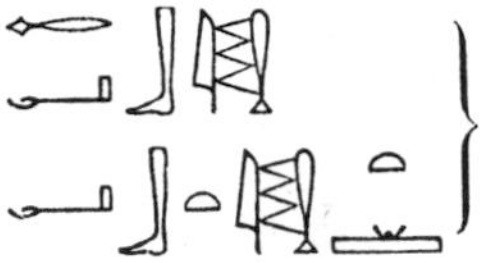 offering, sacrifice; plur. 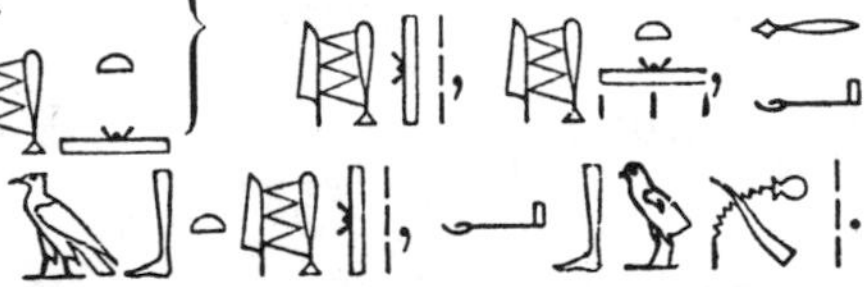

ābai (**āabai**)  sacrifice, offering, 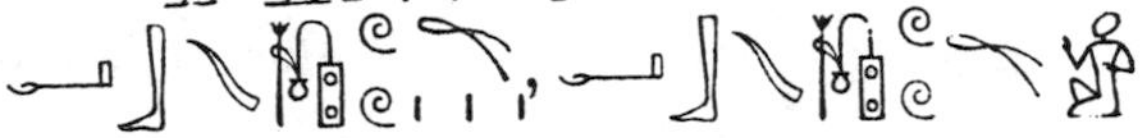 a priest who read the Liturgies.

āb (**uāb**), **ābu** (**uābu**), **ābet** (**uābet**)  clean, pure, holy, to be pure, to purify, to sprinkle or wash ceremonially.

āb (**uāb**)  libation, purification; plur. 

āb (**uāb**) 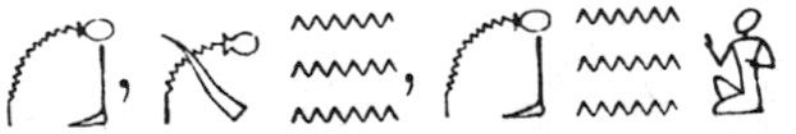 libationer, a man ceremonially pure.

āb (**uāb**)  pool of water used for purificatory purposes.

ābu (**uābu**)  clean raiment, holy apparel.

ābet (**uābet**)  water-house, bath, clean place; plur. 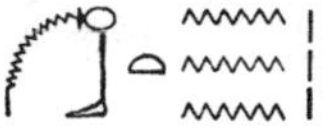; great pure place 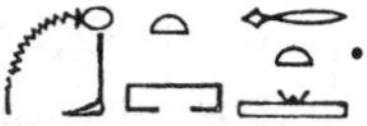

ābti (**uābti**) 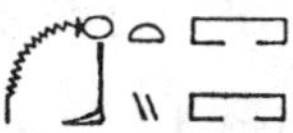 double holy place.

āb (**uāb**) **āāui**  clean-handed.

āb (**uāb**) **ru**  clean-mouthed.

āb (**uāb**) **ḥeru**  clean-faced beings.

ābu (**uābu**)  propitiatory offerings.

Āb-ur (**Uāb-ur**) 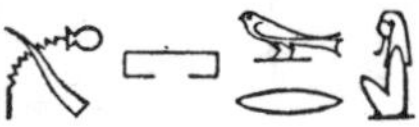 a title of Osiris.

āba (**uba**)  to open or force a way, or passage, through something.

āba (**uba**) **ru**  to open the mouth.

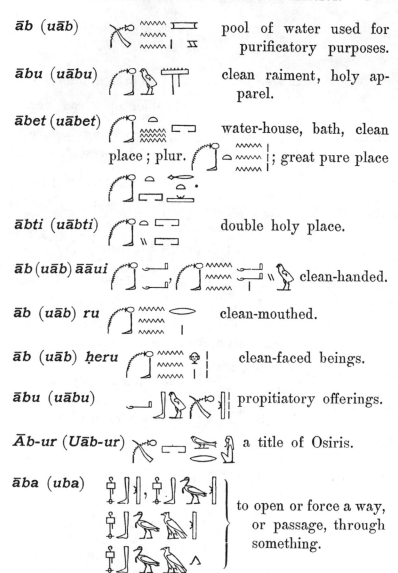

āba (*uba*) 

ābet (*ubet*)  entrance, opening.

ābata (*ubata*) 

āba  to see.

ābat (*ubat*) 
 fore-court of a temple.

Āba-ta (*Uba-ta*)  "Opener of the Earth", a name of a god.

Ābau-taui  the name of a god.

āb  horn;  two-horned; plur. ;  broad-horned; *neb ābui*  "lord of two horns" = Dhu 'l-Ḳarnên, a title of Alexander the Great.

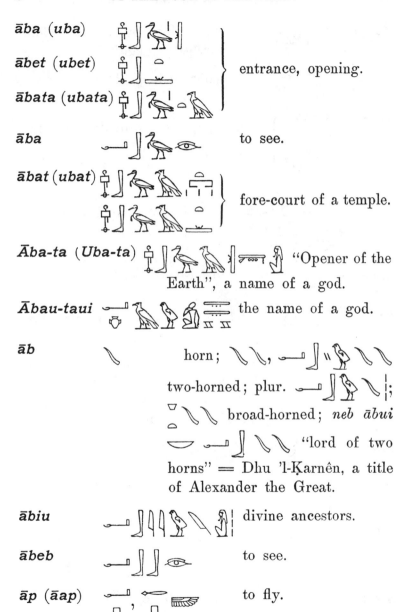

ābiu  divine ancestors.

ābeb  to see.

āp (*āap*)  to fly.

Āpep the arch-enemy of Rā. Copt. ⲁⲫⲱⲫ "giant".

Āpef name of a fiend.

āper to be equipped or provided with, furnished with; provided.

Āper, ***Āpert*** the name of a city and city-god.

āpesh tortoise, turtle.

āpshait a kind of beetle. Perhaps the weevil, the Muta Jambi, or "head of God", of the Bakuba of the Kasai District in the Congo Free State. (See T. A. Joyce in *Man*, vol. IX, No. 1, p. 3.)

āfa filth.

āfau food.

āfent wig, headdress; plur.

āftet place, abode, chest.

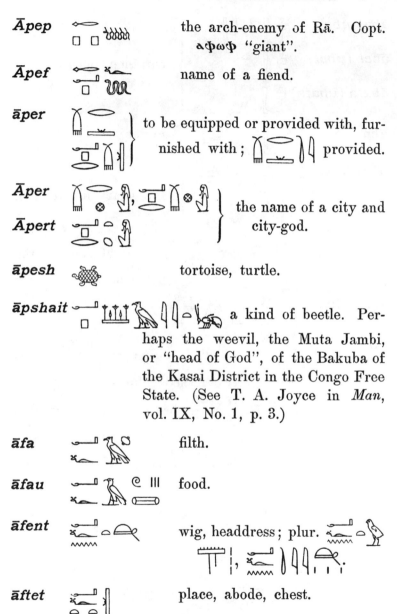

āfṭet 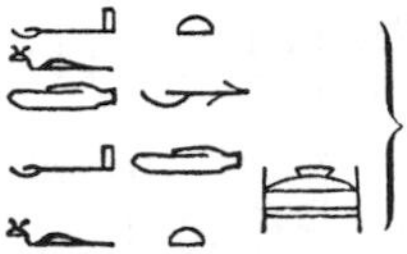 place, abode, chest.

ām  to eat, consume, devour; 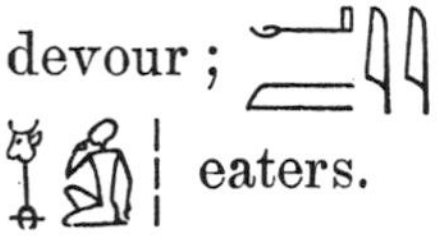 eaters.

āmam  to eat, to understand, to comprehend.

āmt  what is eaten, food.

ām ȧb  "to eat the heart", *i. e.*, become angry and rage.

āmam-ȧrit  "Eater of the Eye"; name of a god.

Ām-āu 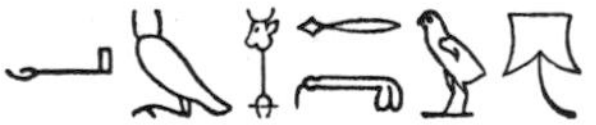 "Eater of the Ass"; name of a fiend and enemy of Rā.

Ām-ȧsfetti  "Eater of Sinners"; name of a god.

Ām-baiu  "Eater of souls"; name of a fiend.

Ām-ḥeḥ  "Eater of eternity".

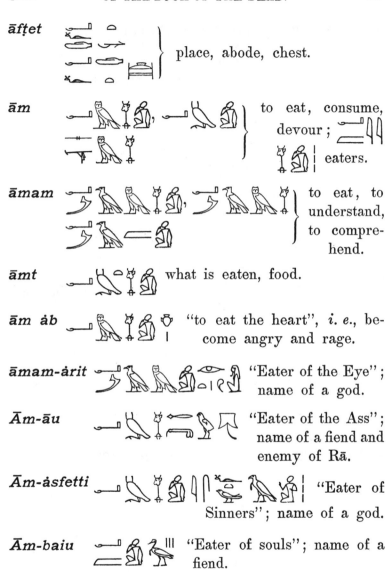

Ām-khaibitu  "Eater of Shades"; the name of one of the Forty-two Judges in the Hall of Osiris.

Āmām 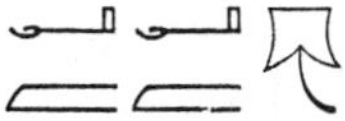 "Devourer"; the name of the Eater of the dead.

Ām-mit  "Devourer of the dead".

Ām-mit  a consuming serpent goddess.

Ān  a proper name.

ān, ***āni*** 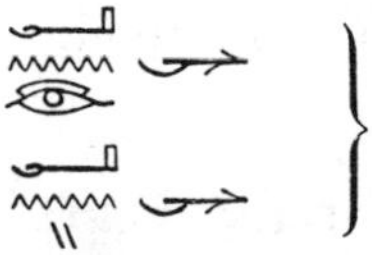 tablet, board, writing palette.

ān  to turn back. Partic. plur. 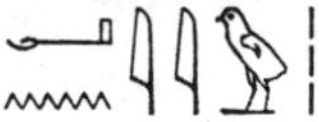 those who turn away, or return.

ānu  a mythological fish.

Ānpet  a name of the city of Mendes.

ānkh  to live, to live upon, to feed upon, life, living one, living; ,  alive. Copt. ωnϩ.  the living one, a name of Osiris.

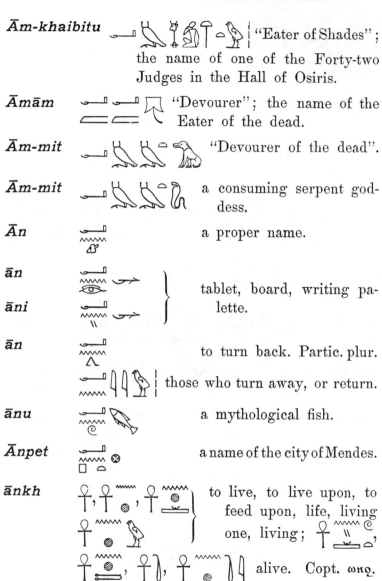

ānkhu, *ānkhiu*  the living, men and women, title of the blessed dead.

ānkh tchetta 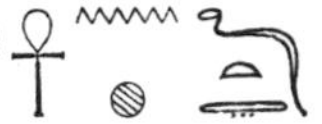 the living for ever. 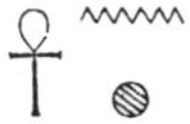 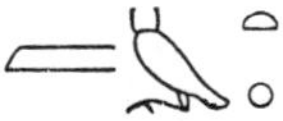 life from death.

ānkh user  life and power.

ānkh utcha senb 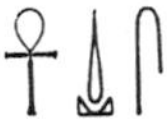 life, strength and health.

ānkhet  life.

ānkhet 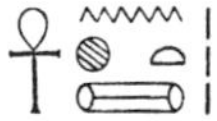 victuals.

Ānkhti 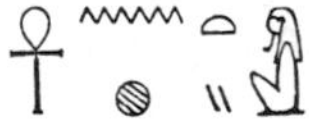 a name of Osiris.

ānkh  a kind of unguent.

Ānkhet pu ent Sebek neb Bakhau   a proper name.

Ānkh-em-bu  "Eater of abominable things".

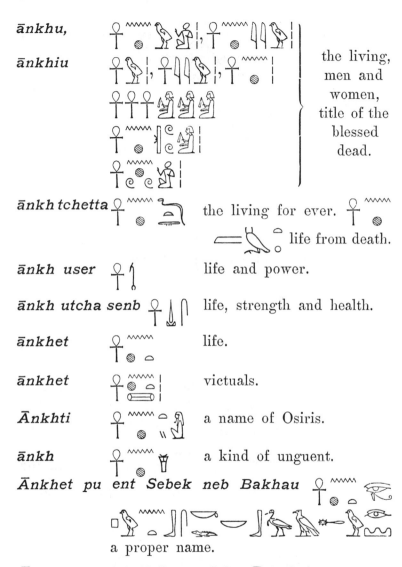

Ānkh-em-fentu  "Eater of worms"; name of the warder of the Fifth Ārit.

ānkhui  the two ears.

ānkhȧmu  flowers, or aromatic plants.

ānt  ring.

ānt 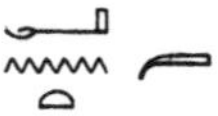 to be covered with something.

ānt  claw, talon, hook, nail of the hand or foot,  "Claw of Ptaḥ"; a proper name.

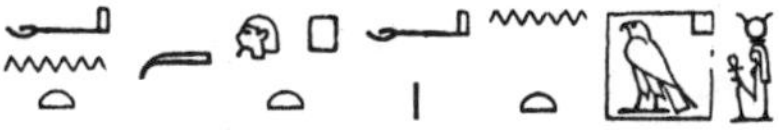 "Claw on the hand of Hathor"; a proper name.

ānti 

ānṭ 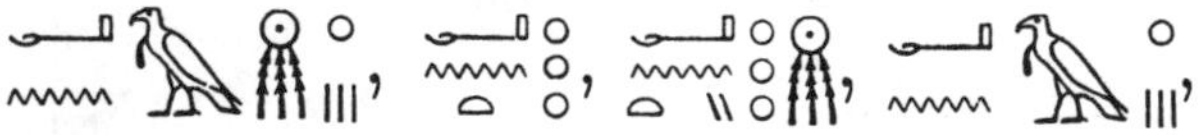

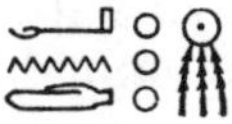 myrrh, unguent (?).

ānti — a preparation of myrrh used by women.

ānṭu — light, radiance.

ānṭ — evil.

ānṭu — darkness.

Ānṭi — the name of one of the Forty-two Judges in the Hall of Osiris.

ār — an animal of the goat species.

ār — to approach, to bring, to come, to arrive; ; divine beings who approach.

āră — to find (?).

ārār — jawbone.

ārārt — uraeus.

ārāti — two uraei goddesses.

two very large uraei.

the living serpent goddesses.

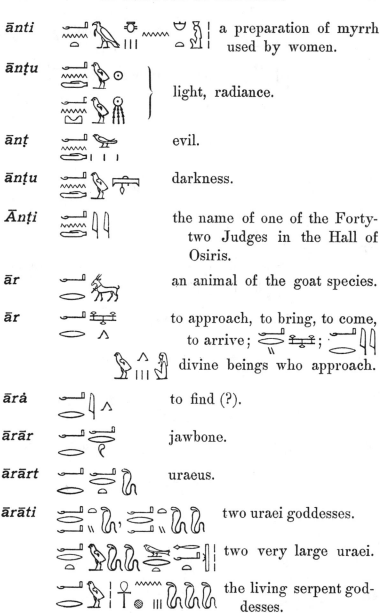

ārit tool, lintel of a door.

ārit hall, chamber; plur. The Seven Ārits

ārfi bundle, purse.

ārrt, **ārrit** hall, mansion; plur.

Ārq to bind, to tie, girdle, to be completed.

ārq to swear.

Ārq-ḥeḥ name of a city.

ārq end; end of the earth.

ārqi last day of the lunar month.

ārt jaw, jawbone.

ārti the two jaws.

ārtu houses, abodes, mansions.

āḥ moon.

āḥ 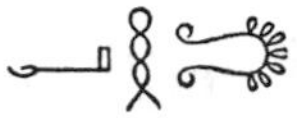 to surround, embrace.

āḥa, **āḥau**  to fight, do battle, wage war;  fighter,  fightings.

āḥa-ā  to fight bravely (?).

āḥa-tu  fight, contest, struggle.

āḥau  fighting implements, weapons.

āḥaui 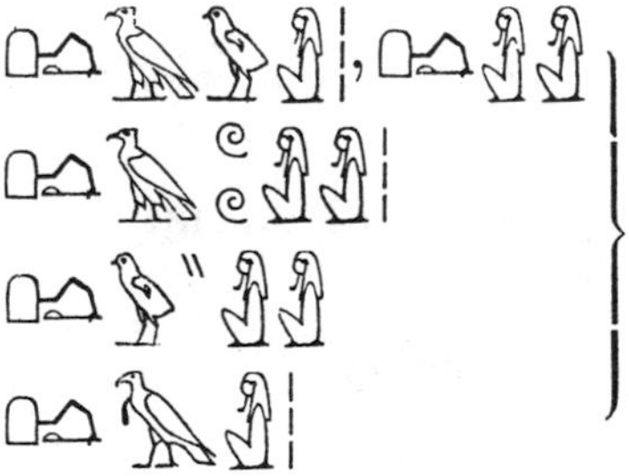 the two Fighters, *i. e.*, Horus and Set.

Āḥau ḥeru  "Fighting faces", a name of certain gods.

āḥāt 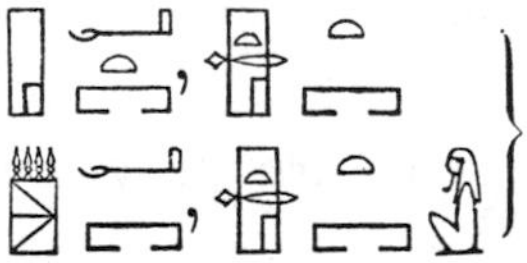 great house, palace.

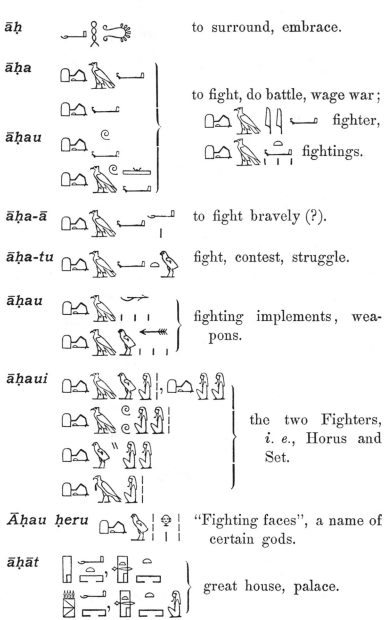

āḥā — to stand up, to withstand.

āḥā — as an auxiliary verb: and see *passim*.

āḥā — stability.

āḥāu — condition, state, position.

āḥā
āḥāu
āḥāt — time, season or duration of life, life, a contemporary.

period from life, or in life.

period of eternity.

āḥāu — noon-day.

āḥāu — supports.

āḥāu — stores, food, provisions.

folk who are provisioned.

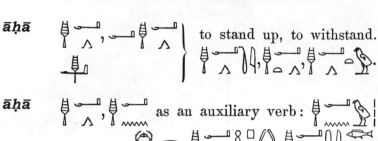

āḥāit  boat.

āḥāt  tomb.

ākh  to spread out the heavens, or sky.

Ākhtuset  a class of divine beings. The variants are:

 *ākhmiu.*

 *àukhu-seku.*

 *ākhsemiu.*

ākha  to fly, to soar; *ākhai*  flying.

ākha  to sleep.

ākhan 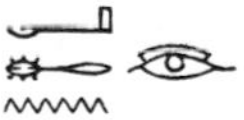
ākhanet 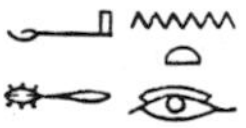 } to close the eye.

ākhu  } fire-altars.

ākhem 
ākhemu  } to quench, to extinguish;  quenched.

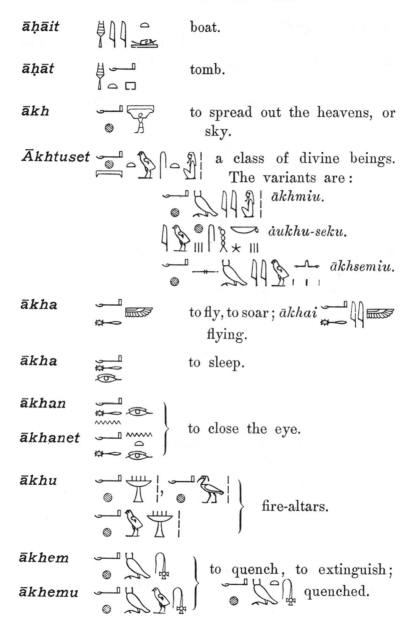

ākhemu, ***ākhmiu*** quenchers, those who extinguish.

ākhem figure of a god.

ākhemu figures of gods.

ākhmet river banks.

Ākhen-àriti*(?)-*f a proper name.

ākhekhau serpent-fiends, monsters.

ākhekhu "Darkness"; a proper name.

āsha to be much or many, manifold.

many reeded.

of multitudinous festivals.

of many forms.

loud voiced to speak.

āshau, ***āshat*** crowd, multitude.

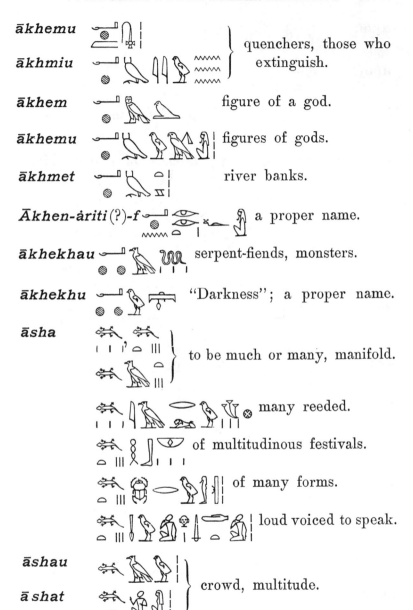

āshat  crowd, multitude.

āsh  to call, to invoke, to cry out.

āshu 

 evil speech.

āsh  cedar, or acacia, tree, cedar gum.

āshāsht 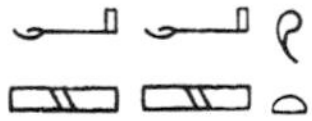 part of the body.

āshāt 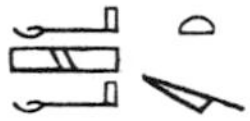 knife.

āshem  the forms in which the gods appear upon earth.

āshemu
āshemiu  crocodiles. A variant gives 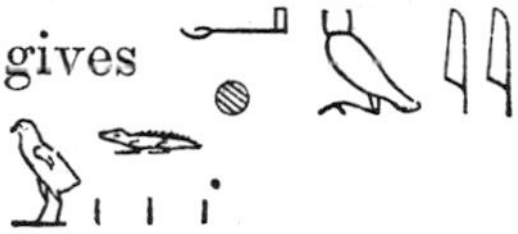.

āshashat  gullet.

Ākesh  name of a city.

āq  to enter, go in.

āqiu those who enter.

āqet things which enter.

āq pert entrance and exit.

Āq-ḥer-àmi-unnut-f "He who enters in his hour"; a proper name.

āqu cakes, loaves of bread.

āqa to present bread (?). Chap. XCIX, 3.

āq maāt (?) exact truth (?), just.

āqa to keep the mean, right, exact, true, just, truth, to be in the middle.

to be exactly over the heart.

āqau truth, right, justice.

Āqan the name of a god.

āqi part of a boat.

āq, āqa 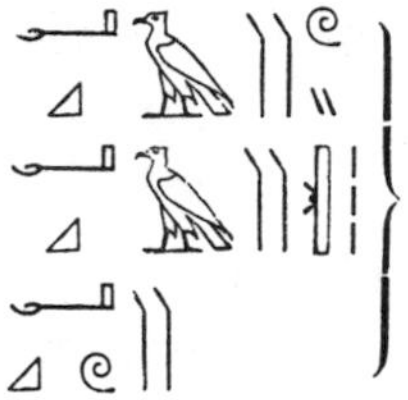 rope, cordage, tackle of a boat.

Āqennu  the name of a city.

āḳa  unguent.

āḳu  to be burned.

āt  domain.

āt  hall, palace.

āt  member, limb; plur. , .

Āti  name of the ninth nome of Lower Egypt.

āteptu  grain, seeds.

āter  provisions.

āṭ (ānṭ) 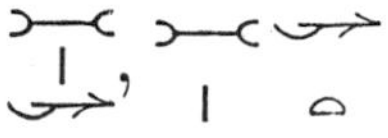 pole of a net with curved ends.

Āṭ (Ānṭ)  name of a god.

āṭ (ānṭ)  domain, territory, soil.

āṭ (*ānṭ*) 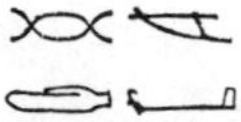 to split, to divide.

Āṭ (*Ānṭ*) 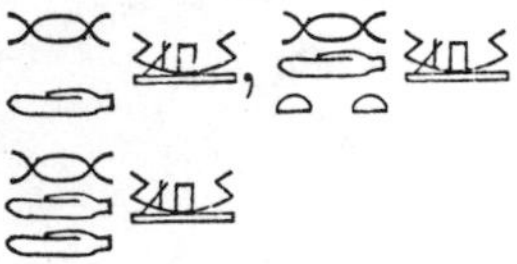 the morning boat of the sun.

āṭu  name of a mythological fish.

āṭurtu  (a mistake ?)

Ātch-ur 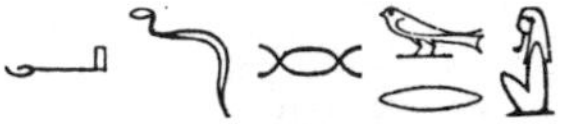 "Great splitter"; name of a god.

ātchet (*āntchet*) 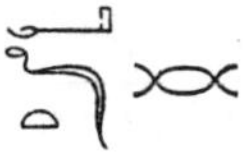 fixed, firm.

 U.

. . . . . . 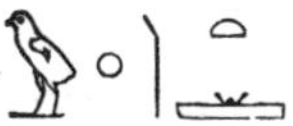 . . . . . . Chap. CLXVIII. Circle X, 14, 2.

u  they, them, their.

u 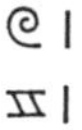 district, region.

Ua  a proper name.

ua
uau  to depart, go away, be afar off; 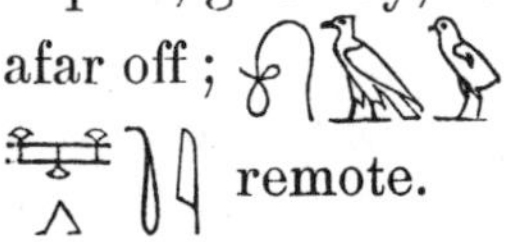 remote.

ua / *uau*  way, path, road; plur. 

uau  waterway, stream.

uauau  radiance, light.

uau  flame, fire.

uau  chains, fetters.

uauu  to speak evil, blaspheme.

uauiuait  hair.

uai  to destroy, overcome, gain the mastery over.

Uaipu 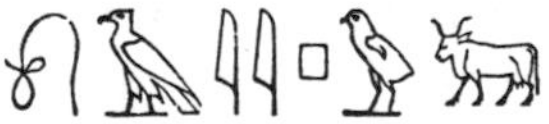 a cow-goddess.

uab  flower, blossom.

Uamemti  the name of one of the Forty-two Judges in the Hall of Osiris.

uart  ropes, cordage.

Uarekht (?) 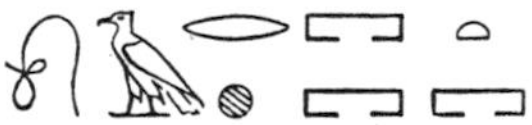 a mythological region.

Uart-neter-semsu a proper name.

uaḥ to place, to set, to fix, to add to, permanent, abiding.

to add to something.

uaḥit libation vessels.

uaḥuu mummy bandages.

uaḥtu to mummify.

uakh, ***uakhet*** "Green"; the name of a pool in the Elysian Fields.

uas sceptre.

uas contentment, happiness.

Uast Thebes.

uash to worship, be adored; two-fold worship.

Uaḳ the name of a festival.

uat ,  way, road, path; plur. , 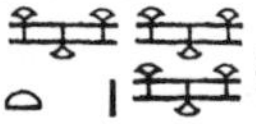;  great roads, 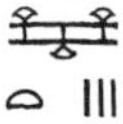  good roads,  all roads,  ways of the dead; 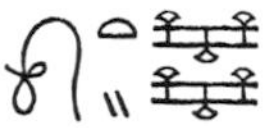 the two roads.

 eastern roads.

 western roads.

 northern roads.

 southern roads.

uatch  sceptre, staff, stick.

uatch  tablet of green faïence, amulet.

uatch  unguent, sulphate of copper eye-paint.

uatchu  sulphate of copper.

uatch shemāt  sulphate of copper of the south.

uatchet  a kind of linen.

uatch  to make to flourish, be green, vigorous, to blossom, be new, fresh.

uatchet  green.

uatchet  green things, plants, herbs.

uatchu 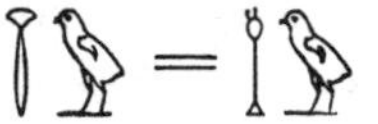 *q. v.*

Uatch-ȧriti (?)  "Green Eyes"; a proper name.

Uatch-ur 
Uatch-urȧ  "Great Green Sea"; *i. e.*, the Mediterranean.

Uatch-nesert 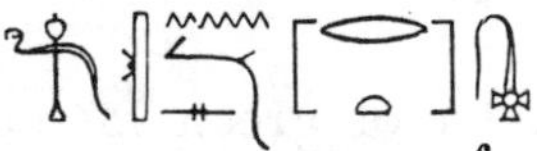 "Green Flame"; the name of one of the Forty-two Judges in the Hall of Osiris.

Uatchit 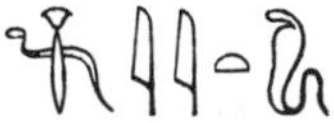 a goddess of fire.

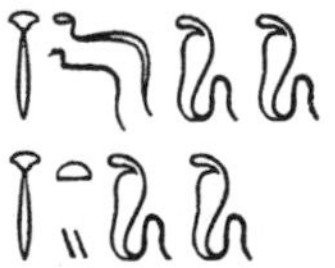 the two fire-goddesses, Isis and Nephthys.

uatchit  abode, house.

uȧ  I, me.

uȧa — boat, boat of Rā.

uȧaui — the two boats of Rā, the boats of morning and evening.

uȧa en Maāti — the boat of Maāt.

uȧa en ḥeḥ — "Boat of Millions of Years".

uȧn — to become worms.

uā, *uāu* — One, the One, *i. e.*, God. One of the gods;

One God (Osiris); One (fem.).

uā — one; fem. ; , being one, or alone; to be one .

uā—ki — one ... the other; one embraced the other; fem. ... ; one in one; one of one.

uā = indefinite article ,

uā neb any one, each one, every one.

uā uāu one alone, only one.

uāu alone. Also and .

uāuti solitude.

uā with at once, all at once; and compare , .

uāt in a piece of cloth.

Uāau the herald of the Third Ārit.

uār passage.

uār to depart.

uārt passage, the name of a place.

uārt thigh; the two thighs.

"thigh" of water.

"thigh" of the lake.

"thigh" surrounding.

"thigh" of iron whereon is the station of the gods.

that "thigh" of Kher-āḥa.

that "thigh" whereon is the House of the Moon.

uārt stream.

uu evil, evil one.

uu region, district;

ui sign of the dual. two very mighty gods.

Ui — a proper name.

uit — chamber.

uben — to rise (of a luminary), to shine; rising and setting;

ubennu, *ubentu* — rays of light.

ubennu — to flow.

ubekh, *ubekht* — to shine, light up, shining, blazing.

ubes — water-flood.

ubesu — beings of fire, sparks (?).

Ubes-ḥer-per-em-khetkhet — "Fiery face, coming forward in retreating"; a proper name.

ubeṭ — to be scalded, to set fire to, to burn up.

ufa to chance on, to light upon.

umet a garment.

umet the middle (?).

umet walls, fortifications, building.

un lightness, defect.

un, unen to be, being, existence, to become, to exist; as an auxiliary verb see *passim*.

unt
unent being, existence; ; plur. ; those who are, things which are.

uniu human beings.

un maā in very truth.

un to open, opener, opening; opened.

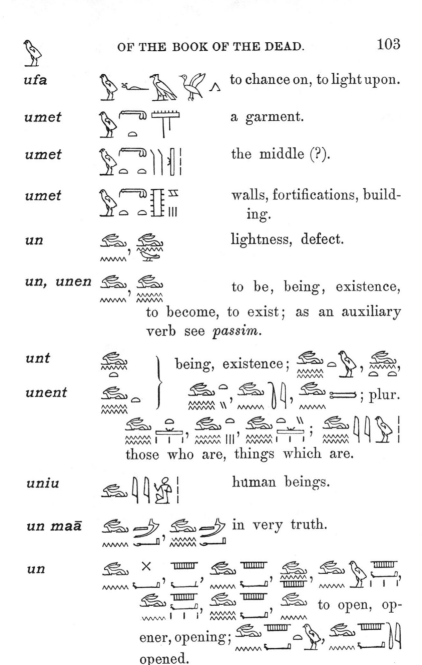

uniu }
uneniu } openers, scatterers.

un ḥer to open the face, *i. e.*, show the face, to appear; ; to open the mouth , .

un shrine.

un shaved.

un }
unnu } to pull out the hair.

un, uni, unt , , to walk, run, rise upright; runners.

unun , , }
unn-unn } to run, stand up.

unun to sow seed.

Unȧset name of a city.

unām unguent.

Uniu, or ***Unniu*** name of a city.

unini light.

uni light, defective.

Unen-em-ḥetep a division of the Sekhet-Åaru.

unb flower, bloom; plur.

unpet flowers, blossoms.

Unpepet ent Ḥet-Ḥeru "Flower of Hathor"; a proper name.

unef to remove, to uncover, to unloose.

unem
unemi
unemt the right side, the right as opposed to left.

unem to eat, see *Åm*.

unnu evil, wrong, defect.

Unnu Hermopolis, the city of Thoth.

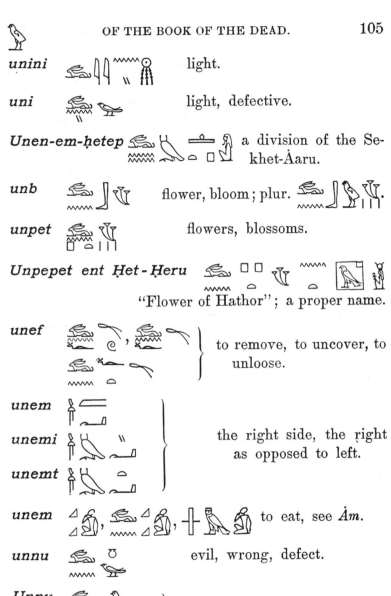

unnuiti sacrificer.

unnut a brief space of time, a moment, an hour, a season, interval. Plur.

Unnut goddess of the hour.

Un-Nefer, *Unen-nefer*, *Unen-Neferu*, *Unen-Neferu* A title of Osiris, meaning something like "the well-doing Being". Coptic forms of the name are ⲟⲩⲉⲛⲉⲃⲣⲉ, ⲟⲩⲉⲛⲟⲃⲣ, ⲟⲩⲉⲛⲟⲃⲣⲓ, ⲱⲛⲟⲫⲣⲉ, etc.

Un-Nefer-Rā.

Un-Nefer, son of Nut.

Un-ḥāt a proper name.

unkh, *unkhu* to dress, to array oneself, to put on a garment.

unkh to tie, untie, set loose.

unkh a garment.

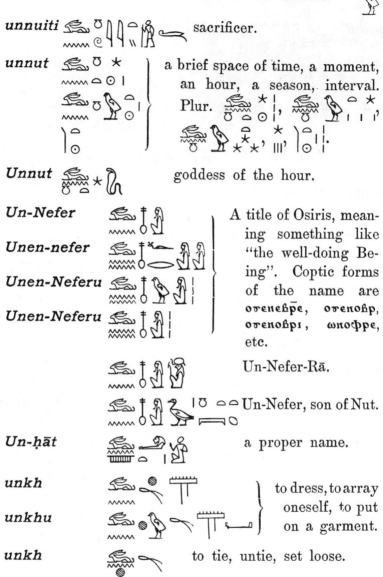

Unes — the metropolis of the XIXth Nome of Lower Egypt.

unshu — wolves.

Unt — a city of the Twelfth Ȧat.

Unti — the name of a god.

un tini — be ye.

unṭu — mankind, people, kinsfolk, relatives.

Unth — name of a district or country.

ur — to be great, great, mighty, supreme, powerful.

ur, uru — great one (God); plur.

urt — great one (fem.), goddess.

uru — dual masc. "two great".

urti  dual fem. "two great goddesses".

 two very great goddesses.

ur  great man, chief, prince, nobleman, master;  princess. Plur. masc.   ; plur. fem. 

ur sep sen 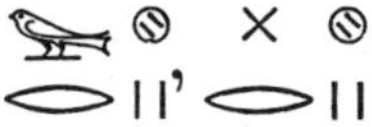 doubly great.

ur  as comparative,  greater than.

ur  as superlative,  greatest of 5 gods.

ur  in titles etc.:

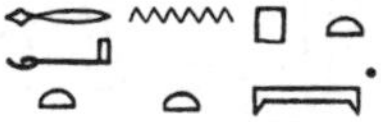

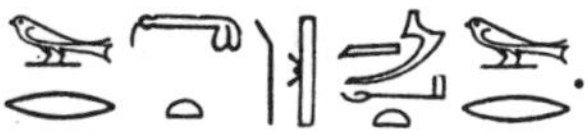

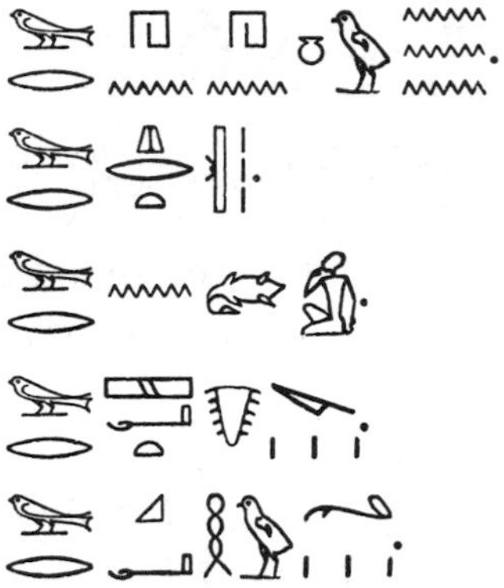

ur  a joint of meat, haunch, carcase;  

Ur-at  "great of moment", a proper name.

Urit  name of a city.

urit 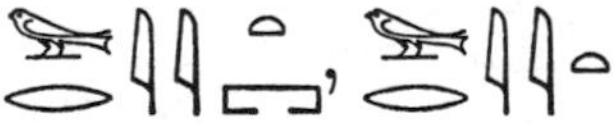 hall, house, room.

Ur-årit-s 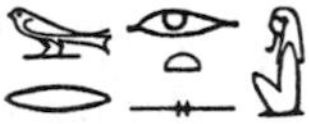 a proper name.

Ur-peḥui-f  a proper name.

Ur-ma  title of the high-priest of Heliopolis (?).

Ur-maat  a proper name.

Ur-mertus-ṭeshert-shenu

Ur-mertis-ṭeshert-shenu "The red-haired one who is greatly beloved"; name of one of the Seven Cows.

Ur-ḥekau a deity who is mighty in words of power, a god or goddess of magic.

Ur-kherp-ḥem "chief master of the blacksmith's tool"; a title of the high-priest of Memphis.

Ur-senu chief of the physicians.

urer

urert the name of a crown. the gods who wear the *urert* Crown.

urertu

urḥ

urḥu to smear or rub with unguent, to anoint.

Urḥetchati two goddesses of Heliopolis.

urs		a pillow, head-rest.
ursh	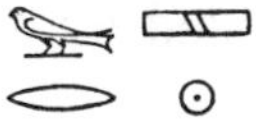	to pass the day, to watch;  watchers.
Urek		
urt	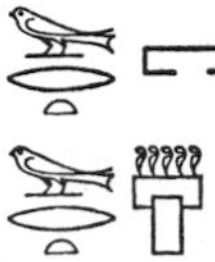	hall, palace.
urt		funeral chest, or coffer.
urt	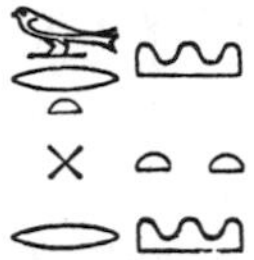	funerary mountain, cemetery.
urt		flood.
urt	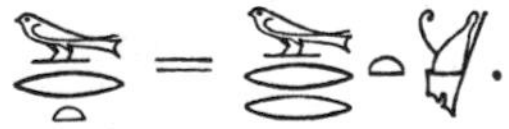	
Urt-urt		a proper name.
urṭ, urṭu		to be inert, motionless, helpless, to rest.
Urṭ-àb		"He whose heart is still"; a title of Osiris.

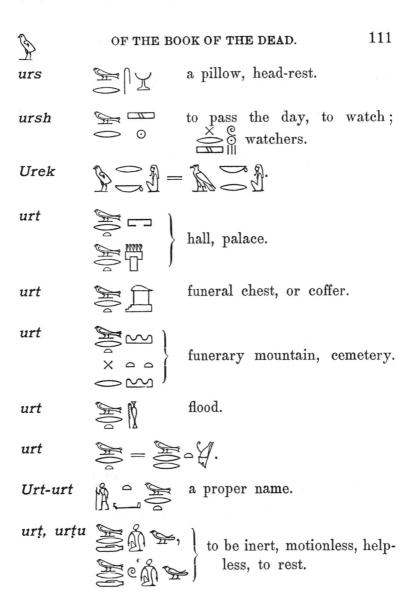

urṭu , see .

uh  to be troubled?

uhau  to supplicate.

uhaȧu  to fail.

uhem
uhemu
uhemm  to repeat, to report, to narrate;  to repeat; .

 to speak again.

 to renew life, live again.

 a new form.

 to renew protection.

, with , a second time, again.

uhem-ā  anew, afresh.

Uhem-ḥer  a proper name.

uhen  decay, failure.

uhen  to overthrow;  be overthrown.

uḥā  to unloose, be set free from, to return (in the evening).

uḥā  cord, rope.

uḥā  to catch fish, to snare game, fisherman, fowler.

uḥeset  to beat down, to slay.

uḥet  baked meats, stew (?).

ukha  to lay down, set down, to seek after, search for.

ukha  darkness, night.

ukha  pillar.

ukhakh  to seek after.

ukheb  to shine.

ukhert  wooden implement.

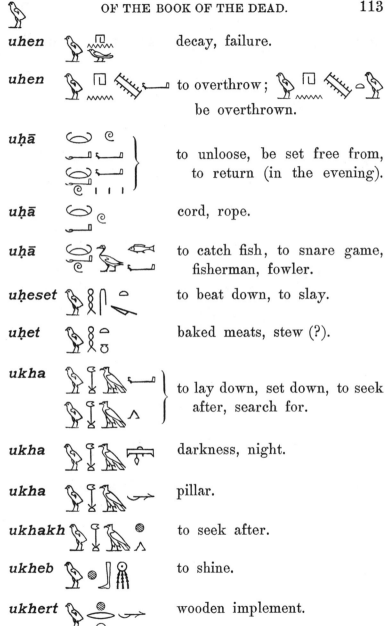

ukheṭ to be angry, be pained, disgusted.

ukheṭet boat.

us to do away with.

usfau idle, lazy.

user to be strong, mighty, strength, might, power, strong; .

useru powers, mighty beings (human or divine).

usert strength.

usert skull, top of the head; plur. .

User-àb "Strong-heart"; a proper name.

User-ba "Strong-soul"; a proper name.

useru oars, rudders, steering poles.

useru to steer a boat.

Usert the name of a goddess.

useḥ to advance.

usekh collar, neck ornament, pectoral.

usekh to be in a wide space, to be wide or spacious, breadth, broad.

Usekh-nemmet "He of the long stride", the name of one of the Forty-two Judges in the Hall of Osiris.

Usekh-ḥer "Broad Face", a name of Rā.

usekht the wide space of the sky, a large hall or room; the great double hall.

Usekht Maāti the name of the double Hall wherein Osiris judged the dead.

Usekt Shuu	the Hall of Shu, *i. e.*, heaven.
Usekht Ḳeb	the Hall of Ḳeb, *i. e.*, earth.
usekhu	plated (?).
usesht	urine.
usesh	to micturate.
usten, *ustennu*	to walk, to follow.
Usṭ	a proper name.
ush	to cry out.
ush	misery.
ushau	night, darkness.
ushā	te eat, to gnaw, crunch bones.
usheb	to answer, to eat (?).
	to make an answer at the right time.
usheb	to beget, begotten.

ushen 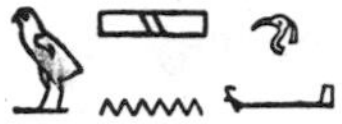 to net, to snare.

ushenu  feathered fowl.

uḳ  to burn, be burned.

uḳa  name of a festival.

uḳaiu  wooden pegs or legs.

ut  the city of embalmment, the abode of Anubis.

utu  embalmment.

utu  the god of embalmment, *i. e.*, Anubis.

ut  coffin, mummy bier.

uta 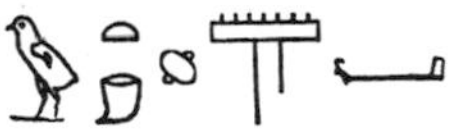 to embalm, swathe a mummy.

Ut (*Uḥet* ?) *meḥt*  the Northern Oasis (Baḥrîyah).

Ut (*Uḥet*) *res*  the Southern Oasis (Khârgah).

Utau  a class of divine beings.

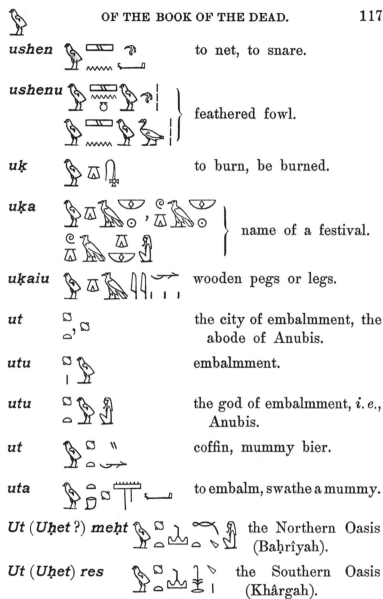

utu to set out on a journey, to make an expedition.

utu
uṭeṭ to issue an order or command, to decree, to ordain.

utet
uṭeṭt commands, behests, things ordered or decreed, records, documents, deeds, copies of deeds.

Utu-nesert the name of one of the Forty-two Judges in the Hall of Osiris.

Utu-rekhit The name of one of the Forty-two Judges in the Hall of Osiris.

utu

utu flowers.

utuit oar rest.

Utent the name of a country.

utet 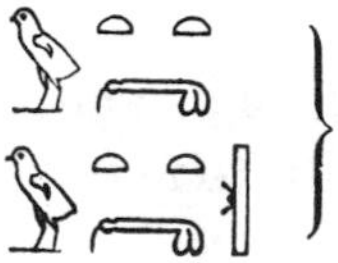 to beget.

 begetter.

Utet 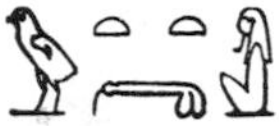 "Begetter", a name of Osiris.

Utet-Ḥeḥ 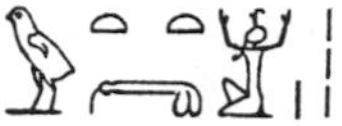 "Begetter of millions of years"; a proper name.

uṭ, *uṭet* 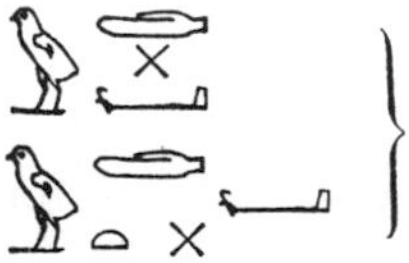 to cast down or out, to shoot out, dart forth, to utter a cry.

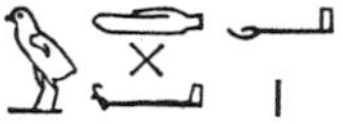 to lay violent hands on some-one.

uṭaiu  strong ones.

uṭit  chamber.

uṭebu  mutable.

uṭeb  to go round, turn about.

uṭeb, *uṭebu* 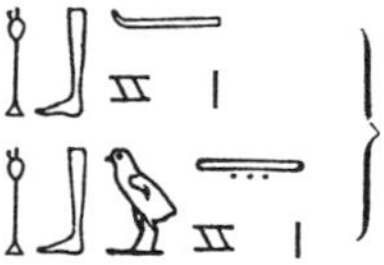 furrow; plur. , .

uṭebtu 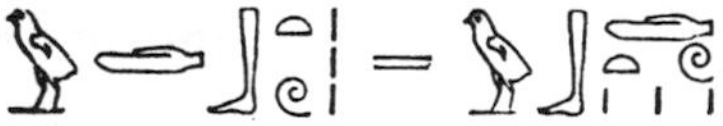 burned.

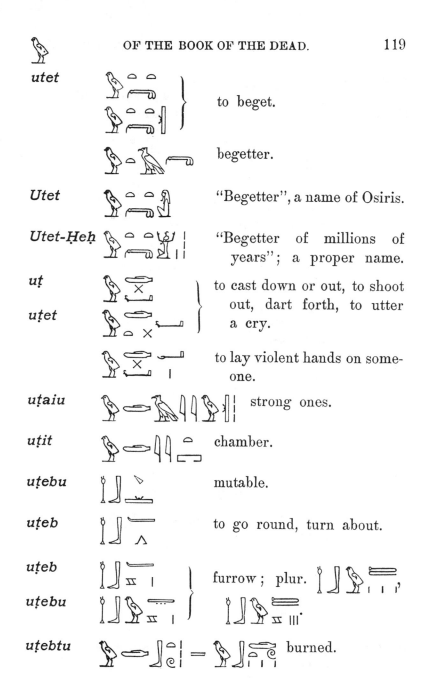

uṭen, ***uṭenu*** to bring something as a gift, to make an offering;

uṭenu, ***uṭent*** offerings, things given as offerings.

uṭeḥ altar, table of offerings; plur.

uṭeṭ to void, shoot out.

uthes to raise up, to lift up, support.

utcha to go out, set out, to begin a journey.

utchat a journey, a going forth.

utcha to be in a good state or condition, sound, healthy, well.

utchau strength, power.

utchau  amulet, object of power.

 magical powers.

Utcha-re  "Strong-mouth"; a proper name.

utcha sep  strong with good fortune.

utchat  the "strong", *i. e.*, the Eye of Rā, whence came all power, strength, health, protection, etc.

utchat  the Utchat with legs and wings.

utchat  the Utchat of Sekhet, the great lady, the mistress of the gods.

utchati "the two Utchats", *i. e.*, the two Eyes of the sky, or the Sun and Moon.

utchā — to weigh, to estimate, to consider, to reckon up, to decide.

— to consider or weigh deeds or words.

utchā senemm — to weigh hair?

utchā — making the water to balance his throne, or making his throne to balance on the water.

utchāiu — to estimate the fields; weighers, those who try something in a balance.

utchāt — judges.

utchāti — judgment, decision.

Utchā-aābet — "computer of the offering", name of a god.

utchfau — to delay, to tarry.

utcheṭ — to walk.

I.

i, *iu* — to come, come, come!

i-tu, *iu-tu* — coming, a coming, advance.

it — a coming.

iu — comers; comers with glad tidings.

iu — to end (of a book) it has gone out in peace.

iu āq — going in and coming out, entrance and exit.

Iu pastu — a class of divine beings.

i, it — hail, O.

iu — O verily.

iumā — sea, lake, river, any large collection of water.

Ir-qai — a name of Ȧmen-Rā.

ikh to stretch out the heavens.

isu abodes, chambers.

B.

ba one of the two souls of man, the heart-soul, which was intimately connected with the *ka* and the heart, as opposed to the spirit-soul *khu*. Plur.

ba mentioned with and ; with , with , with and .

a perfect soul.

an equipped divine soul.

a living soul.

a living heart-soul and a perfect spirit-soul.

soul of souls.

my soul is the souls of the gods.

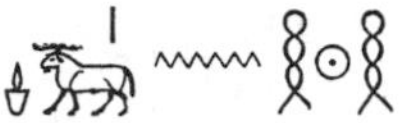 soul of eternity.

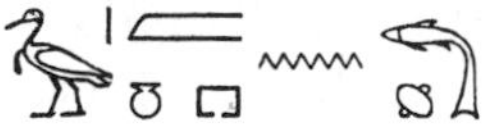 soul in the body.

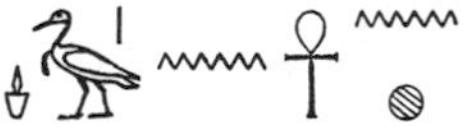 soul of life.

 a soul [made] of gold, an amulet.

 thy soul is to heaven, thy body is under the ground.

ba  the divine Soul, or soul of God.

ba 

 soul of Osiris;

 of Rā;

ba  soul in Shu;

ba  soul in Ḳeb;

ba 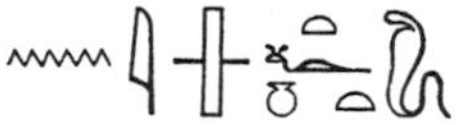 soul in Tefnut;

 Holy Soul, a name of Osiris.

 Holy Soul, a name of Osiris.

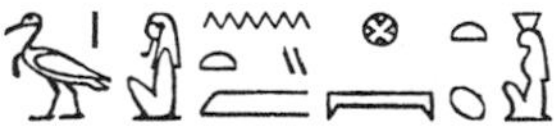 the Soul which is in Nut.

 the Soul of the gods who exist in the body of Osiris.

 the Soul of the Great Body which is in Saïs, Neith.

 the Living Soul in Suten-ḥenen.

 the Soul of Ȧmenti.

baiu  divine souls, souls of gods.

 the souls in the gods.

 the souls of the gods of the East.

 the souls of the gods of the West.

 the souls of Heliopolis.

 the souls of Pe-[Ṭep] (Buto).

 the souls of Nekhen.

 the souls of Hermopolis.

 living souls.

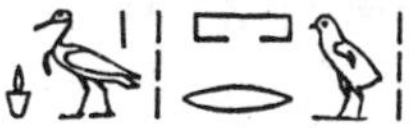 souls who have appeared.

 souls of the dead (*i. e.*, damned).

 souls of his father (Osiris).

baui  the double soul.

 the double soul in the Tcha-fui, *i. e.*, the souls of Osiris and Rā.

Bai  the Soul-god, or the Divine Soul, or the Ram-god;  the double-soul god.

Bati  a name of Osiris.

Ba  divine soul with plumes .

Ba  the metal-god; a proper name (?).

ba  to be endowed with a soul.

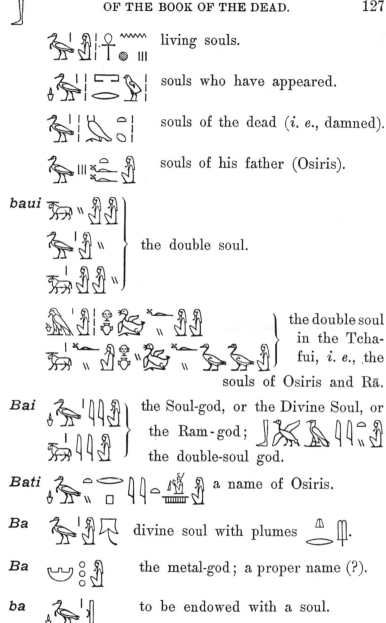

ba  to cleave, make a way through something.

Bau  a proper name.

baba  to work.

babau  cavern, cave, den or lair; plur. 

Baba  the name of the first-born son of Osiris.

Ba-neb-Ṭeṭṭeṭ 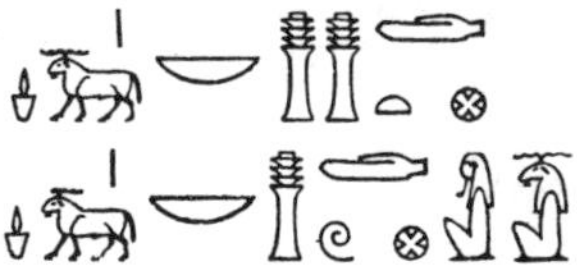 Soul-god, or Ram-god, lord of Ṭaṭṭu (Mendes), a title of Osiris.

Barekathȧ tchaua  a proper name.

baḥ , or , with  before, in front of.

Bakhau  the Mountain of sunrise.

Bast  the city of Bubastis in the Eastern Delta, the modern Zaḳâziḳ.

Bast  the goddess of Bubastis.

Bast  Bast dweller in Thebes.

Basti  the name of one of the Forty-two Judges in the Hall of Osiris.

bak  to work, to toil, to serve.

 works, labours.

baq  olive tree.

baḳ  to be weak, weary, feeble, helpless.

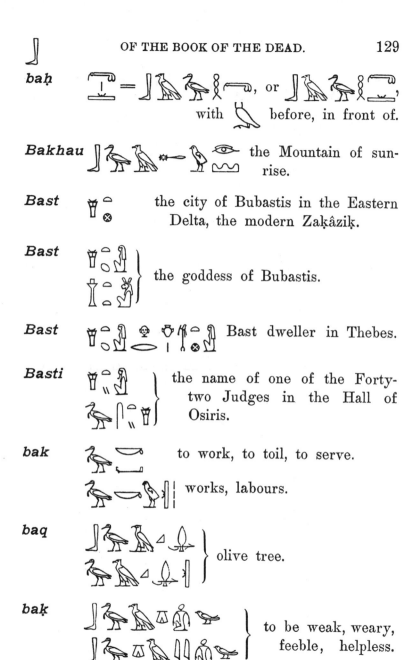

baḳ  weak one, the helpless one (*i. e.*, the mummy); plur. .

bat / *bȧat*  plants, boughs, branches.

Bati 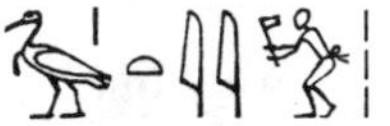 name of a fiend, or of a group of fiends.

bȧa 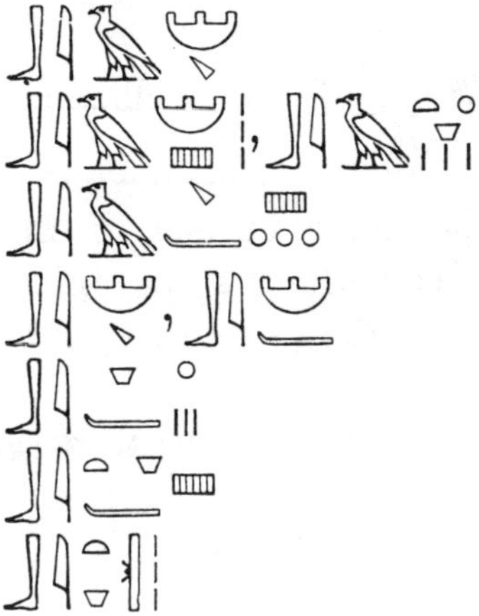 the ore of a metal, iron, copper, etc., a metal tool, a name of the sky or firmament.

bȧa en pet 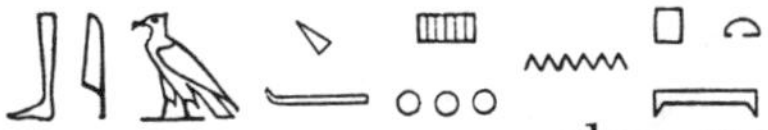 metal of the sky, meteoric iron (?).

 that iron in the sky.

bȧat shemāu  "the metal of the south", iron.

bȧat shemāu 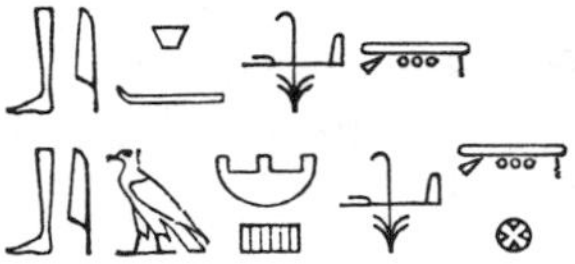 "the metal of the south", iron.

bȧau, *bȧat*  wonders, wonderful things.

bȧaq  a kind of grain, or fruit.

Bȧbȧ  the name of a god, Baba (?).

bȧbȧ  a cry of joy.

bȧn  evil, wickedness.

bȧk  hawk; plur. .

 the double divine hawk.

Bȧket  the city of the divine hawk.

bȧt, bȧti  king of the north.

Bȧti  a proper name.

bābāt  water-flood, stream.

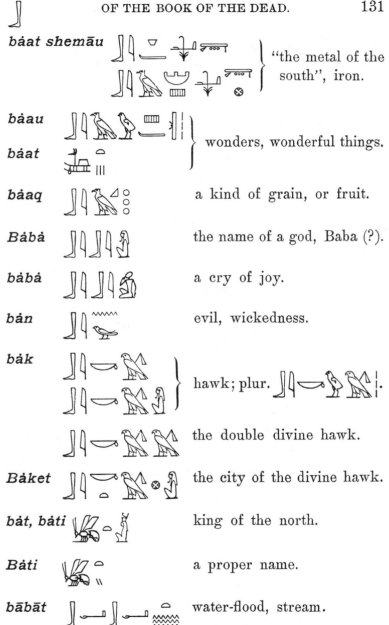

bāḥ 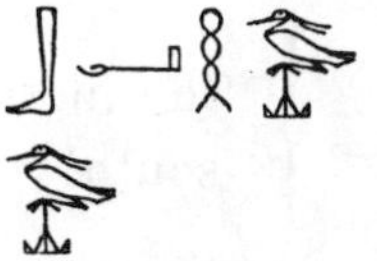 to be flooded, inundated.

Bāḥ 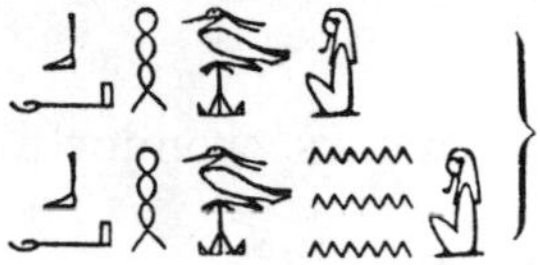 the god of the Inundation.

bi 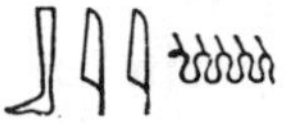 name of a fiend.

biu  strength.

bu 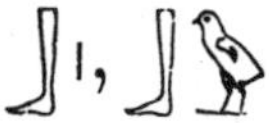  purity,  oneness (?), altogether,  lawfulness, legality, truth,  this place (?).

bu neb  everywhere, every place.

bu nebu  all men, all people, everyone, folk in general.

bu nefer  prosperity, happiness.

bu ṭu  evil thing, calamity.

bu  not, it is not; 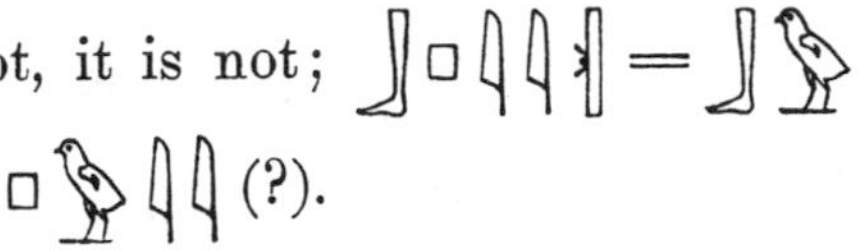 (?).

bu-pu 

but  evil thing, abomination.

but  offering.

bebait  the mantis.

bebuu  strong.

Bebi  the name of a god.

bebet  flowers.

bebet  fountain head.

bebet  hollow place, cavity.

ben  not.

benānā 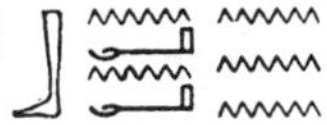 to bathe.

benben  a kind of wood.

benben  bier, funerary couch.

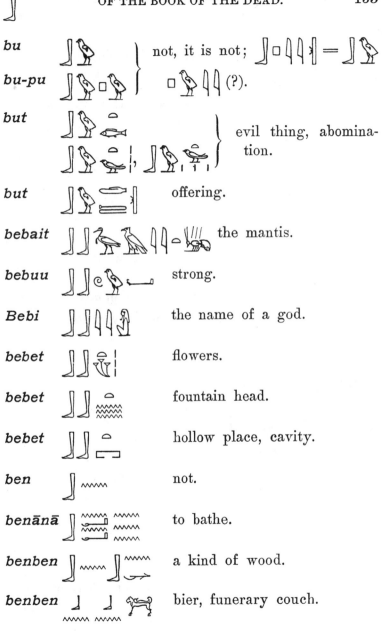

benbent  hall, pylon chamber.

ben  to pass away, to dissolve, to go on.

ben, ***benen*** 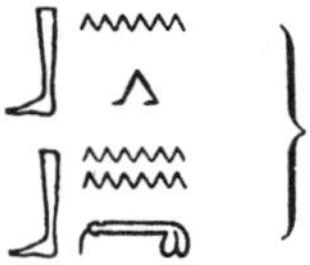 to beget, to be united with, union.

benen 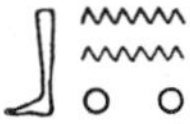 ring.

benen  a kind of wood.

bennu  a bird commonly identified with the phoenix.

 the Bennu, the Soul of Rā.

bennut  matter, pus.

bennu, ***bennut***  cakes (?), bread.

Bener  the name of a city.

benrȧ  to be sweet, pleasant.

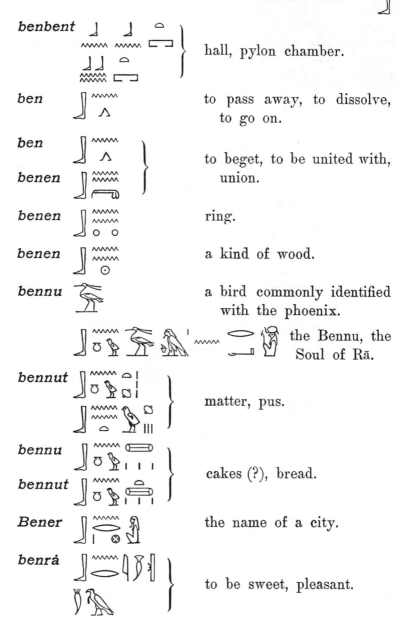

benrȧu — sweet things, dates, date wine, pleasant, nice.

benshu — bolts.

bent, *benti* — divine apes, incarnations of the spirits of morning.

beḥ — to cut, to split.

beḥen — baleful one.

beḥen — to cut, to pierce; — murderous.

beḥennu — animals of the wolf or dog species.

beḥes — calf.

Bekhennu — a proper name.

bekhekhu — fire.

bes — form (?).

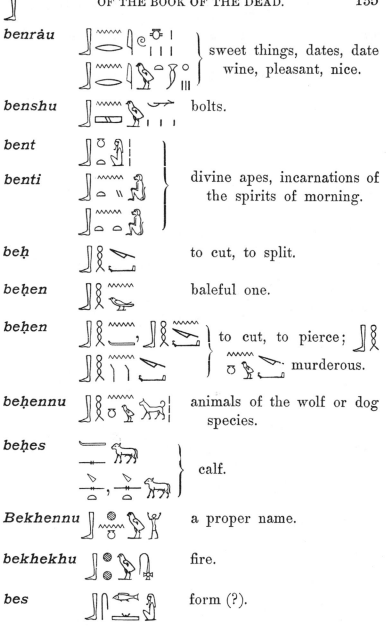

bes — to enter, to pass in, to rise (of the river).

— increase.

bes
besu — flame, fire, blaze.

Besu-Aḥu — a proper name.

Besu Menu — a proper name.

bessu — humours, excretions, filth.

Besek — Sebek, the Crocodile-god.

besek — intcrnal organ of the body; plur.

besh — to vomit.

beshu (?) — metal plates, scales.

beka — pregnant.

beka — to shine, the dawn, to-morrow.

bekau — weakness.

beq olive tree, olives; the olive tree in Heliopolis.

beq a proper name.

beqsu eyeball, skin (?).

beqsu balance, scales.

Beqtui a proper name (?).

beḳ misery.

beḳi helpless one, sinner.

beḳa defect, sin, crime, evil, sinner; plur.

beḳa, **beḳai** evil man, sinner.

beḳasu . . . .

beḳsu part of a boat.

beḳset . . . .

bet place, every place, everywhere.

bet 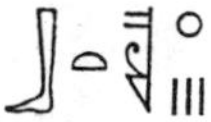 incense.

bet  grains, seed.

bet  flower.

beta  to sin, commit a fault, do wrong.

betau, *betu*  sin, wrong, abominable thing; plur. 

Betȧ  name of a city.

betennu, *betnu*  swift.

beṭ  incense.

beṭ, *beṭ-ti*  barley.

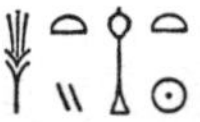 white barley.

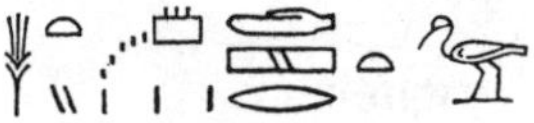 red barley.

beṭesh 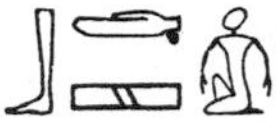 to be weak, powerless, but disposed to do evil.

beṭesh, ***beṭeshet*** 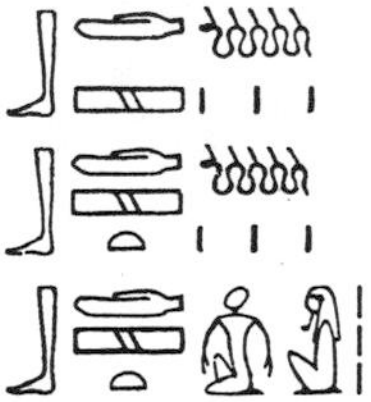 impotent fiends; fem. sing. 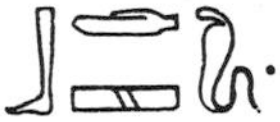.

Beṭshu  the name of a city.

Beṭ-ti 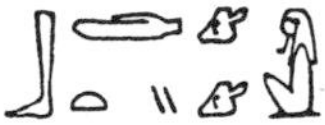 a proper name.

bethet (?) 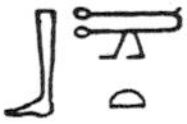 brought.

betcha 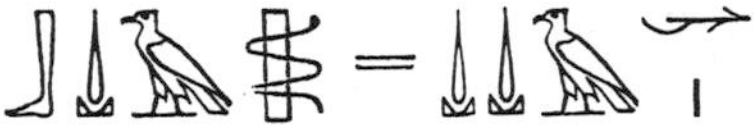 a tool or instrument.

□ P.

Pe  One half of the city of Buto (Per-Uatchit).

Pe . . . . .  the little Pe (?).

p  the.

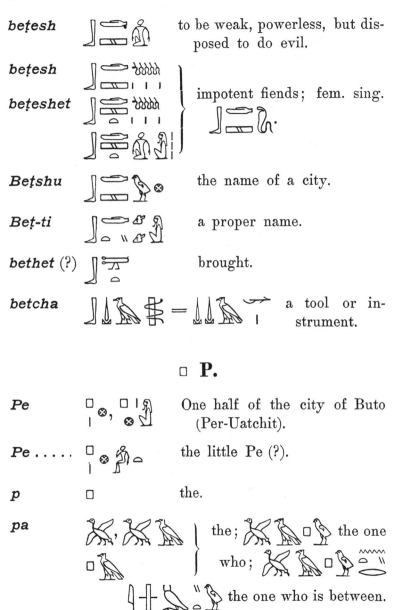

pa  the;  the one who;   the one who is between.

pai-à  my.

pai-f  his.

pa, *pai*  to fly, flight.

pait  bolt hole.

paut  stuff, substance, matter, cakes, offerings in general.

paut 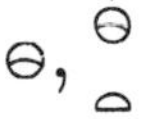 primeval matter, the material out of which the gods and the universe were formed.

pauti 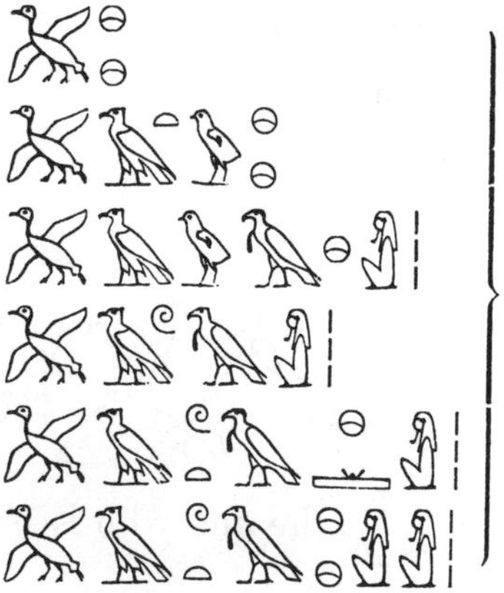 the god of primeval matter, the chief Egyptian god of the Predynastic Period.

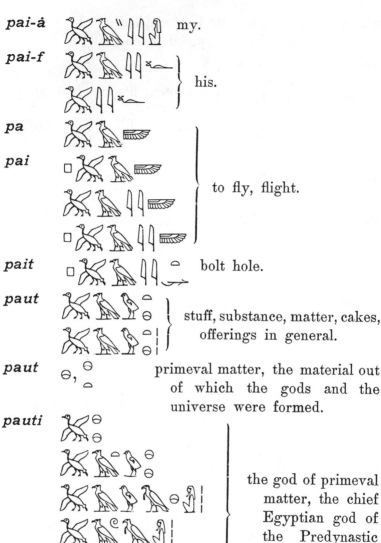

paut neteru 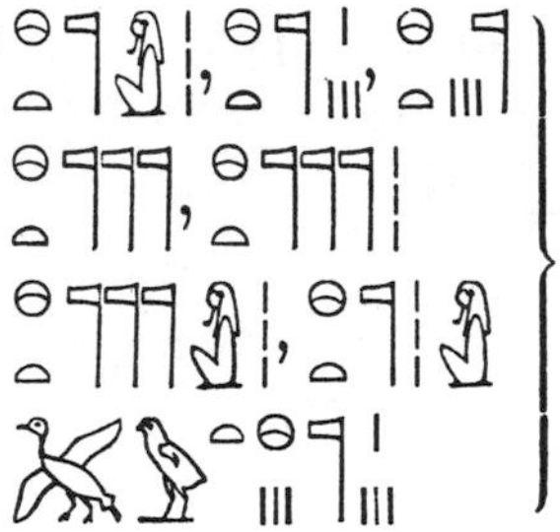 the whole company of the primeval gods, *i. e.,*  . The 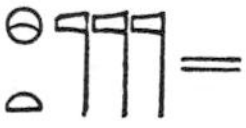 = the names  of Nu.

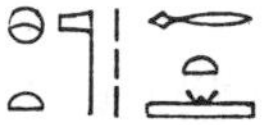 the Great Company of the gods.

 the Little Company of the gods.

 the complete Company of the gods.

paut-ti 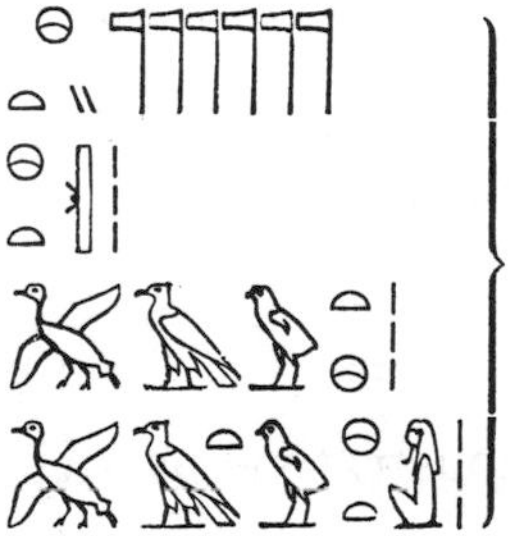 the Great and Little Companies of the gods.

pan 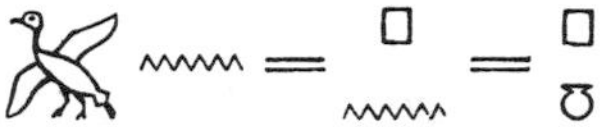 this.

Par, or ***Pal***  a proper name.

Parehaqakheperu  a proper name.

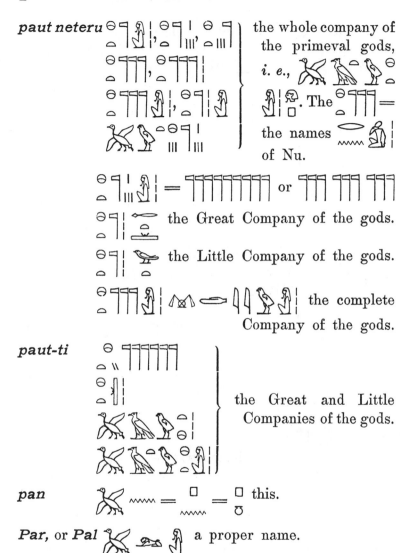

pas an ink jar.

pasekh = .

Pashakasa a proper name.

pat (?) light.

pā spark, flame, fire; plur. .

pāt men and women, people, a class of people.

pāit ḥer-f human-faced.

pu , a mark of emphasis: ; .

puȧau cakes.

pui a demonstrative particle.

Punt

Punṭ the region whence came *ānti* (myrrh) and other aromatic gums and spices, a region in Africa near the southern end of the Red Sea. The district of Punt proper was probably situated some distance inland.

putrȧ (Nebseni Papyrus), an interrogative particle. What is this then? *i. e.*, what does this mean?

pef
pefa
pefi
pefat — a demonstrative particle.

pefes
pefses — to burn, be hot, fiery, a spark, to cook, bake.

pefsit baked.

Pen
Pen-ḥeseb (?) — a proper name (?).

penā to overturn, capsize (of a boat), to invert a matter.

peni land (?).

penu rat, mouse.

pens . . . . . .

penq 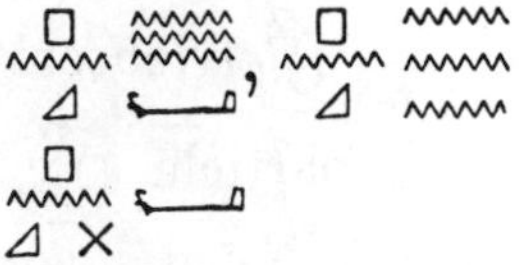 to beat to pieces, to macerate.

Penti 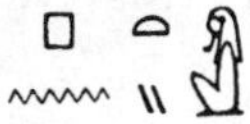 the name of a god.

pert  a season of the Egyptian year.

per  house, abode, temple, habitation; plur. 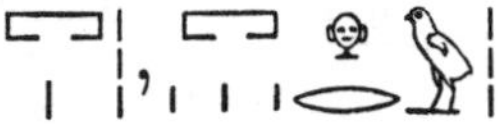 celestial mansions.

perui  double house.

per āa  "great house" פַּרְעֹה.

Per-àbu  the temple of hearts, *i. e.*, the judgment hall.

per Àsàr  temple of Osiris.

Per-Àst 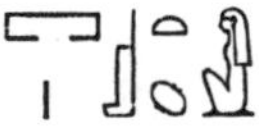 the temple of Isis.

Per-Àsṭes 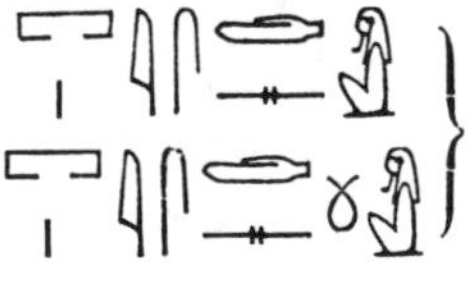 the temple of Àsṭes.

Per-Unnut  the temple of the Hour-goddess.

Per-ur 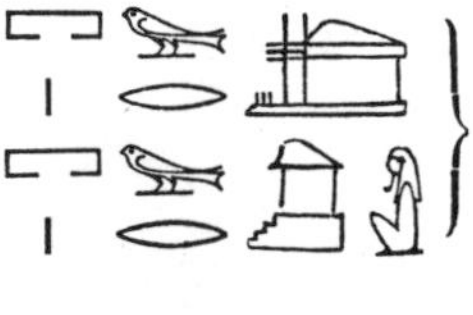 the "great House", *i. e.*, the tomb.

Per-Ptaḥ 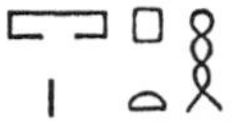 the temple of Ptaḥ at Memphis.

Per-Menȧ 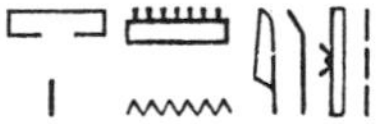 the house of coming into port, *i. e.*, the tomb.

Per-Menu 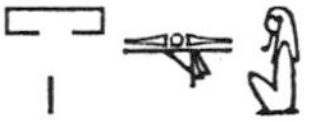 the temple of Menu.

Per-neḥeḥ  the house of eternity, *i. e.*, the tomb.

Per-neser  the house of fire.

Per-neter 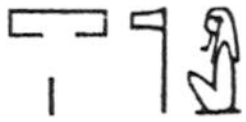

Per-neter-āa 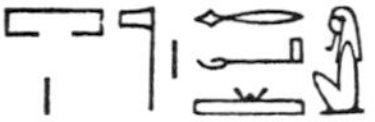 the temple of the god, *i. e.*, Osiris.

Per-Rerti (?) 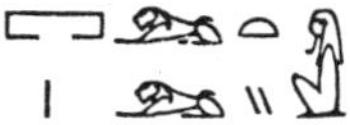 the temple of Shu and Tefnut.

Per-Ḥapṭ-re  the temple of Ḥapṭ-re.

Per-ḥāt  the temple of hearts, *i. e.*, the judgment hall.

Per-Ḥepṭ-ur  the temple of Ḥepṭ-ur.

Per-Ḥeru  the temple of Horus.

Per-Ḥetch 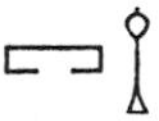 the "White House".

Per-Khenti-menȧtu-f 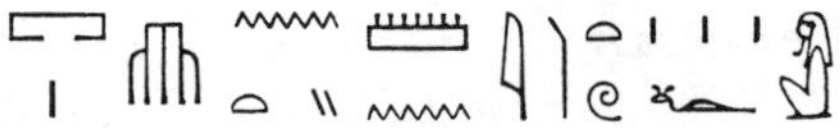 the temple of the "President of his dead".

Per-Sabut  the house of Sab (or Ḳeb), the earth (?).

Per-Sati  the temple of Sati.

Per-suten  the house of the king, *i. e.*, palace.

Per-seḥeptet 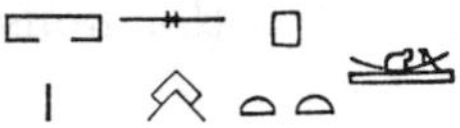 the temple of Seḥeptet.

per-shāt (?) 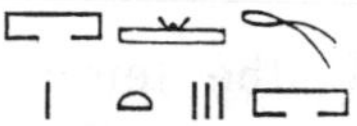 the house of books, *i. e.*, library.

Per-Kemkem  the temple of Kemkem.

Per-Keku  the temple of darkness.

per qebḥ  the house of coolness, *i. e.*, bath (?).

Per-tep-ṭu-f  the temple of him that is on his hill, *i. e.*, Anubis.

Per-Tem  the temple of Tem.

Per-Ṭeḥuti  the temple of Thoth.

per , — *peru* , — *perr* — *perru* — to come forth, to rise up, to appear, to make oneself manifest; to come forth retreating; to appear in the presence.

, comer forth; plur. , things which appear, manifestations; to come forth; , appearance, exit.

per-ā — to come forth boldly, brave.

per ḥer ta — to be born on the earth.

pert em hru — to come forth by, or in, the day; the title of several groups and Chapters of the Theban Recension of the Book of the Dead.

pert — offspring.

pert — *pertu* — things which appear, *i. e.*, offerings.

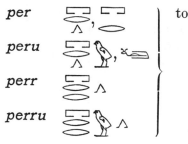

pert er kheru 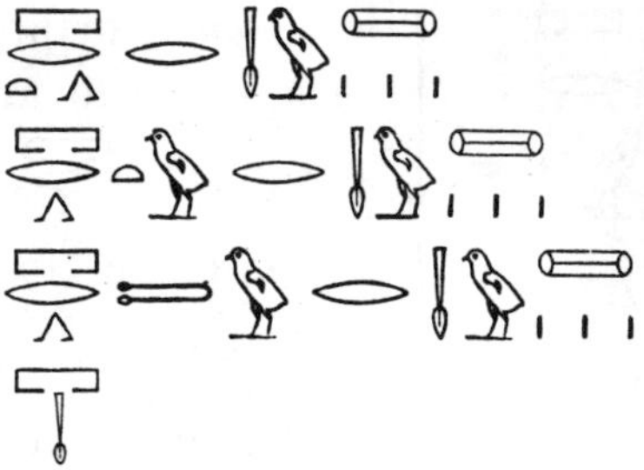 "things which appear at the words", *i. e.*, sepulchral offerings of bread, beer, oxen, geese, unguents, etc. Determinatives of these objects are usually added to  thus: 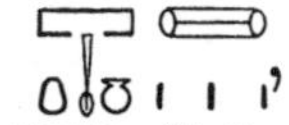, 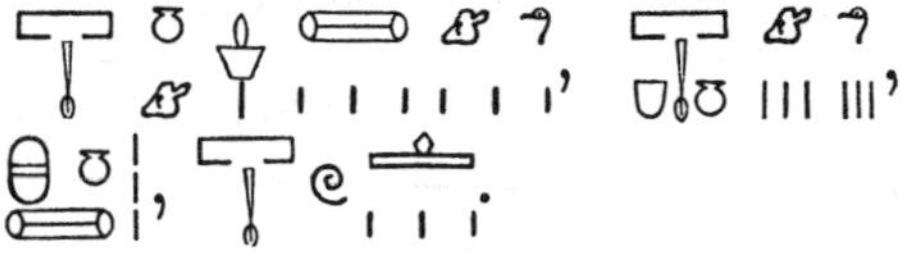.

perit  temples.

peri  strip of linen, bandage.

persen 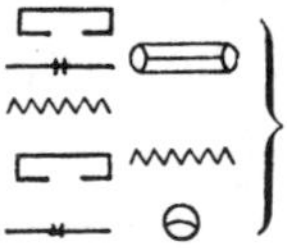 a kind of cake; plur. 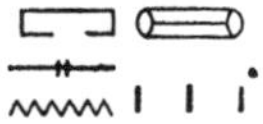.

pert  [1] corn, grain in general.

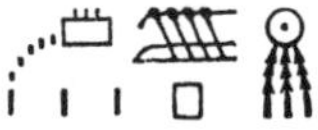 white grain.

1. Perhaps "measures of grain" *ḥeqat.*

	black grain.
	red grain.
peḥ	to arrive at, attain to, to reach the end.
peḥu	
peḥuut	
peḥt	
peḥu	the back part, the end.
peḥi	the lower part of the back, the buttocks, thighs.
peḥui	
peḥti	
peḥuit	stern of a boat.
peḥu	swamp, marsh.
peḥrer	to run.

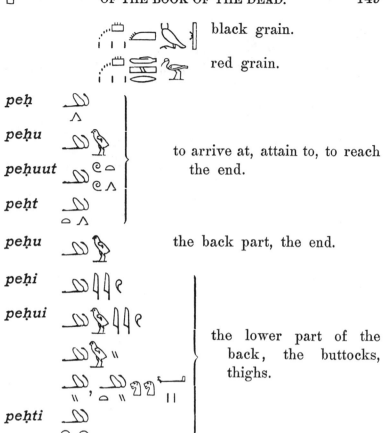

peḥreru  runners, a class of beings.

Peḥreri 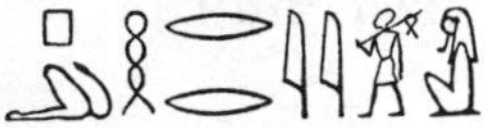 "Runner", a name of Rā.

peḥti 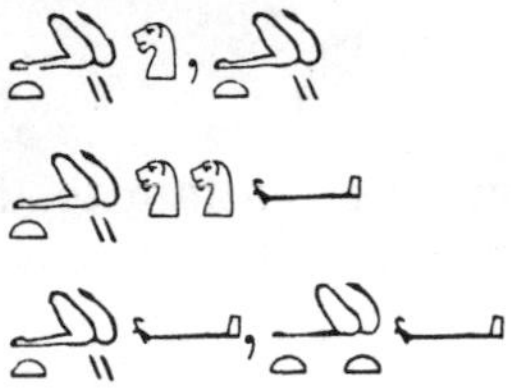 strength of the thighs originally, then strength, might, power, in general.

pekha  to separate.

Pekhat  the name of a goddess.

pekhes  to cover over, fall on.

pes 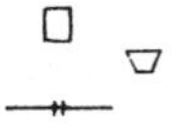 ink-jar.

pesakes 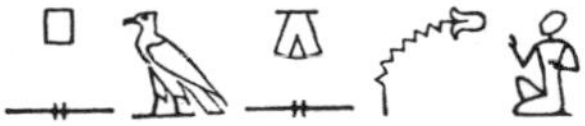 a mistake for   to spit.

peseḥ 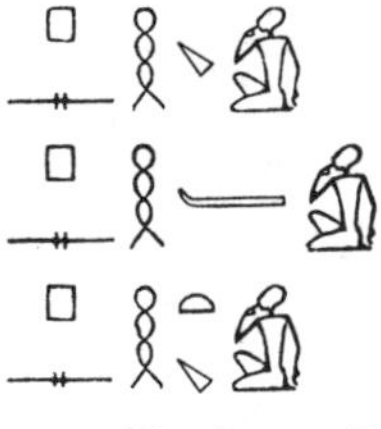 to eat, to bite (of an insect or animal), to sting.

Peskheti  a divine envoy.

pesesh 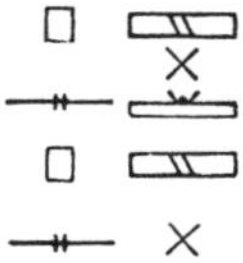 to divide, to cleave, to allot.

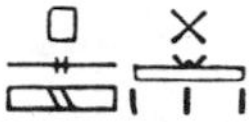 divisions.

pesḳ  to spit.

Pesḳ-re  a proper name.

pesṭ (*pestch*) ||| ||| |||,  nine, 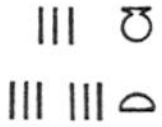 ninth.

pesṭ 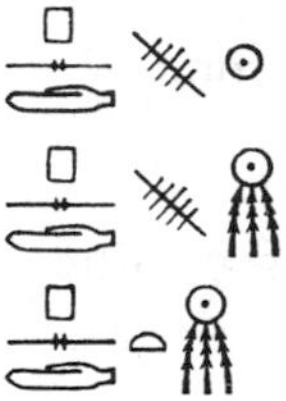 to shine, to illumine.

pesṭ / *pesṭtu* 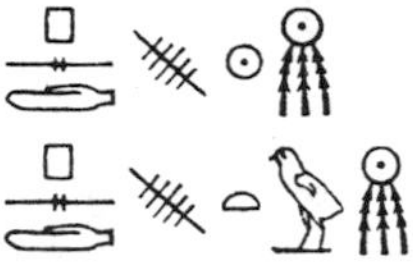 rays of light, radiance, brilliance.

Pesṭu  the god of light.

pesṭ  to spread out like light.

pesṭ / *pesṭu* 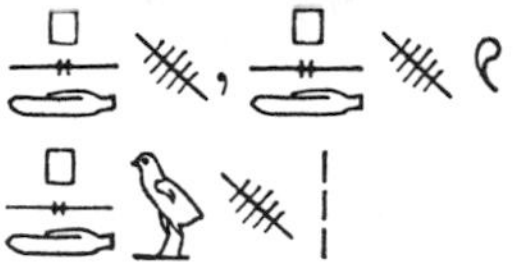 back, backbone; 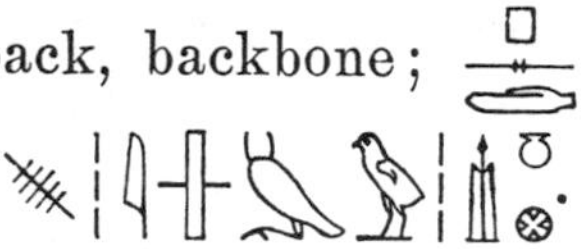

pesṭ tep  to move the head.

pesh  to spread out.

peshen 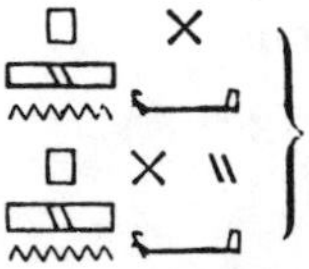 to divide, to cleave.

Peshennu 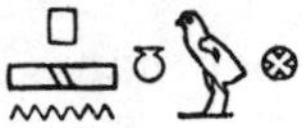 name of a city.

Peq  a region near Abydos.

pequ
peqt  cakes, food.

peqt 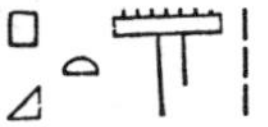 apparel of fine linen.

peḳ  to explain.

peḳ  byssus, very fine, semi-transparent linen.

Peḳa  name of a city.

peḳes
peḳas  to spit upon.

Peḳes 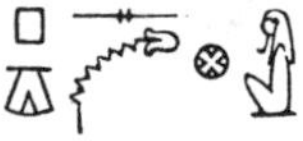 name of a city and a god.

pet  the sky, heaven;  the heaven of Rā.

pet 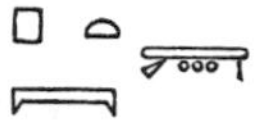 heaven and earth.

 heaven, earth and the Other World,

petti  heavenly beings, denizens of the sky.

pet  eastern heaven, or sky.

 western heaven, or sky.

 northern heaven, or sky.

 southern heaven, or sky.

petpet 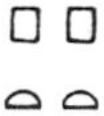 to crush, break.

Peti  a proper name.

pet  to see.

peti 

peter 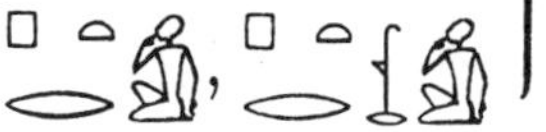 who? what? an interrogative particle.

 what then is it? *i. e.*, what does this mean?

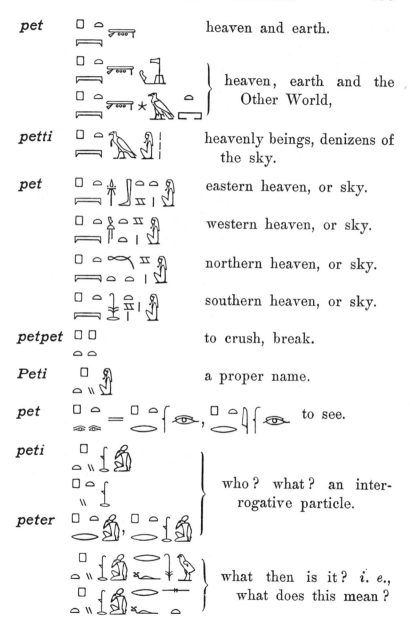

peter, *petrà* 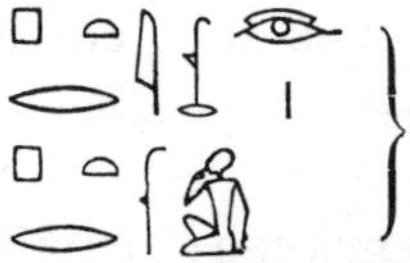 to see, look at, observe.

Petrà  the name of a god.

Petrà-sen  the name of a river.

Ptaḥ  Ptaḥ, the blacksmith-god of Memphis. 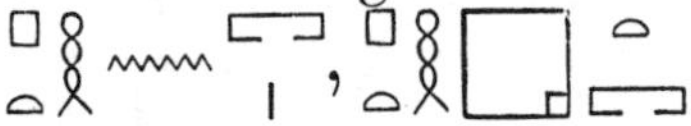 the temple of Ptaḥ.

Ptaḥ-ḥet-ka  or Ḥet-ka-Ptaḥ, "House of the double of Ptaḥ", a name of Memphis. The common name of Egypt, Ἀιγύπτος, appears to be derived from these words.

 Memphis of the Other World.

Ptaḥ res ȧneb-f 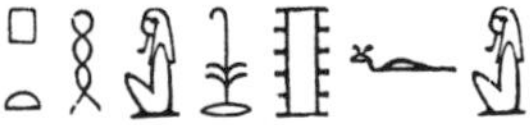 "Ptaḥ [to the] south [of] his Wall", Ptaḥ of Memphis.

Ptaḥ-Seker, *Ptaḥ-Sekri* 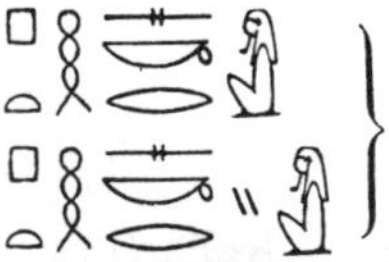 a dual god formed of Ptaḥ of Memphis and Seker, the old god of the Other World of the region of Memphis and Ṣaḳḳârah.

Ptaḥ-Sekri-Tem  a triad formed formed of Ptaḥ of Memphis, Seker, and Temu, an old god of Ȧnu, or Heliopolis.

Ptaḥ-Tanen  a dual god formed of Ptaḥ of Memphis and Tanen, an old cosmic god of the region.

Ptaḥ-mes  a proper name.

peṭ  to open out, to extend, to stretch out.

peṭ  a kind of unguent.

Peṭeṭ  name of a god and city.

peṭsu  to break open, opener.

Peṭ-mer  "Broad Lake", the name of a shrine.

F.

f  he, him, it, its, his.

fa

fat  to bear, to carry, be carried, to lift up, to diminish through decay.

 bearers, carriers.

Fa-ā  to raise the hand.
 the god of the lifted hand.

Fa-ākhu  a proper name.

Fa-pet  "Supporter of the sky"; the name of the god of the Seventh Àat.

Fa-Ḥeru  "bearer of Horus"; a name of Osiris.

Fat-Ḥeru  "the city of the bearer of Horus".

Fau-ḥeru-sen  "those who lift up their faces"; a class of divine beings.

fau  riches, wealth, abundance.

fenkhu  offerings.

Fenkhu  the name of certain dwellers in Syria.

fent 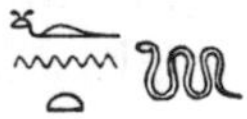 worm, serpent, reptile; plur. 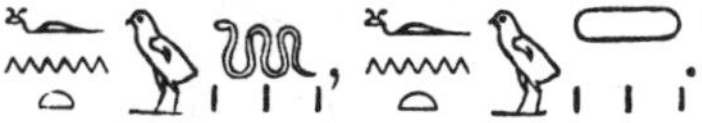.

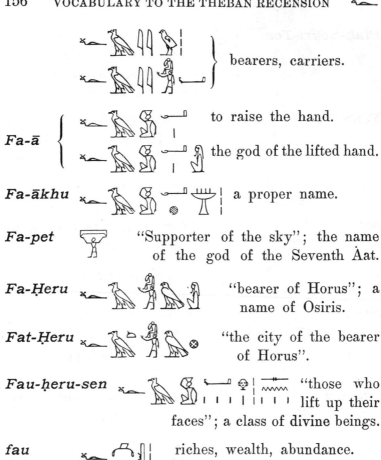

fenṭ 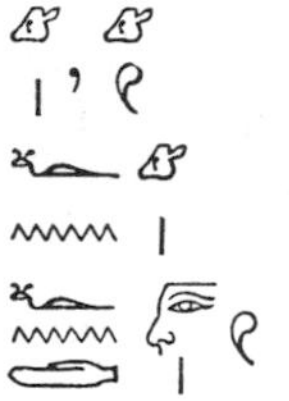 nose; plur. 

Fenṭi  a form of the god Thoth; the name of one of the Forty-two Judges in the Hall of Osiris.

fekh 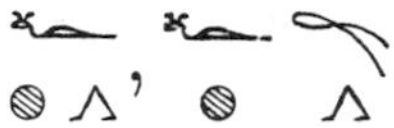 to untie, unloose, destroy.

fekhekh  to burst through.

feqat  a bread-cake, food in general.

feḳa  to make water.

fetu 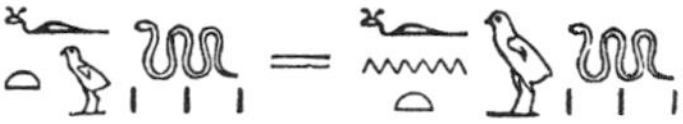 worms.

fettu  fish.

feṭ-àb  languor, disgust, weariness.

fṭu — four; fourth.

feṭqu — destruction, damage.

M.

em — sign of the present participle.

em — particle of negation, no, not; let not make to stink (my name).

em — in, into, from, on, at, with, out from, of, upon, as, like, according to, in the manner of, among.

em āb — opposite, in front of, confronting.

em ābu

em āb sa

em baḥ — before, in the presence of; the old form is .

em baḥ ā  before, in the presence of.

em paitu  before, when not yet.

em nem (uhem) 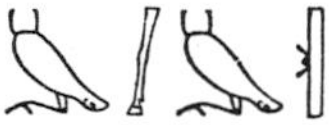

em nem (uhem) ā  } a second time.

em ruti  outside.

em ḥāt 

em ḥāti ā  } before.

em ḥer  upon.

em khen 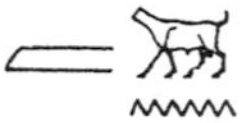

em khennu 

em khennu ā  } inside, within.

em khert 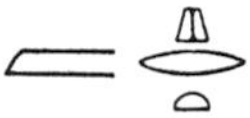 on behalf of.

em khet 

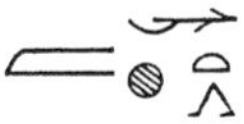 } behind, after, in the train of.

em sa  at the back of, behind, after.

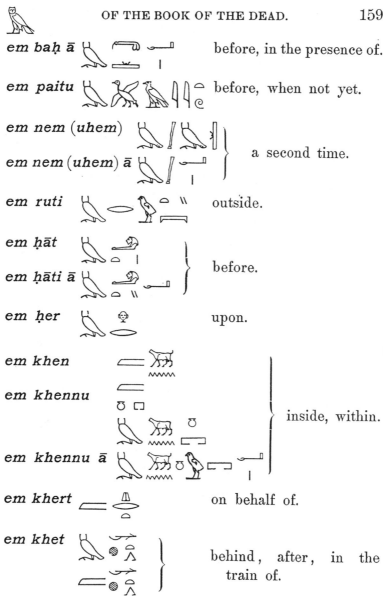

em qeṭ round about, throughout.

ma part of a boat.

ma, *maui*, *mat* to be new, to renew, made new, new.

maa, *maau*, *maat* to see, to look upon, to behold, observe, perceive; seen, observed; plur. part.

maa sight, view, glance.

maat (or ***ȧrit***?) eye; eye to eye; an eye.

maati (or ***ȧriui*** ?)  the two eyes.

maat  eyes.

maat nebt  every eye, *i. e.*, every body, all people, folk, mankind.

maat Rā 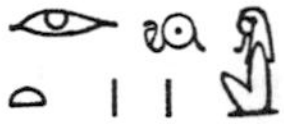 eye of Rā.

 right eye of Rā.

maat Ḥeru  eye of Horus, the name of offerings.

maat Shu  eye of Shu, *i. e.*, the sun.

maat Tem 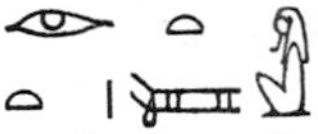 eye of Tem, *i. e.*, the sun.

maa-ȧnt-f  the name of a plank, or peg, in the magic boat (Chap. XCIX).

maa-ȧnuf  the name of one of the Forty-two Judges in the Hall of Osiris.

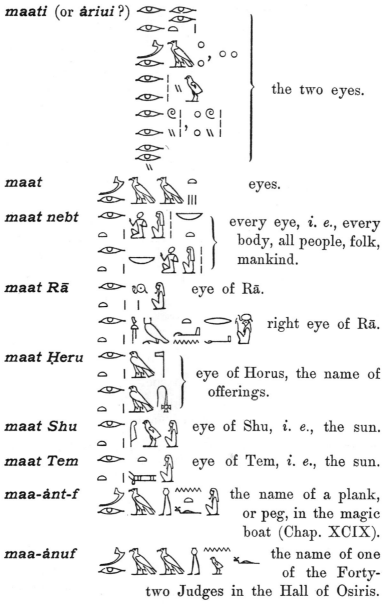

Maa-àtef-f-kheri-beq-f  the name of one of the spirits who guard the bier of Osiris.

Maati-f-em-khet  "he whose two eyes are of fire"; the name of one of the Forty-two Judges in the Hall of Osiris.

Maati-f-em-ṭes  "he whose two eyes are like knives"; the name of one of the Forty-two Judges in the Hall of Osiris.

Maa-em-ḳerḥ-ànnef-em-hru 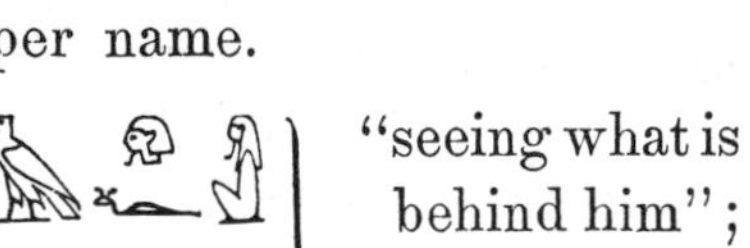 "he who seeth in the night what is brought to him in the day"; a proper name.

Maa-ḥa-f, ***Maa-ḥa***  "seeing what is behind him"; a proper name.

Maa-ḥeḥ-en-renput  "seeing millions of years"; a proper name.

Maatuf-ḥer-ā  a proper name.

Maaiu-su (?)  a proper name.

Maa-thet-f 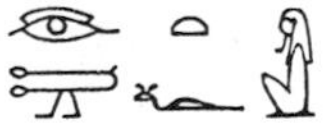 a proper name.

maar 
maȧr  restraint, misery, affliction, wretched one, oppressed one.

maȧ  lion.

maȧuti 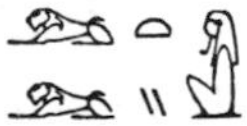 the lion-lioness god, *i. e.*, Shu and Tefnut.

maā 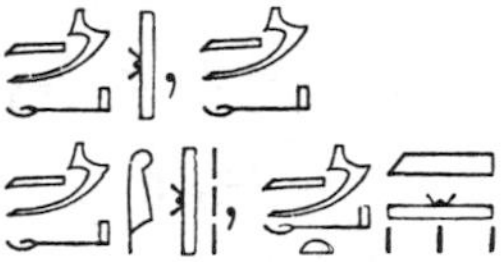
maāu  to be right, straight, just, true, to pay which is legally due, or what it is right to pay, to give a statutory offering.

maā-kheru 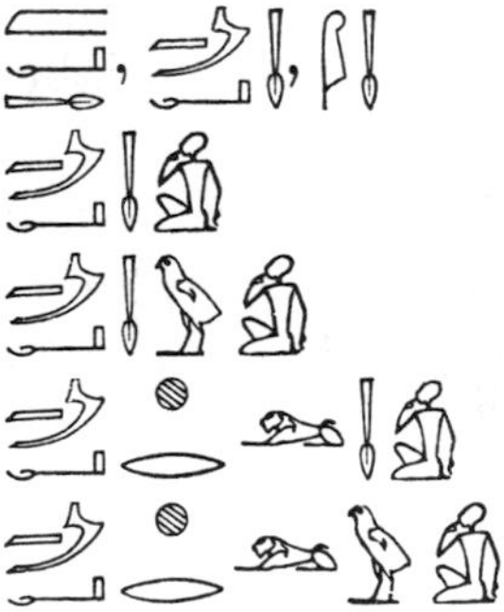
maāt-kheru 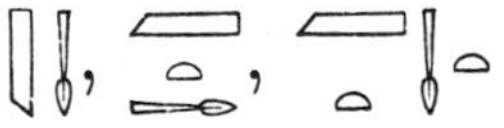 "true word", or "true of word", or "true voice", or "true of voice", he whose word when spoken is followed unfailingly by the effect desired. These words are placed after the

names of the dead, and appear to mean something like "triumphant", 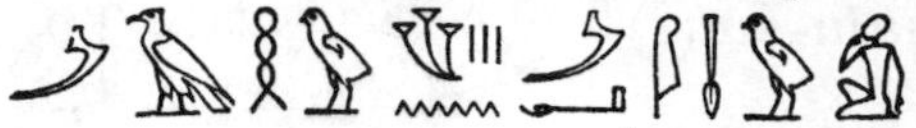 a crown of triumph; 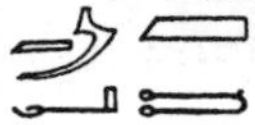 to be right.

maāt 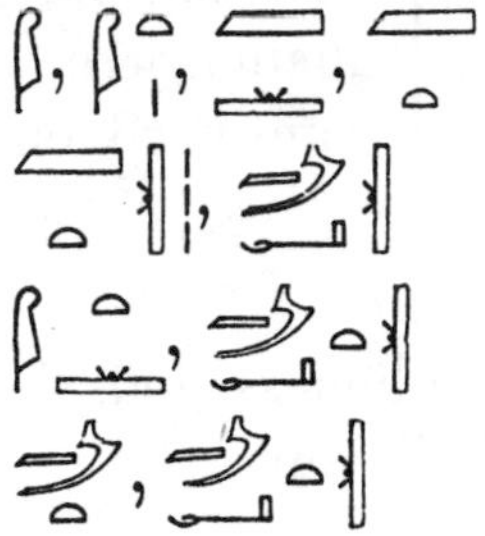 truth, what is right, true, straightness, law, order;  doubly true:   the scales balance exactly. 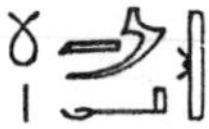 "[with] the cord of maāt", *i. e.*, uniformly and regularly;  beautiful truth.

 a righteous judge.

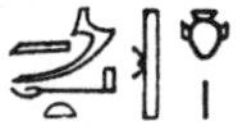 true, right of heart.

 real lapis-lazuli.

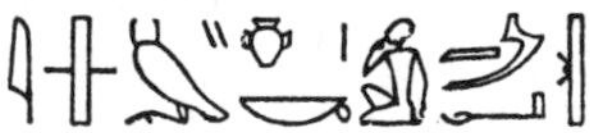 thy genuine friend.

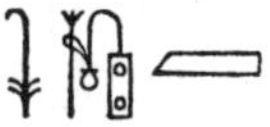 real royal scribe.

 in very truth.

 really true.

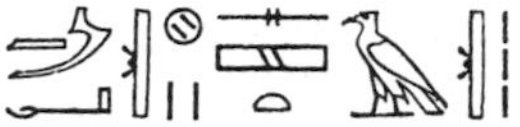 most truly a mystery.

Maāt 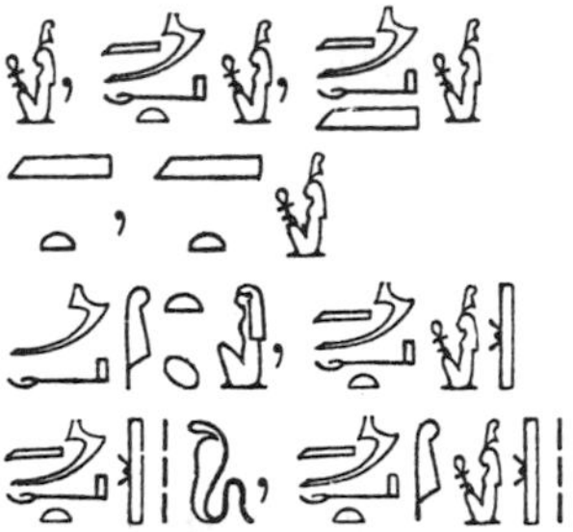 the goddess of truth, law, order, etc.

Maāti  the two goddesses of truth, law, order, etc.

maāti  truth, right.

Maātiu  the gods of truth, law, order, etc.

maāt  a district, or region.

Maāti 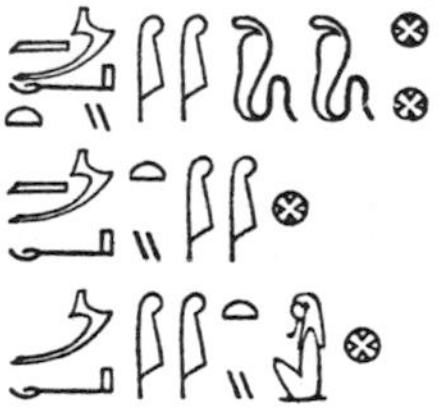 the cities or districts of the two Maāti goddesses.

maā  limb.

maā 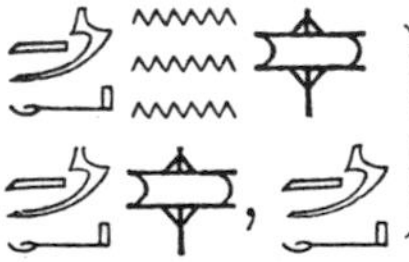 windsail, wind, breeze; plur. 

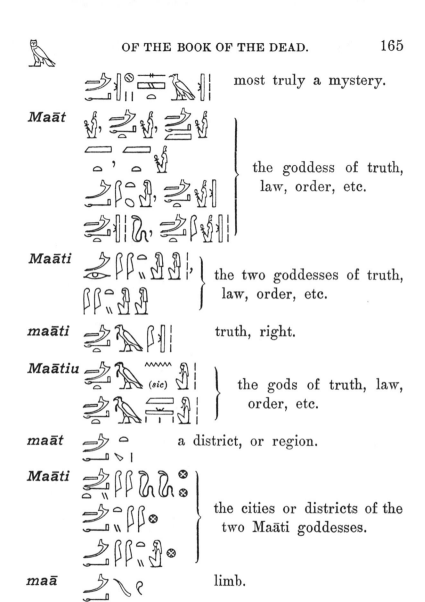

maā  to stretch out (?).

maā  to journey.

maautu  stalk.

maftet  lynx.

mama  palm (?) tree.

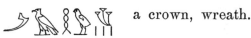

Manu  the Mountain of Sunset.

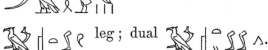

maḥa  a part of the head.

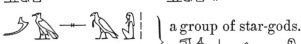

maḥu 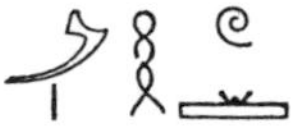 part of a boat.

maḥu  a crown, wreath.

mast  leg; dual 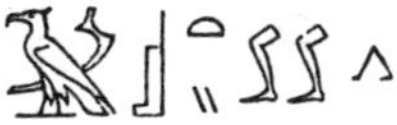.

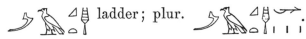

Mastiu 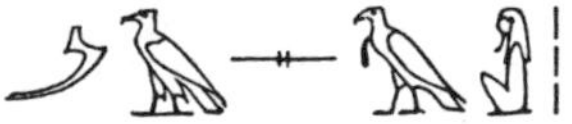  a group of star-gods. .

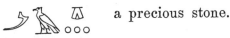

maqet  ladder; plur. .

maḳ  a precious stone.

maut / *matu*  incense.

Matchat  the name of a city.

mȧ 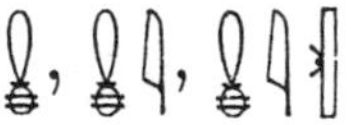 as, like, concerning, even as. .

 like that same one.

 inasmuch as, even as.

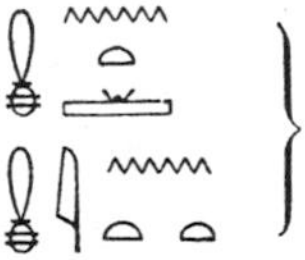 like that which.

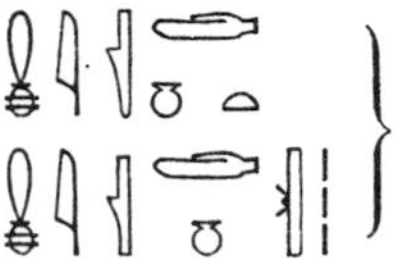 after the manner of.

mȧti  a person or thing resembling another person or thing, type, copy.

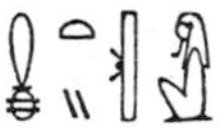 divine image; 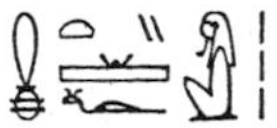 his divine images.

mȧtet  picture, likeness, similitude, like unto, copy of;  likewise.

mȧn  to-day.

mȧnt  with  daily.

mȧu  to be like 

mȧu  cat, cat's skin.

mȧu  lion;  lions.

mȧu  to knead, to mould, to fashion.

mā  give, grant, let there be! who? what? behold!  behold thou! 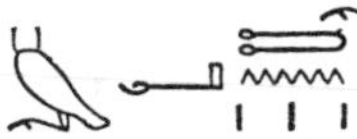 behold ye!

mā, *māȧ*, *māȧi* 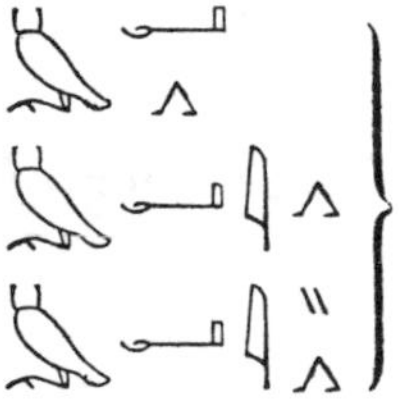 come! give! bring!  

Māau-taui  name of a god.

māāt 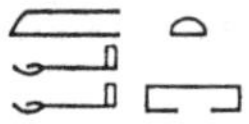 place.

māāat  name of a place.

māb  thirty.

mābiu  the thirty great gods.

mābit — name of a place or building.

māfket — turquoise.

Mānāat — ?

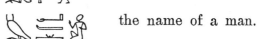

Mārqathȧ — the name of a god.

māhaiu — people, tribe, generations (?).

māhaṭti — fire.

māhui — milk vessels, udders (?).

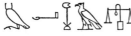

māhenȧ — milk vessel.

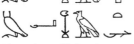

māḥā — standard.

Māḥu — the name of a man.

mākha — to weigh.

mākha, ***mākhat***, ***mākhaȧt*** — a pair of scales, a balance; the balance of the earth.

mākhatu 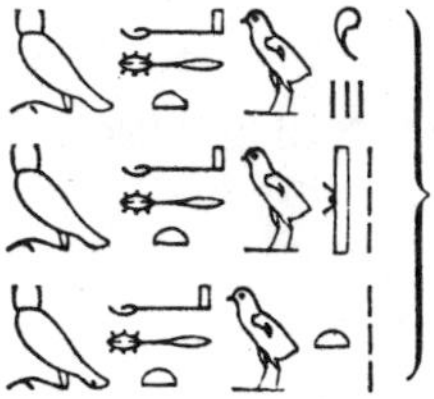 intestines.

mākhait  sledge for a sacred boat or god.

mākhiu  altars with incense burning on them.

mākhent 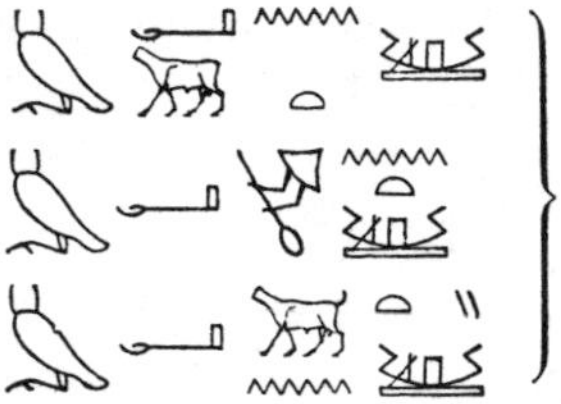 a boat.

māsheru  evening, eventide.

mākat  place.

māku  to protect, protection.

māki  protector.

māket  a thing which protects, amulet.

mākefitiu  objects made of turquoise.

mākḥa 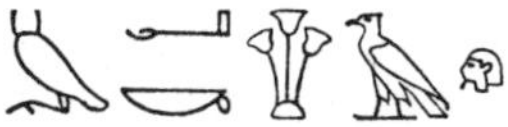 to turn round, or behind, back of the head.

māket  station, place.

māqet  ladder.

mātau  weapons, short spears, harpoons.

mātenu  ways, roads, paths.

Māṭes 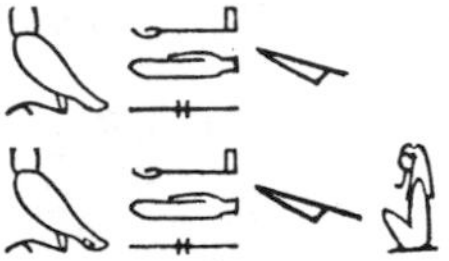 a proper name.

Māṭes-årui (?) 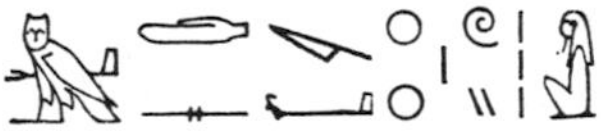 the gods with knife-like eyes.

māṭet (*māntchet*) 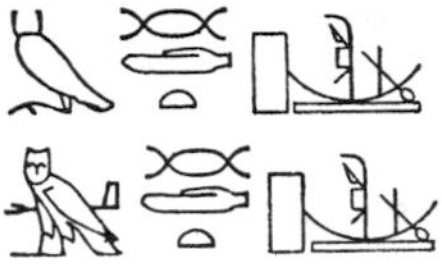 the boat in which the sun sailed from sunrise to noon.

māthennu  ways, roads, paths.

mātcha  phallus.

mātchabu 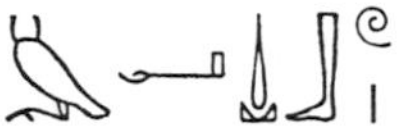

mātchabet  chain, fetter.

mātchabet  part of a ship.

Mātcheṭ  a proper name.

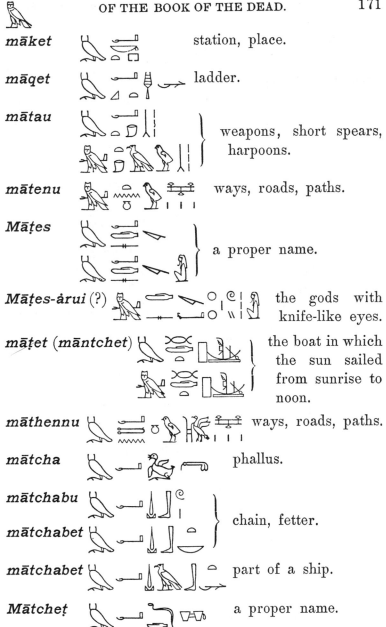

mātcheṭ to use force, to compel, to constrain.

Mi-sheps a proper name.

mu water, essence.

pool; the pool of the well of Åmenti; the pool of Kher-āḥa.

the god of the water, or divine essence; essence of Rā.

brow (surface?) of the water.

what is in the water.

m[u]it water.

mu a decoction, as in:—

ānkham flower water.

myrrh water.

saltpetre water.

incense water.

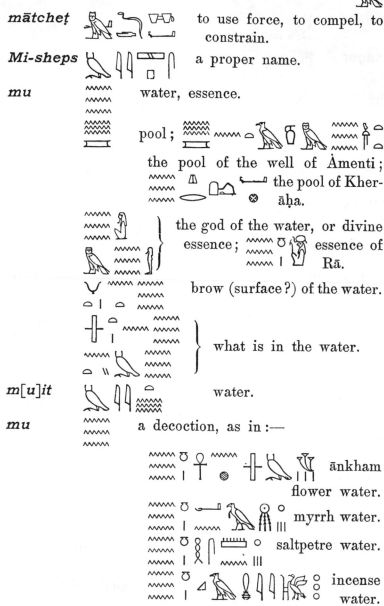

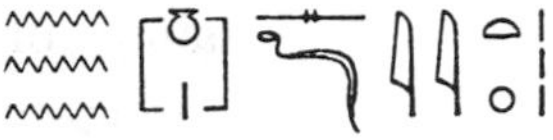 incense water.

 dirty water.

mut  mother.

muti  parents.

Mut 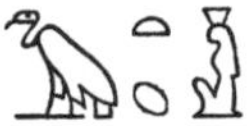 the Mother-goddess *par excellence* of Egypt;   "Mut in the horizon of heaven". 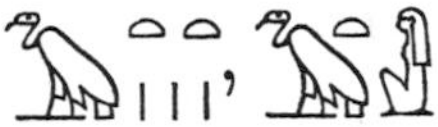  mother-deities.

mut  weights for scales.

Mut-restȧ  a proper name.

Mut-ḥetepth  a proper name.

mut  to die, death, the dead, the damned; plur. , , .

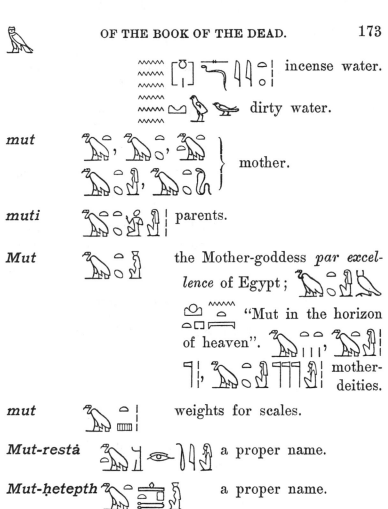

Menu name of a god of generation and fertility.

Menu-Ḥeru Menu + Horus.

Menu-suten-Ḥeru-nekht a name of Osiris.

Menu-qeṭ a proper name.

men, *ment* to be permanent, stable, firm, to be fixed, to remain; abiding, fixed.

menu possessions, things which abide.

menu chamber.

menu bases, pedestals.

Ment name of a god.

menti, *mentiu* the two thighs.

men to be in pain, sick.

ment, *menut* pain, sickness, disease.

men 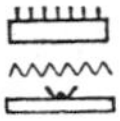 such and such an one.

Menȧ  name of a god or city.

menȧ 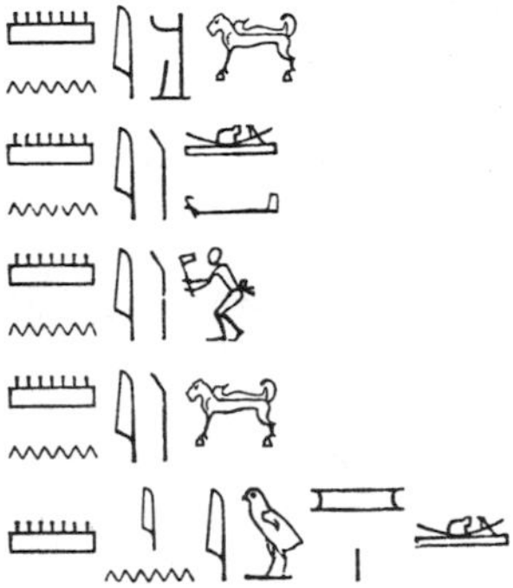 to tie up a boat to the mooring post, to come into port, to land, to die; 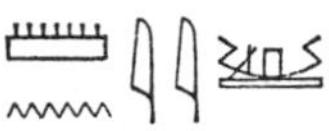 arriving.

menȧ 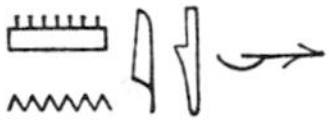
menȧt  post to which boats are tied up or moored.

menȧu  mooring posts, stakes of death.

menȧ 
menȧt  end, ending 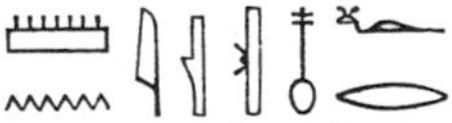 a happy ending, or death.

menȧ 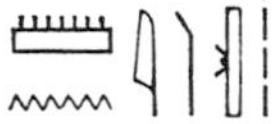
menȧ-tu 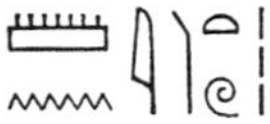 the dead.

menȧt 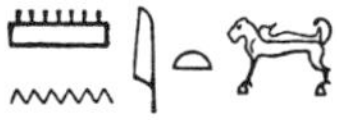 funerary bed, bier, death.

meni 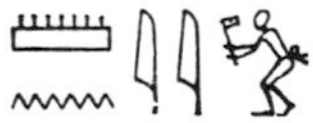 to slay, put to death.

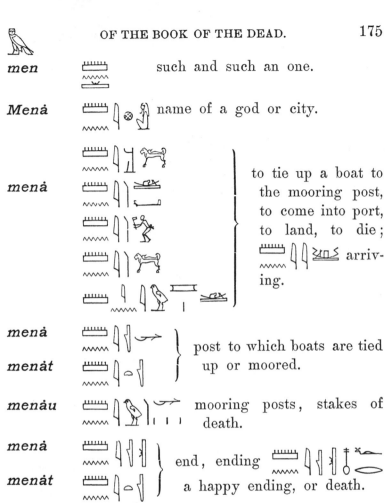

menȧt a musical instrument.

menāt breast.

menu ministrants.

menmen to go about.

menment cattle, farm stock.

menḥ wax.

menḥu to offer up.

Menḥu name of a god.

menkhu , to work, wrought, well finished, excellent, worked or inlaid, perfect, well disposed, well-doing; perfected; valuable things.

Menkh the beneficent god (?).

menkhet apparel, clothes, garments.

Menqet  the name of a goddess.

Ment  a proper name.

ment  swallow.

menṭ-t 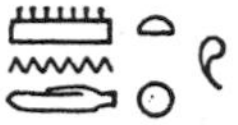 apple of the eye.

menṭi 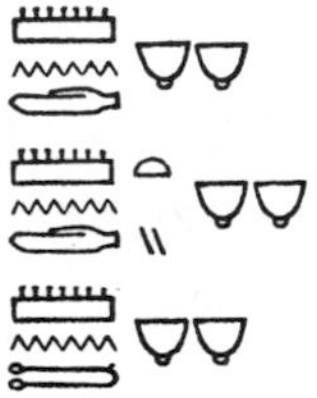 the two breasts.

Menthu 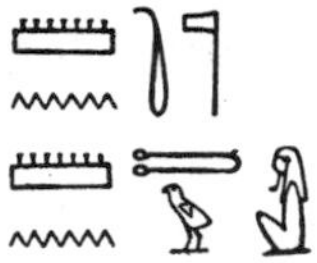 the War-god of Hermonthis, who was at a later period identified with Rā.

Mentchat  the name of a city.

mer  overseer, superintendent.

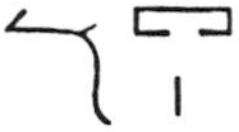 major-domo, steward.

 officer of soldiers.

 overseer of the granaries.

mer  a water-course, canal.

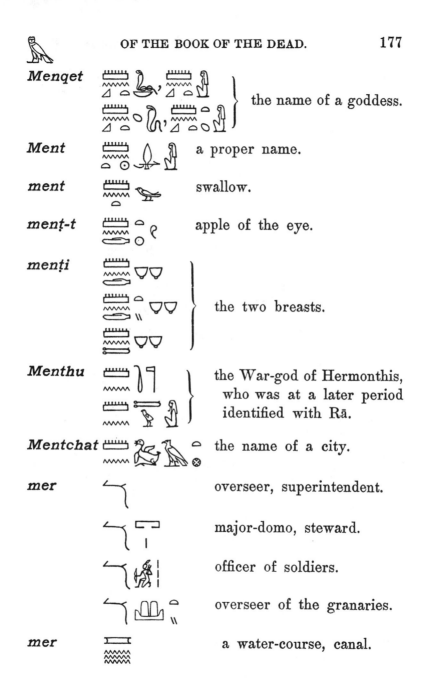

mer  pool, tank, cistern; plur. 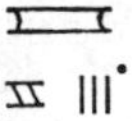

 swamps, lakes.

 Lake of Maāt.

 Lake of the Maāti gods.

 Lake of the geese.

 Lake of the horizon-gods.

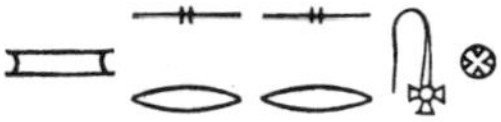 Lake of Fire.

 name of a mythological Lake.

meru  peasants, agricultural labourers.

mer  to be sick, ill;  sick; 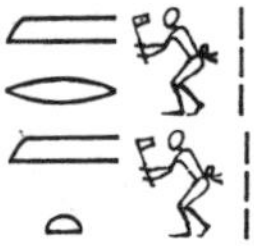 diseased, or perhaps = the dead.

meru 
meràu 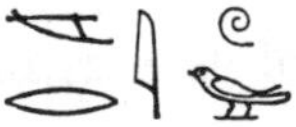
} pain, sickness, disease, decay.

Mer  a proper name.

mer, *meru*, *merr*, *merru* — to love, to desire, to wish for, to will. loving, lover, beloved; lover, beloved; lovers.

mertu, *mert*, *merit*, *merrt* — love, desire, wish, will.

Mer — a proper name.

Mert — name of a goddess.

Meritti — a group of gods.

Merti — two goddesses.

mer — to bind, to tie.

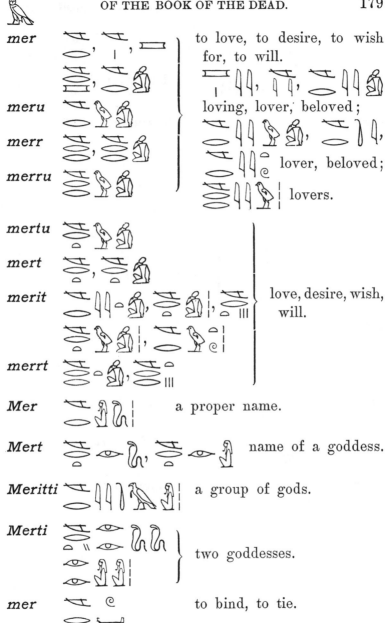

meru		swathing, bandage.
Mer-ur		the Mnevis Bull.
merāḥāt	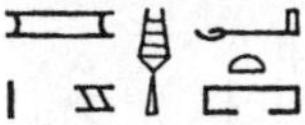	tomb, sepulchre.
meruḥ		oar, paddle.
meriut		a kind of tree.
Meres		a proper name (?).
Meri-s	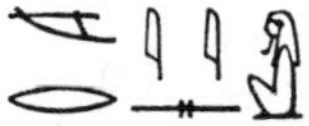	
merḥ	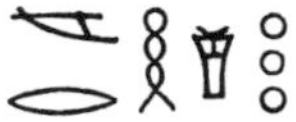	wax.
merḥet	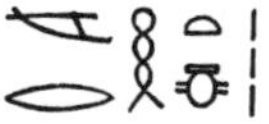	
mert	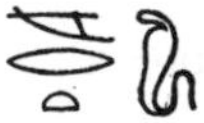	the name of a part of a boat.
Mert		name of a city.
Mert		a proper name.
mehait		roof.
meḥ		cubit, 

meḥ  to fill. be full; , full; filling, filler; the filling of the Ut-chat, *i. e.*, full moon; the filling of the Eye of Horus; a stream filled with flowers.

meḥ sa  to be complete.

meḥ 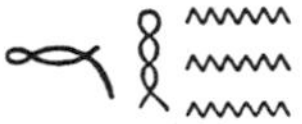 to be inundated, submerged, drowned.

meḥit  flood.

Meḥ-urt
Meḥt-urt 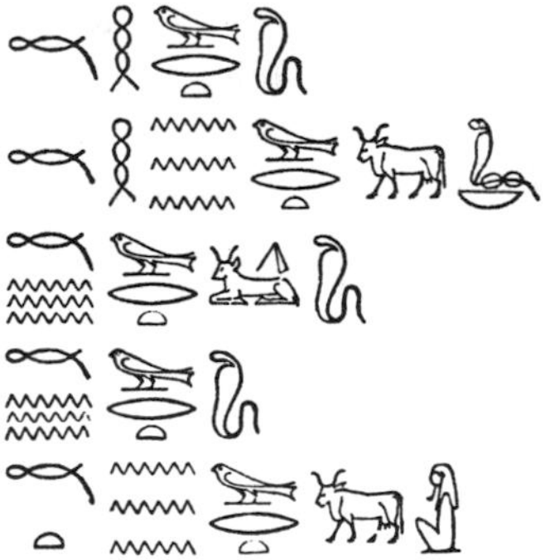 a very ancient sky goddess, afterwards identified with Nut.

meḥ 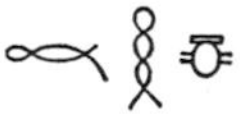 unguent (?).

meḥ wing, pinion.

meḥ garland.

Meḥānuti-Rā a proper name (?).

meḥut offerings.

meḥuti oil.

Meḥi
Meḥiu } a proper name.

meḥit fish.

meḥef a kind of stone.

Meḥen
Meḥent
Meḥenit } name of a god and goddess.

Meḥenet name of a city.

meḥenet the north wind.

meḥt placed before numbers;

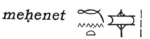

meḥt vessel, plaque (?).

meḥt

meḥti the north in general, the north of Egypt, *i. e.*, the Delta; north-west.

meḥtiu northern beings, men or gods, , lords of the north, *i. e.*, in late times, the Greeks; nest of the northerners.

Meḥt the goddess of the North.

meḥt

meḥit the north wind.

meḥuiu(?)

meḥu

meḥti oil.

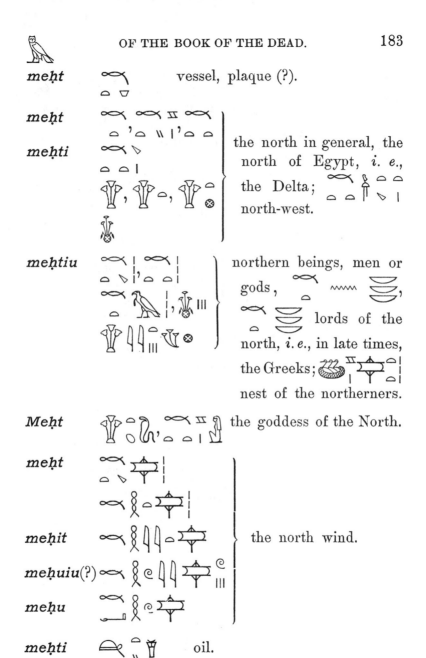

Meḥti (?)-***sāḥ-neter*** the name of one of the Seven Cows.

meḥṭet to bathe.

Em-khent-maati (?) = (?).

em khennu within.

mekhsef name of a wooden instrument.

mes
mesu to bring; bringer, bringing.

mest to walk, approach.

to give birth to, to bring forth, to produce, to fashion; , born of; born; giving birth a second time to mortals; ; .

mest , genetrix.

mest  birth; plur. , 

mestu  birthday.

mes  child, offspring.

mesu

mesesiu  children.

mesu nebu  all who are born, *i. e.*, the human race.

mesu beṭesh  malicious but powerless fiends.

mesu ent Nu 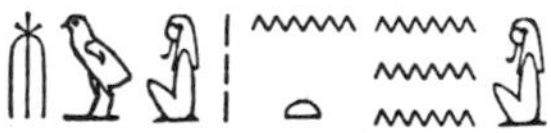 children of the divine water, *i. e.*, plants.

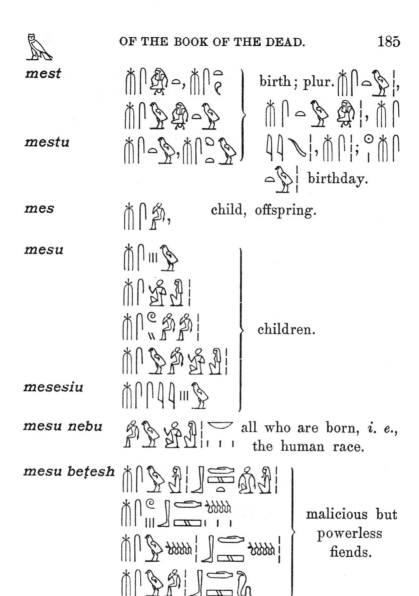

mesu Nut children of the Sky-goddess.

mesu Ḥeru children of Horus (Kesthȧ, Ḥāpi, Ṭuamut-f, Qebḥsennuf).

mesu Serȧt beqet . . . .

mesit cakes eaten in the evening.

mesbeb (?) banded (?).

Mes-peḥ a proper name.

Mes-Ptaḥ a proper name.

Mes-em-neter a proper name.

mesmes to count (?).

mesmes Vol. II, p. 251, l. 2.

mesnekht birthplace.

emseḥ, ***emseḥu*** crocodile; plur. , eight crocodiles .

emseḥu  to slay.

meskhen / ***meskhent***  the birth-place of a god or goddess; a region in the Sekhet-Ȧaru where the gods were produced;   the four birth-places of Abydos.

Meskhen-āat 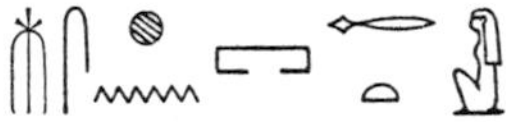 the name of a goddess of birth, or of a birth-place.

Meskhen-ment 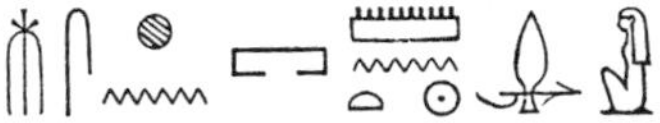 the name of a goddess of birth, or of a birth-place.

Meskhen-nefert 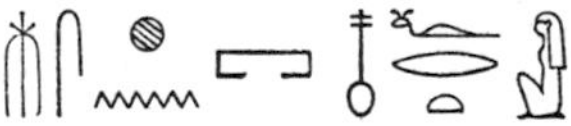 the name of a goddess of birth, or of a birth-place.

Meskhen-Seqebet 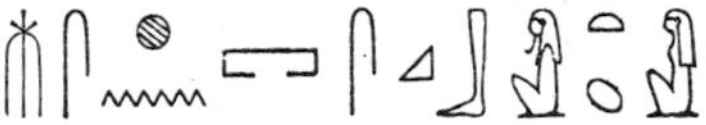 the name of a goddess of birth, or of a birth-place.

Mesespekh 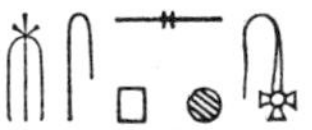 a proper name.

Messhenu 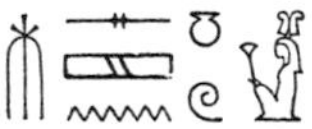 = Meskhenu.

meska  skin.

Mesqen 
Mesqet 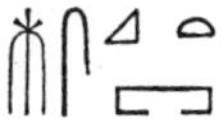 } a region of the Other World through which the deceased must pass before he could reach the Sekhet-Ȧaru.

mesqet 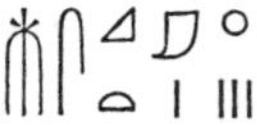 weapons.

mesṭemu  to paint the eyes with *koḥl.*

mesṭemet  eye-paint, stibium, *koḥl.*

mesṭet  leg.

mesṭ 
mesṭeṭ 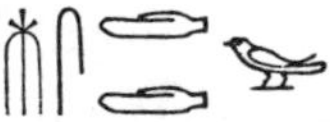
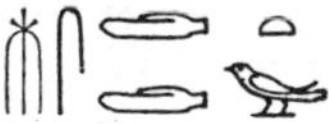 } to dislike, to hate.

mesthȧ  palette. The true reading is Ḳesthȧ, *q. v.*

Mesthȧ 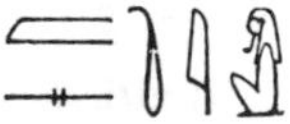
 } one of the four sons of Horus. The true reading is Ḳesthȧ, *q. v.*

mestcher  ear.

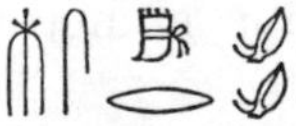
 } the two ears.

mestchetch  to hate.

meshā  bowmen, soldiers.

meshen  Chap. CX. B. 16.

Em-qeṭqeṭ 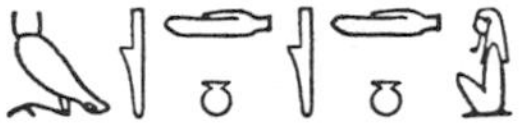 the name of a spirit, or god.

met (***mut***)  the dead, the damned.

met  ten. 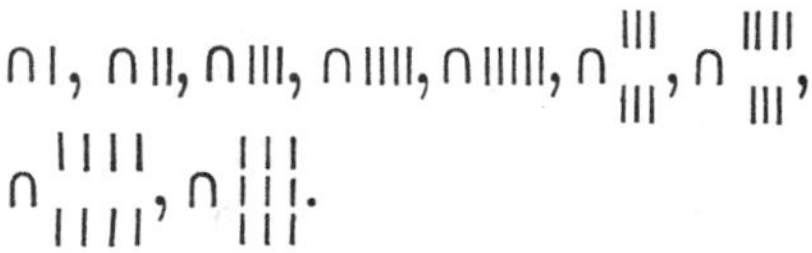

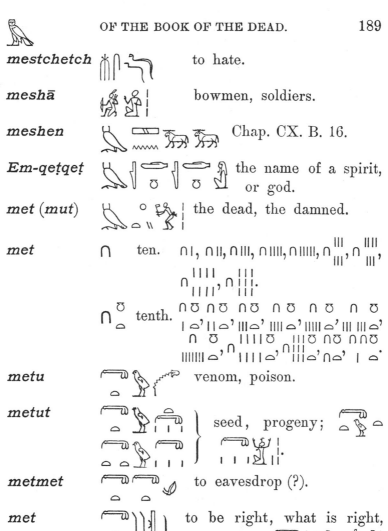

 tenth. 

metu  venom, poison.

metut  seed, progeny; 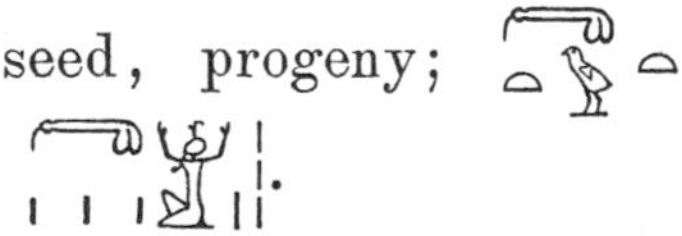

metmet  to eavesdrop (?).

met
meti 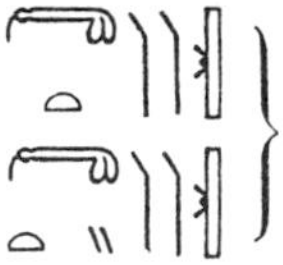 to be right, what is right, the mean; 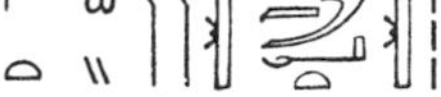 the exact truth (?).

meter
metru  to bear witness, to testify, to give evidence.

meṭu  to speak, to talk, tell, declare.

meṭ, meṭu  word, speech, talk, declaration; pronouncement.
meṭet

meṭut 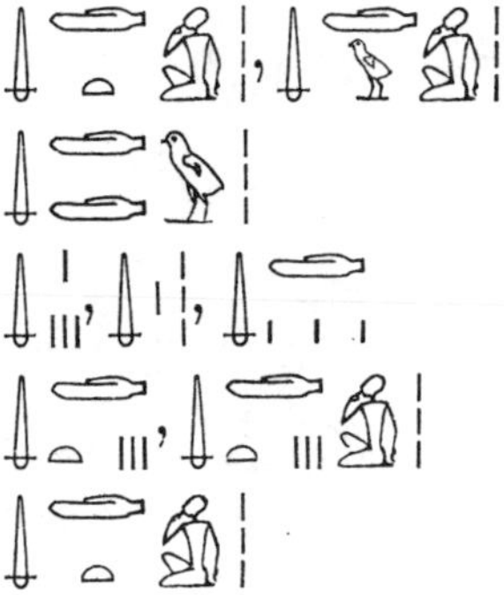 words, speech, things (like the Hebrew דָּבָר);  word of wisdom; 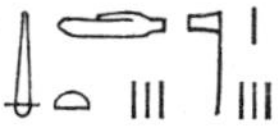 words of the gods;  words of truth;   words of evil, blasphemy.

Meṭu-ta-f  a proper name.

Meṭes-ḥer-àri-mer  "Knife-face, guardian of the Lake"; the name of the doorkeeper of the Sixth Ārit.

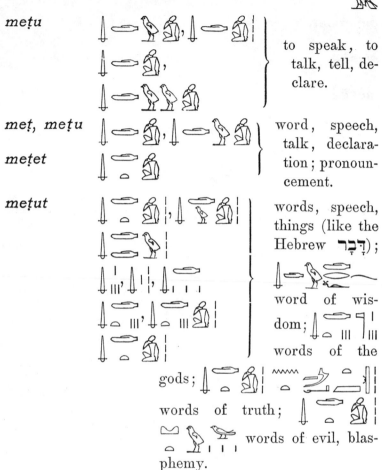

Meṭes-sen — the name of the door-keeper of the Seventh Ārit.

metch — to be deep; deep; very deep.

metchtu — abyss.

deeps, depths.

metchaub — to fetter.

metchet — salve, ointment, oil.

N.

n — a preposition, in, to, for, because. With additions :—

n — of; with plural following,

n  we, us.

n  no, not = 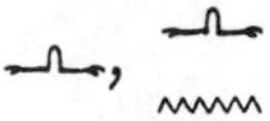;  = 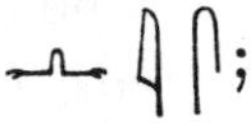;  invisible.

na  those, the;  those who are after.

naiu  those of;  those of thine;  those belonging to.

na 
nai 
nȧu 
} air, wind.

Naȧrik  a proper name (?).

Naȧrruṭ 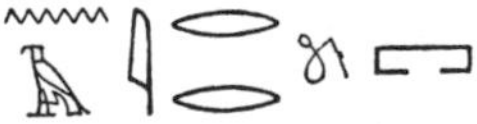
Naȧrruṭf 

Nanȧaruṭf 
Nȧareruṭ 
} "the place where nothing grows", a name for a region of the Other World. See Ȧn-ruṭ-f.

Nasaqbubu	name of a god.
Nak (?)	=en Aker (?).
Nathkerthi	name of a god.
n-ȧ	I, me, my.
nȧh	injury.
nȧs	to call, cry out, invoke; invoked.
nȧsu	
Nȧk	the name of a fiend and enemy of Rā.
	fiends, enemies.
nā	to journey, to travel, to come, to arrive, to advance.
nāai	
nāt	
Nāȧu	name of a god or devil.
nāu	fiend, devil; plur.

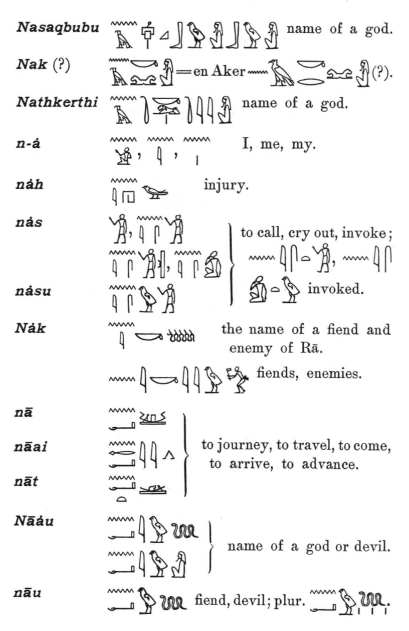

nāā  a decree (?), a design, picture.

nār  a reed pen, painting reed.

Nārt 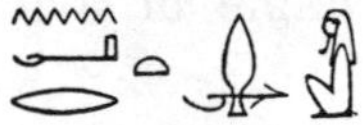 a proper name.

Nārtiānkhemsenf  name of a fiend.

nāsh  mighty one.

nāḳ  to break open, to split.

nāḳeḳa  to cackle.

ni (?)  in 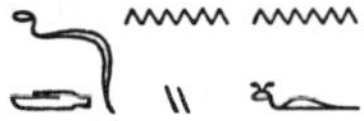 and .

nimā  who?

nini  to salute, to acclaim.

nu  of. 

Nu  name of a scribe.

nu — the watery abyss of the sky.

Nu — the Sky-god.

nu — these; these very ones; these; these who.

nu — season, period, time.

nu — to see, to watch, to observe.

nu — to go away, go about.

nu — to be strong, to strengthen.

nu — hours.

nu (?) — adorations, praise, worship.

nuit — weapon, knife, short dagger.

nub — gold; fine gold; golden light.

Nub-ḥeḥ — "Eternal gold"; a name of Osiris.

nub, *nubȧu* — to mould, to shape, to fashion, to form; fashioned, inlaid.

nubḥeḥ — blossom, flower.

Nubti — name of the god of Ombos, *i. e.*, Set.

nun — to pay homage.

nur — a kind of bird.

nuḥ — to masturbate.

nuḥ — to bind, to tie, to fetter.

cords, cordage, rigging, tackle.

nuḥu — flower, blossom.

nuḥti — pair of horns.

nukh — to be burnt.

nuk — I. I, even I.

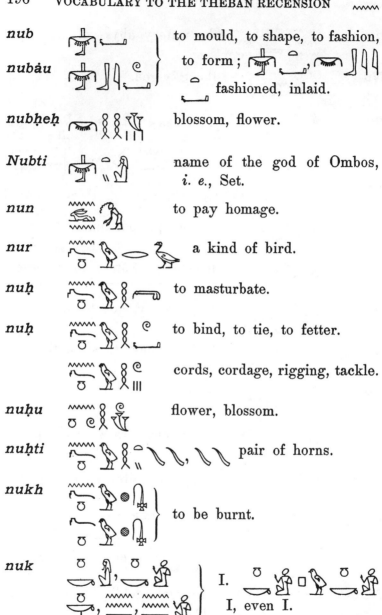

nut  the sky, heaven.

Nut 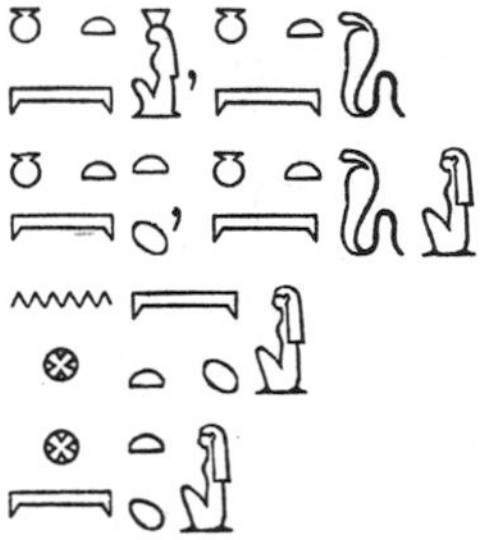 the Sky-goddess, the wife of Seb, or Ḳeb; the name of a sail in the magic boat.

Nut  the night sky.

nut  cords, ropes.

nut  city; plur. ;  city of god.

nuti  citizens.

nui

nut  canal, stream, river, flood, any large collection of water.

Nut-urt "great city"; the name of a lake in Sekhet-Åaru.

Nutu-ḥru a proper name.

nuti sweet air (?).

nuṭ to bear, to carry, to journey.

Nuṭiu a class of divine beings.

neb
nebt (in late times or), each, every, any, all; plur. , , ; every kind of evil thing.

neb with *bu*, , everywhere. See also under .

neb lord, master, sovereign; plur. , ,

nebt lady, mistress; in late times "lord".

neb lord of, possessor of, owner of, *e. g.*, , , ; compare the use of בַּעַל.

neb àbu  "lord of hearts"; a name of Àḥi.

neb Àbti  "lord of the East"; a title of Rā.

neb àmakh  "lord of veneration", *i. e.*, one to whom service is rendered and homage paid; .

neb Àmenti  "lord of Àmenti"; a name of Osiris;  the lords of the Other World;  "lady of Àmenti", a title of Hathor.

neb āāui  "lord of the two hands".

neb ābui 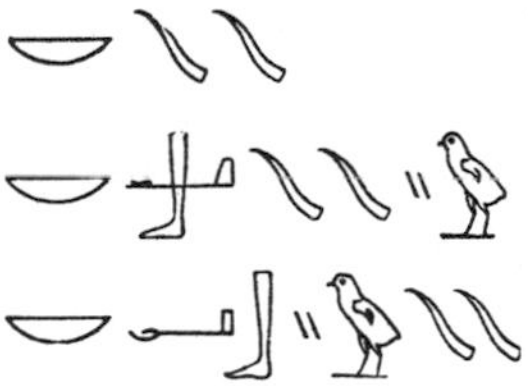 "lord of the two horns"; a title of Àmen; the name of one of the Forty-two Judges in the Hall of Osiris.

neb ānkh  "lord of life"; a title of Osiris.

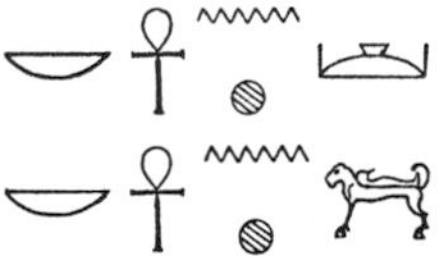 the title of the sarcophagus and the bier; late form 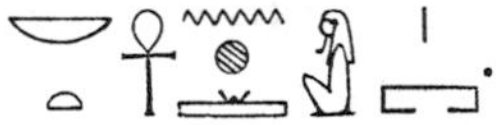.

nebt ānkh	"lady of life"; a title of Isis.
nebt unnut	"lady of the hour"; a proper name.
neb urert	"lord of the *urert* crown"; a title of Osiris and of Horus.
neb useru	"lord of strength, or powers"; a title of the Sun-god.
neb baiu	"lord of souls"; a title of several gods.
neb pāt	"lord of mankind"; a title of Horus.
nebt per	"lady of the house", *i. e.*, a married woman, house-wife. It is possible that is not intended to be read, and is only a determinative. The Egyptian to-day speaks of his "house", meaning his wife, or his wife and family.
neb mau	possessor of many eyes, or good sight.
neb maāt	possessor of truth or law, , .
neb Maāti	lord of the double City of Truth.

nebt māket 

nebu en meḥt  "lords of the north"; the peoples of the Delta; in late times the Greeks.

Neb nebu  "Lord of lords"; the name of one of the Forty-two Judges in the Hall of Osiris.

neb nefu  "lord of winds"; a title of Osiris.

neb nemt 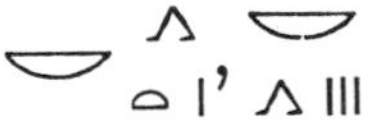 "lord of steps", *i. e.*, one who has the power to walk.

neb neru  "lord of victories"; a title of the heart of Osiris.

neb neter meṭut  "lord of the words of the god", *i. e.*, one who understands the hieroglyphic language.

neb renput  "lord of years", *i. e.*, aged one.

neb rekhit  "lord of the *rekhit*", a class of men.

neb Re-stau  "lord of Re-stau", *q. v.*, a title of Osiris.

neb henu  "lord of praises", *i. e.*, he who is praised.

neb ḥeru 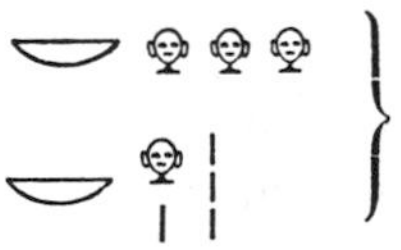 "lord of faces"; the name of one of the Forty-two Judges in the Hall of Osiris.

neb ḥeḥ "lord of eternity"; a title of Osiris; plur.

Neb khat the goddess Nephthys (?)

nebu khaut "lords of altars", *i. e.*, gods to whom altars have been dedicated.

neb khāu "lord of crowns, or risings"; a title of Rā.

neb khut "lord of the horizon"; a title of Rā.

neb kheperu "lord of transformations", *i. e.*, he of many changes.

neb khet "lord of things", *i. e.*, lord of creation; plur.

nebu Kher-Āḥa "lords of Kher-āḥa", *i. e.*, Temu and his fellow deities.

nebt Sau the "lady of Saïs", *i. e.*, Neith.

neb setut "lord of light", *i. e.*, giver of light.

neb senṭ "lord of fear", *i. e.*, he who inspires fear.

neb sekhti 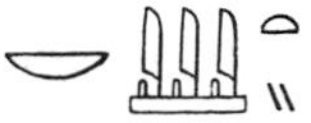 "lord of the field", *i.e.*, master of the field, a title of the Bull-god.

nebt Seḳer  "lady of silence"; a name of the Other World.

nebu kau  "lords of food", *i.e.*, gods to whom food offerings are given.

neb kesu  "lord of bowings", *i. e.*, he to whom homage is paid.

neb qerset  "lord of the bier"; a title of Osiris.

neb taui  "lord of the Two Lands", *i. e.*, of Upper and Lower Egypt.

neb taiu  "lord of the lands", *i. e.*, of the world, a title of Osiris.

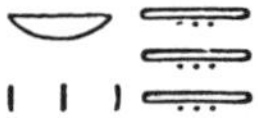 "lords of lands".

Nebt-taui 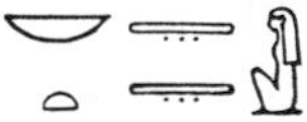 the name of a lake in the Sekhet Ȧaru.

Nebt-taui em karȧ  the name of the mooring post for the magic boat.

Neb ta ānkhtet  "lord of the Land of Life", *i.e.*, the Other World.

Neb ta tchesert  "lord of the Holy Land"; a title of Osiris.

neb tau  "lord of cakes".

neb temu  "lord of mankind".

nebu ṭuat 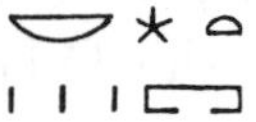 "lords of the Other World".

neb ṭeshert 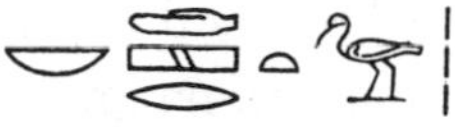 "lord of the red things", red clouds, or desert (?).

neb tchefau  "lord of divine food".

neb tchetta  "lord of eternity", *i. e.*, Osiris.

Neb-peḥti-petpet-sebȧu  "lord of might, crusher of fiends"; a proper name.

Neb-peḥti-thes-menment 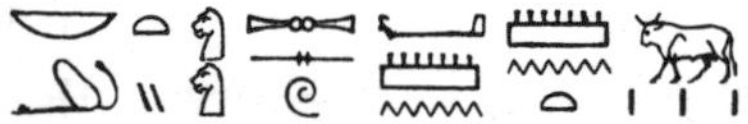 "lord of might, roper in of cattle"; a proper name.

Neb-maāt-ḥeri-reṭui-f  a proper name.

Neb-er-tcher  "lord to the boundary", *i. e.*, the Lord of the Universe, a title of Osiris.

Nebt-er-tchert 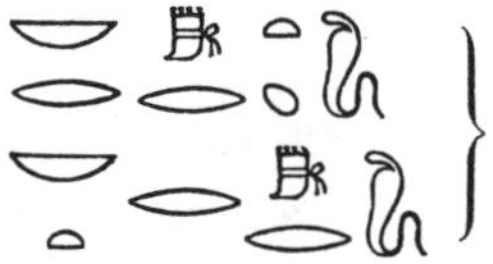 fem. of preceding.

Nebt-ḥet 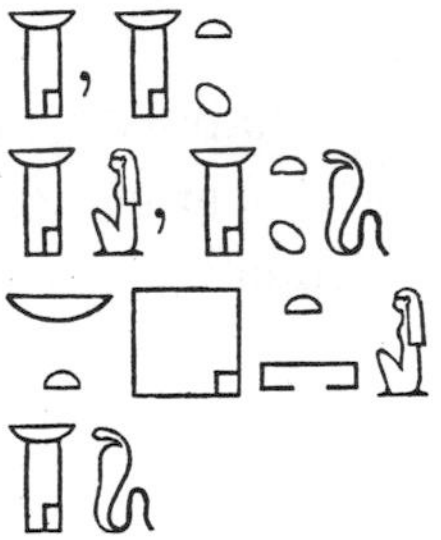 the goddess Nephthys, sister of Isis.

Neb-s 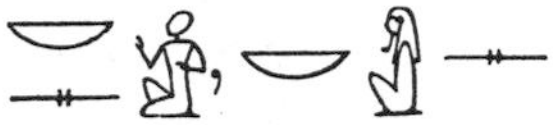 a proper name.

Neb-seni 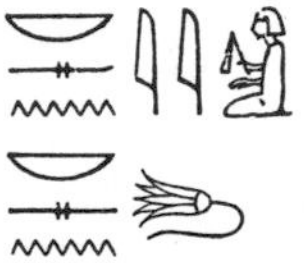 the name of a famous scribe.

Neb-qeṭ  the name of a scribe.

neba  a weapon or tool, a pole.

Nebȧ  the name of one of the Forty-two Judges in the Hall of Osiris.

nebȧu 

nebȧnȧu  flame, fire, a burning.

nebȧt 

nebȧu 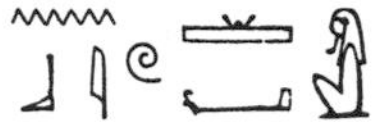 fashioner, moulder.

nebeḥ  a kind of bird.

nebti 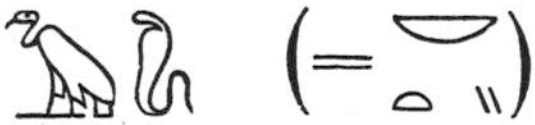, the two goddesses Nekhebit and Uatchit.

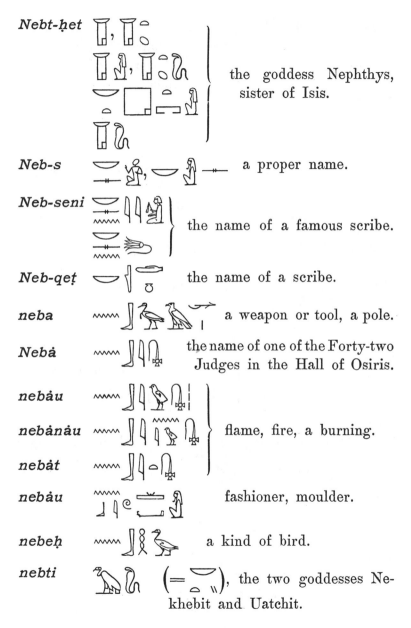

nebṭ, ***nebṭet*** — lock of hair, tress; the name of a storm cloud; the name of a fiend.

nepu — a part of the body.

neper — grain, wheat, barley, dhura.

Nepraȧ — the Grain-god.

nepert — corn-land.

Nepert — the name of a city.

nef — he, him.

nefa — a sign of the demonstrative, this, that; plur. .

nefu — air, wind, breath; breath of life.

nefu — sailor.

Nef-ur — the name of a city or district.

nefer — to be good, to be happy, to be beautiful, good, pretty, gracious, well-doing; beautiful, good; twice good, very good; good one or thing; fine gold; gracious speech.

with , happiness, joy, gladness,

neferu, *nefert* — beauties, splendours, fair things, good things.

Nefer-ḥer — "fair face", a title of Rā and of Ptaḥ.

Nefer (?) — the name of a lake.

neferu — to be glad (?).

Nefert — girl, maiden; a proper name.

nefert  name of a tree.

Nefer-uben-f  a proper name.

Nefer-sent  name of a city.

Nefer-Tem  name of a god, the son of Ptaḥ and Sekhet.

nem  to defraud =  (?).

Nem 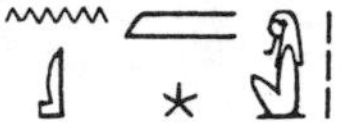 a proper name.

nem 

nemȧ 

nemnem 

nememti 

} to walk, to stride, go about, wander about.

nemt 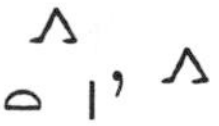 step, stride; plur. 

nemā  who? 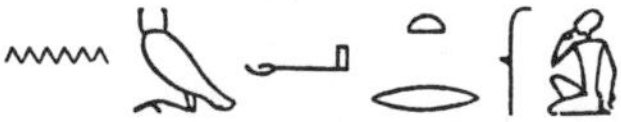 who then?   who then art thou?

nemm to lie dead.

nemmȧt bier.

nemmȧ pygmy, dwarf.

nemeḥ to understate the reading of the tongue of the balance, to be young, lowly, poor, humble.

nemes the name of a crown, tiara, or fillet for the head.

nemt block for slaughter, the chamber in which the damned suffered decapitation and mutilation; plur.

nemtchet a place of slaughter.

nen a sign of the demonstrative; this is he who; these who;

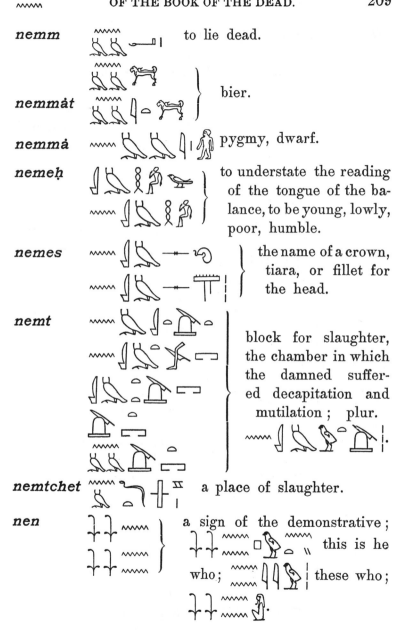

nen 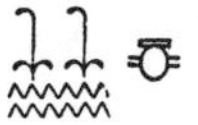 unguent.

nen 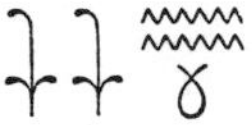 a kind of stuff, linen.

nen 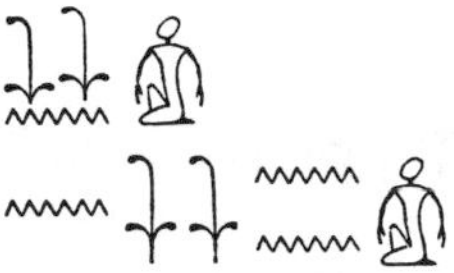 to be weak, helpless, exhausted.

neni, ***neniu***  weak or helpless folk, fiends, etc.

nenaiu  winds.

Nin-ȧrruṭ-f (?), ***Nen-aȧrruṭ-f*** 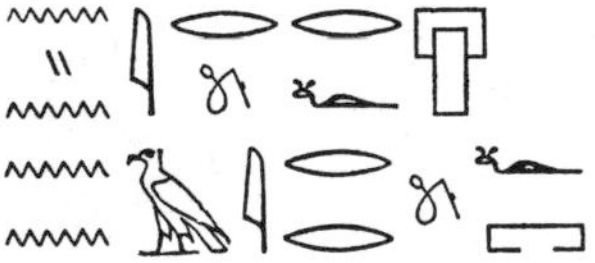 see Ȧn-ruṭ-f.

Nenunser 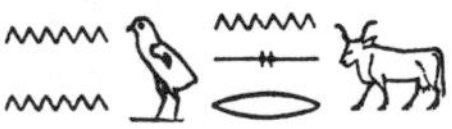 name of a Cow-goddess.

nenmet  (a late form) bier.

Nentchā 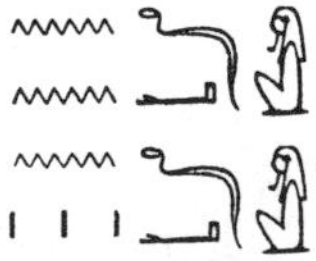 the name of a god.

Ner  name of the Herd-god; a proper name.

Nerȧu  name of the Herd-god; a proper name.

ner, nert  men and women, mankind.

neru, ***nerȧu***, ***nerr***  to be strong, to strike fear into any one.

nerȧut, ***nert***  victory, conquest; plur. 

Neri  "mighty one"; name of a god.

Nerȧu-ta  a proper name.

nerȧut  vulture.

neh  to conquer.

neha  to alight.

neha  to advance.

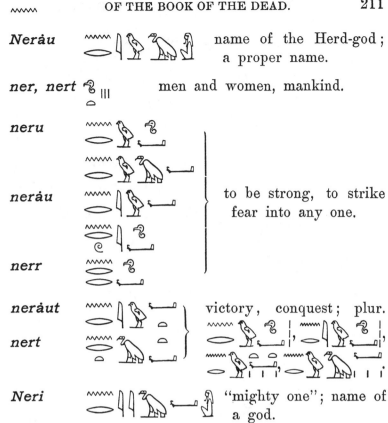

nehaȧs  to awake.

nehapu  to shine, give light.

nehat  sycamore, fig-tree; 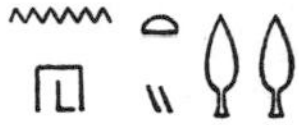 the two sycamores, fig-trees.

Nehatu  the name of a city.

nehep  to copulate.

nehep 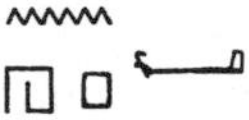 to have power over.

nehpu  strength.

nehpu  light, fire, to shine.

nehem  to rejoice.

 rejoicings.

nehemnehem  to destroy (?).

neheh 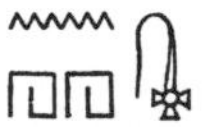 fire.

nehhu  needy one.

nehes	to wake up, rouse up.
Nehesu	a group of divine beings.
Nehes-ui	a proper name.
Neḥ	the name of a god.
neḥ	to beseech, pray, entreat.
neḥa	to be bad, stinking.
Neḥa-ḥāu	"stinking limbs"; a proper name.
Neḥa-ḥer	the name of one of the Forty-two Judges in the Hall of Osiris.
neḥait	flowers.
neḥit	time, eternity (?).
neḥeb	to coerce, put the yoke on some one.
neḥebet	neck; plur.

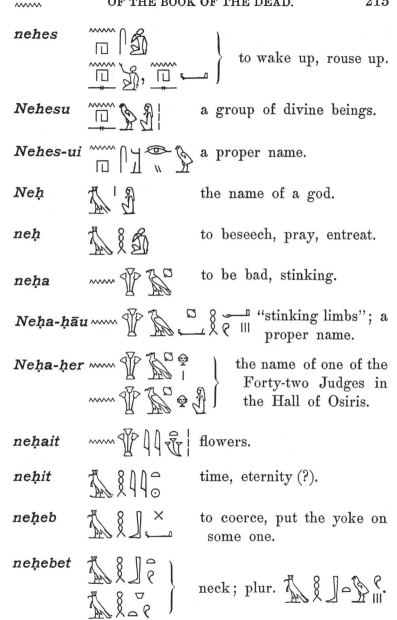

Neḥeb-nefert  the name of one of the Forty-two Judges in the Hall of Osiris.

Neḥeb-ka 

Neḥeb-kau 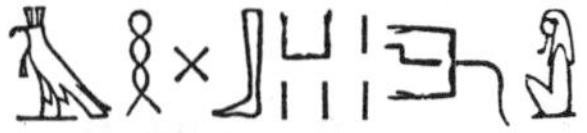

"he who yokes together the Kau"; a proper name.

neḥep 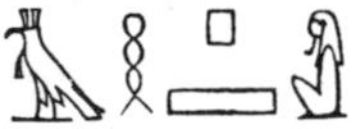 the divine potter's table.

neḥem 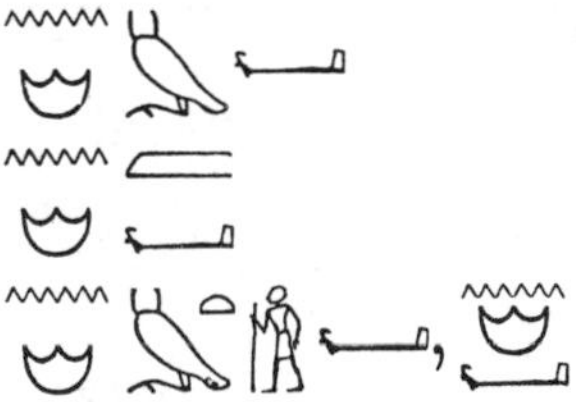 to carry off, to plunder, to deliver, release;  deliverers;   delivered.

neḥeḥ 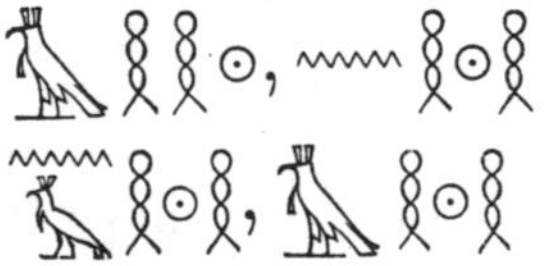 eternity, for ever; with  time without beginning or end.

neḥeḥ  to invoke, entreat.

neḥes 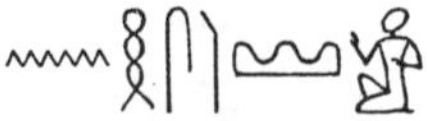 negro, a Sûdânî man in general.

neḥṭ-t 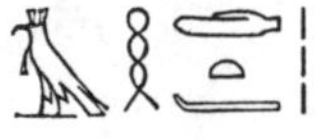 jaw teeth (?).

neḥṭ-ui  the two jaws (?).

 . . . . . .

nekh  to cry out, complain.

nekha  a sharp knife.

nekhakhat 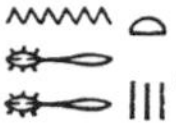, humours (?), variant .

nekhȧu  protector.

Nekhebet  the goddess of the city of Nekheb (Al-Kâb).

nekhebet  flowers.

Nekhen 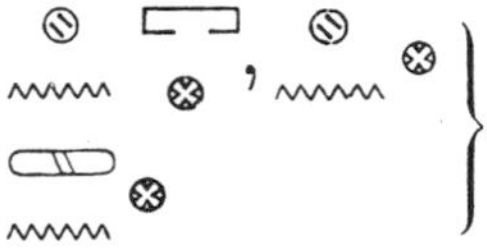 a city of Upper Egypt,  the god of Nekhen.

nekhen  babe, child.

nekhenu ,  children.

Nekhenu  the name of one of the Forty-two Judges in the Hall of Osiris.

nekhenit  girls (?).

nekhekh  old man.

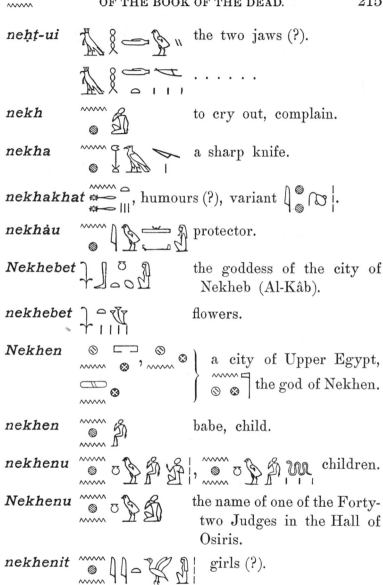

nekhekh 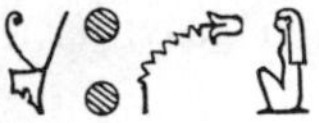 Vol. II, p. 251, l. 10.

nekhekh 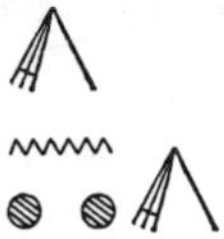 whip, flail.

nekht  to be strong, strength, powerful.

nekhtu  valour, bravery, conquest.

Nekht  a proper name.

nekht  strong (in a bad sense).

Nekhtu-Åmen 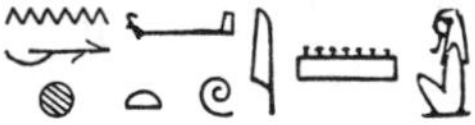 a proper name.

nes 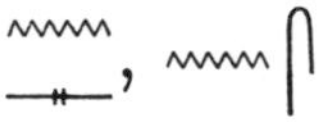 she, her, it.

nes  to belong to.

 belonging to him.

nesu  . . . . . . 

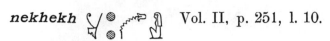

nes *nesau*		tongue; 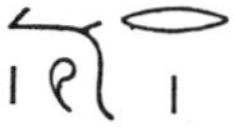; plur. .
nes		to eat, devour, consume.
nes		to arrange (?), order (?).
nes *nesnes*	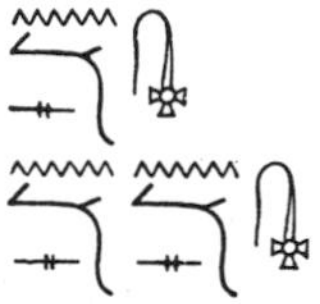	flame.
nes		grain (?).
nesut		weapons of war.
nesb		to eat; .
nesbit		to eat, devour.
Nesbu		devouring gods.
nespu		slaughter, wound, knives.
nesert		flame, fire.

Nesert a fire-goddess.

Nesersert the Fire-city.

nest throne; plur.

Throne.

nesti a class of divine beings.

nest cakes (?).

nesh to walk (?).

neshau plates of metal.

neshu a weapon (?).

neshi — to make the hair bristle.

neshep to snuff the air.

neshem, ***neshmet*** a precious stone.

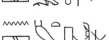

neshmet the name of a sacred boat.

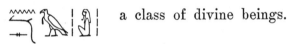

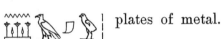

neshni 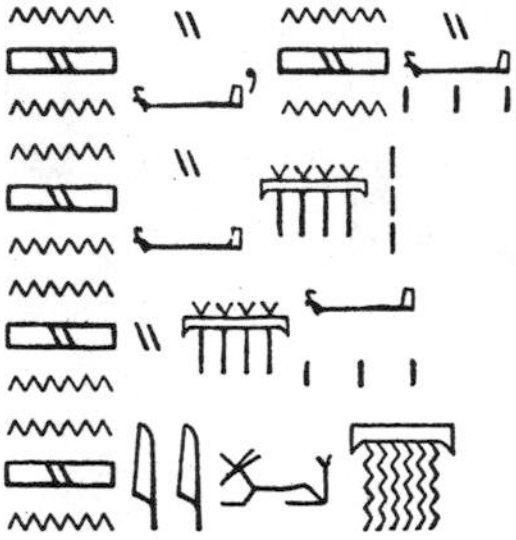

neshen 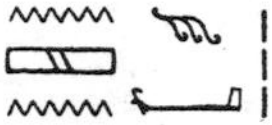

neshenu 

to be stormy, to revolt, a thunder-storm, destructive winds, whirlwind, tempest in general, revolt; 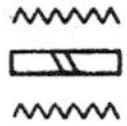 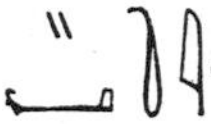.

nek  thou, thy.

nek  to copulate;  to have union with himself.

nekek 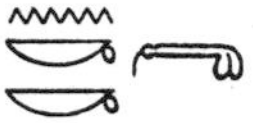 to commit sodomy.

nek nekek  to have union with a sodomite.

nekau  . . . . . .

nekai  injury.

 ill-doing fiends.

Nekȧ 

Nekȧu 

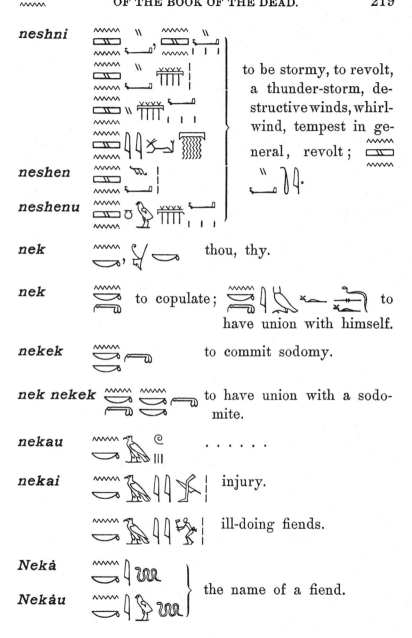

the name of a fiend.

neken	to do harm or injury to anyone.
nekent	injury; plur.
nekenu	injury, evil, harm.
neqāut	shackles.
neqāiut	those who steal away.
neḳa	to chew.
Neḳau	a Bull-god.
neḳeḳ	to cackle.
Neḳeḳ-ur	"Great Cackler"; name of the Goose-god.
Net	Neith, the great goddess of Saïs.
ent	of.
net	water, stream.

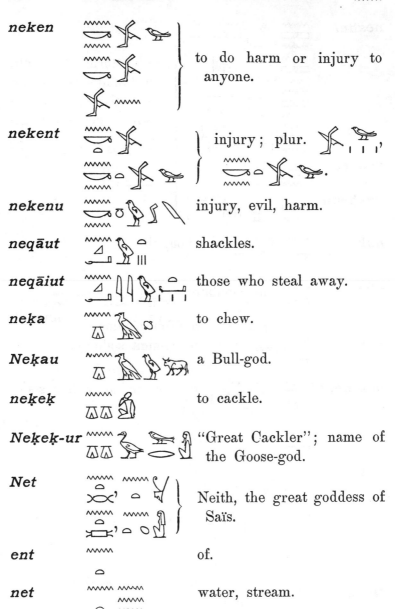

ent-ā 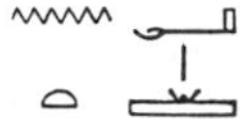 to ordain, order, ordinance, decree, customary rite; 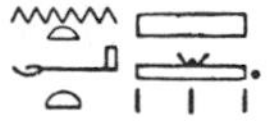.

enti  who, which, that which; plur. .

entiu, ***entet***  things which exist, persons or beings who are.

enti  sign of the negative, no, not, without.

neti  to vanquish, conquer.

Enti-mer-f 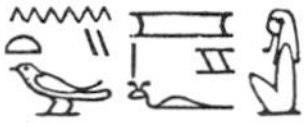 a proper name.

Enti-ḥer-f-emm-mast-f  a proper name.

entu 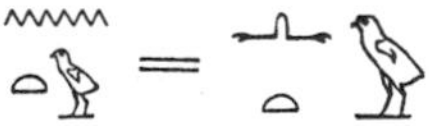

netu  fastenings, cords.

entuten  ye, you.

entef  he.

netnet  that which flows.

neter god, Copt. ⲛⲟⲩⲧⲉ great god; self-created, great god; god One; the City-god; god with a dog's face.

neteru gods, all the gods of the Three Companies, *i.e.*, Heaven, Earth, and the Ṭuat; all the gods.

the father-gods.

the mother-goddesses.

the Four gods.

the Forty-two gods.

gods celestial and gods terrestrial.

gods of heaven and gods of earth.

gods of the Ṭuat.

gods of the Qerti.

gods guides of the Ṭuat.

gods of the East.

gods of the North.

gods of the West.

gods of the South.

neter-ui the two gods Horus and Set; the two divine eyes, *i. e.*, Sun and Moon.

netert goddess, late form ; plur. , , .

netri to be a god or like unto a god, divine , , , divine.

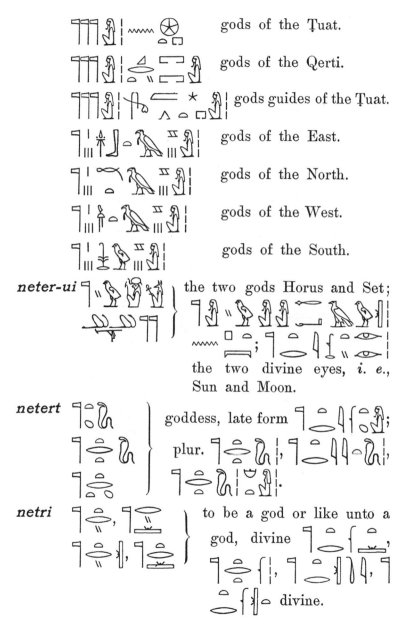

he who is divine ; , "divine god".

neter àtfui the two divine fathers.

neter meṭu "the words of the god", *i.e.*, hieroglyphic writing.

neter nemt the block or execution chamber of the god (Osiris).

neter ḥāu the body, or limbs, of the god.

neter ḥet "god-house", *i. e.*, temple.

neter ḥetepu "god-offerings", holy offerings, sepulchral meals.

neter khert , "underworld of the god" ; a name for the grave and for the place of departed spirits.

neter khet "god-property", *i. e.*, things dedicated to the service of the god.

neter shems "god-follower", a member of the god's "body-guard".

neter ṭuai "god-star", the morning star, Venus.

neter ṭuau  "god-adoration", to give thanks to God.

neter ṭept 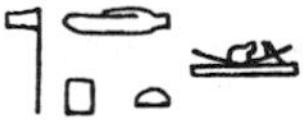 "god-boat", divine barque.

neter tcheṭ  "god-word", sacred speech.

Neter  name of a lake in the Other World.

Neteru 

Netri 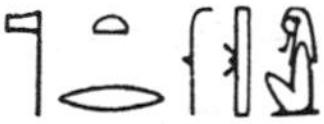 name of a town or city.

Netert-utchat  name of a place.

entes  she.

ent-sen 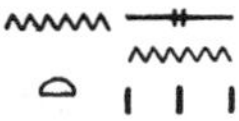 them, they.

entek  thou (masc.).

Netqa-ḥer-khesef-àtu  the name of the herald of the Fourth Ārit.

ent  thou (fem.).

netet  cattle for sacrifice.

entet  which, that which is.

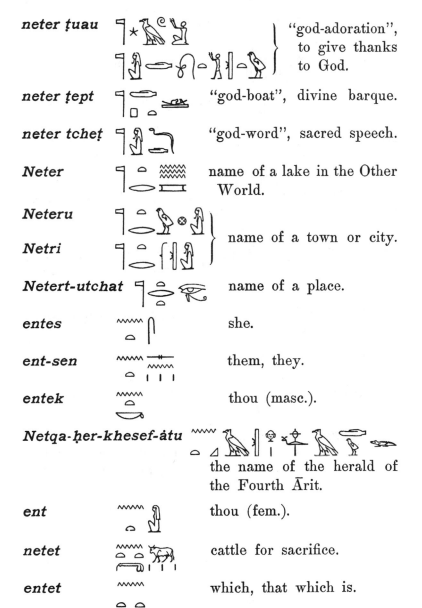

neṭ 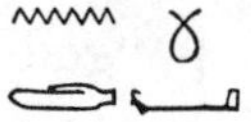 to bandage, to tie.

Neṭit 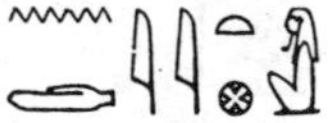 a proper name.

Neṭbit  name of a town or city.

Neṭet  name of a town or city.

netch, *netchet* 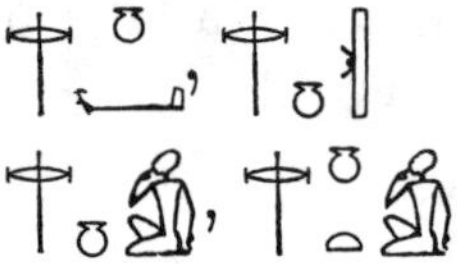 to protect, guard, avenge.

netch ḥer 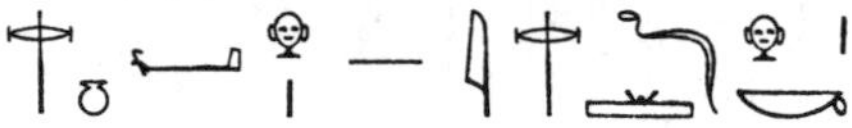 "homage to thee", a form of salutation to gods.

netchti  protector, advocate, avenger.

netch meṭu, *netchtu re*  to discuss a matter with someone, to converse, to take counsel.

netchnetch 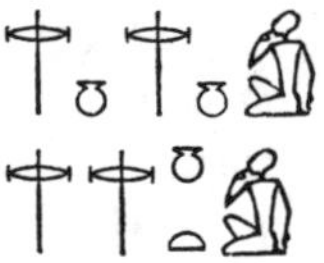 to take counsel with someone, to discuss a matter.

Netcheb-àb-f  a proper name.

Netchfet  name of a town and its god.

netchem  to be sweet, pleasant, to rejoice, be glad;  very pleasant;  pleasant things.

netchemu

netchemet

netchemmit  love-making, the delights of sexual love.

Netchem  the god of love.

netcher  to grasp, hold fast.

netcheriu 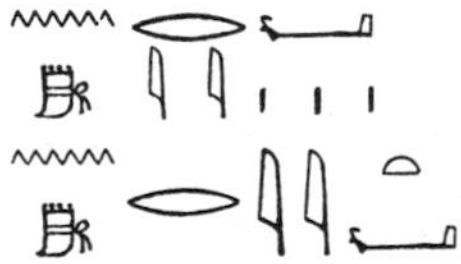 clinchers, grapplers.

netcherit

netcherȧ  to hew, to carve.

netchḥet  to strengthen.

Netcheḥ-netcheḥ 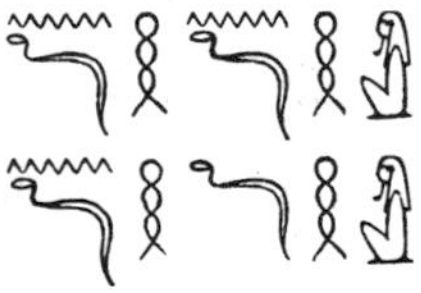 the name of one of the Seven Spirits who guard Osiris and his bier.

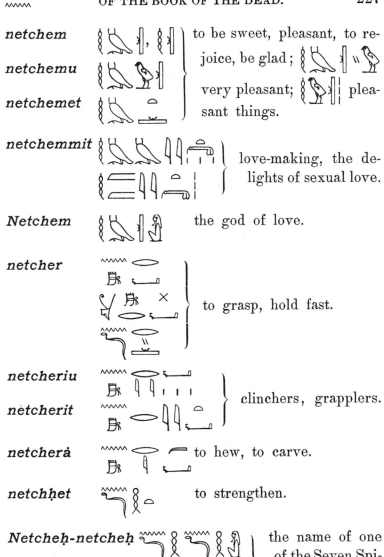

Netcheḥ-tcheḥ

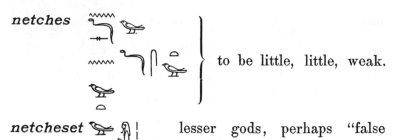

netches	to be little, little, weak.
netcheset	lesser gods, perhaps "false gods".
Netchesti	a name of Osiris.
Netchses	a name of a god.
Netchet	a name of a town or city.

R or L.

er	at, to, with, into, among, against, from, according to, near, by, towards, upon, concerning. With compounds :—
er ȧmi	among.
er ȧmi tu	among, between.
er ȧmi thu	among, between.
er ȧsu	in return for, as reward or recompense for.
er mā	with, near.

er men 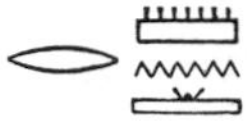 as far as.

er entet 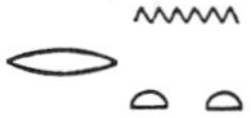 because.

er ruti  outside.

er ḥāt  before.

er ḥenā 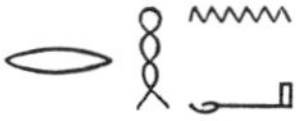 with.

er ḥer  away from.

er ḥeru  above.

er kheft ḥer  in the face of.

er kher  under.

er kherth 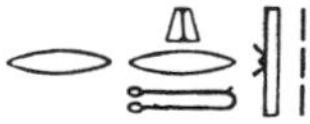 on behalf of.

er sa  by the back of.

er ḳes  near, by the side of, in the track of.

er  sign of the comparative: more than, *e. g.*,

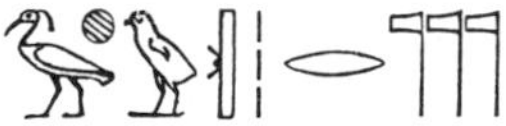 glorious more than the gods.

 divine more than the gods.

 swift more than greyhounds.

 swift more than the shadow.

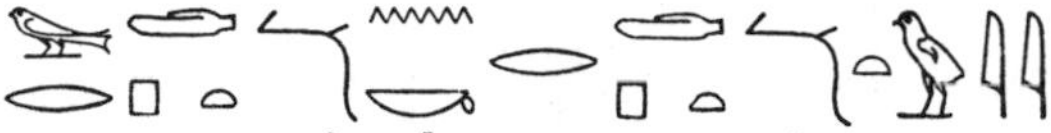

great is the taste to thee more than that taste.

Horus is bolder than all the gods.

 provided more than the gods.

 a name greater than yours.

 stronger than the gods.

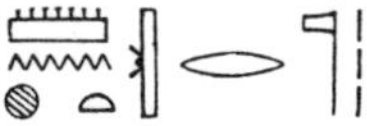 more gracious than the gods.

 brighter than the House of the Moon.

thy speech is more piercing than the [cry of] the *tcheru* bird.

er 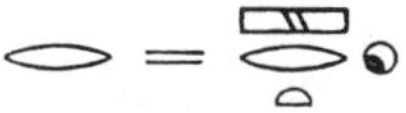 cake, offering.

re  goose.

re — worms (?),

re — door, opening, entrance, mouth, speech, chapter; plur. ; opening of the mouth, appearance; strong of mouth; doors of the Ṭuat; chapters of commemorations; a single chapter; a chapter of words; a chapter of mysteries; to set the mouth in motion against any one, *i. e.*, to slander.

re ȧpt (?) — brow.

Re-āa-urt — "opening of the great door"; the name of a town.

re-uat — entrance to the roads.

re Ḥāp — mouth of the Nile.

re Khemenu — the entrance to the city of Hermopolis.

re Sekhait 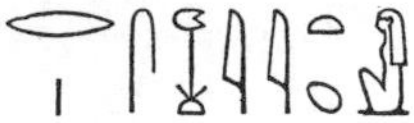 mouth of the goddess Sekhait.

Re-stau 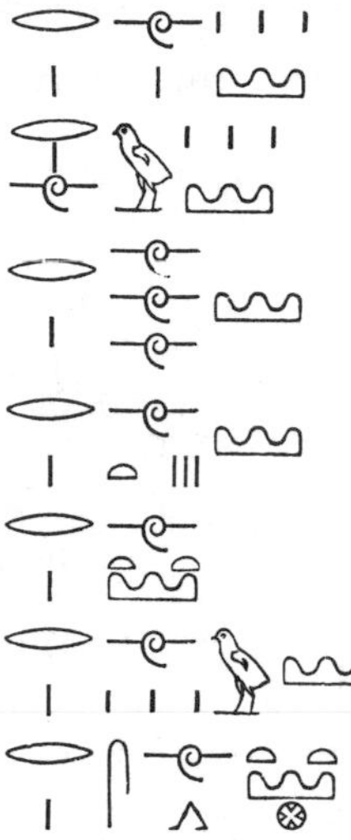 the "entrance to the corridors" in the Other World of Seker at Ṣaḳḳârah.

re-pu  or.

re-per 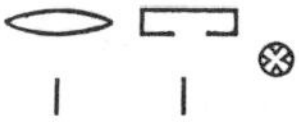 temple.

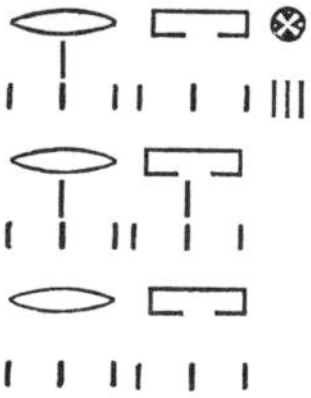 temples;  temples of the South and North.

Re (***Maȧu***?)  the Lion-god.

Re (?)-***Iukasa***  the name of a god.

Re (?)-***Rā***  the Lion-god Rā.

rā 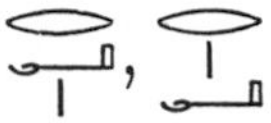 work.

Rā  the Sun-god *par excellence*;  like Rā.

rā  day. 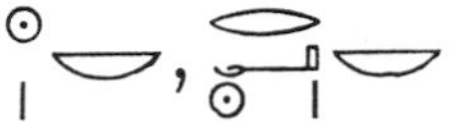 daily, every day.

Rā-Åsår  Rā-Osiris, the Sun-god of day and night.

Rā-Ḥeru-khuti  "Rā-Horus of the two horizons", Rā-Harmachis.

Rā-Tem  Rā-Tem, the Sun-god of day and night.

Rā-Maāt-men  the prenomen of Seti I.

Rā-men-kau 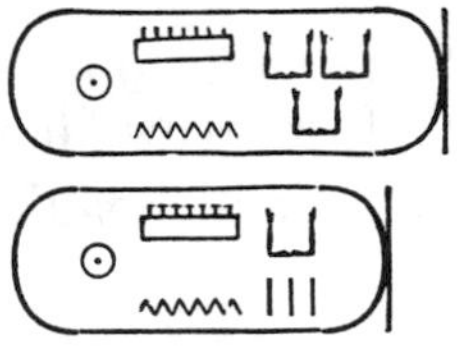 the Mykerinos of the Greeks.

Rā-mes-meri-Åmen-meri-Maāti 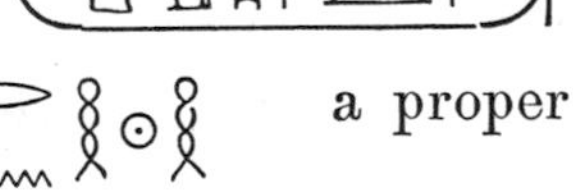 Rameses IV.

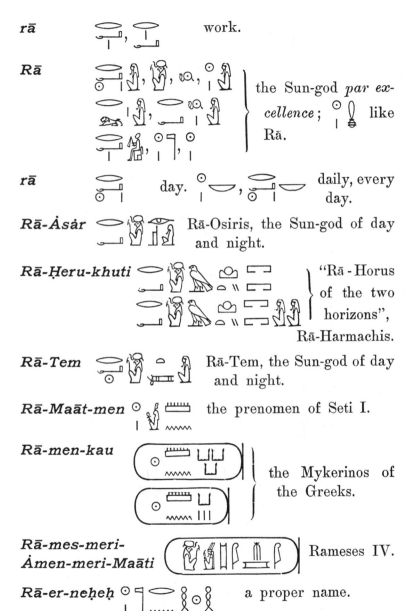

Rā-er-neḥeḥ a proper name.

ri 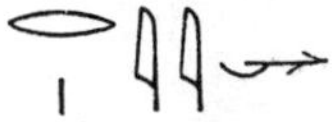 door.

ri 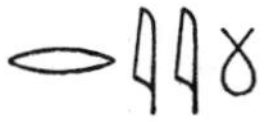 bandage, swathing.

riu  emanations.

ru  . . . . . .

ru  . . . . . .

ru  to fall, drop (of the wind).

ruȧ, *ruȧa*  to separate from, move away from, depart.

rui  journey, departure.

ruti  the two leaves of a door.

ruṭ  to grow, flourish, to be firm and healthy, to be taut (of ropes and sails); 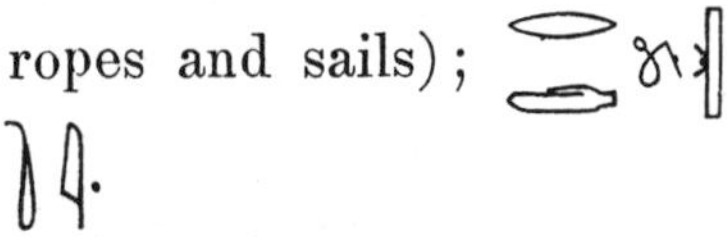.

ruṭi  strong, vigorous.

ruṭ | plants, things which grow.

ruṭu |

Ruṭ-en-Ȧst a proper name.

Ruṭu-nu-Tem a proper name.

Ruṭu-neb-rekhit

a proper name.

ruṭu | superintendent, overseer.

ruṭ staircase.

eref an intensive particle, then, therefore.

erpā |

erpāt hereditary tribal chief.

erpit image, statue, august person.

erpti the two august goddesses, *i. e.*, Isis and Nephthys.

remu fish.

Remu the "town of fish"; a proper name.

Remi  the Fish-god.

rem 
remu  } to weep.

remt  tear; plur. .

rem-tȧ  studded (?).

ermen 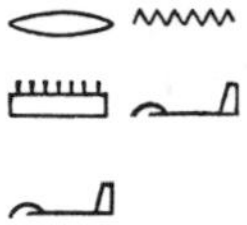 } arm, shoulder, one side of the body.

ermenui  } the two arms, shoulders.

 the two sides of a ladder.

ermenu 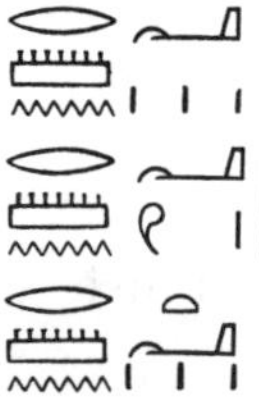 } shoulders, arms, supporters, the branches of a tree.

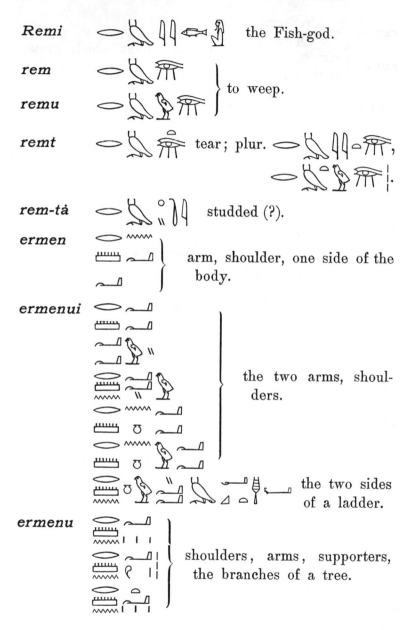

ermen  to carry away, to bear, to remove something, to shoulder.

Remrem  the name of a god.

ren  name; plur.  .

ren  to nurse (see *renen*).

renp  to be young or youthful, renewal of youth, to become young;  youthful one.

renp-tȧ  youthful, made young;  very young.

renpit  year; plur. *renput* .

renpit 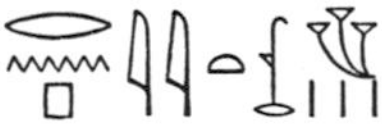 plants, vegetables, fruits.

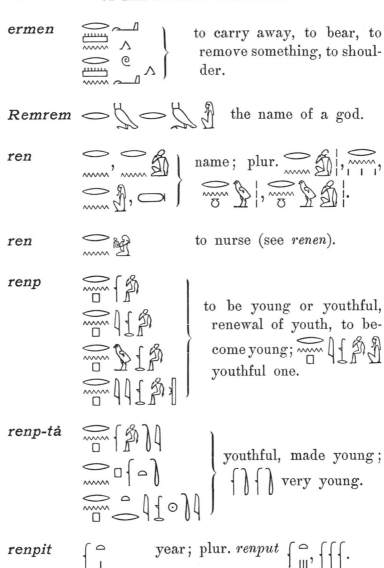

Renen 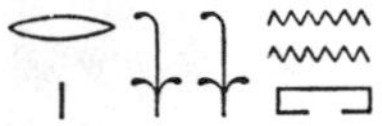 the name of a god.

renen  to nurse, to suckle.

Renenet 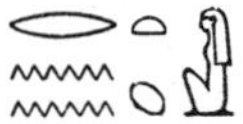

Renutet  } the goddess of grain crops and the harvest.

rer (*peḥer* ?)  territory, a place for walking about.

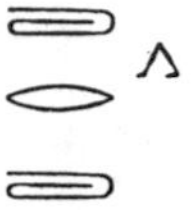

rer 

reru  } to walk about, to go round about, to revolve, to encircle; *thes rer* 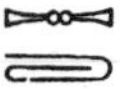 again, repetition, conversely.

rertå 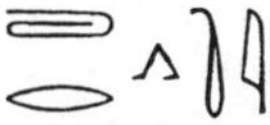 encircled.

reri 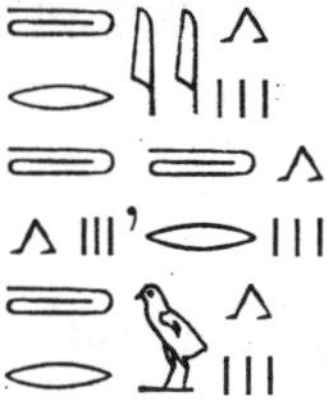 } those who revolve, or go about.

rer khet  going about retreating.

rert 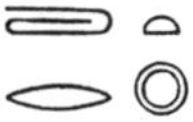 circle.

rert 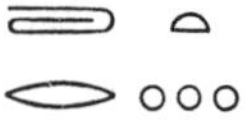 drugs, medicine.

rer  pig.

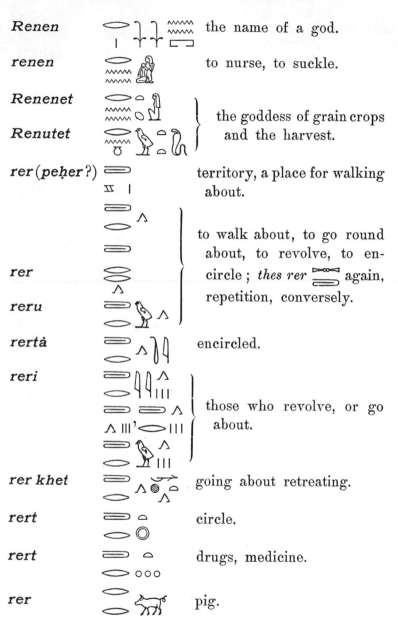

reru  . . . .

reru  . . . .

rert  mistake for  or  men.

Rertu-nefu 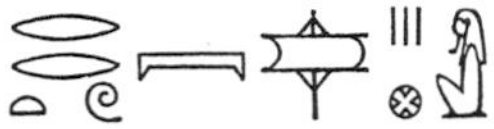 a proper name.

Rerek  name of a serpent fiend in the city of Åses.

Rerti (?) (***Maȧuti***?) 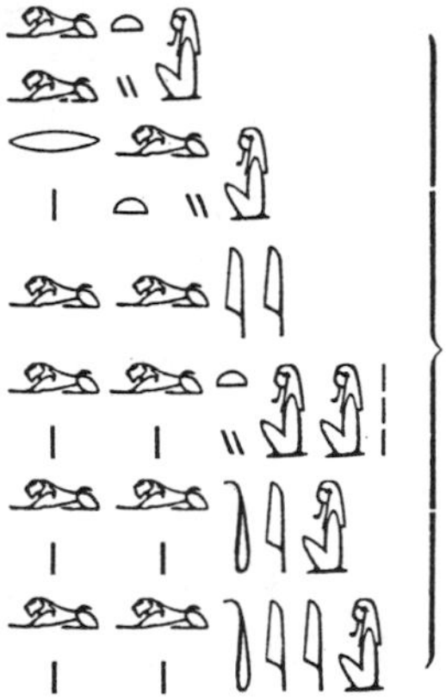 the Lion-god and Lion-goddess, *i. e.*, Shu and Tefnut (?). The name of one of the Forty-two Judges in the Hall of Osiris.

rehebu  flame, fire. Compare Heb. לָהַב.

rehen 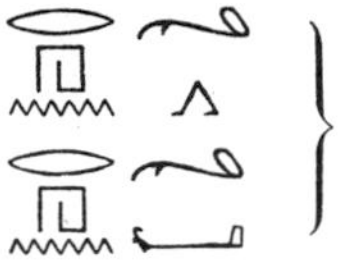 to rest upon, to support.

reḥ  to enter.

reḥu  a man deified, later a god.

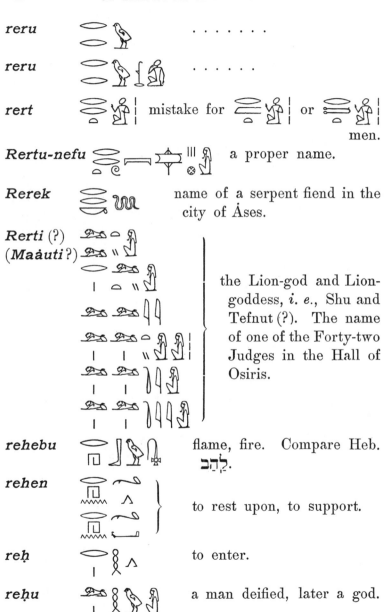

reḥui 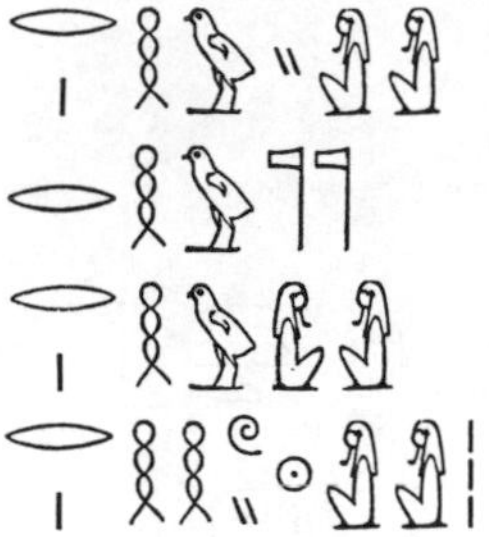 the two combatant gods, Horus and Set.

reḥti  the two combatant sister goddesses, Isis and Nephthys.

Reḥui  the town of the two combatant gods.

Re-ḥent  a proper name.

Re-ḥenent 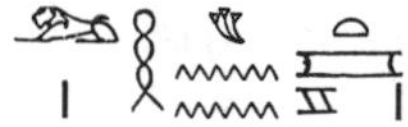 name of a lake or canal.

Re-ḥenent  the name of a town or its god.

rekh 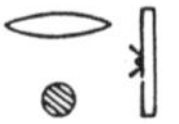 to be wise, to have knowledge; 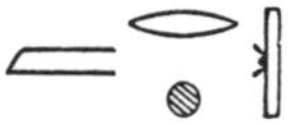 knowingly, with intent; ,  known; 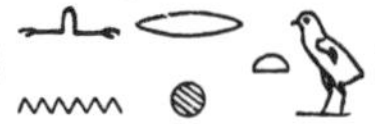 unknown.

rekht  knowledge, a list, inventory, total.

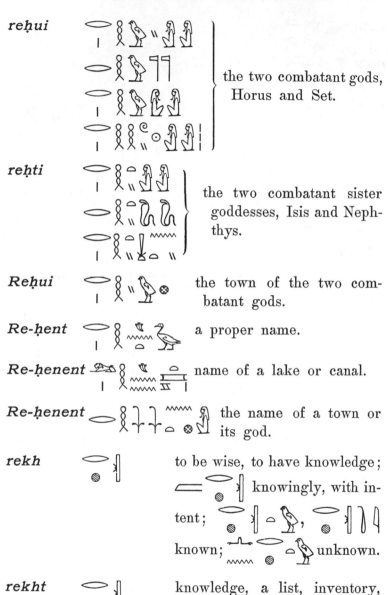

rekh åb to understand.

rekhu khet "knowers of things", *i. e.*, the wise gods.

rekhit beings of knowledge, rational beings, men and women, people, mankind.

rekhes to sacrifice, to slaughter.

Rekhti the two goddesses Isis and Nephthys.

Rekhti-Merti-neb[ti]-Maāti the two goddesses who were the ladies of the city of Maāt.

res, ***resu*** to watch, be awake; awake; rouse up! wake up!

resit the nine watchers.

restu night watchers.

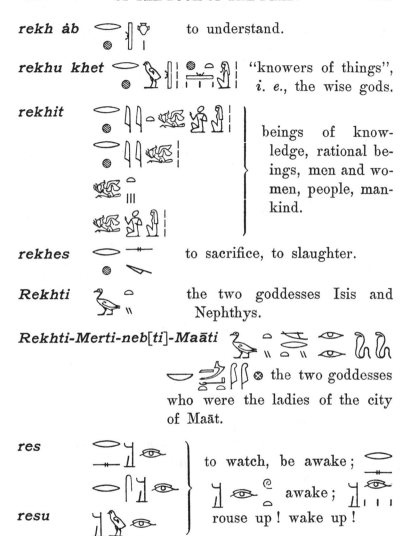

Res-àb 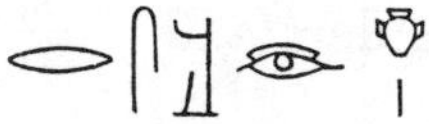 the warder of the Fourth Ārit.

Res-ḥer 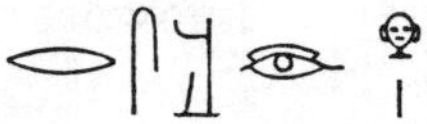 the warder of the Third Ārit.

res 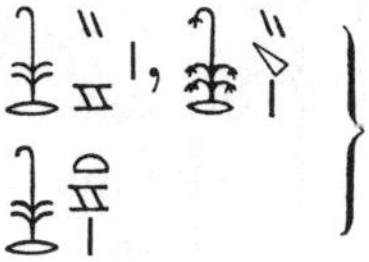 south, southern;  South and North, all Egypt.

resiu 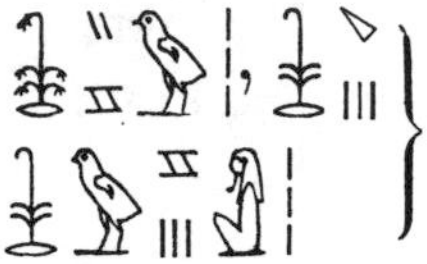 southerners, southern gods.

Resu  a proper name; fem. .

resu  south wind.

Resenet (?)  a proper name.

resh 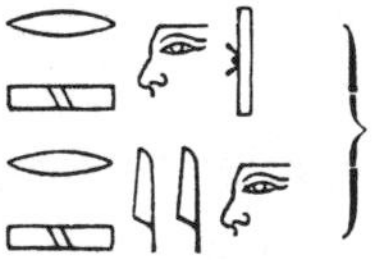 to breathe with joy, to rejoice.

resht  gladness, joy, to snuff, to inhale.

reshui  the two nostrils.

rek  then, an emphatic particle.

rek  time.

rekḥ 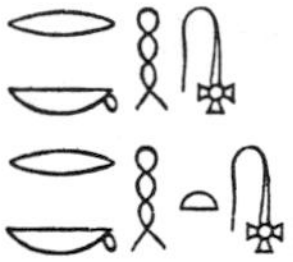 to burn, to be hot.

rekḥu  fire, flames.

Rekes 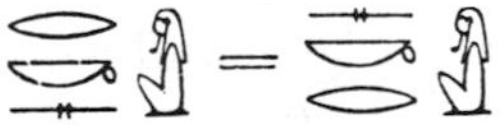

req
reqa  to incline away, fall away from ; .

reqi  fiend, enemy.

reqau  (or ) fiends, enemies.

ret 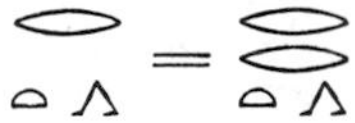 *i. e.*, *reret*, or *peḥrert*.

ret (***remt***)  men and women, people, mankind.

 everybody.

Retasashaka  a name of Åmen.

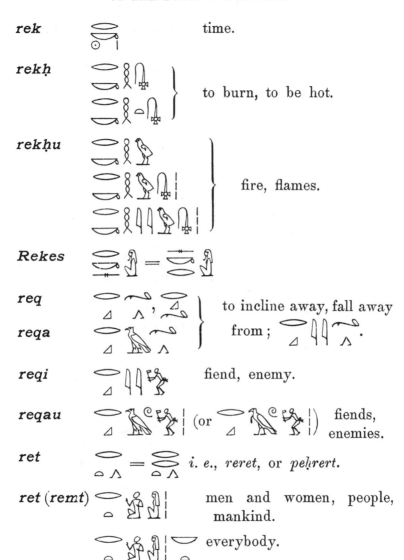

reti the two leaves of a door.

reṭ leg, foot.

reṭui

reṭi the two feet.

reṭȧu feet.

***reṭ* (*remt*)** men and women, people, folk, mankind.

reṭ steps, staircase.

erṭā

erṭāt to give, to set, to place, to put, to cause or make to happen;

As an auxiliary verb:

and see *passim*.

Erṭā-nefu a proper name.

Erṭā-ḥen-er-reqa a proper name.

reṭut places, abodes.

reṭu . . . .

reṭu emanations, effluxes, droppings.

reth men and women, people, folk, mankind.

everybody.

H.

ha interjection, O! Hail!

ha to be strong; strength.

ha	to descend, to go down into a place, to embark on a ship, to fall, to go in, enter, advance into; those who enter.
hai	
hait	
hau	time, period, reign.
Haȧker	name of a festival.
Hai	"phallus"; the name of one of the Forty-two Judges in the Hall of Osiris.
hai	interjection, O! Hail!
hai	to shout with joy, rejoice.
haiu	the gods who rejoice.
hait	a large chamber, heaven (?).
hab	to send, to send forth, to go forward.

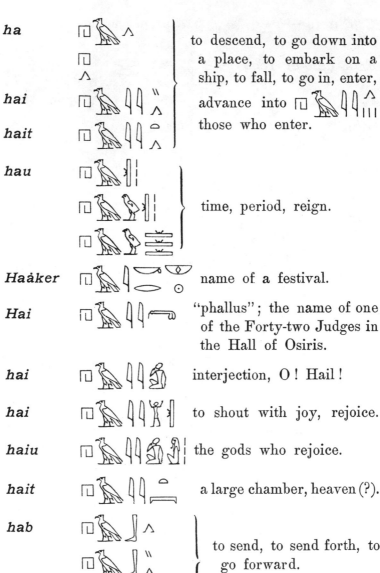

habu those who fall down.

Hab-em-atu "advancing at the moment"; a proper name.

habeq to fail.

hamu blemish, defect, sin.

Hart-ȧb to please.

Hahuti-ȧm- ..... the name of a fiend.

Haḥetep a proper name.

Hakheru a proper name.

Hasert a city in the Seventh Ȧat.

haker the name of a god and of a festival.

haq

Haqahakaḥer a proper name.

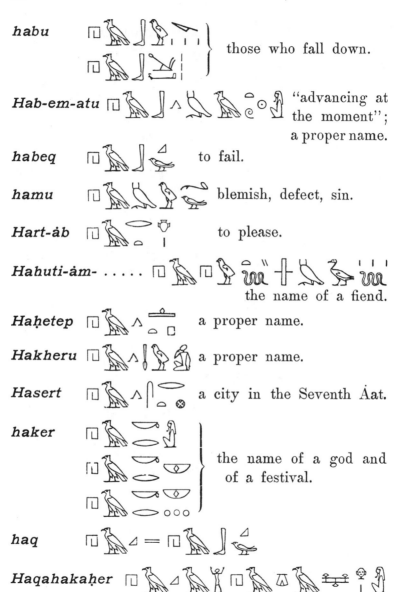

hat		interjection, O!
hat		descent, entrance, embarcation.
hatu		brow (?).
haṭ		to suppress, to beat down, subdue.
hi		to rejoice.
hu		to enter, descend, fall.
Hunefer		the name of a scribe.
Hu-kheru		the name of the herald of the first Ȧat.
heb		ibis, the bird sacred to Thoth.
heb		to send out, to go forward.
hebt		
hepu		laws, ordinances, regulations.
hem		fire.

hemu  men and women, folk, people: see also ***ḥenmemet.***

hemhem  to roar, cry out, bellow (of a bull).

hemhemet  outcries, roarings.

Hemti  runner.

hen 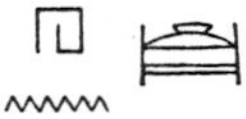 funeral chest, coffin.

Henȧ  the name of a city.

henȧnȧu 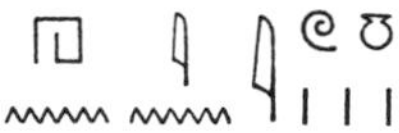 pleasant things.

henu  to sing songs of joy, to praise.

henu  praises, shouts of joy, singers.

henhenu 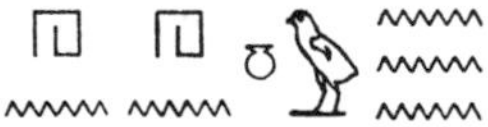

henhenit  the watery abyss of heaven, flood.

hensheses 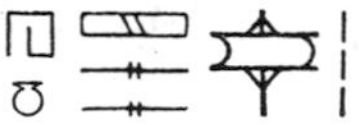 the east wind.

her  to be content, pleased.

her-åb
hert-åb 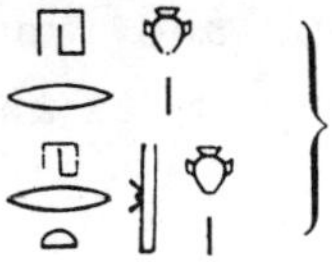 pleased in heart, content, pleasure.

herå  a vessel.

heru  day; plur. .

 this day, to-day.

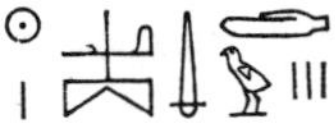 judgment day.

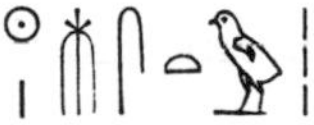 birthday.

 birthday of Osiris.

 day of the funeral.

 every day, daily.

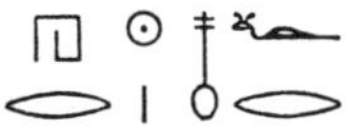 a happy day.

 daily, course of each day.

heriu 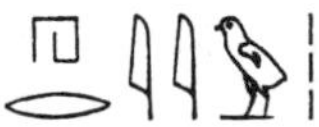 those who are content (?).

herret 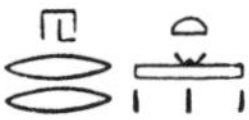 things which please.

heh  flame.

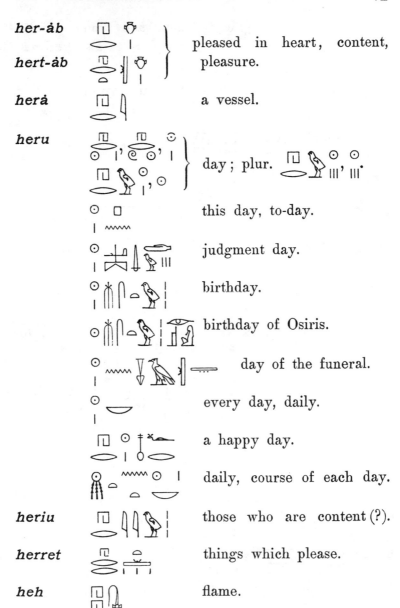

heker / ***hekeru*** 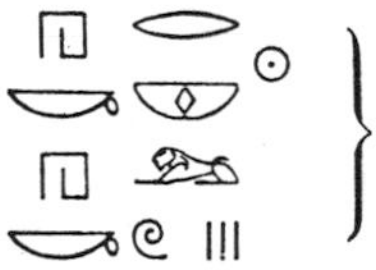 name of a festival.

heq 

hetu  to be addressed.

hethet  to go round about.

heṭ 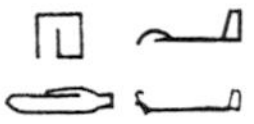 to subdue. 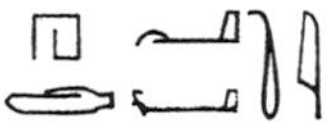 subdued.

 Ḥ.

. . . . . . 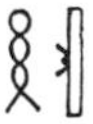 with  . . . . . .

ḥa  behind, get back! back thou! (in addresses to fiends).

ḥa  back of the head and neck.

ḥa  a cry, a precative particle.

Ḥaȧs  a proper name.

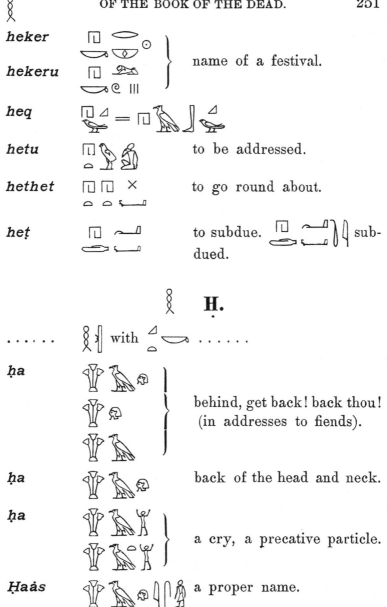

ḥaȧu  the dwellers in the Delta and in the marshes near the sea-coast.

ḥai  to be bright, to shine.

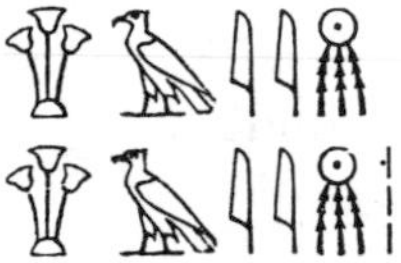 light.

Ḥai 

Ḥait  a proper name.

ḥait  to grasp.

ḥau

ḥauu 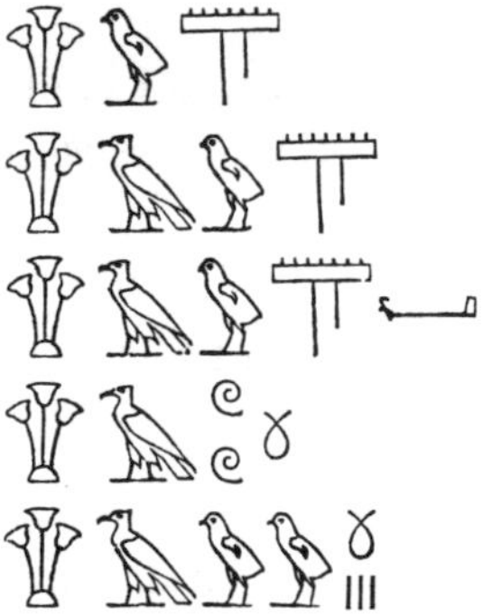 to be unclothed, to strip off apparel.

ḥaui  naked man.

ḥau  addition, increase, things added.

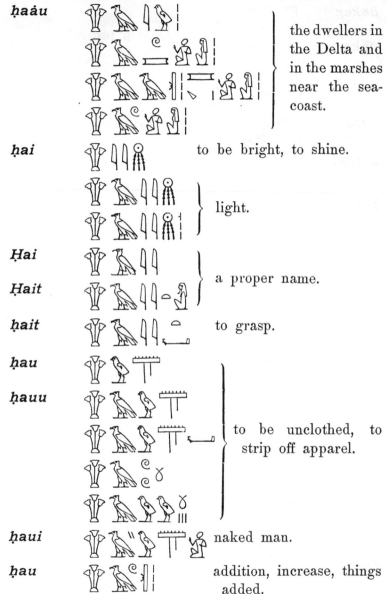

ḥauatu 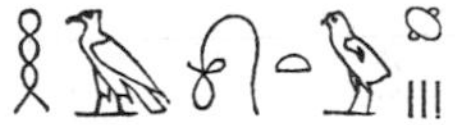 filth, dung.

ḥan-re  to have a care for, assuredly.

Ḥa-ḥer  a proper name.

ḥap

ḥapu 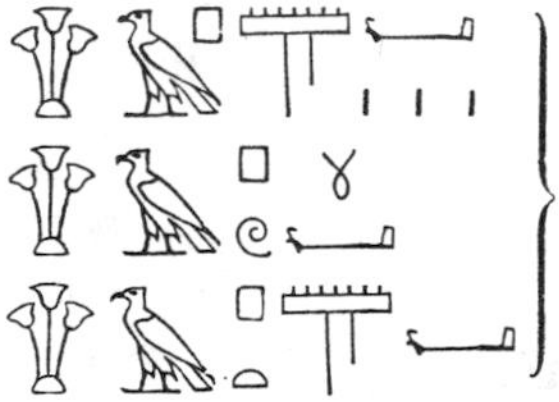 to enshroud, to hide, to cover over.

ḥapt

ḥap  to advance, move forward.

ḥaputi  runner (?).

Ḥap  the Bull Apis;  .

Ḥap

Ḥapi  one of the four sons of Horus who protected one quarter of the body of the deceased.

ḥapu  oar, steering pole, rudder.

ḥaptu 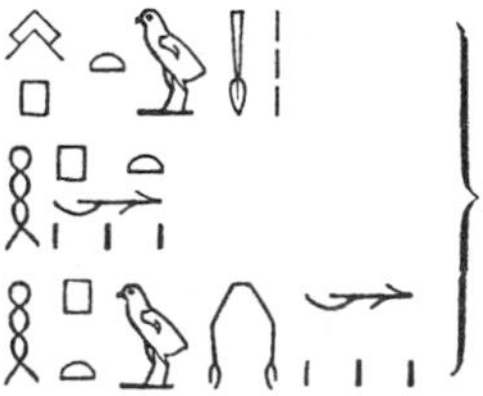 oars, paddles.

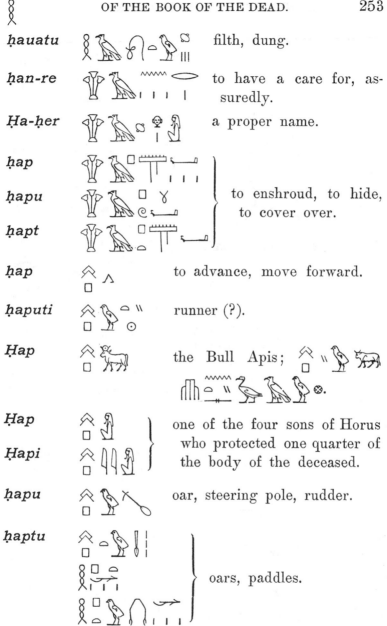

Ḥapu-en-neb-sett 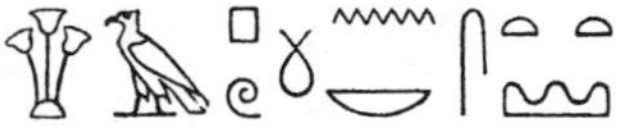 a name for the cemetery.

Ḥapṭ-re  a proper name.

ḥam 
ḥamt  } to net birds and fish.

ḥamiu 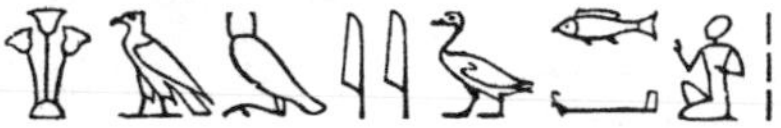 fishermen, fowlers.

Ḥarpuḳakashareshabaiu  a proper name.

Ḥareti  a proper name.

ḥaqet  to capture, make prisoners, captives.

ḥaqet  fetters.

ḥaqu  name of a plank or peg in the magic boat.

ḥat  pit.

ḥaṭ  tomb.

ḥaṭ 
ḥaṭu 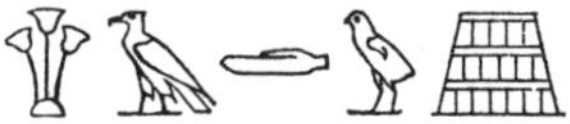 } net.

ḥatȧ, *ḥatȧtu*, *ḥattui* 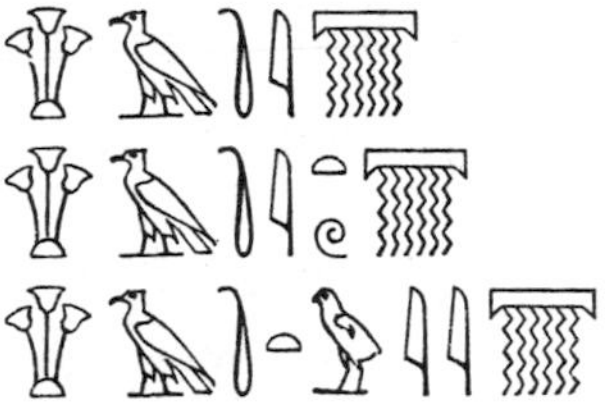 storm, whirlwind.

ḥā, *ḥāa*  to rejoice, be glad; , 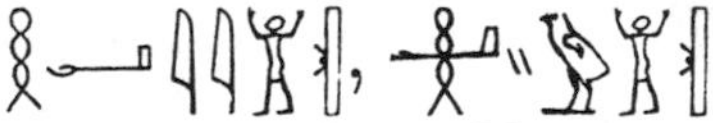, rejoicing;  glad.

ḥāiu 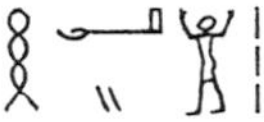 rejoicings.

ḥāā  to rejoice.

ḥāāiu, *ḥāātu* 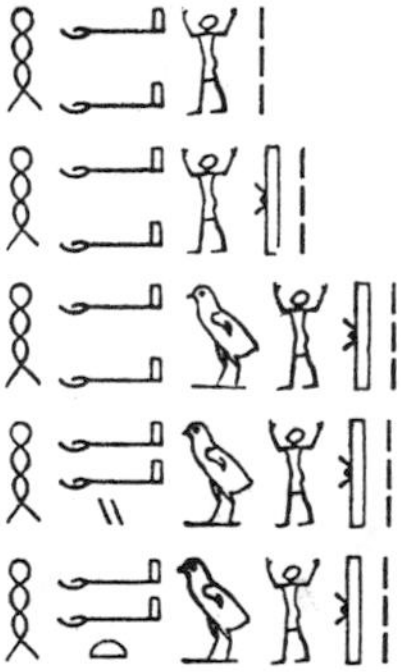 rejoicings, those who rejoice.

[*ḥā* 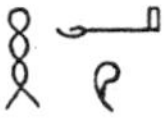 limb, member of the body, the body itself.]

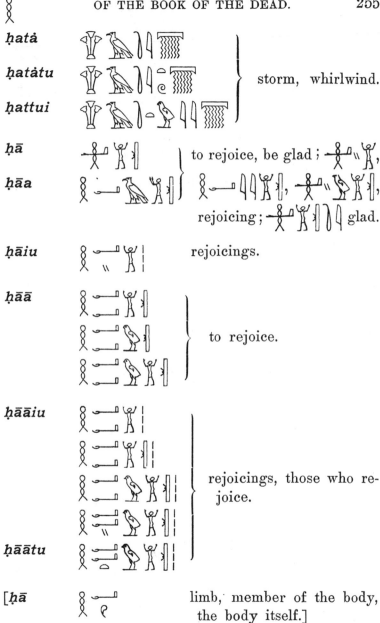

ḥāu
ḥāt

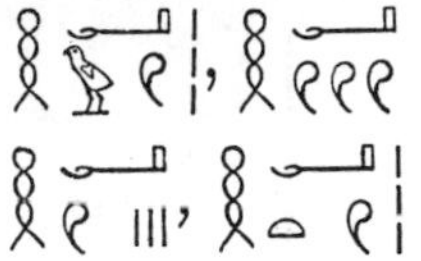

limbs, members of the body; 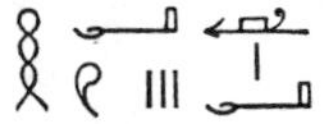 one body; 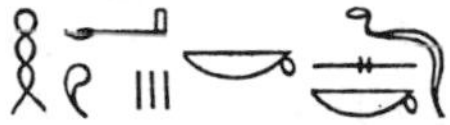 thy own self.

Ḥāp
Ḥāpi

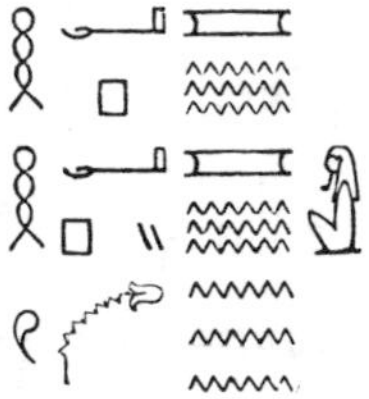

the Nile.

Ḥāp-ur  the Great Nile.

ḥā[t]-ā  the beginning or front of anything; the opening words of a book.

ḥāt  the beginning or front of anything, bows of a boat, the breast; 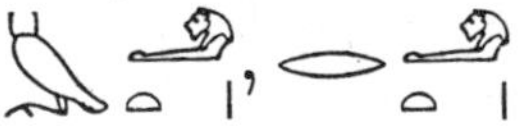 before.

[*ḥāt-ā*  prince, chief]  the two divine princes.

ḥāti

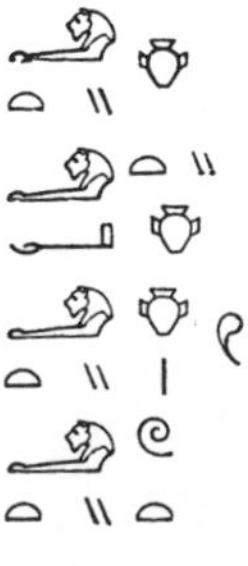

the heart; plur.  .

ḥātet  a rope in the bows of a boat.

ḥāti — unguent of the best kind.

Ḥi-mu (?) — the name of one of the Forty-two Judges in the Hall of Osiris.

Ḥit — a proper name.

ḥu — a mistake for [hieroglyphs].

ḥu — hair, tresses.

Ḥu, *Ḥui* — the god of food, divine food.

ḥu — to smite, to strike; [hieroglyphs] smiting (*i.e.*, clapping) their hands; [hieroglyphs] smiting.

ḥut — a smiting.

ḥuit-Rā — smiters of Rā.

Ḥu-tepa  a proper name.

ḥua  to be filthy, in a stinking, corrupt, or rotten state.

ḥuaat 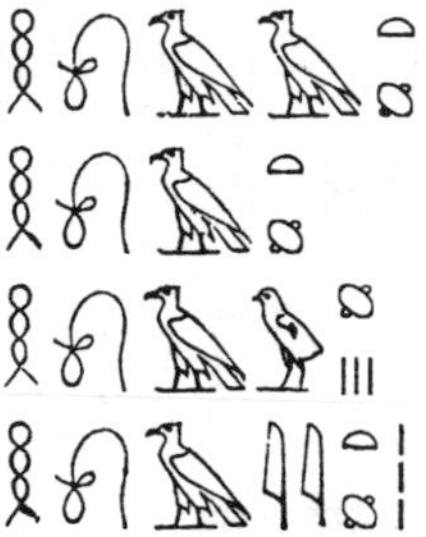 filth, dung, offal; 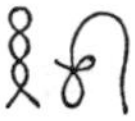  "filthy cat".

ḥui 

ḥuia  to decree, issue a command.

ḥun  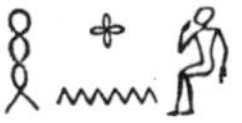 to be in the state of a child; boy, child, young man; plur. 

ḥunu  

ḥunen  

ḥunt  maiden, girl.

Ḥunt-Pe-...  . . . .

ḥuḥu  waterflood, a large mass of water.

ḥeb — festival.

ḥebu, *ḥebit* — festivals.

ḥebt — the book containing the words of the festival service.

ḥeb — fowls and fish for the festival.

ḥebā — to play (at draughts).

ḥebt, *ḥebbet* — stream, flood.

ḥebenut — a cake, confectionery.

ḥebs — to be clothed; clothed, a garment.

ḥebs — garment, clothing, a swathing; plur.

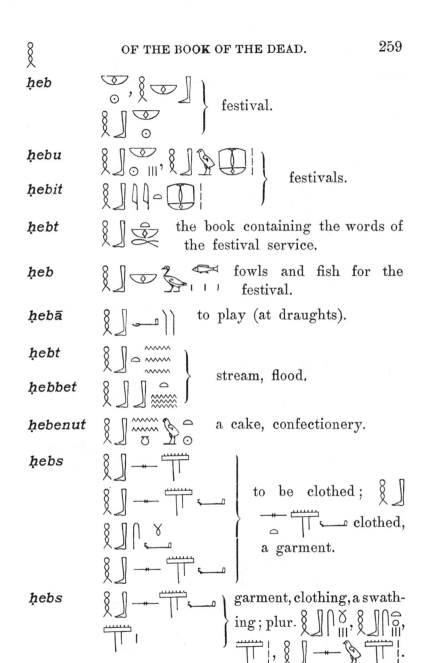

Ḥebṭ-re-f a proper name.

ḥept for *q. v.*

ḥept to embrace, embrace ; .

ḥept breast (?), embrace.

Ḥept-ur a proper name.

Ḥept-shet the name of one of the Forty-two Judges in the Hall of Osiris.

ḥeptu oars of a boat, doorposts.

ḥept , to move forward, advance; see ad-vancing.

ḥeptet a course, a place for walking.

Ḥepṭ-ur a proper name.

Ḥepṭ-re a proper name.

ḥepṭ-re to shut the mouth, to gnaw (?).

ḥefau  serpent, snake.

ḥefi  a serpent with two legs.

ḥefait 

ḥefiu 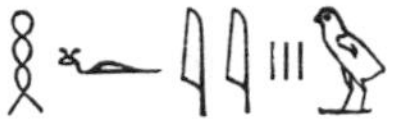 } . . . .

ḥefen 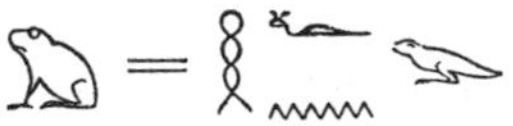 one hundred thousand.

ḥefṭ  to sit down, to rest.

ḥem  a particle.

ḥem  to retreat, make to go back.

ḥem  to steer, or paddle a boat.

ḥemu 

ḥemi  } paddle, oar, rudder, steering pole.

ḥemu 

ḥemit 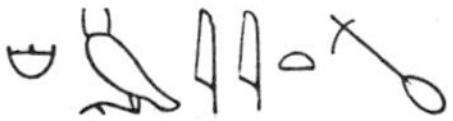 } paddles.

ḥemaḳa  to grasp.

Ḥemaḳa  the name of a town and of a god.

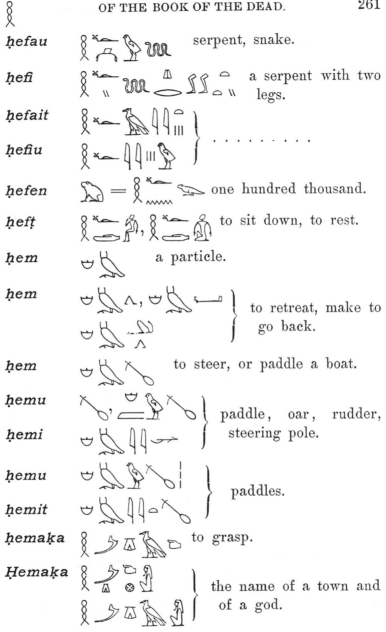

ḥematet name of a chamber.

ḥemu artificer, workman.

ḥemt work, handicraft.

ḥemt a mineral.

ḥemt copper, bronze.

ḥemen slaughter.

Ḥemen the name of a god.

ḥement forty.

ḥems to sit, be seated, to dwell; sitting, sitting ones; seated.

ḥemset a sitting, seat.

ḥemt woman, wife; plur. , .

woman belonging to a man, wife.

king's woman, *i. e.*, queen.

god's woman, *i. e.*, priestess.

Asiatic woman.

women goddesses.

a proper name (?).

ḥemt cow, cow-goddess; plur.

ḥen servant, slave; plur.

ḥent servant (fem.), slave.

ḥen neter god's servant, *i. e.*, priest.

ḥen ka priest of the *Ka*, or double.

ḥen majesty;

ḥen
ḥenen
ḥenḥen to go forward, to run.

ḥen
ḥenu to bestow, to be given or provided with, ordered, arranged.

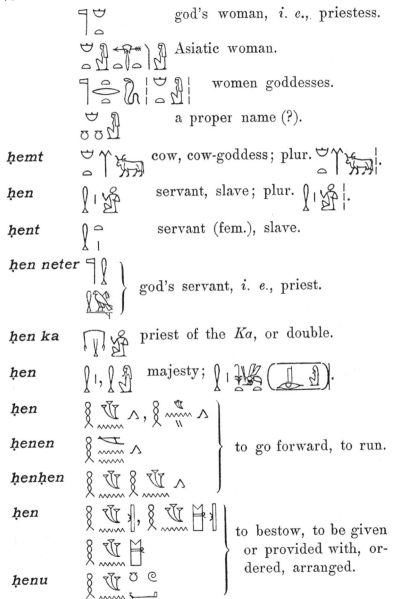

ḥen, ḥeni flowers, plants, blossoms.

ḥen to praise;

ḥenā with, along with, and; with; triumphant with you; god spake with god.

ḥenu
ḥeniu offerings, gifts.

ḥenu pillars.

ḥenu to draw to oneself.

ḥenbet corn-land.

ḥeneb offerings of grain produce.

Ḥenbi the god of the cultivated lands.

ḥenmemet also men and women, folk, people, mankind.

ḥenemnemu	devourers (?).
ḥenen	to labour, toil.
ḥenen; *ḥenu* (or *ḥennu*)	phallus; phallus of Rā.
Ḥenu; *Ḥennu*	name of a sacred boat which was drawn round the sanctuary at dawn at Memphis.
ḥennui	to go about, to wander, move forward.
ḥennui	the beginning and end of time or of eternity.
ḥennuti	crocodiles.
ḥennuit; *ḥennut*	fraud, deceit.
ḥennuti	two horns, a pair of horns.
ḥens	to block the way.

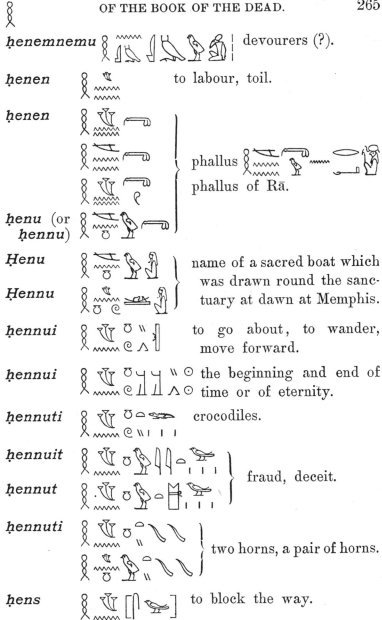

ḥenseki 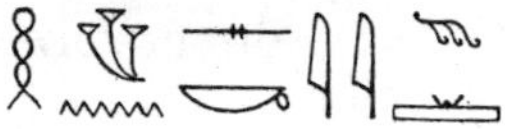

ḥensekit 

ḥensekt 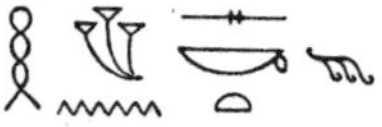 hair, lock of hair, tress.

ḥensekti 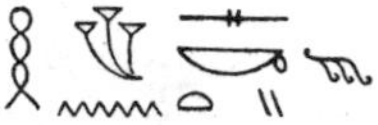

ḥenkesti 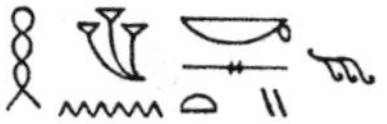 (*sic*)

Ḥensek  a god with much hair.

Ḥensektiu 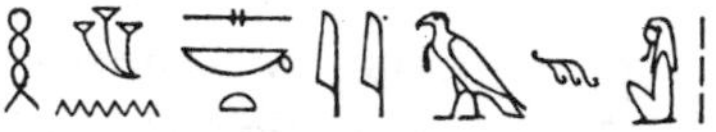 the gods with much hair, *i. e.*, the gods with long hair and beards.

Ḥenseket-menȧt-Ȧnpu-em-kat-en-utu 

name of a rope.

ḥenk   to give, present, offer; 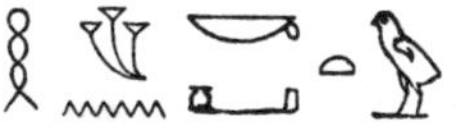 offered, given.

ḥenket 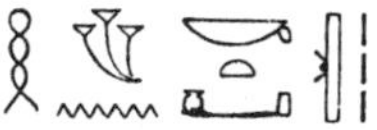 offerings.

Ḥenku-en-Ȧrp 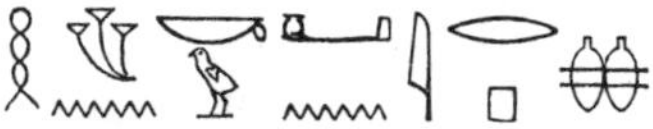 a proper name.

Ḥenku-en-fat-Maāt 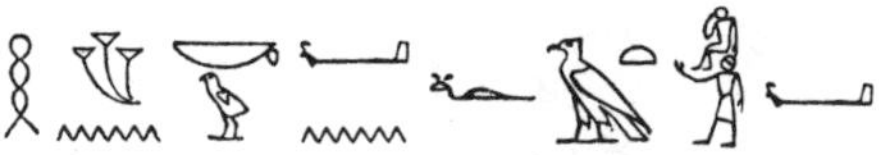
 a proper name.

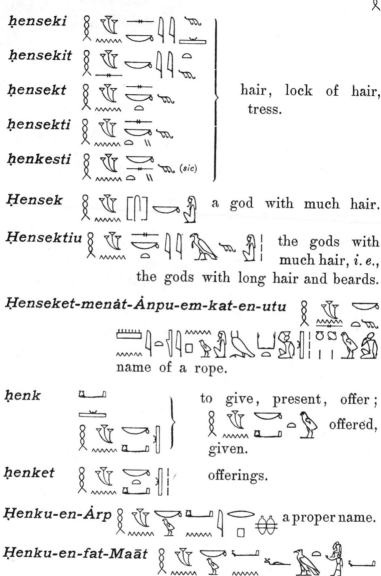

ḥenku  balance.

ḥenket 
ḥenkit 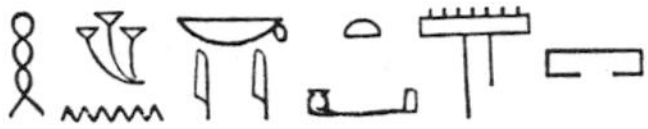 } the funerary bed, or chamber.

Ḥenket  the name of a town.

ḥent  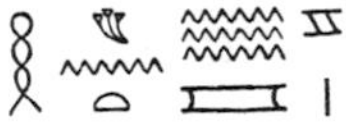 } lake, canal, stream, pool.

ḥent   } to be hostile.

ḥent 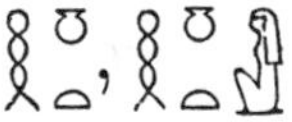  } mistress, lady, sovereign, queen.

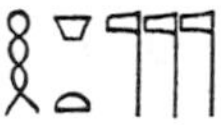 queen of the gods.

 lady of the crowns of the South and North.

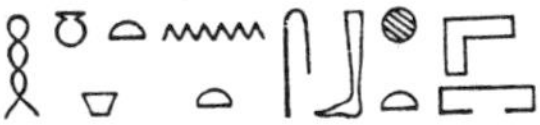 mistress of the pylons.

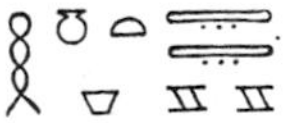 queen of the Two Lands.

Ḥent  crocodile.

ḥenta  to fall into oblivion, or decay.

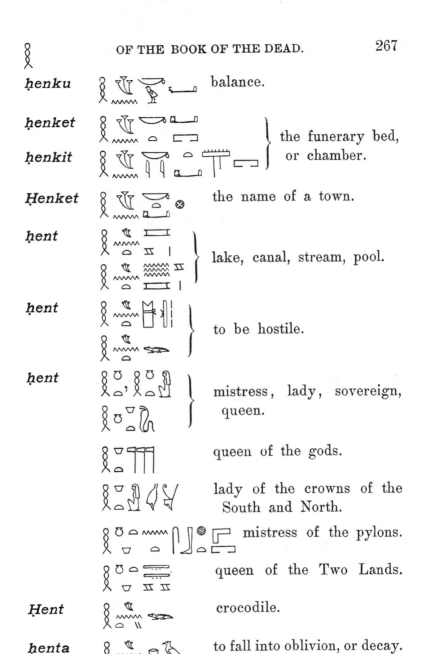

Ḥenti — god of the two crocodiles, a name of Osiris.

ḥenti — crocodile.

ḥenti — a pair of horns.

— the two-horned gods, or the two two-horned gods.

ḥenti — the beginning and end of time, or of eternity.

ḥenti pet — the two ends of heaven.

Ḥenti-requ — a proper name.

Ḥent-khent-ta-meru — a proper name.

ḥer — in, at, upon, on, by, etc.; *en ḥer* upon.

ḥer-ā — on the hand, *i. e.*, straightway, immediately.

ḥer-àb — in the middle of, dweller in; plur.

ḥer-àbt

Ḥer-àb-uàa-f "within his boat"; a proper name.

Ḥer-àb-àrit-f "within his eye; a proper name.

Ḥer-àb-karà-f "within his shrine"; a proper name.

ḥer mā straightway, forthwith.

ḥer entet
ḥer enti sa } because.

ḥer sa besides, in addition to.

ḥeri he who is above, or over, chief of, principal of.

chief scribe; chief of the writings; chief of the altar; chief of the altars.

ḥeriu those who are over, those who are above, celestial beings; chiefs.

ḥeriu
ḥertu  those who are over, those who are above, celestial beings; chiefs.

ḥeru  the upper regions, what is above; 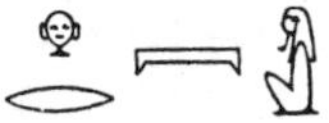 heaven, .

ḥeri tchatcha  chief, governor, president.

 chieftainess, goddess.

ḥert  the upper regions, the sky, heaven.

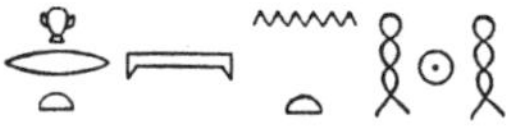 the heaven of eternity, *i. e.*, the everlasting heaven.

Ḥeri-aḳebȧ-f  "chief of his ocean"; a proper name.

Ḥeri-uatch-f 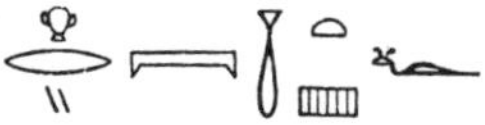 "chief of his sceptre"; a name of Horus.

Ḥeri-uru  "chief of the great ones"; the name of one of the Forty-two Judges in the Hall of Osiris.

Ḥeri-sesh "chief of the writings"; a proper name.

Ḥeri-sep-f "chief of his time"; a proper name.

Ḥeri-sesh[*eta*] "he who is over the secrets"; *i. e.*, secretary.

Ḥeri-shā-f "he who is on his sand"; a title of Osiris.

"those who are on [their] sand"; a name of the dwellers in the desert.

Ḥeri-ta "governor of the land".

Ḥeri-tchatcha-taui "governor of the Two Lands"; *i. e.*, Egypt.

ḥer and.

ḥer face; plur. , ; two faces; the divine face.

ḥer em ḥer face to face.

ḥer neb every one.

ḥeru nebu , folk, all men, mankind, all the people.

Ḥerui  the god of the two faces.

Ḥerui-f  he of the two faces.

Ḥer-uā  a proper name.

Ḥer-f-em-qeb  the name of a fiend.

Ḥer-nefer 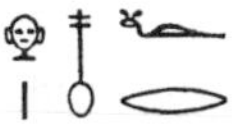 "beautiful Face"; a name of Rā and Ptaḥ;  

Ḥer-f-ḥa-f  "he with his face behind him"; the name of one of the Forty-two Judges in the Hall of Osiris.

Ḥer-k-en-Maāt  a proper name.

ḥer 
ḥeru 
 } to terrify, be frightened.

ḥerit  terror, fright.

ḥeri 
ḥeru  } to go away, depart, be away, be afar off; 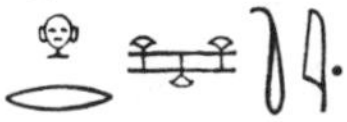.

Ḥer  the ancient name of the Sun-god; applied to the king as the representative of the Sun-god on earth.

Ḥerui  the pair of Horus gods, *i. e.*, Horus and Set.

Ḥerui-senui  the two Horus brethren.

Ḥeru-āa-ȧbu  "Horus, great one of hearts".

Ḥeru-ȧmi-ȧbu-ḥer-ȧb-ȧmi-khat  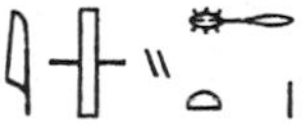 "Horus, dweller in hearts, he who is in the intestines".

Ḥeru-ȧmi-ȧthen  "Horus, dweller in the Disk".

Ḥeru-ȧrit (?)  the "Eye of Horus".

Ḥeru-āḥāi 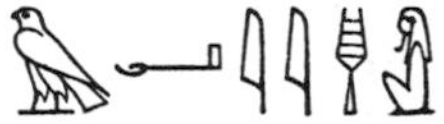 Horus the Fighter (?).

Ḥeru-Un-nefer 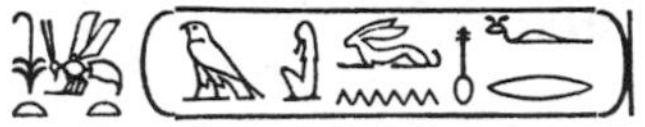 "King of the South and North, Horus Un-nefer".

Ḥeru-ur  The elder Horus as opposed to Horus the son of Isis.

Ḥeru-merti  Horus of the two Eyes, *i. e.*, Sun and Moon.

Ḥeru-em-khebit  Horus of the North.

Ḥeru-em-khent-en-merti .

Ḥeru-neb-urert  "Horus, lord of the Urert-crown".

Ḥeru-netch-ḥer-ȧtef-f  "Horus, the advocate of his father".

Ḥeru-ḥer-neferu  "Horus on the pilot's place [in the Boat of Rā]".

Ḥeru-khuti  Horus of the horizons of sunrise and sunset.

Ḥeru-Khuti-Kheperȧ 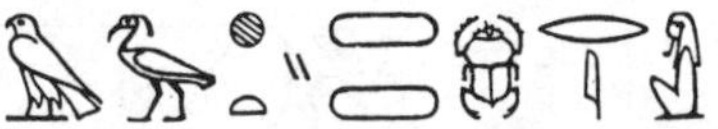 Harmachis Kheperȧ.

Ḥeru-khenti-ȧn-Merti (?) 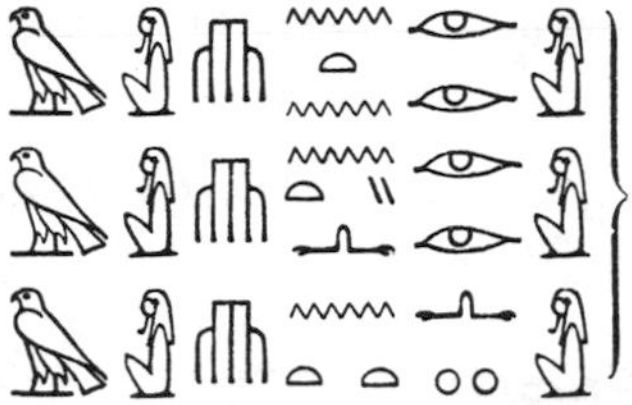 "Horus dwelling in blindness", *i. e.*, Horus (the sky) when neither the sun nor moon is visible.

Ḥeru-khent-Ḳhaṭti 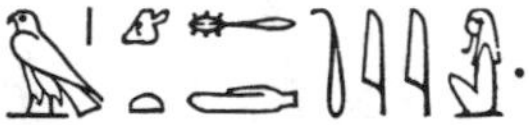.

Ḥeru-khenti-ḥeḥ  "Horus, governor of eternity".

Ḥeru-khenṭ-ḥeḥ  "Horus, traveller of eternity".

Ḥeru-khenti-Sekhem 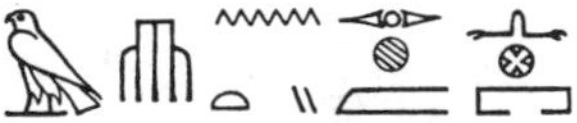 "Horus, governor of Sekhem" (Letopolis).

Ḥeru-khesbeṭ-merti  "Horus with eyes of lapis-lazuli", *i. e.*, blue-eyed Horus.

Ḥeru-sa-Ȧst  "Horus, son of Isis".

Ḥeru-sa-Ȧsȧr  "Horus, son of Osiris'.

Ḥeru-sa-Ḥet-Ḥeru  "Horus, son of Hathor".

Ḥeru-sekhai 

Ḥeru-sheṭ-ḥer  an obscure form of Horus.

Ḥeru-Ṭeḥuti  "Horus-Thoth".

Ḥeru-ṭesher-merti  "Red-eyed Horus".

Ḥeru-shemsu  "followers of Horus", or "body-guard of Horus"; a class of mythical beings.

Ḥeru ṭāṭāf 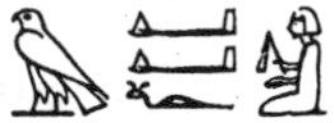 a son of King Khufu who "found" certain Chapters of the Book of the Dead.

ḥerset  crystal.

ḥeḥ  million, a number past counting; plur. . Two millions (?) .

ḥeḥui  . . . .

ḥeḥ en sep 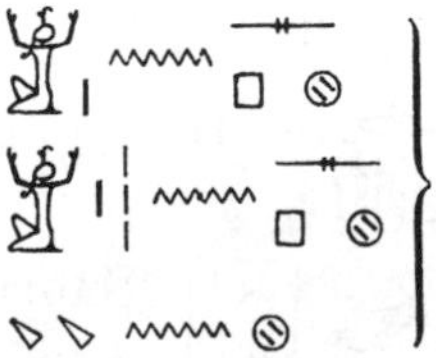 a million times, millions of times.

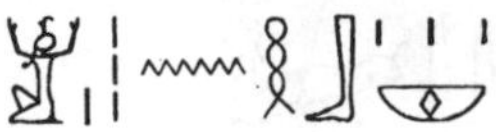 millions of festivals.

ḥeḥ . . . .  the land of millions of years.

ḥeḥ 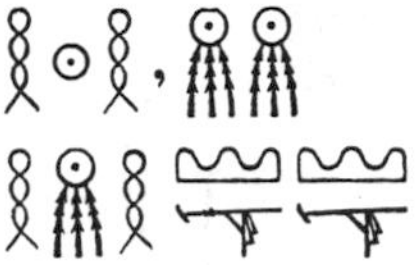 eternity, everlastingness.

 for ever and ever.

Ḥeḥi 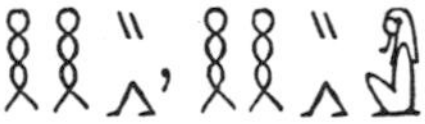 the name of a god.

ḥeḥi 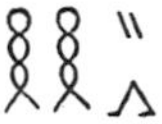 to hasten after, search for; .

ḥes 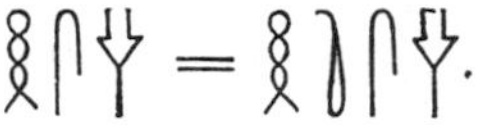.

ḥes 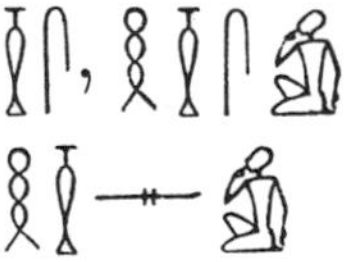 to praise, be praised, to give a reward as a sign of praise; 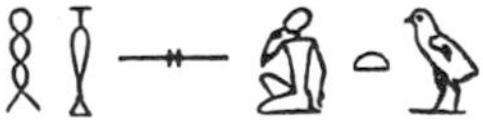 praised.

ḥesu
ḥeset  favour, act of grace, the gift of praise.

 favours, praises.

ḥesi  he to whom favour has been shewn by the king or god.

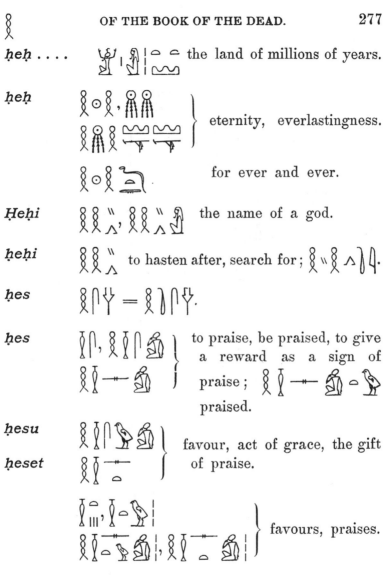

ḥesiu } plur. of preceding.

ḥesuiu

ḥesu a hymn of praise; the 70 hymns of praise of Rā.

Ḥest } name of a very ancient goddess.

Ḥes-ḥer
Ḥesi-ḥer } "savage face"; a proper name.

Ḥes-tchefetch "savage eye"; a proper name.

ḥesu } dirt, filth.

ḥeseb faïence (?).

. . . .

ḥeseb  to count up, reckon, estimate, calculate;   reckoned up.

ḥesbet 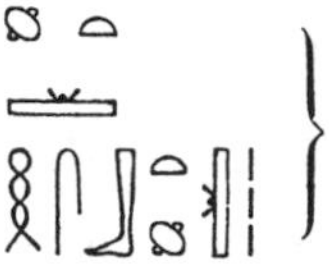 a reckoning, an account.

 computer of holy offerings.

ḥeseb qeṭu 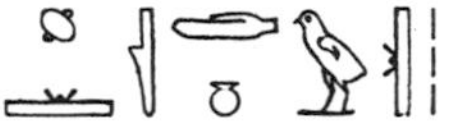 he who estimates characters or dispositions.

ḥeseb**.....** 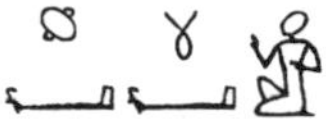 accountant of the linen cloths.

ḥesbet  knife (in the passage  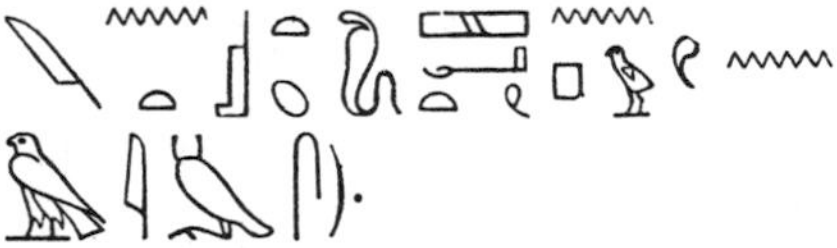).

ḥesepu

ḥespu  nomes.

ḥespet  gardens.

Ḥesepti 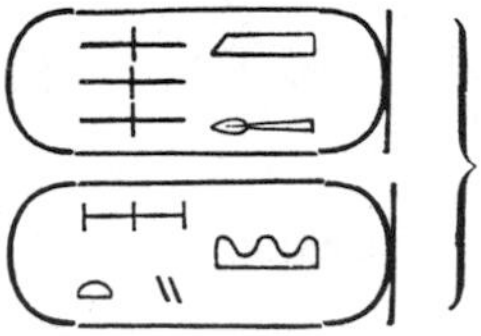 a king of the 1st dynasty. The true reading of this name is Semti, *q. v.*

ḥesmen	natron.
Ḥesert	the name of a town sacred to Thoth.
ḥesq	to cut, be cut, cut off, to wound, to mow. Compare cut.
ḥesqet	knife.
Ḥest	the name of a city.
ḥest	libation vase.
ḥekau, *ḥekat*	incantations, enchantments, magical formulae, charms, amulets.
[*ḥeken*]	to praise.
ḥekennu	a hymn of praise, praise.
	praises, songs of praise.

 those who praise, singers.

ḥekennu 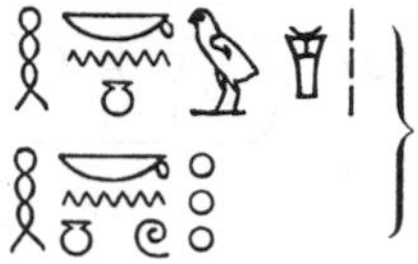 an unguent or salve.

Ḥekennut  the name of a city.

ḥeq 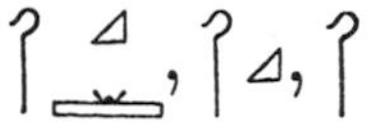 to rule, give commands.

ḥeq  ruler, governor; plur. .

ḥeqet 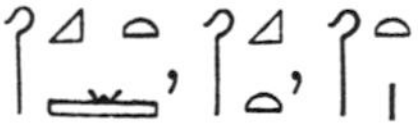 rule, sovereignty, dominion.

ḥeq 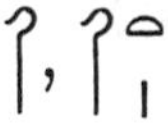 sceptre, emblem of rule.

 ruler of Åmenti.

 governor of towns.

 governor of the Two Lands.

 governor of the world.

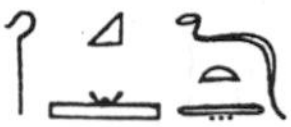 governor of eternity.

Ḥeq-ānṭ 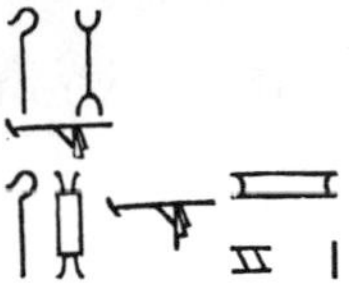 the XIIIth nome of Lower Egypt (capital Heliopolis).

Ḥeq-Maāt-Rā setep-en-Āmen  prenomen of Rameses IV.

ḥeq / *ḥeqt*  ale, beer.

ḥeqr 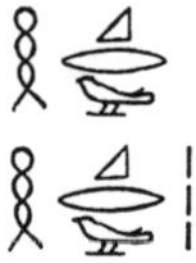 to be hungry.

ḥeqr  hunger.

ḥeqr 
ḥeqrȧu  hungry man.

Ḥeqtit 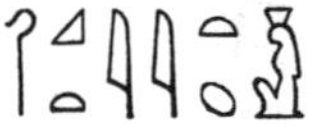 a goddess.

ḥet  to rejoice.

ḥet  house, section of a book, chapter. Compare the Arabic بيت *bêt*, couplet, stanza, portion of a poem. 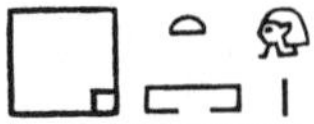 first section, , , etc.

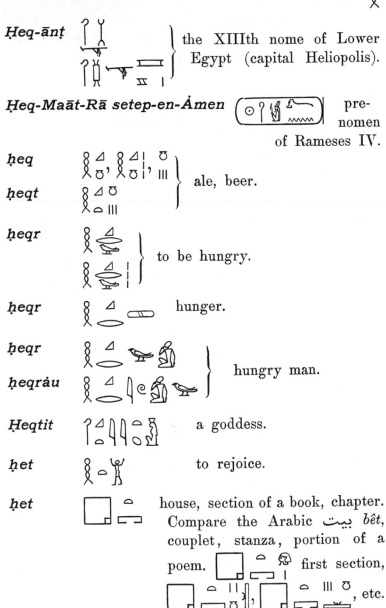

ḥet  house, temple; plur. 

Ḥet-ȧāḥ 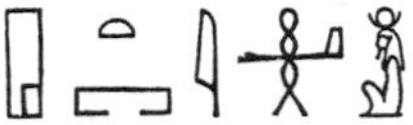 House of the Moon-god.

Ḥet-Ȧsȧr 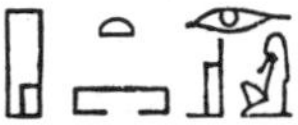 House of Osiris.

Ḥet-Ȧmen 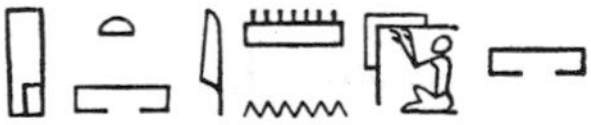 the Hidden House.

Ḥet-Ȧnes  House of the Ȧnes garment.

Ḥet-āshemu 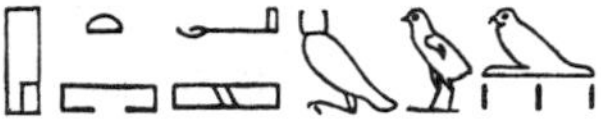 House of the statues of the gods.

Ḥet-ur  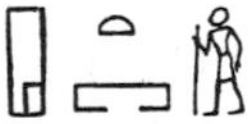 House of the Prince.

 city of the Prince.

Ḥet-uhem-ḥer  House of the Face Renewer.

Ḥet-Usekh-ḥer 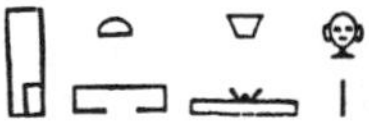 House of Broad-face, *i. e.*, Rā.

Ḥet-Ba  House of the Soul.

Ḥet-Bȧti  House of the king of the North.

Ḥet-Benbent 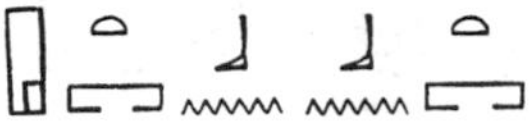 House of the Obelisk.

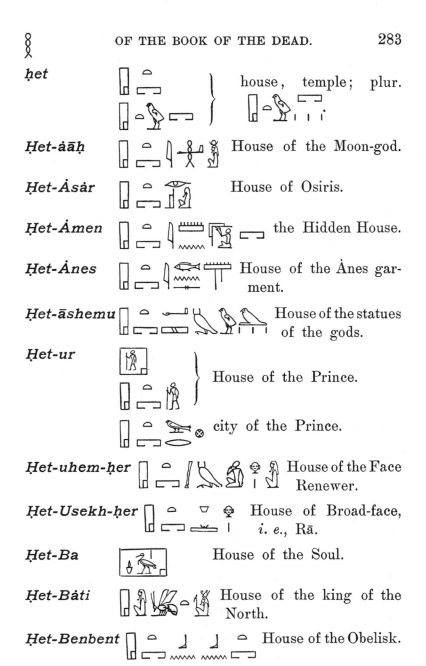

Ḥet-ka-Ptaḥ 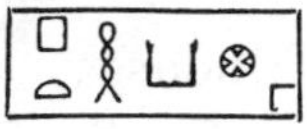 House of the Ka of Ptaḥ, *i. e.*, Memphis.

Ḥet-nemt 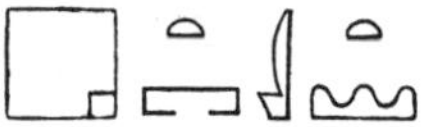 House of the . . . . .

Ḥet ent Ȧnpu  House of Ȧnpu.

Ḥet ent ḳem-ḥeru  House of the gods who have . . . . their faces.

Ḥet-nub 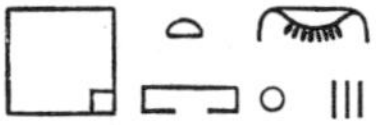 House of gold, *i. e.*, sarcophagus.

Ḥet-nemes  House of the Nemes tiara, or headcloth.

Ḥet-Ḥeru  House of Horus, *i. e.*, the goddess Hathor.

Ḥet-Kheperȧ  House of Kheperȧ.

Ḥet-seru  House of the Ram-gods.

Ḥet-kau-Nebt-er-tcher 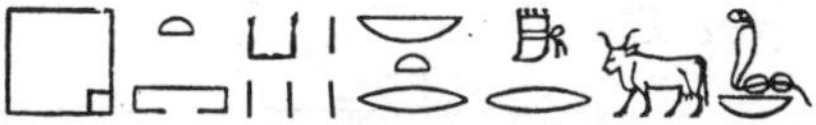 House of the Kau of the Universal Lady.

Ḥet-ṭesheru  House of the red-gods.

ḥeti smoke.

ḥeti a wooden pole.

ḥeti heart.

ḥeti = strength.

ḥeti , throat, gorge.

ḥetit

ḥetep , to be at peace, to rest, be satisfied or content, to be at peace with anyone, to remain in one place, to set (of the sun); , satisfied, content; setting in life, *i. e.*, alive when setting; "I make Rā to set like Osiris, and Osiris to set as Rā sets".

ḥetep peace, content; peace

ḥetepu of heart; at peace on truth, or resting on truth.

in peace;

ḥetep — a table of offerings.

ḥetep, *ḥetepet* — food which is offered to the gods and the dead.

ḥetep neter — offerings, sacrifices, temple property in general.

ḥetep, *ḥetepet* — offerings of cakes, ale, oxen, fowl, etc., offerings of propitiation.

Ḥetep — the god of offerings; plur.

Ḥeteptiu  gods who are regularly provided with offerings.

Ḥetep 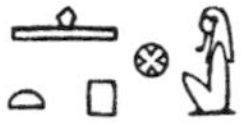 the town of the god Ḥetep.

ḥetepu  geese.

Ḥetep-mes  a proper name.

Ḥetep-Ḥeru-ḥems-uāu  a proper name.

Ḥetep-sekhus 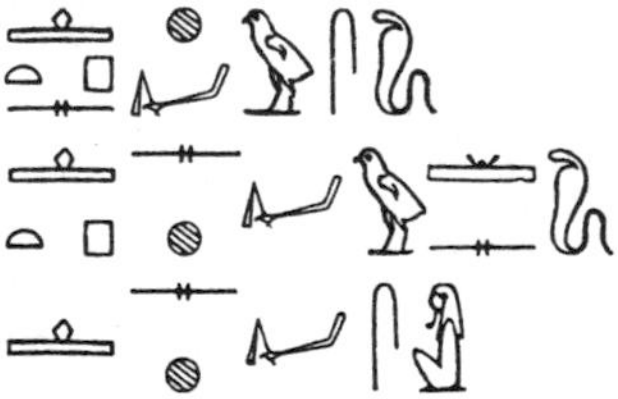 the name of a goddess.

Ḥetep-ka 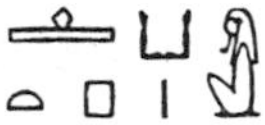 a proper name.

Ḥetep-taui  a proper name.

ḥetem  to destroy, be destroyed.

ḥetemu  destroyers.

ḥetem  to be filled with, provided with;   provided.

Ḥetem-ur  "great destroyer"; name of a god.

Ḥetemt-ḥer  "destroying face"; name of a god.

ḥeter  to pay something which is obligatory, legal due, something like tithe.

ḥetru  impost, tax.

ḥetes  to be lord of.

ḥeṭeṭ  scorpion.

Ḥeṭeṭ-t 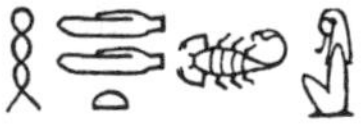 Scorpion-god.

ḥetch  to do evil, to plunder, steal, waste, destroy, filch away.

ḥetchet  theft, wickedness.

ḥetch 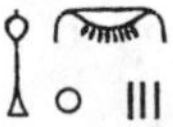 white metal, silver.

ḥetch 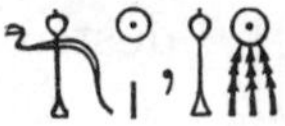 to be bright, to shine.

ḥetch ta 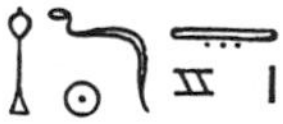 dawn, daybreak.

ḥetchu  light.

Ḥetch-åbeḥu 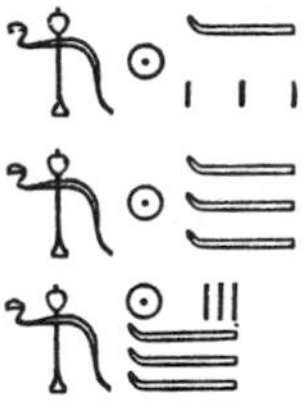 "White teeth"; the name of one of the Forty-two Judges in the Hall of Osiris.

Ḥetch-re 

Ḥetch-re-pesṭ-tchatcha 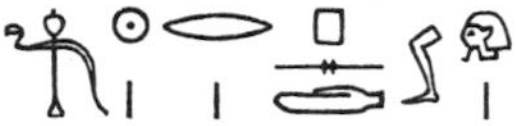

} a proper name.

ḥetch-ḥetch  light.

ḥetchet  white.

ḥetchet  the White Crown, or Crown of the South.

ḥetchti  white sandals.

ḥeṭṭ 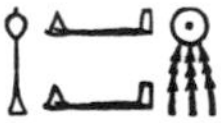 light.

ḥetchu  loaves.

ḥetchas  . . . .

KH.

kha one thousand; two thousand; plur.

kha chamber.

kha, ***khat*** the material body, dead body; divine corpse; plur.

khaā to set aside, cast away, to throw.

khāā emissions.

khaām to hasten.

khaāmt throat.

khaibit shade, shadow; plur.

khaitiu slaughterers.

khau  fire.

khaut  fire-altar, altars for burnt offerings.

khaut  festival of burnt offerings.

khau  evil, sin.

khau  basins, bowls.

khau  to be plentiful, abundant.

khaui  darkness, night.

khaut  fiends, the dead.

Khau-tchet-f  a proper name.

khabesu 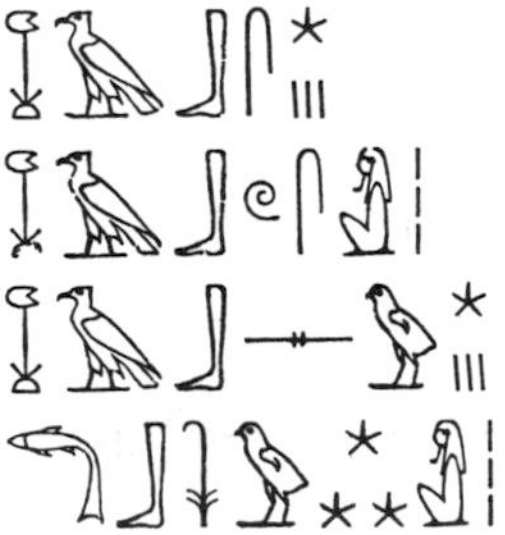 the stars, the thirty-six dekans; the sing. is .

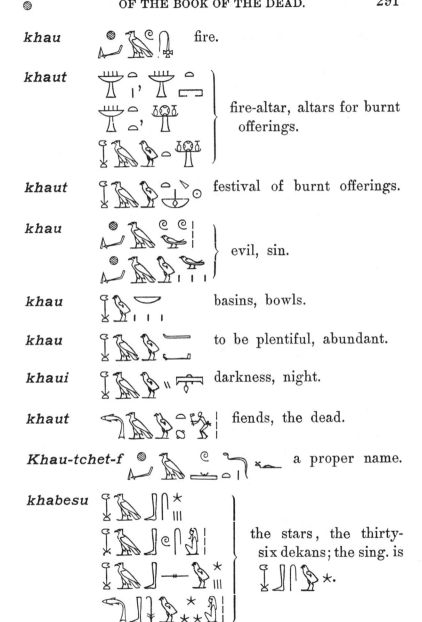

khabet  fraud, deceit.

khapa  a portion of the body, the navel; plur.   buttocks (?) *pudenda muliebris* (?) thighs (?).

Khap-khap  a part of the sky, the god of the Ecliptic (?).

kham  to subdue, be submissive.

khamesu  ears of corn.

khart 

kharu 
} a kind of bird with a piercing cry.

Kharsatȧ  a proper name.

khakh 

} to seek, run after.

} swift.

khasu  the lower eyelids.

khasi bad, evil, wicked, cowardly.

khast territory, country. Perhaps the reading of .

khak-àbu the timid-hearted, enemies.

khaker to be decorated, pretty.

ornaments, decorations.

Khatiu a class of divine beings.

khat fire altar.

khat body, belly, womb; core of the sycamore; plur. , ,

khat the XVIth nome of Lower Egypt (?).

khat a kind of ground.

khatu dead body.

dead bodies.

khatememti nostrils.

khā, ***khāu*** — to rise like the sun, to ascend the throne, to be crowned, to appear (of the king or god). he who rises; one who rises; rising; risen, crowned; beautiful appearance.

khāu — risings, splendours, coronations.

khāu — crowns, diadems.

khāi — crown.

khi — babe, child.

Khiu — the name of a god.

khiuaut — perfume.

khu — to dress.

khu / ***khui*** / ***khaui***

to protect, strengthen, to do good to.

khu / ***khut***

protection.

khu

the spirit soul of man which was immortal, as opposed to the  or heart soul which fed upon offerings and lived with the Ka.

the equipped soul.

the perfect soul.

khu

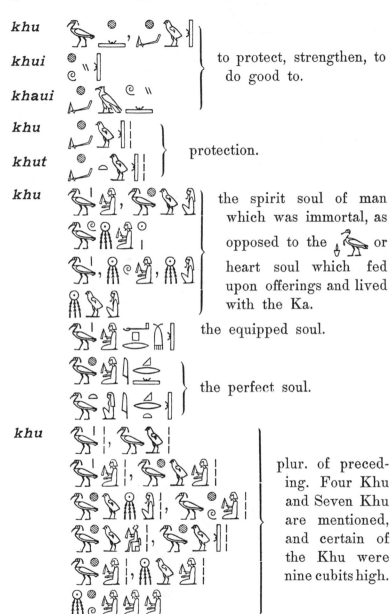

plur. of preceding. Four Khu and Seven Khu are mentioned, and certain of the Khu were nine cubits high.

khu — the spirit soul of Osiris, or Rā. … is a title of Osiris.

khu — to shine, be glorious.

khu, ***khut*** — glory, splendour, radiance, brilliant things, light.

khu — words of power.

khut — the name of a light-goddess.

Khu-kheper-ur — a proper name.

Khu-tchet-f — a proper name.

khunt — drink offerings.

khus  to construct a building, make a cistern.

khut  fire.

khut  the place in the sky where the sun appears on the horizon in rising or setting, the horizon.

 northern horizon.

 western horizon.

 eastern horizon.

 the horizon of the mountain of sunset.

 the hidden horizon.

khuti  the gods or beings of the horizon.

khui  words of power.

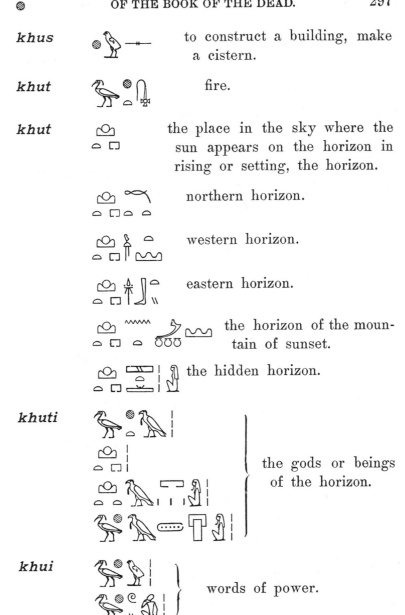

kheb 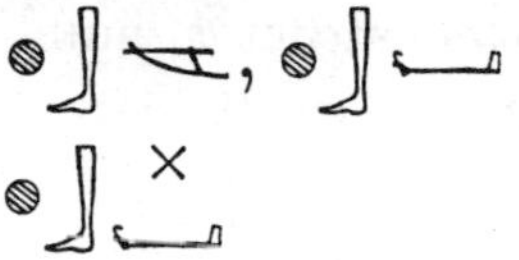 to defraud, pilfer, steal.

kheb  slaughter.

kheb 
khebȧ  to be defeated, overthrown.

khebu 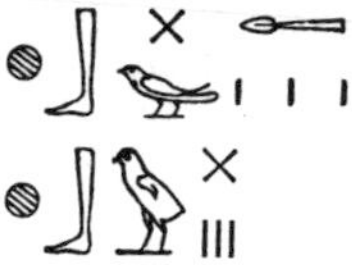 defeat, defeated ones.

kheba  to destroy.

khebu  to be dipped into some liquid, steeped.

Khebent  a proper name.

khebent  evil, wickedness.

khebenti  evil doers.

khebkheb  to destroy.

khebkhebt  destruction.

khebkheb  torture chamber.

khebs 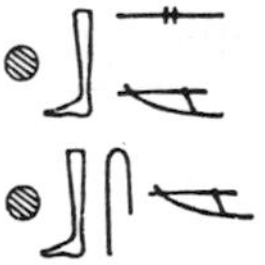 to plough; 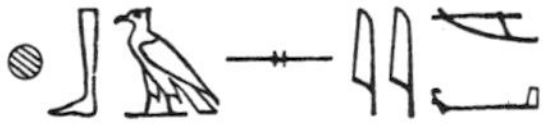 plougher.

khebs ta  the ceremony or festival of ploughing the earth.

khebsu  devourer (?).

khebs  star, lamp.

 stars, the Thirty-six dekans.

khebt 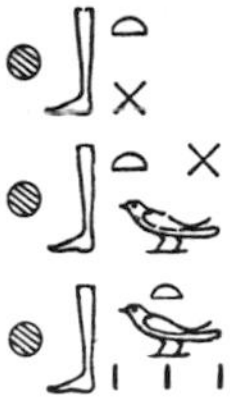 loss, injury, damage;  destroyer.

khebt  dance.

khebt 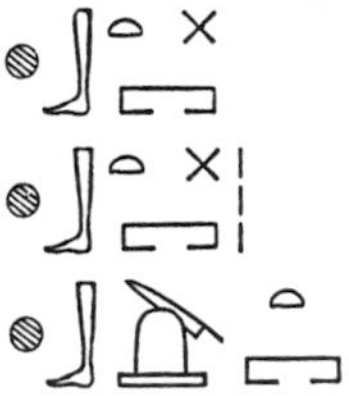 torture chamber, slaughter house.

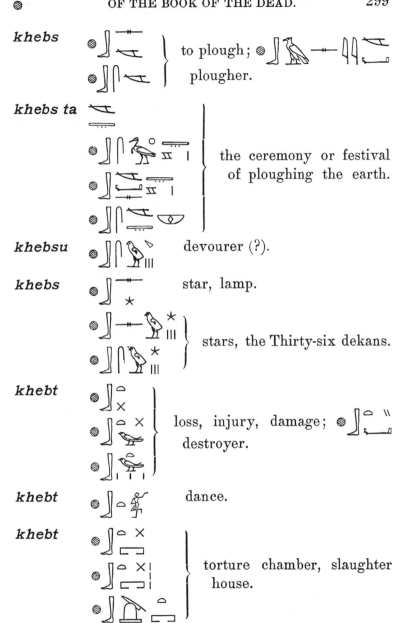

khep	◉ ▢ ⋀	to travel, journey.
khept	◉ ◠ ▢ ⋀	journey.
khep	◉ ▢ ℓ	a part of the body, navel (?).
khepu	◉ ▢ 𓅭 ⌣ = ◉ ▢ ⌣.	
Khepiu	𓅭	the gods who are.

kheper
kheperu

to come into being, become, exist, subsist, to turn into something, to create, to form, fashion; non-existent; when takes place, when it happens; to be or become satisfied; is thy name what? those who become.

self-created.

khepert

that which is, what exists, thing.

kheperu 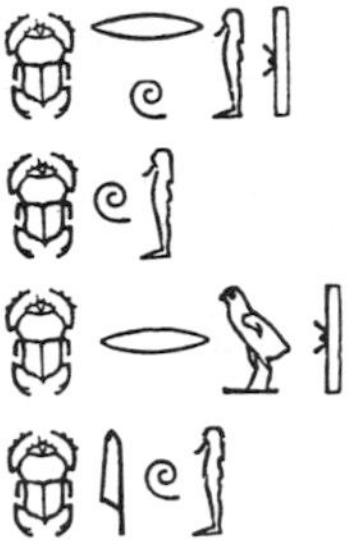 form, phase of being, something evolved, transformation, change.

kheperu 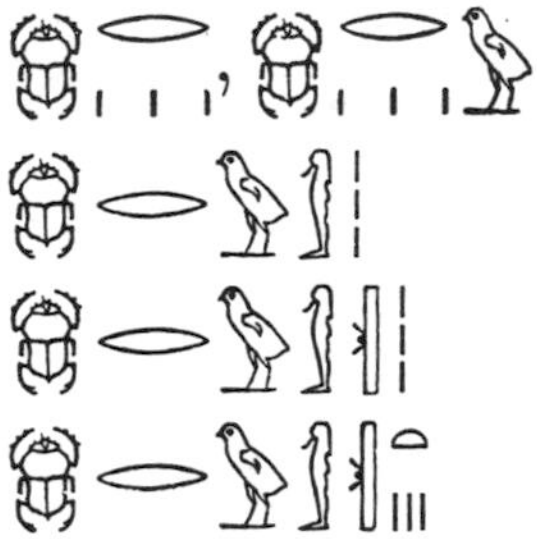 forms, transformations.

kheperut

kheper  scarab, beetle.

khepprer

Kheperȧ / ***Kheperrȧ*** (?)  the Beetle-god, a form of the Sun-god.  .

khepesh  thigh; plur. 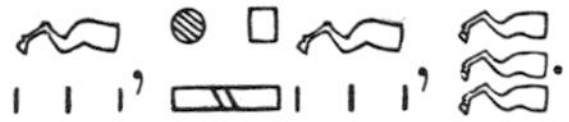.

Khepesh 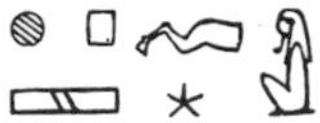 the constellation of the Thigh.

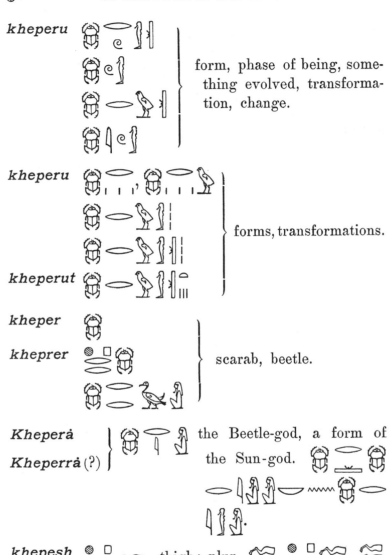

khept

kheptet — buttock; plur.

khept

khefa — food.

khefā — to grasp, to seize with the hand;

khefā — fist, grasp.

khefāt

khefit — quay, river bank.

kheft — in front of, according to, conformably to, when.

kheft ḥer — opposite to, before the face of.

khefti — enemy, fiend.

kheftiu — enemies.

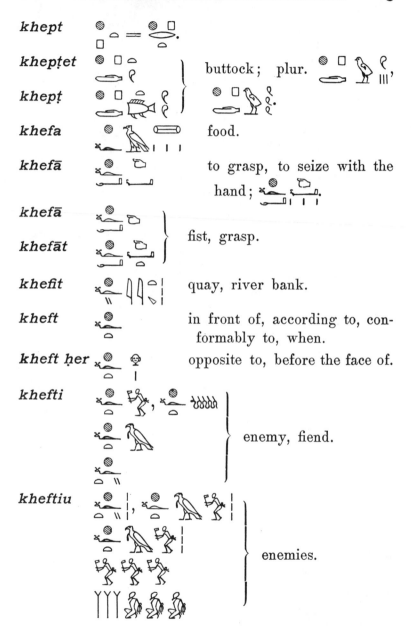

khem  to burn.

khem  shrine.

khem  to be ignorant, to put an end to (?); 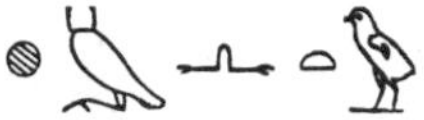 ignorant, helpless;  unknown is his name.

khem  an ignorant man.

khem 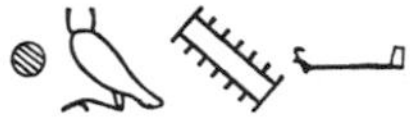  to overthrow, destroy.

khemiu  
khemit  overthrower, those who overthrow, destructions.

Khemi  the name of one of the Forty-two Judges in the Hall of Osiris.

khemā  to lay hold of, to seize and carry off.

khemāu  snatchers, seizers.

khemu  wind, air.

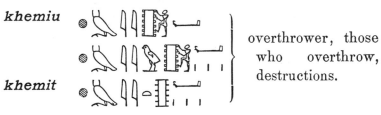

khemenu eight; eighth.

Khemenu the eight gods of the Company of Thoth who dwelt at Hermopolis.

Khemenu the city of the Eight gods, Hermopolis.

khemt three; third.

khemt to think, to know, to intend. is sometimes written by mistake for .

khemt the god of thought.

khen
khenn
khennu to hover over, to flutter like a bird when alighting on a tree, to perch on something.

Khenit the goddesses who fly or dance.

khen	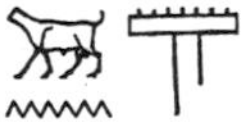	to be dressed, garment.
khen	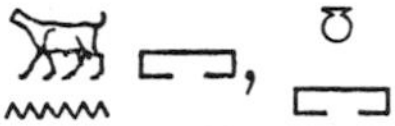	the inner part of a house, house.
		within.
Khennu		the name of a city in the Sekhet-ḥetep.
khen / *khenn*	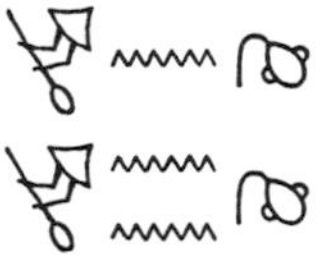	to decay, to rot, to wither.
khen		to break, smash, destroy, stir up strife, disturb, trouble.
khennu	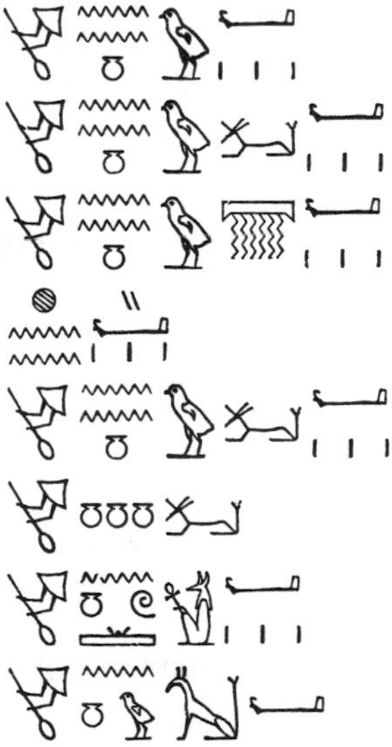	trouble, revolt, destruction, storm, opposition.
khenui		rebels.

khen 

khenen  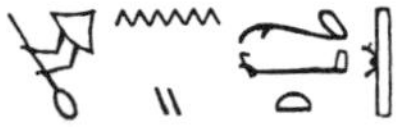  to ferry across a stream, to transport by water, to row, to paddle.

khent  a passage, a journey.

khenen  sailor.

khenȧ    to lock up, shut up, keep in captivity.

khenp  to draw out, pluck out.

 a tearing; 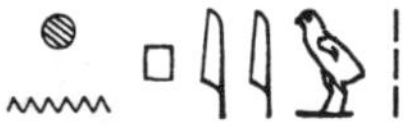 tearers, renders.

khenf  a bread-cake.

khenem  jasper, carnelian.

khnem  to form, join up or together.

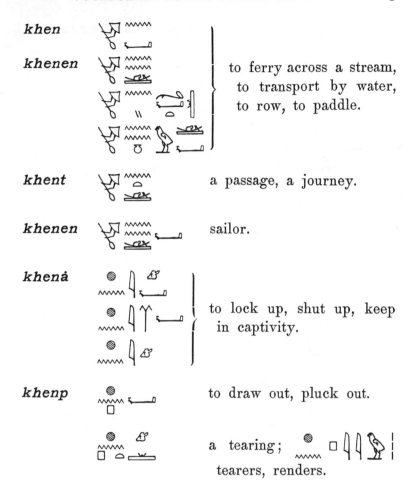

Khnem  the god Khnemu, the Potter-god.

Khnemu-Ḥeru-Ḥetep  the name of a god.

khnem  well;  a proper name (?).

Khnemet-urt  a proper name.

Khemet-em-ānkh-ȧnnuit 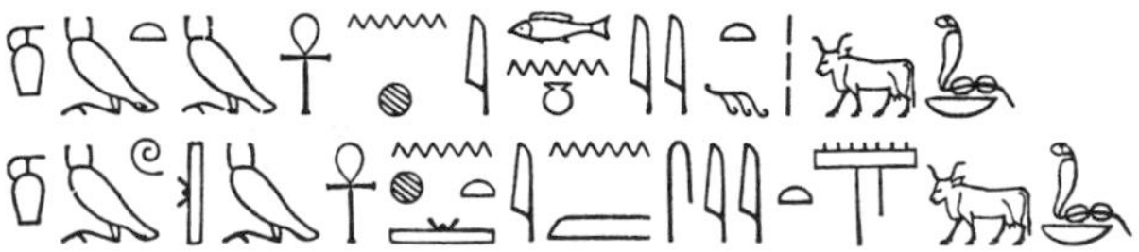 the name of one of the Seven Cows.

khenem 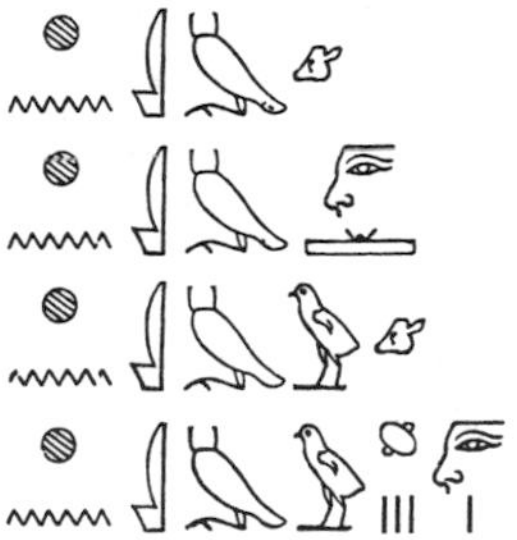 to snuff the air, to smell, scent out.

khenemti  nurse, servant, companion.

khenemu  . . . .

Khenem-nefer  a proper name?

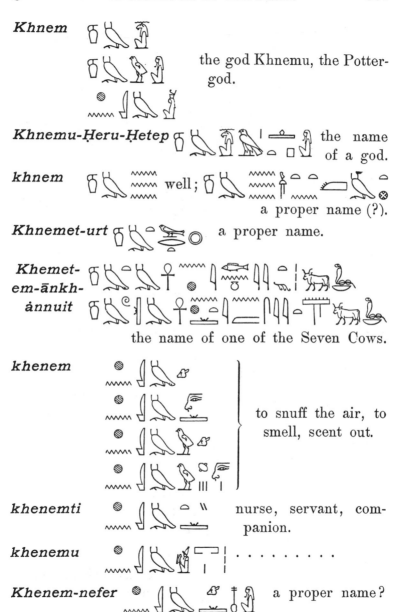

khenemem  to smell, feed upon (?).

Khenememti  the two ministering goddesses, Isis and Nephthys.

khenemes 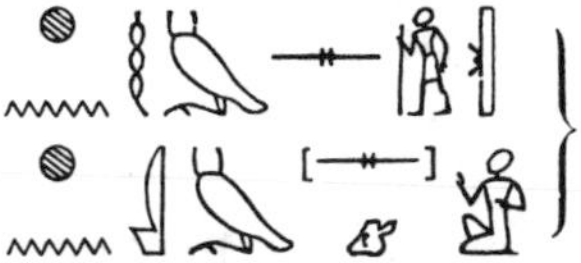 protector, friend.

khennu  those who cry out.

khennu 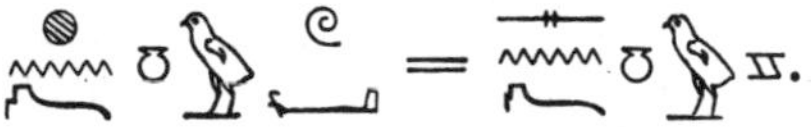

khennu  injury, evil hap.

khenrȧ  to shut in, imprison.

khenrȧ  fiends.

khenrit 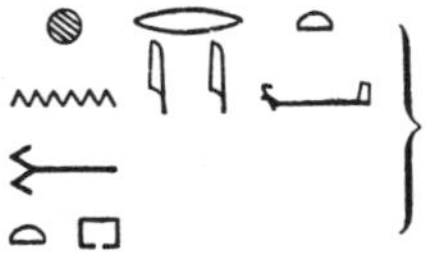 prison.

khens 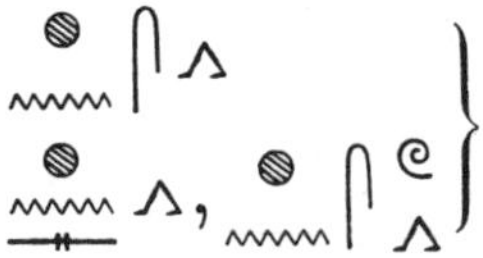 to stride about, to journey, travel.

Khensu  "traveller", a name of the Moon-god.

Khensu-p-åru-sekheru em Uast 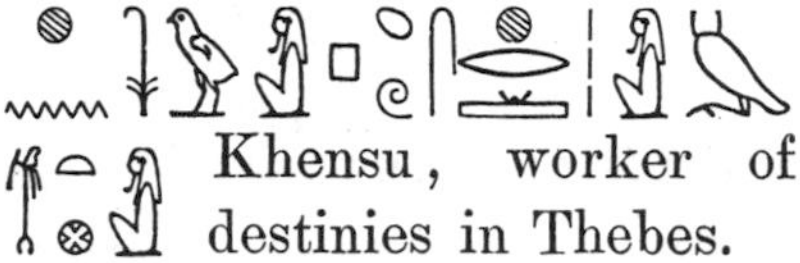 Khensu, worker of destinies in Thebes.

Khensu em Uast Nefer-ḥetepi  Khensu in Thebes, Nefer-ḥetep.

khent 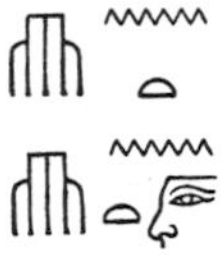 the nose.

khent  the fore part of anything, the front, in front of, before.

khenti  he who is in front, or at the head, chief, governor.

Khenti Åmenti  He who is at the head of Åmenti and of those who are therein; a title of Osiris.

Khenti Āḥa  he who is chief of the fighting.

Khenti-aḥāt 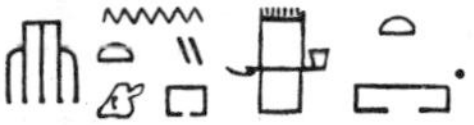

Khenti-āt-àment 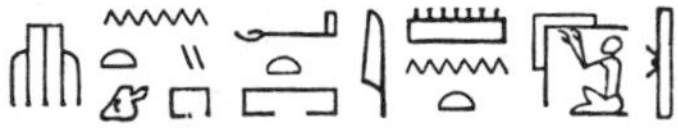 a title of Osiris.

Khenti-Un  a title of Osiris.

Khenti-Peḳu  a title of Osiris.

Khenti-menȧtuf 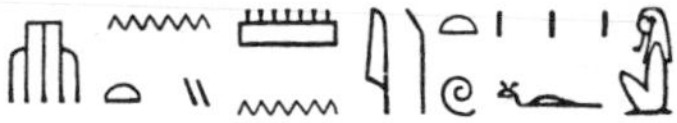 a title of Osiris.

Khenti-Naȧreṭ-f  a title of Osiris.

Khenti-nut-f  a title of Osiris.

Khenti-nep  a title of Osiris.

Khenti-n-merti (?)  a title of Horus.

Khenti neter ḥet 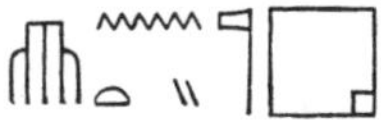 "Chief of the god-house".

Khenti neter seḥ  "Chief of the god-hall".

Khenti Re-stau  "Chief of the funerary corridors"; a title of Osiris.

Khenti-hetut-f  "Chief of his fire".

Khentiu ḥensekti  "Chiefs of long hair and beards".

Khent ḥeḥ 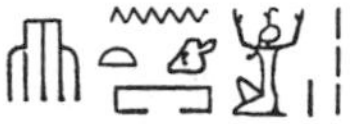 a title of Osiris.

Khenti Ḥeq-ȧnṭ  a title of Osiris.

Khenti ḥespu 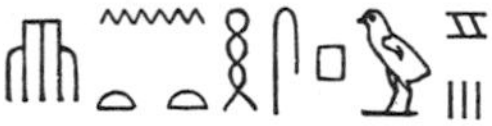 the name of the bows of the magic boat.

Khenti-khas  a name of a god.

Khenti-Khati
Khent-Khaṭti  "the dweller in the belly"; a title of Horus.

Khenti-Suten-ḥenen 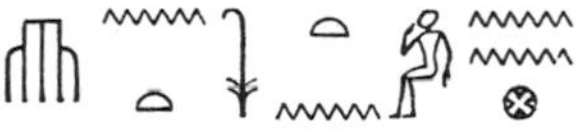 a title of Osiris.

Khenti-Sekhem  a title of Horus of Letopolis.

Khenti-seḥ-ḥemt 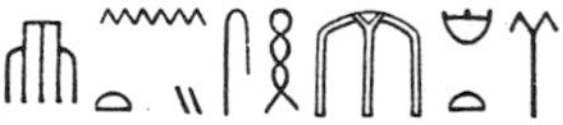 "chief of the house of the wife"; a title of Osiris.

Khenti-seḥt-kaut-f  "chief of the house of his cows"; a title of Osiris.

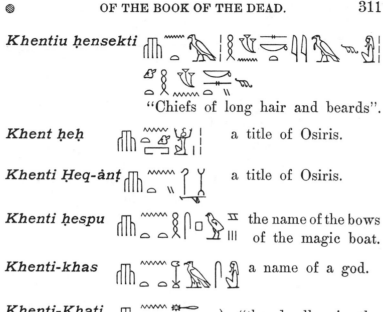

Khent-she (or ***mer***)-***Āa-perti*** "chief of the Lake of Pharaoh"; a title of Osiris.

Khenti-Tenent a title of Osiris.

khent abode, the private portion of a palace or temple; plur.

khent
khenti to sail upstream, usually to the south;

khentiu sailors.

khenti a mineral colour.

khenṭ to travel, journey.

khenṭi traveller.

khenṭi to ascend.

khenṭ 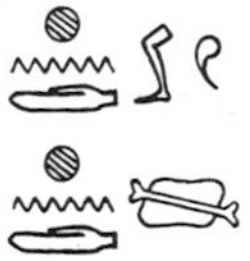 thigh, haunch.

Khenṭ-Ḥepiu  name of the steering pole.

khentch  to travel.

kher  a preposition, with, before, etc.;  under the Majesty of, in the reign of.

khert  the things of, the affairs of, property of; 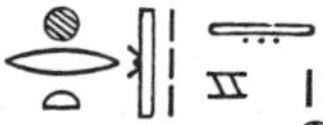 the affairs of the country;  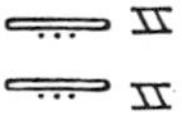 the business of the Two Lands.

kher  under, beneath;  things or beings who are below.

 under the favour of.

 before.

kheri  low-lying land, the earth as opposed to the sky; plur. .

kheru  men and women in subjection, serfs, vassals, or perhaps the tillers of low-lying lands.

kher  to have, hold, possess.   "heaven hath thy soul, earth hath thy form".

khert 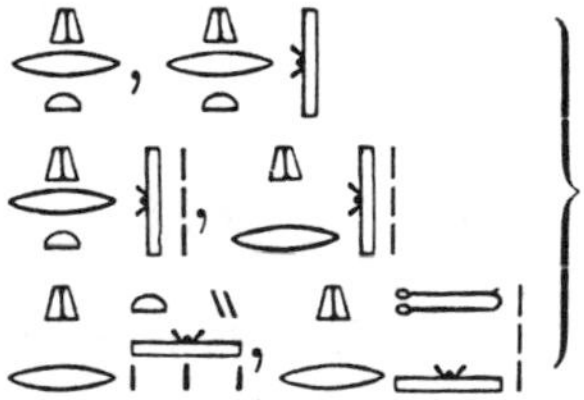 goods, possessions, share, portion, lot, what belongs to someone, property, wealth, products of.

khert hru  the things of the day, what belongs to the day, daily round or routine.

 every-day matters.

kher
kherui  testicles.

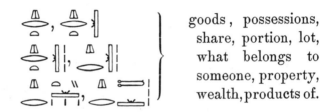

kher 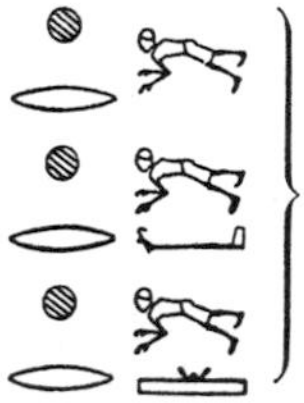 to fall down, to happen.

kheri 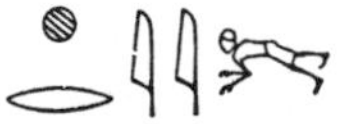 fallen one, foe.

kherit 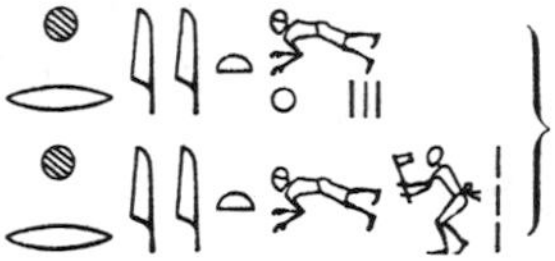 the dead, the damned.

kherit 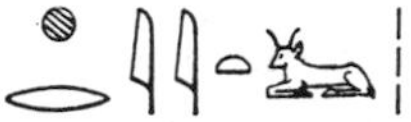 victims for sacrifice.

Kher  the name of a god.

Kherȧ  a proper name.

kheru 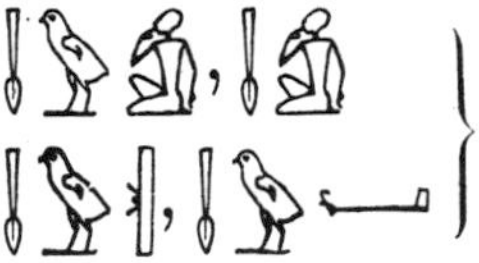 voice, word, speech, sound; plur.  reading unknown.

 loud-voiced.

 a man's voice.

 multiplying the sound of words, *i. e.*, talking overmuch.

kheriu  enemies, hostile attacks.

Kher-āḥa  a city near the site of the modern Fusṭâṭ, or Old Cairo.

kherp  to be chief or master, to direct, be in command, to present an offering.

Kherp  Prince, Chief; plur. .

Kherp-nest  title of a priest.

kherpu  steering pole.

kherefu  two Lion-gods.

kher ḥeb  the priest who recited religious compositions and the Liturgy.

Kherserȧu  a proper name.

khersek to destroy;

Khersek-Shu a proper name.

khert course.

khertu it is said, speech.

kherṭ child; plur.

a title of the scribe Nebseni.

khekh to run.

khekh, ***khekhi*** throat.

khekhu darkness.

khes to slay.

khesu ritual, a book.

khesbeṭ blue stone, lapis-lazuli;

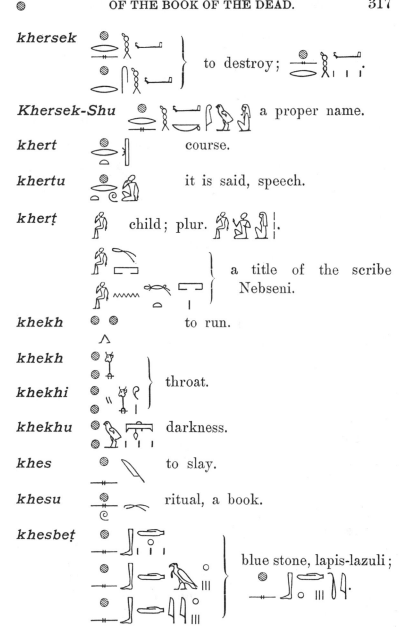

real lapis-lazuli as opposed to blue paste.

blue-eyed.

khesef to meet, to oppose, to drive back, repulse; repulse; irresistible.

khesef-ā

kheseft repulse.

khesefu adversaries, foes; hostile faces.

bowings down before.

Khesef-aṭ a proper name.

Khesef-ḥer-āsh-kheru a proper name.

Khesef-ḥer-khemiu the name of the herald of the Seventh Ārit.

Khesem Letopolis.

khesṭeḥ to destroy.

khet steps, throne.

great stairs of Osiris.

khet fire, flame.

khet wood, tree, stick, staff, sceptre, board; planks of a ship; rod.

khet mast.

khet, ***khetkhet*** to retreat, go back.

khet back, behind.

behind, in the following of.

followers.

khet, ***khetu*** to write, to cut on wood or stone; cut, engraved.

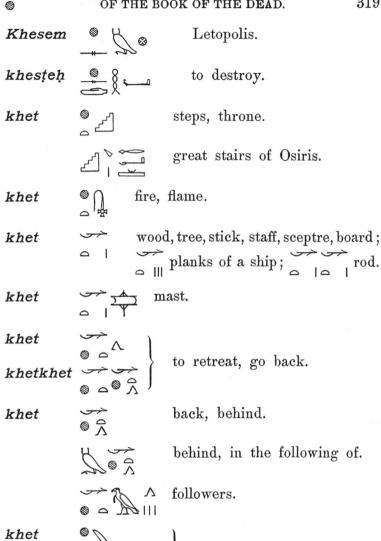

khet  things, affairs, cases, goods, property.

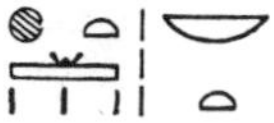 everything.

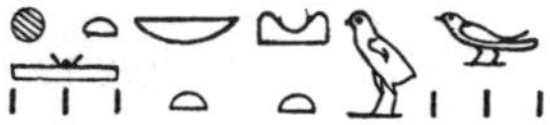 all sorts of bad things.

 everything beautiful and pure.

 all most beautiful things.

 sweet things.

 everything bad and evil.

 weak things.

 things about Osiris.

 things on the altars.

 things of Horus (*i. e.*, offerings, property of).

 things (offerings) of the night.

 things of the festal altars.

 things of his father Osiris.

things of the Eye of Horus.

things of the Boat.

their personal things.

khetu . . . .

khetita fiends, devils.

khetem to shut in, to seal, close the door on;

khetemiu those shut in.

khetemit closed place, prison.

kheṭ to float down stream.

kheṭebet = .

S.

s , her, she, its; .

= .

sa person, man, one.

everyone, everybody.

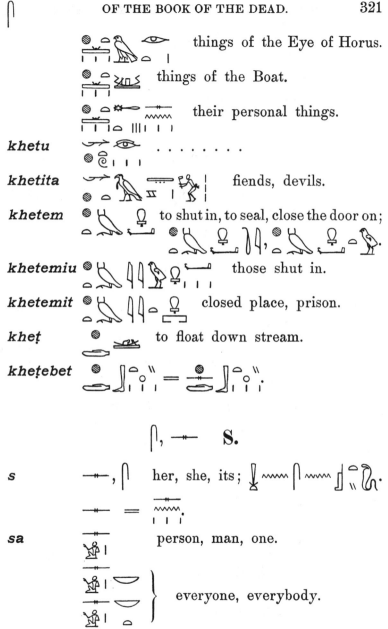

set		woman.
sa		son.
		son of Rā.
		firstborn son.
sat		daughter.
		daughter of Rā.
sati		the two divine daughters, *i. e.*, Isis and Nephthys.
Sa-mer-f		"Son loving him"; title of a priest.
Sa-pa-nemmȧ		a proper name.
Sa-ta	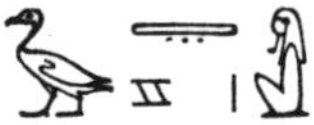	"son of the earth"; the name of a serpent.
sa		side, back.
		in the side.
		afterwards.
		behind.

after.

by the back.

sa chamber (?).

sa to protect, a thing which protects, amulet; plur. , as a protection. See .

sa to perceive, know, recognize.

knower of hearts, trier of reins.

sauu wise man.

Sa, *Sau* the god of knowledge.

Sa-Åmenti-Rā a proper name.

Saau-ur a proper name.

Saa "shepherd"; a name of Osiris.

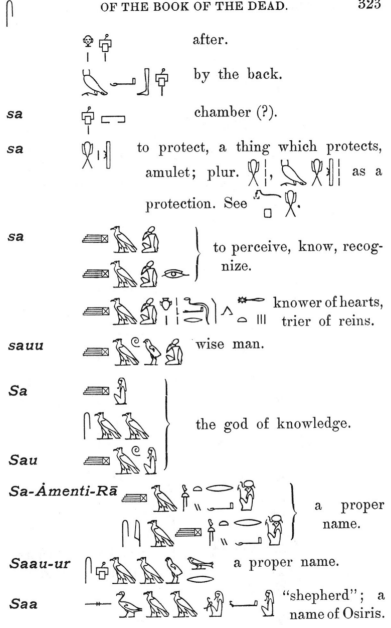

sau 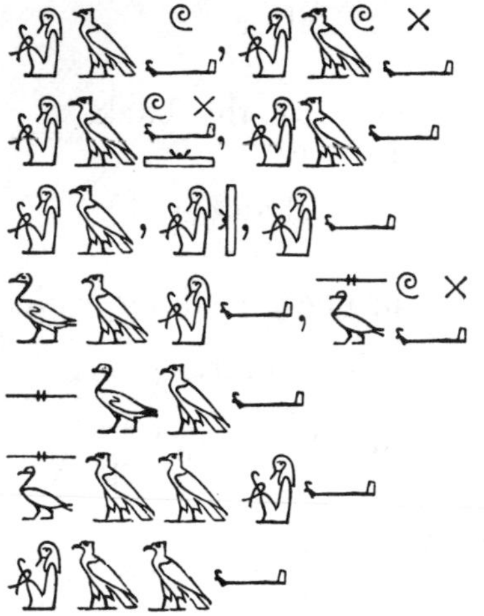 to watch, keep guard over, protect, keep in restraint; to tend sheep.

sau, sai  watcher, guardian, shepherd.

 plur. of preceding.

 people in fetters.

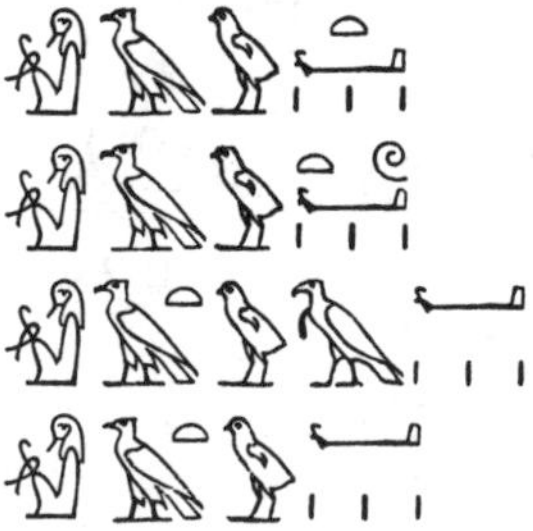 watchers, warders, fetterers, fetters.

sait 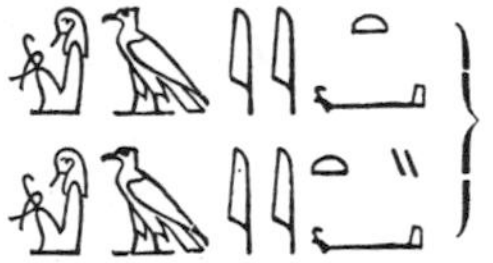 restraint, ward.

sau  corruption.

Sau  the city of Saïs.

 Upper Saïs.

 Lower Saïs.

saāiu 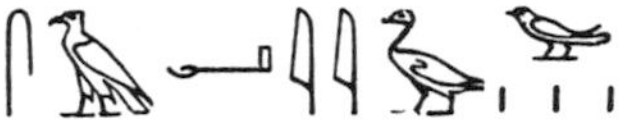 evil ones (?).

s-au  to make glad, to provision.

 wide goings, journeyings.

sauṭ  to transfer.

sab  making to cease.

sab  jackal; plur. .

Sab (?)
Sabȧ 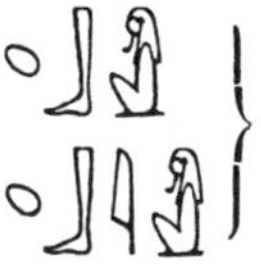 the name of a god.

Sabes  the herald of the Second Ārit.

sam  to consume, burn up.

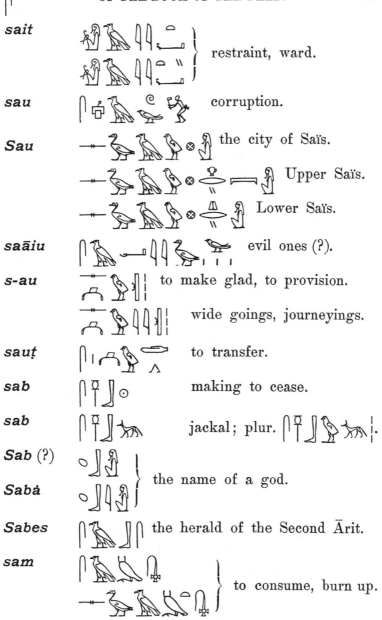

Samiu		a group of gods or fiends.
samiu		the gods with hair.
samut		hair.
samit		tresses, hair.
Saneḥem		the city of grasshoppers.
saneḥemu		grasshoppers.
Sar	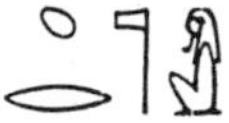	Osiris.
saru		order of dismissal (?).
sariu		evilly disposed persons.
saḥ		to journey, to travel.
saḥt	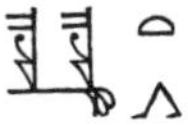	journey.
saḥ		an estate, farm, homestead.
saḥ	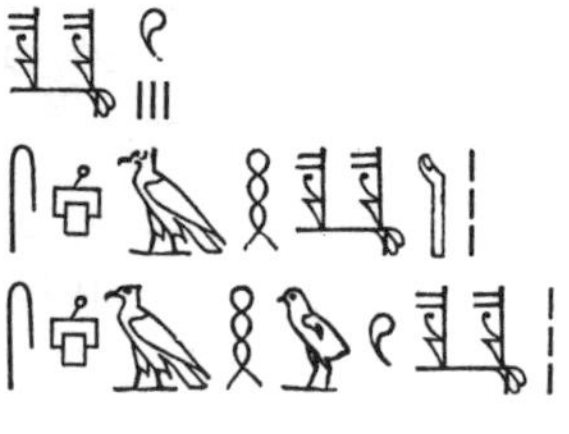	fingers, toes, claws.

Saḥ  Orion.

Saḥ-en-mut-f 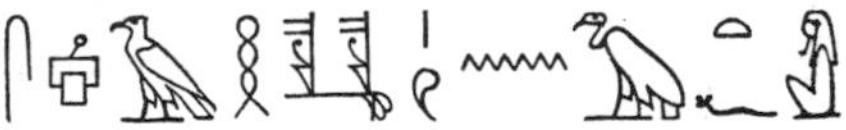 a proper name.

saq  to collect, gather together.

Saq-baiu  "collector of souls"; the name of a boat.

Saqnaqat  a proper name.

sat 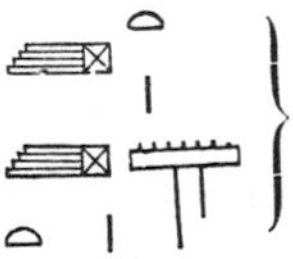 apparel, garment, robe, dress.

sat  to think scorn of the god.

sat  evil, evil one.

satu  wall, building.

sat  earth, ground, floor of a chamber.

sati  threshold.

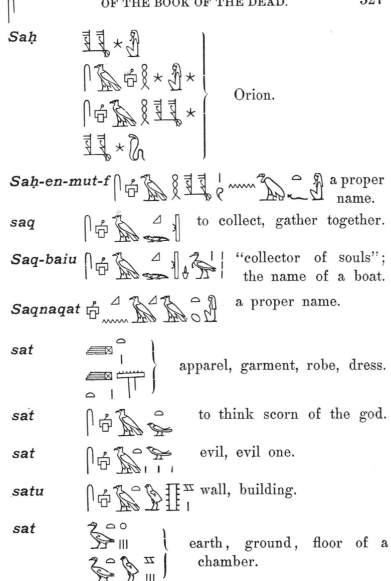

Satiu  the city of Siut, the modern Asyûṭ.

saṭu  terrors.

Sȧ 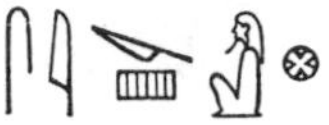 the name of a town and of a god.

Sȧa  the god Sa.

Sȧa  the name of a town and of a god.

Sȧu  to cry out.

sȧat  to encroach, attack.

Sȧatiu  slaughterers.

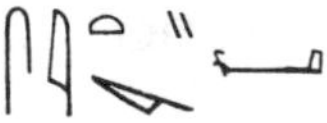; plur. 

sȧu  to drink water.

sȧbit  animals for sacrifice.

sȧb-kui 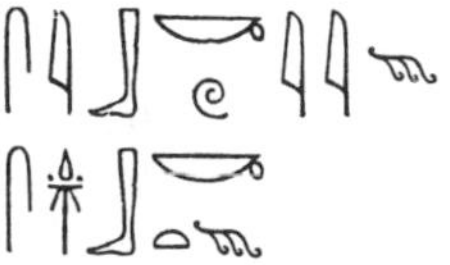 to make to weep.

sȧp  to judge, decide, compute, reckon up, examine, inspect, inquire into; ,  judged, computed.

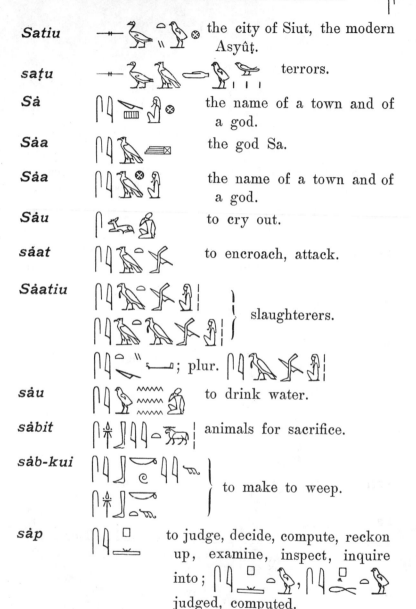

sȧpu judge, judgment; plur.

sȧp, **sȧpti** account, reckoning, a list of goods, property.

Sȧp the name of a god.

sȧpt abode of the god Sȧp.

sȧm (**sȧam**) to shew kindness.

sȧn length, extent.

sȧn to be kind, do good to, benefit, nourish; things which benefit.

sȧn clay.

sȧn to walk, march, pass along.

sȧn to pull, draw.

sȧn to be in good case.

sȧs six; sixth; = $^1/_6$; the festival held on the sixth day of each month.

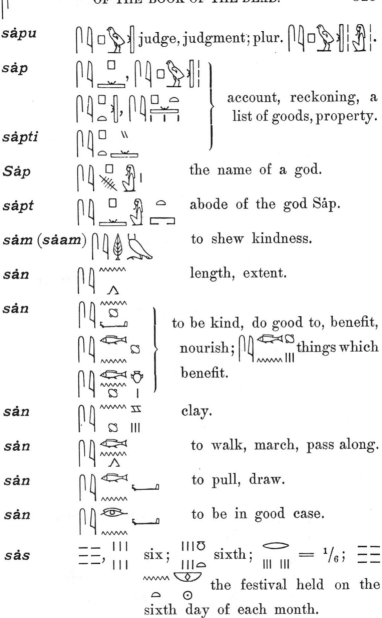

Sȧsȧ the name of a city =

sȧka to afford relief.

sȧqer to make strong, or perfect.

Sȧti the name of a city.

sȧtti (?) executioners.

sȧṭi headsman, executioner.

sȧṭen to transfer.

sāa , to magnify.

sāam to slay.

sāb (***suāb***) , to wash, purify, cleanse.

washed, plated.

sāba to make to enter, force an entrance.

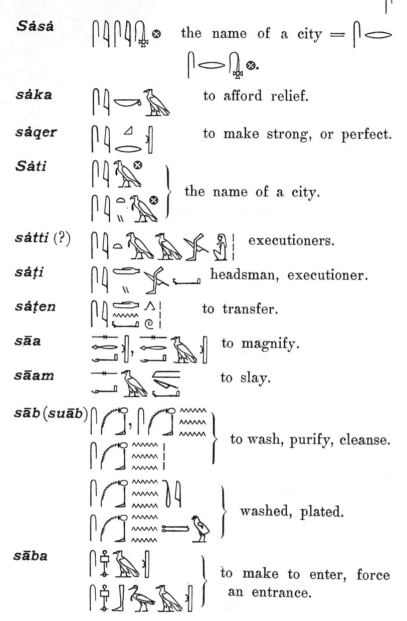

sām  to make to eat or drink, to swallow.

sāmiu  eaters, devourers.

Sām-em-senf  "drinker of blood"; a proper name.

Sām-em-ḳesu  "eater of bones"; a proper name.

sām  flowers, plants.

sāma  . . . .

sānkh 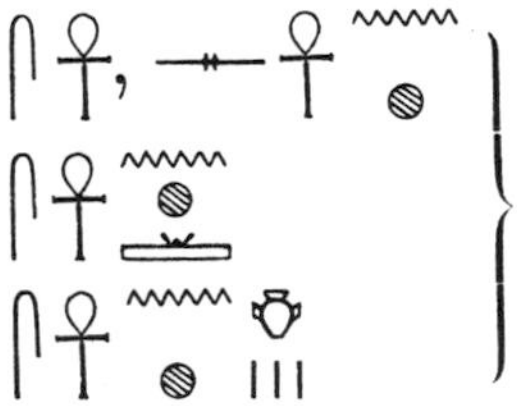 to vivify, keep alive. to support life, to feed, give sustenance to, "vivifier of hearts"; a title of Osiris.

sānṭ  to make strong.

sār 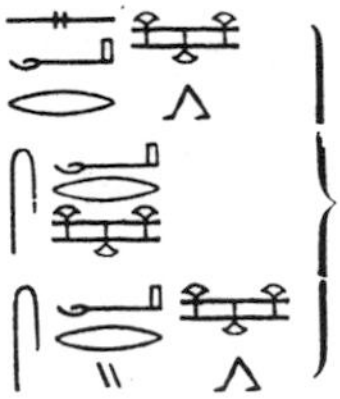 to make to come, to introduce.

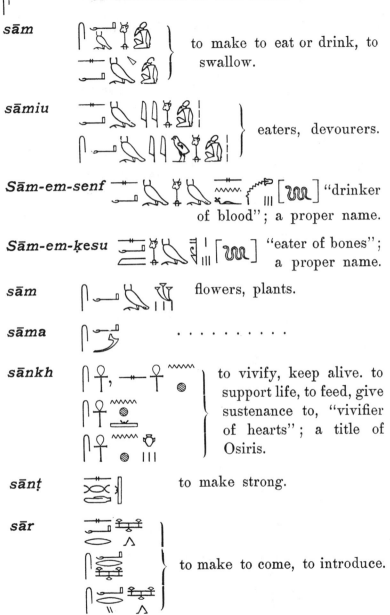

sārt 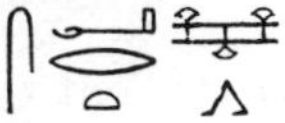 approach, introduction.

sāriu  introducers.

sāḥ, ***sāḥu***  the spiritual body of a man, later the mummy; plur. . Mentioned with the  and the .

sāḥ 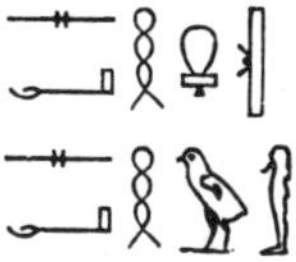 to become a *sāḥ*, 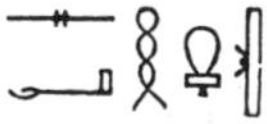 endowed with a *sāḥ*.

sāḥ 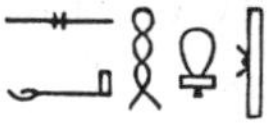 honour.

sāḥā 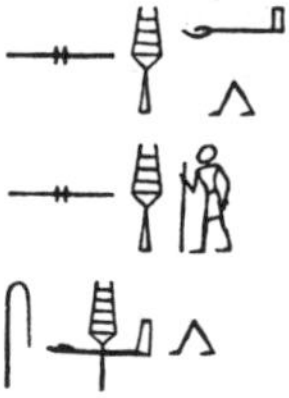 to set up, make to stand up.

 set up a pillar.

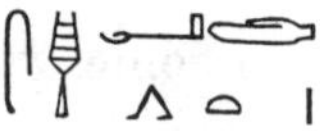 set up the Ṭeṭ.

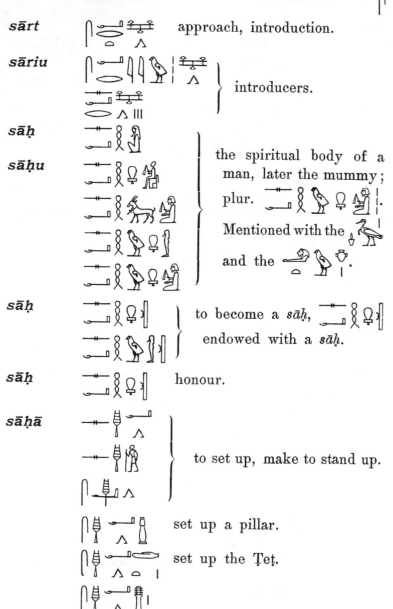

su  he, him; .

su tchesef  he himself.

sua  to pass by.

suash 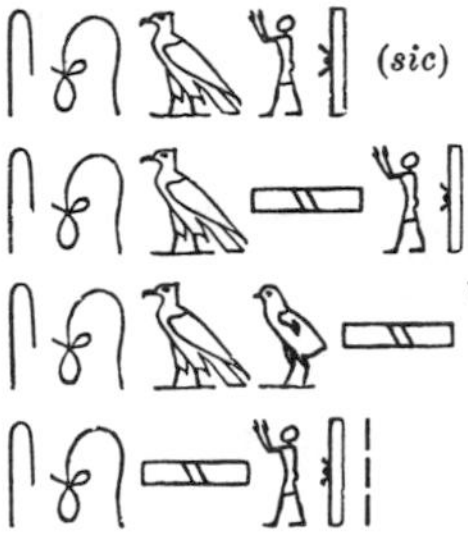 *

suatch 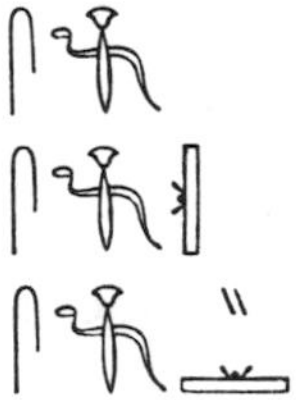 to be green, vigorous, flourishing.

suȧs  decay.

sui 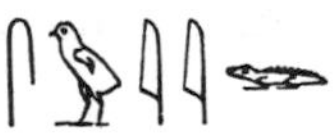 crocodile.

sun 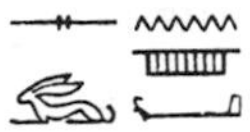 to open.

sun  to be destroyed.

*Definition missing in 1911 edition. May translate as "to praise" or "to adore" and related meanings.

sun / ***sunen*** 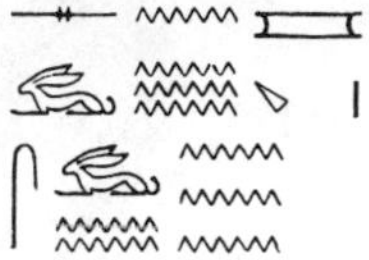 pool, lake, any large collection of water.

sunȧt  unguent.

Sunnu  the city called by the Greek Syene. Heb. סְוֵנֵה.

surȧ 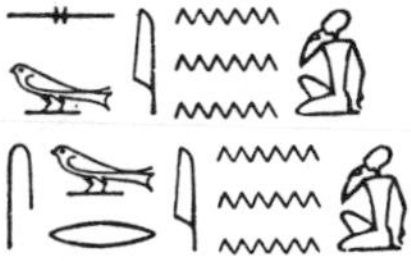 to give to drink, to drink.

suriu  drinkers.

surṭ 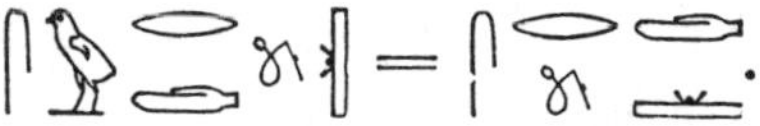.

suha  to supplicate.

suḥ  a garment.

suḥt  egg;  testicles (?).

sukha  evil recollection.

sukheṭ  to embalm, mummify.

suser  to strengthen.

susekh  to make broad, to make wide (*i. e.*, long) the steps.

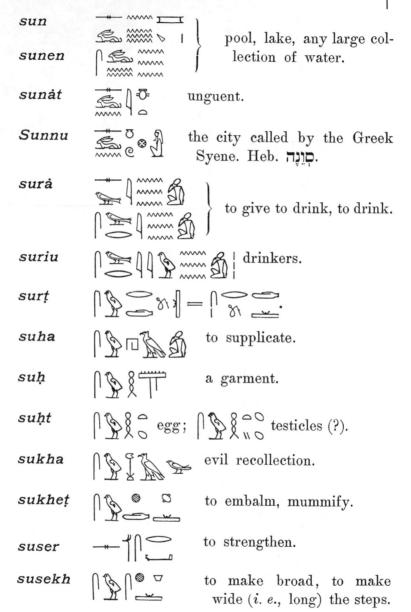

Suķaṭi  the name of a god.

sut  he, it, himself, they, them.

sut  hair.

Sut 
Suti  } the god of darkness and night, and of physical and moral evil.

Suti-mes  a proper name.

suten   } king;  king of the gods.

 the reigning king.

 kings.

 sovereignty, kingship, reign.

sutenit  to reign, sovereignty.

suten bȧti  } King of the South and North.

suteniu bȧtiu   } plur. of preceding.

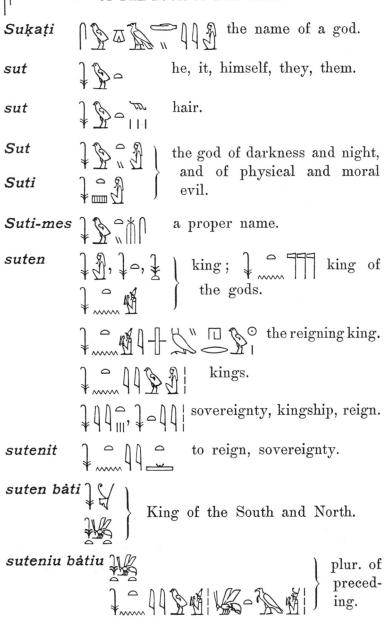

suten bȧt Ȧsȧr  Osiris, king of the Two Egypts.

suten ḥeḥ  "king of eternity"; a title of Osiris.

suten Ṭuat  "king of the Ṭuat"; a title of Osiris.

suten ḥemt  "king's woman", *i. e.*, queen.

suten sesh  "king's scribe", *i. e.*, royal scribe.

suten . . . .  byssus; plur. .

suten ṭā ḥetep   an ancient formula meaning "may the king give an offering", dating from the time when the king sent gifts for the funeral feasts of his loyal servants. At a later period its use was purely conventional in funerary texts.

Suten-ḥenen (or ***Ḥenensu***)  Herakleopolis, the חָנֵס of Isaiah XXX. 4. The Copts called it ϩⲛⲉⲥ, or ϩⲛⲏⲥ, or ⲉϩⲛⲏⲥ, and its Arabic name is اهناس.

sutennu		to extend, walk with long strides.
suṭekh		to treat with medicaments, to embalm.
sutcha		to set out on a journey, to go, travel.
setcha		
sutcha		to be strong, sound, well, to make strong and happy.
setcha	 	
si		it, its, them.
si		fulness, satiety.
sia	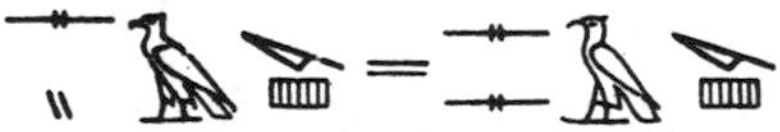	to cut, engrave.
Seb (***Ḳeb?***)		the Earth-god.
Sebu (***Ḳebu***)		
		the abode of Seb (or Ḳeb).
seb		to guide, to lead, to pass by or through a place; 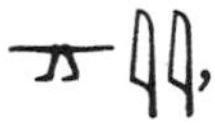, 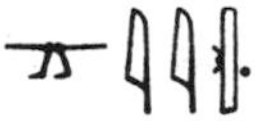.
sebbi		
		passage.

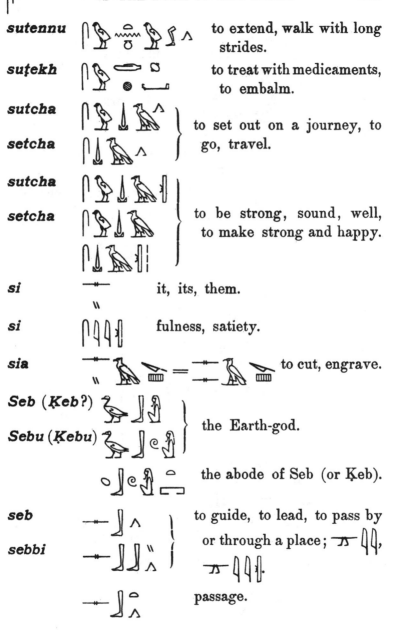

sba  star, Star-god; plur. 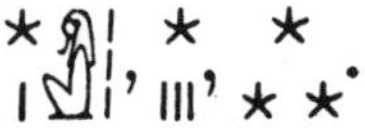

sbaiu  stars.

sba 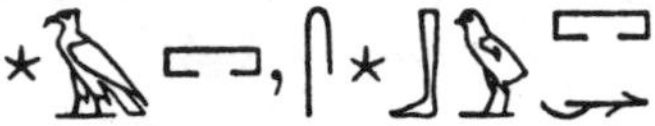

sbau  door, gate, pylon; the forms  also occur.

sbau 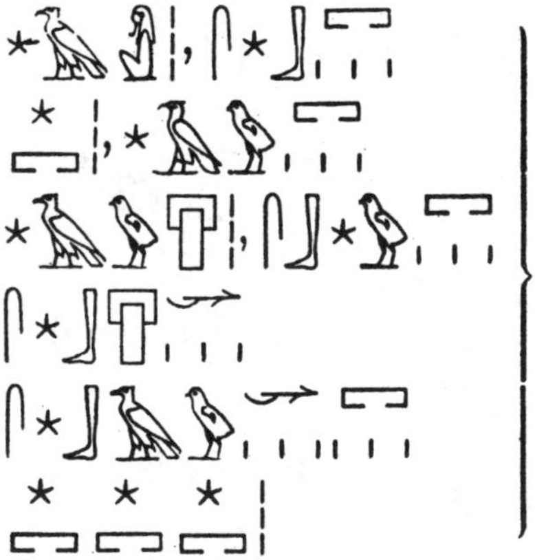 plur. of preceding.

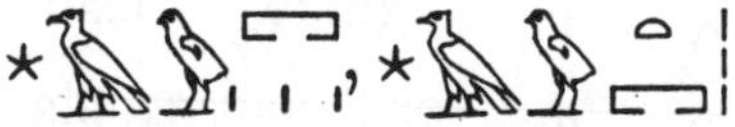 doors of the Other World.

sba  to instruct.

sbaut  to rebel.

sebaḳi  helpless one, inert, weak.

Sebȧ 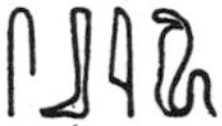 the name of a goddess.

sebȧ  to be an enemy of some one.

sebȧ 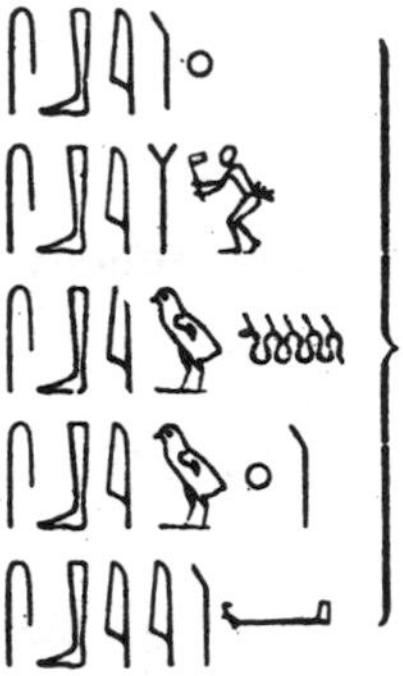 enemy, fiend.

sebȧu  plur. of preceding.

seben  to retreat, depart.

sebeḥ 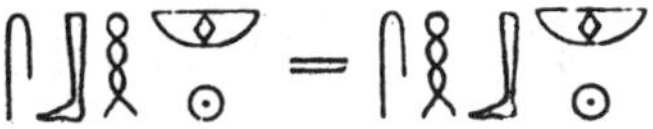 to keep a festival.

sebeḥ  to call upon someone, to invoke.

sebḥet 

sebḥit 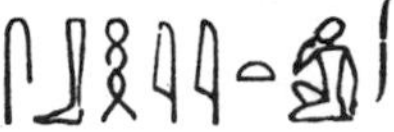 invocation, praise.

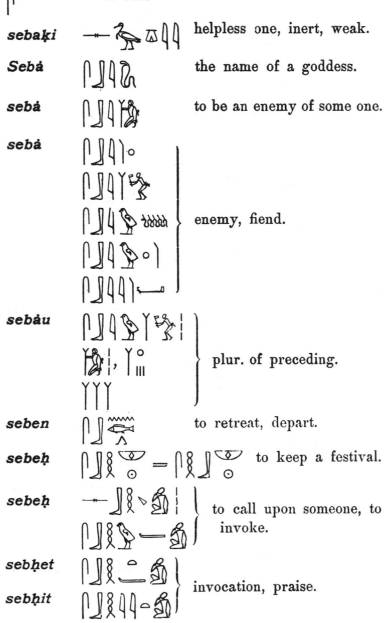

sebekh  be master of, have power over (?).

sebkhet 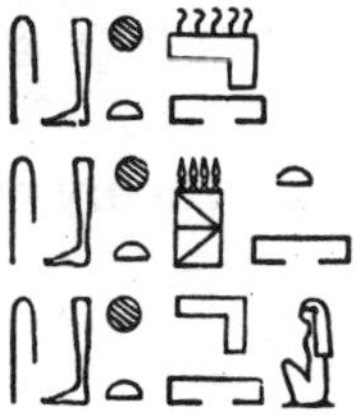 gate, pylon.

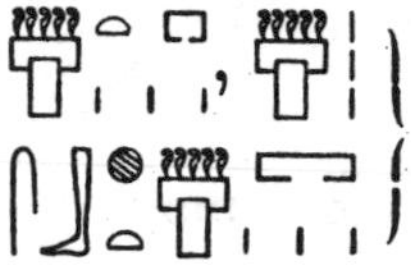 plur. of preceding.

sebekhbekht  to scatter (?).

Sebek  the Crocodile-god, who was a form of the Sun-god.

Sebeku  the Crocodile-gods.

sebeq  leg, thigh.

Sebeq-en-Shesmu  a proper name.

Sebeq-en-Tem  a proper name.

Sebeḳ 

Sebḳa 

Sebaḳu 

the name of a god.

sebt  to be pleased (?), laugh, laughter.

sebt  walls.

sep 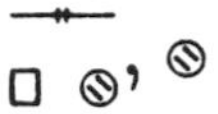 season, luck, fate, occasion, opportunity, circumstance, case, etc.; plur.  .

 a right case, a just trial.

 ill luck, a bad time.

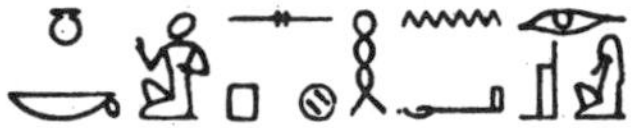 I am Fate and Osiris.

 a prosperous time.

 the occasion of the night.

 likewise, at the same time.

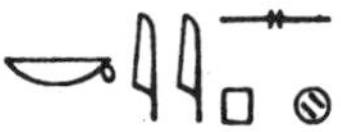 another time or opportunity.

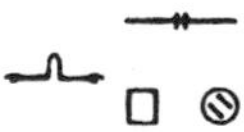 at no time, never.

 primeval time, when the world began.

sep 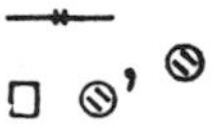 time;  twice;  four times;  millions of times.

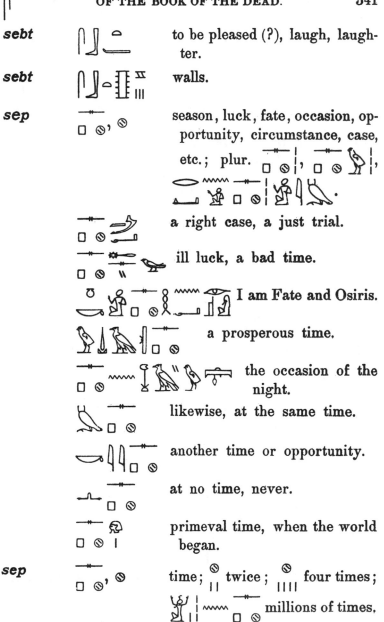

sep sen 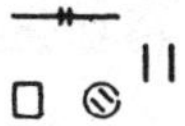 duplicity.

sep  to pass sentence.

sep  crown (?).

Sep  the name of a god.

Sepa 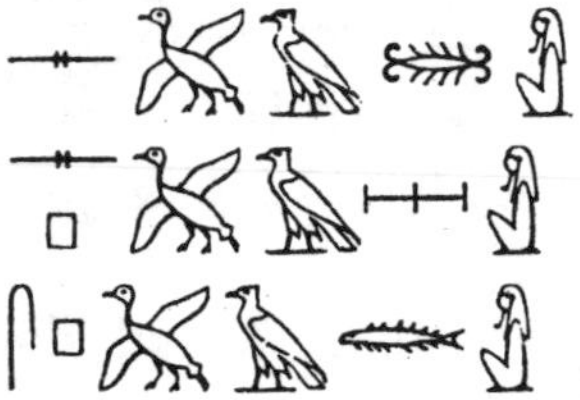 the name of a god.

seppi 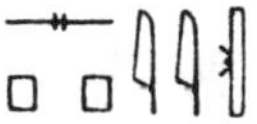

sepi 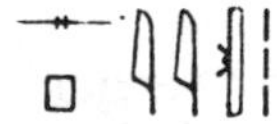 remainder.

seppu 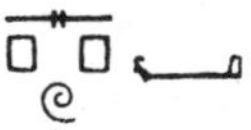 omission.

sper  to come to a place, to arrive at;  comers.

sper  to speak to, address.

speh 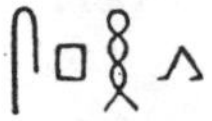 to make to arrive at.

sepeh 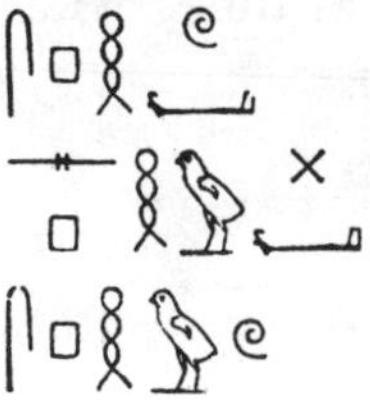 to tie with a rope, to fetter.

sepḥer  to design, make a plan, draw, write.

sepḥer  to make to revolve.

Sepes 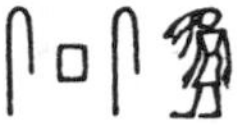 a proper name.

sept  lip;  edge of the water.

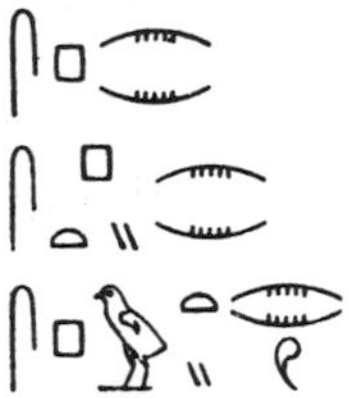 the two lips.

sept  nome; plur. 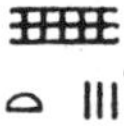.

 the nome of Maāti.

Septu  a god of the Eastern Delta; a form of Horus.

Sepṭ  the star Sirius.

sepṭ  to be ready to do or use something, prepared; to be provided with.  provided.

 prepared for the moment.

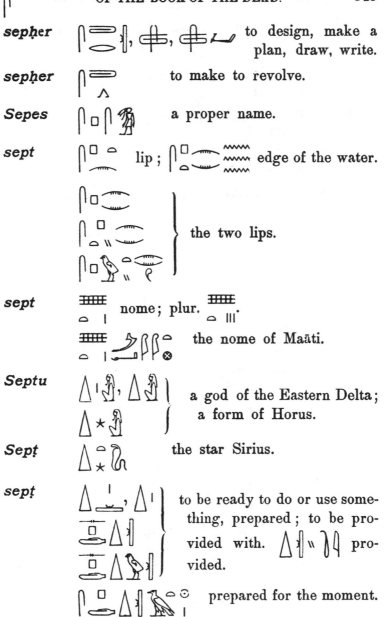

having horns ready to strike.

ready of face, keen, alert (?).

sepṭ a kind of wood.

sepṭ leg.

Sepṭ-kheri-neḥait-àmi-beq a proper name.

Sepṭ-mast-ent-Reruti a proper name.

sef yesterday;

sef maāt . . . . . .

sef ḥer to be gracious, longsuffering.

sefi babe, child.

sefekh seven.

sefekh to untie, undress, set free;

Sefekh-neb-s a proper name.

seft  to slay.

seft  knife, sword.

seft 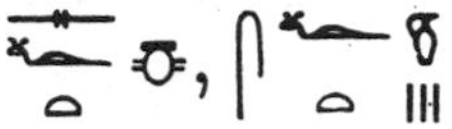 pitch, unguent.

sem  a priest (also setem ).

sma  loin.

sma 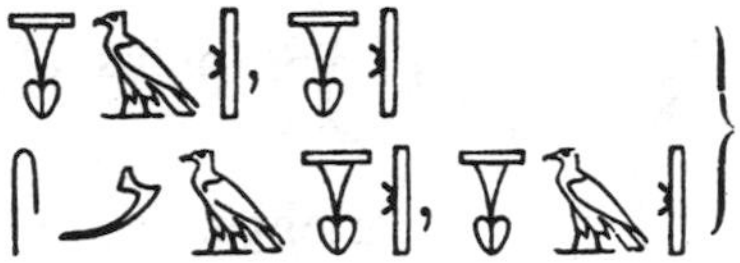 to join together, to unite with.

 union, assembly.

smat (?)  a burial place.

sma.ta 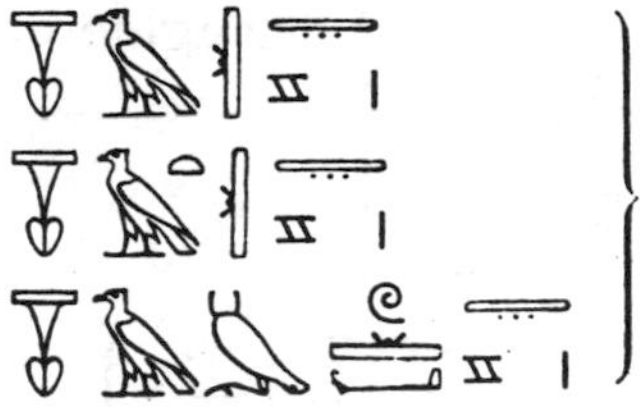 union with the earth, *i. e.*, burial.

 day of burial.

 to unite the Two Lands, *i. e.*, Egypt.

sma  to kill, slaughter.

 slaughterer, butcher.

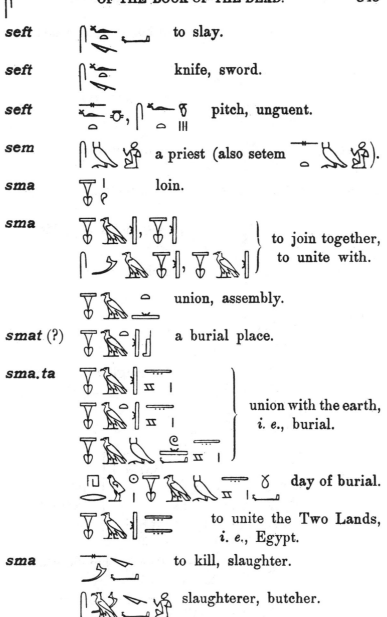

sma  cow or bull bound for sacrifice.

smaui  to renew, remake.

smaȧr  to oppress.

smau  branches.

 poles of a bier.

smaiu  branches.

smaiu 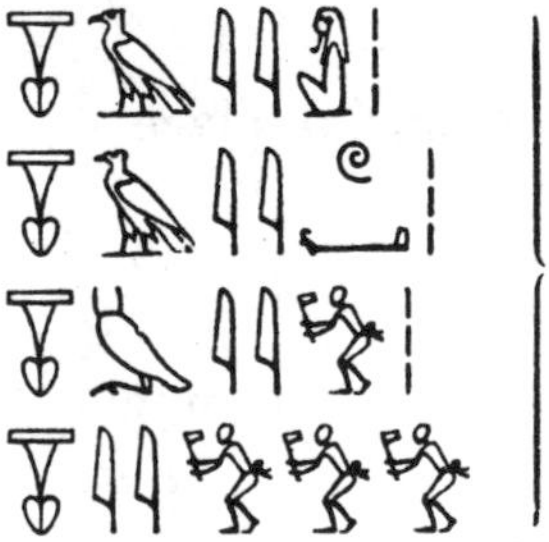 slaughterers, fiends.

 plur. of preceding.

 butchers of Set.

 god of slaughter.

Smait 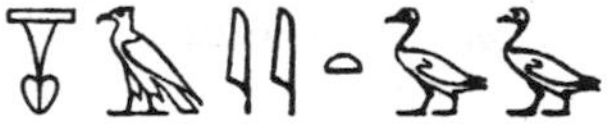 two goddesses of slaughter.

smaā  to pay what is due, make an offering.

smaāiu  slayers.

smaā-kheru 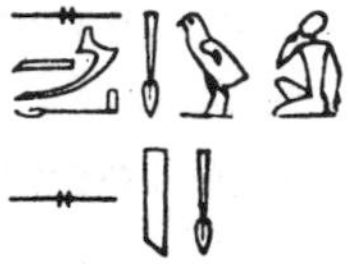 to justify, to make triumphant, to proclaim blessed.

smam  to slay, sacrifice.

smam  butcher.

smamiu  slaughterers, fiends.

smam  a bull for sacrifice.

smamu  cattle for sacrifice, victims.

Smam  the name of a god.

Smam-ur  the name of the Soul of Seb (Keb).

Smam  the name of a lake.

smamu  foliage or branches of a tree.

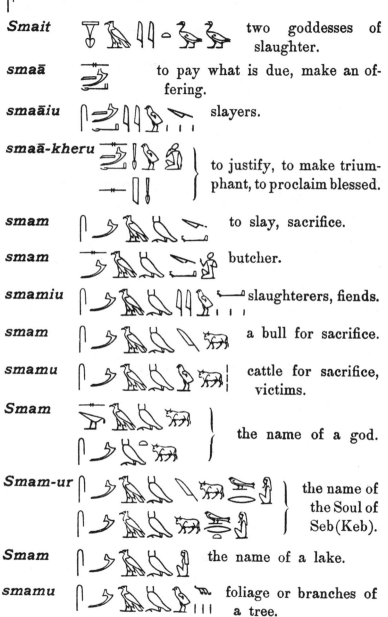

smamu clouds.

smat bows of a boat (?).

smatu torture chambers, shambles.

Smati a proper name.

Smamti a proper name.

smaṭ festival of the half month.

smȧ to report, announce, bear a message; reporting;

smȧ, ***smȧiu*** herald, announcer.

smȧ, ***smȧt*** report.

smȧ leather.

smȧu pieces of leather.

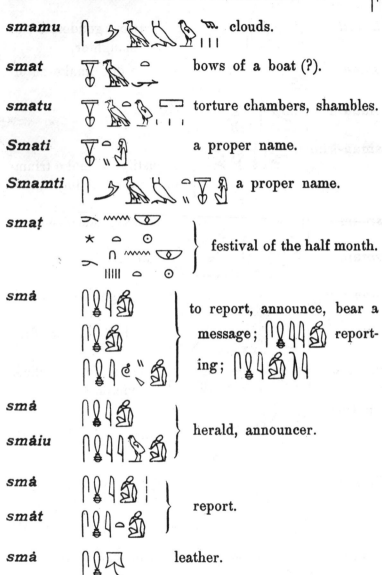

semu  herbs, pasturage.

semiu  devourers.

semi  to entreat.

smemā  to burn up.

smen 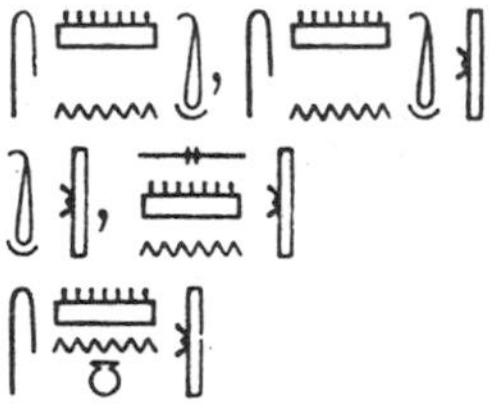 to stablish, be stablished, fixed, made firm.

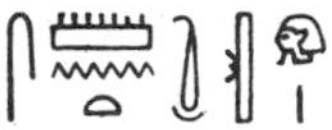 fixed head.

smen  a kind of goose.

smenkh 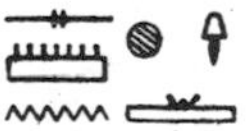 to repair, re-establish, beautify, make perfect.

smert  eyelids.

smer  to inflict or cause pain.

smeḥ 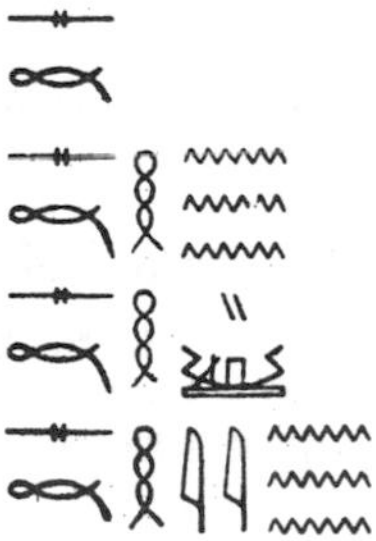 to flood, to submerge, water fields.

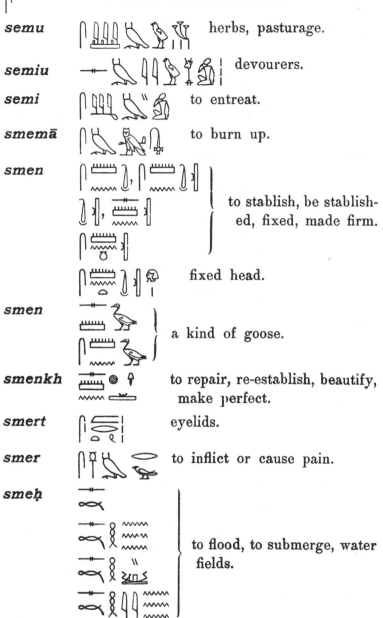

smeḥit	flood.
semkheṭ	. . . .
semes	to make to be born, produce.
semsu	eldest, firstborn.
Semti (?)	a king of the 1st dynasty. This name was formerly read Ḥesepti.
smet	to listen.
smetmet (?)	to pry into.
Smetu	the warder of the First Ārit.
smet	woven with, or shot with (of cloth).
Smet-āqa	the name of a rudder.
Smeti-āqa	name of a part of the magic boat.
Smetti	a proper name.

smetru  to investigate, search out, find the truth.

semṭet  servant, serf.

sen 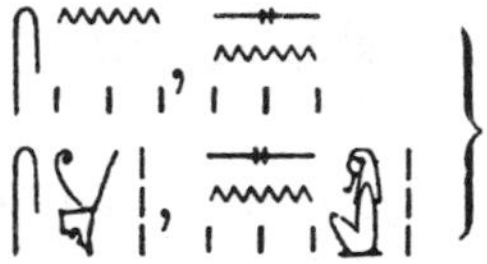 they, their, them.

sen 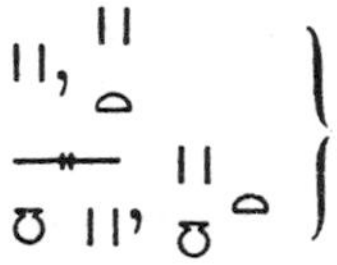 two; second, fellow, equal, companion, like, equal;  two breasts.

sen 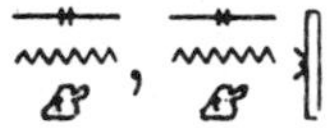 to smell, breathe.

sen ta  to smell the earth, to pay homage.

sen 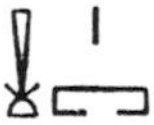 house, abode (?).

sen  brother; dual  ; plur. 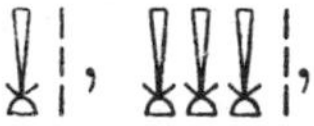 .

sent  sister.

 two sisters, pair of sisters.

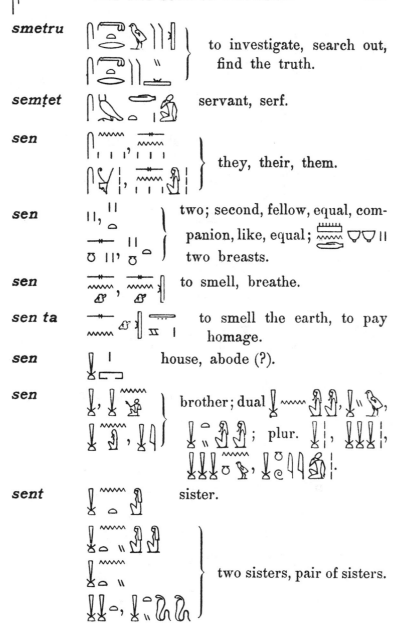

seni  companion, fellow.

sen 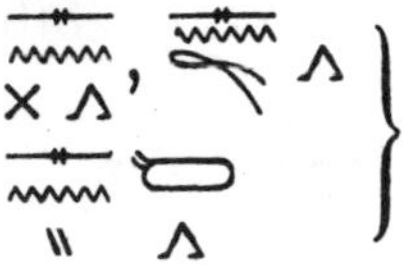 to pass away, depart, to walk.

sen  to slit, to cut.

Senu  a city near Panopolis.

senȧ 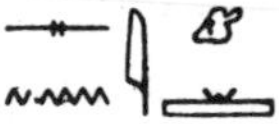 adoration.

senȧha  injury, misery.

senā  restraint.

senāāt  to beautify (?).

senb  to be well, strong, healthy.

senbȧ  health, soundness.

senb 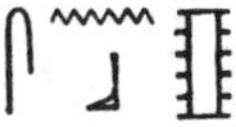 wall; plur. 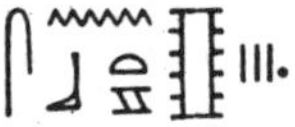

senbet  libation vessel.

senpu  slaughterings.

senf blood.

senfekhfekh to be untied, set loose.

senem abundance.

senem to pray, to adore.

senemȧi to make advance.

Senemti a proper name.

senemem hair.

senen image, statue.

sennu to cut, to sever; those who cut.

sennit . . . .

sennu to gather (?).

sennu cakes, bread-offerings.

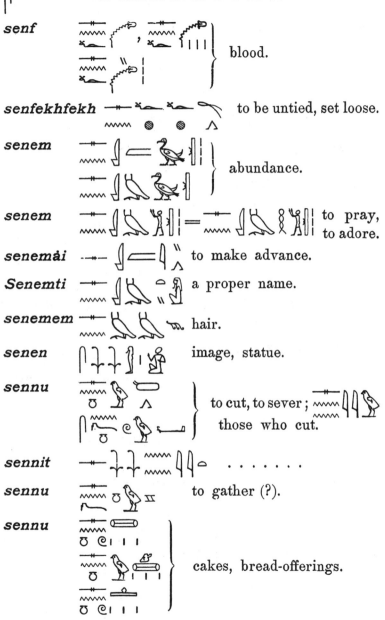

sennȧu — to fail.

sennuṭ — carrier.

senni

Sen-nefer — a proper name.

senneshni — storm.

seneh — to be in servitude.

senehep — to be strong.

Seneh-paqarha — the name of a city.

Senehaparḳana — the name of a city.

seneḥem — to deliver.

senkha — to disembark (?).

senekhekh — to grow old.

senes
sensi } to praise.

sensu — to cry out, invoke.

Senseneb  the name of the mother of Nu.

sensenni 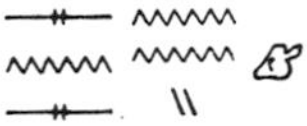 to breathe, snuff the air.

sensen 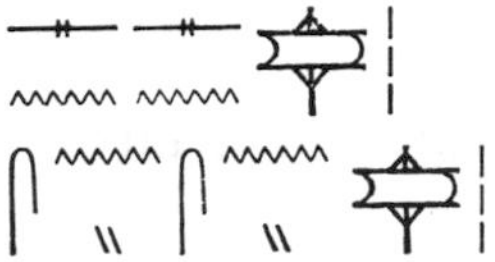 breathings, breaths.

sensen 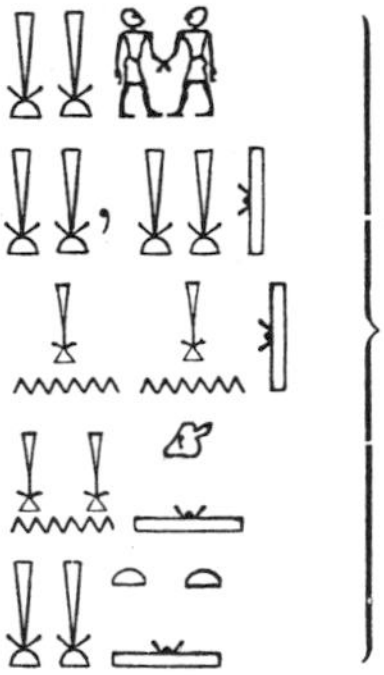 to become friendly with some one, to fraternize; to smell.

sensen 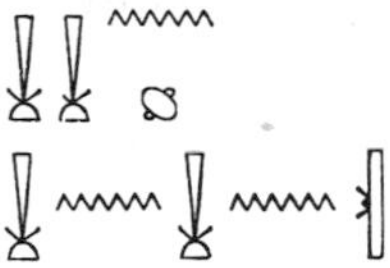 to have a bad smell, to become corrupt, to decay.

senesh 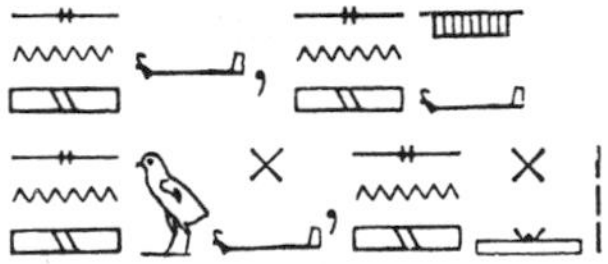 to unbolt, unbar, open.

senshu  bolts (?).

seneshni  storm, hurricane.

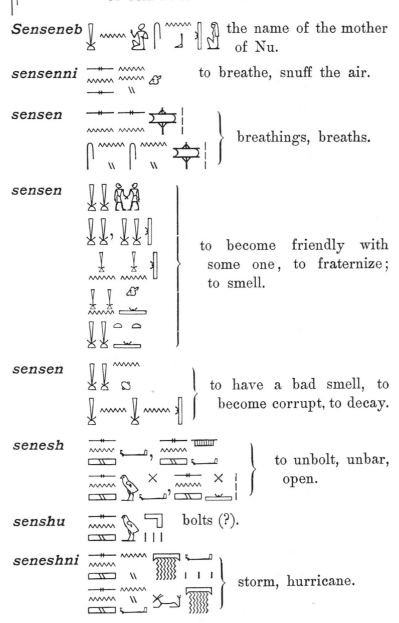

Senk 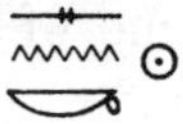 a proper name.

senket  light.

Senket  the name of a city.

senk-ȧb  strong-willed.

senq (?), ***senqet*** 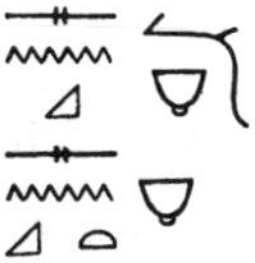 to suckle.

sent  labourers, builders.

sent 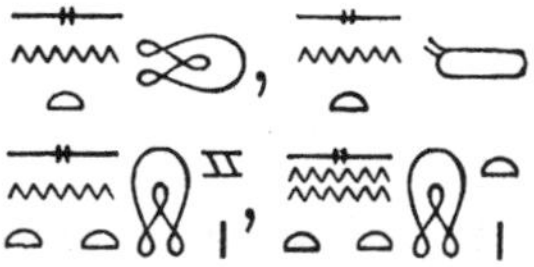 foundation.

sent 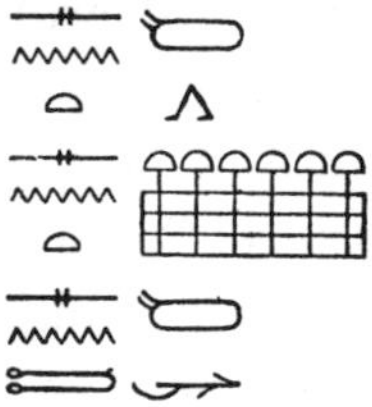 draughtboard, game of draughts.

sent  to pass away.

sent  decay.

sentu  enemies.

Sent-Rā a proper name.

senter / ***senther*** incense offered to the god; censed; to cense the mouth.

senteḥ to have power over.

Sent..... the brother-gods Horus and Set.

sent̤ to fear, be afraid.

sent̤ àb timid.

sent̤ fear.

senetchem to make glad or happy.

pleasure.

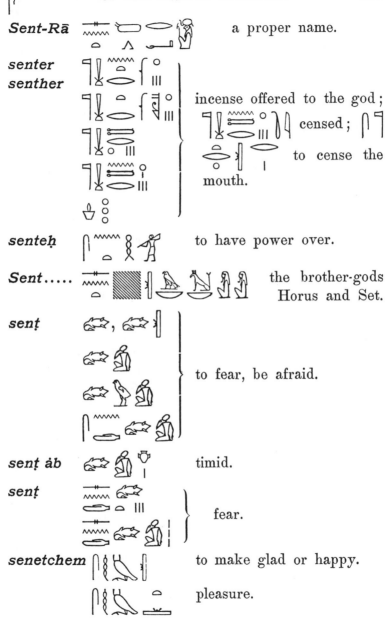

ease.

senetchem to sit.

sentchert restraint.

ser prince, chief; everlasting prince; a proper name.

plur. of preceding.

ser to give orders or directions, to announce, give tidings;.

sert order, announcement.

Ser-kheru
Serȧ-kheru the name of one of the Forty-two Judges in the Hall of Osiris.

Serȧt-beqet the name of a sacred cow.

seru grain, barley.

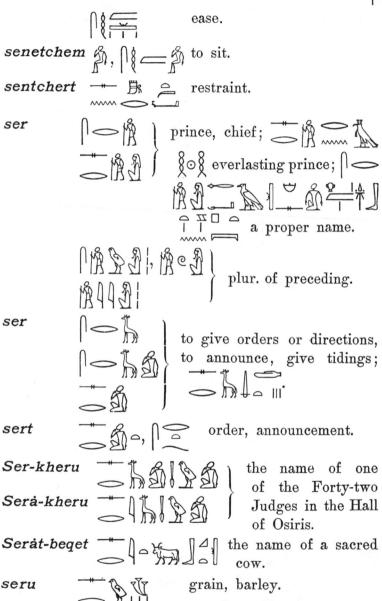

seru  geese of a special kind.

serui (?)  flame.

serukheṭ  to treat with medicaments, embalm.

seruṭ   } to make to grow, to flourish, to perpetuate.

seref 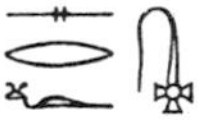 to be hot, flame, fire.

serem  to make to weep.

serenp  to make young.

serḥu (?)  to overthrow.

serekh 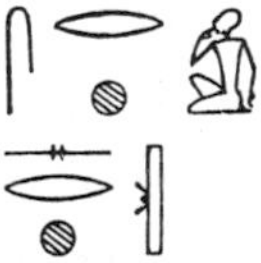 } to make to know, to inform.

serekh  a funerary building, a cognizance.

Serekhi 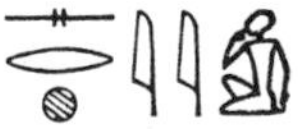 the name of one of the Forty-two Judges in the Hall of Osiris.

seres 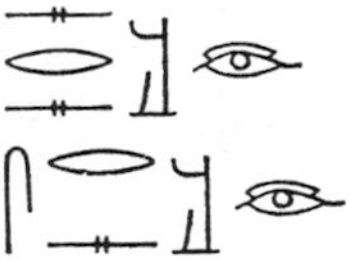 } to be awake, to watch.

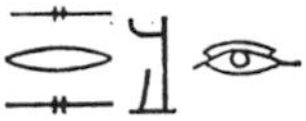 watch, watching, watcher.

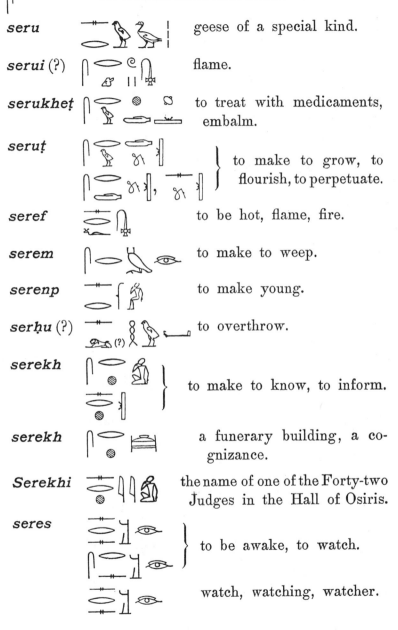

Seres-ḥer 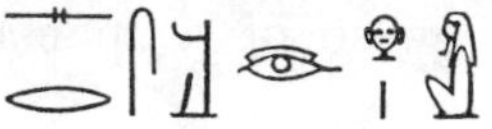 "watching face"; the name of a god.

 "watching faces"; a class of divine beings.

serqaȧu  to be refreshed, to breathe.

Serqet 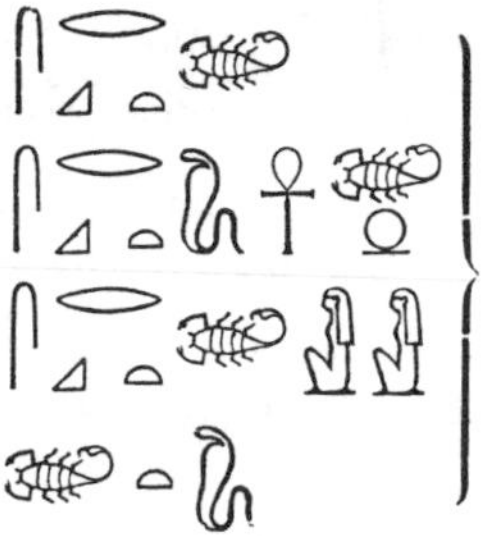 the goddess Serqet.

Sert  a city in the Seventh Ȧat.

sert  "goad"; the name of a part of the magic boat.

serṭ 

Serṭiu  the name of one of the Forty-two Judges in the Hall of Osiris.

sehep 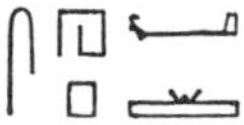 lawgiver.

seher, ***seherr*** 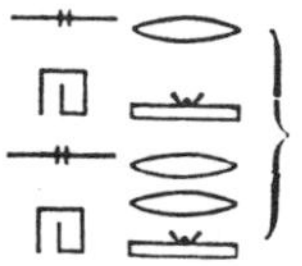 to make quiet, subdue.

sehert  carnelian.

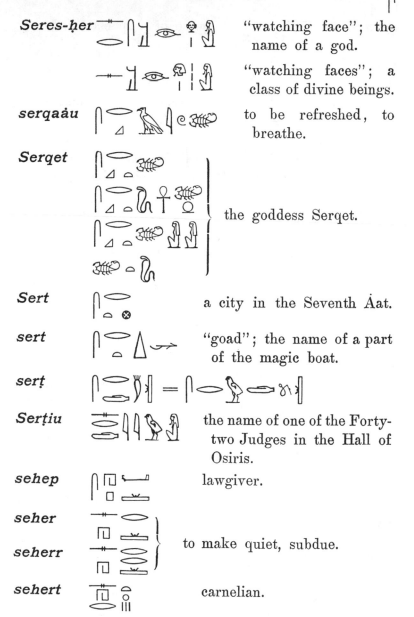

seḥ 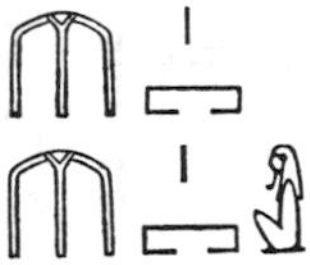 hall; 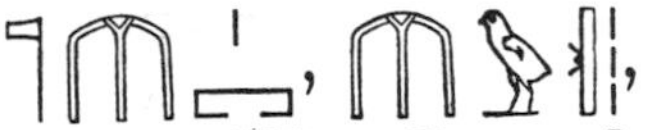 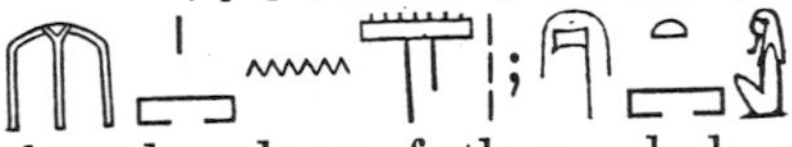 the chamber of the embalmment of Osiris.

seḥap  to hide.

seḥuā  to confuse, disarrange.

seḥui  to gather together, collect.

seḥurȧ 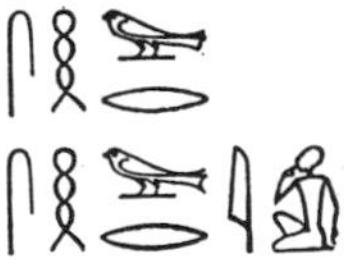 to curse.

seḥeb  to keep a feast, to make festival.

seḥem  to turn back.

seḥeptet  name of a boat (?).

seḥen  to order, arrange (?).

seḥer  to drive away.

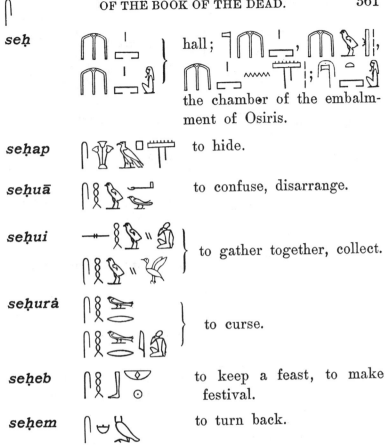

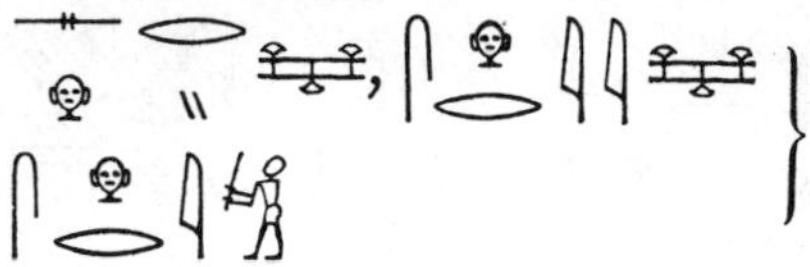 driver away; plur. 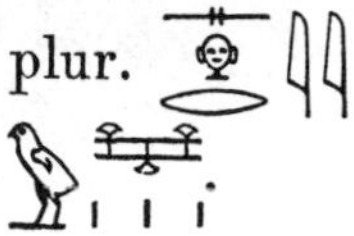

seḥes 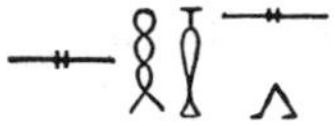 to make to meet.

seḥset 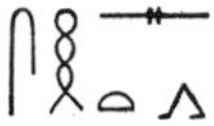 a meeting.

seḥeq  to cut off, hack in pieces.

seḥeq  to appoint to some office.

seḥeqer  to cause to hunger, to keep hungry.

seḥetep 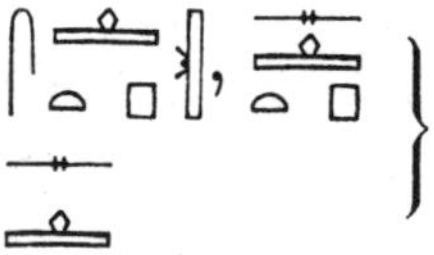 to make to be at peace, to propitiate, to pacify.

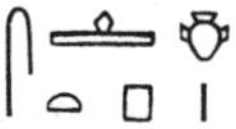 to quiet the heart.

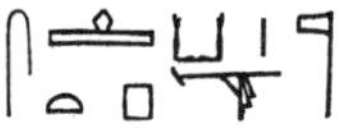 to propitiate the divine Ka.

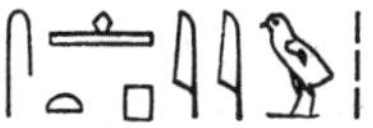 peacemakers.

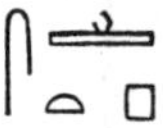 pacification.

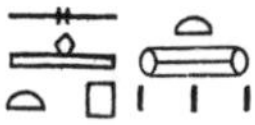 offerings which bring peace.

Seḥetep-taui "pacifier of the Two Lands"; a proper name.

seḥetem to destroy.

Seḥetemet-Au-ā-em-ābet the name of the banks of a river.

Seḥtet a proper name.

seḥetch to emit light, illumine, to shine.

light, radiance, brilliance.

Seḥetch-ur "Great Light", *i. e.*, Rā.

sekh

sekh to break, strike, cut, wound.

sekha to have in mind, to commemorate, to remember.

remembrance for good.

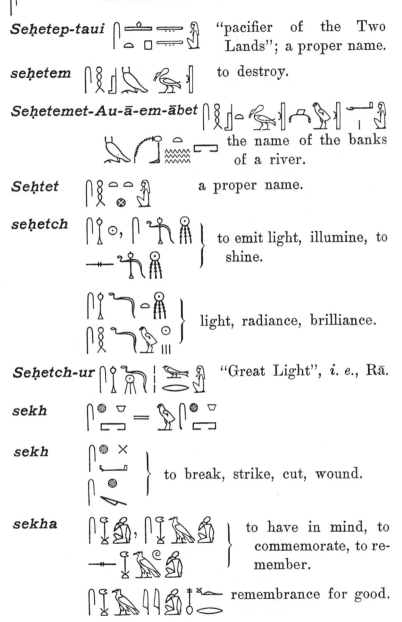

memorial servicces.

remembrance of evil.

sekha to be deaf.

Sekhai a Cow-goddess.

sekhabui eaters (?).

sekhap to swallow.

sekhar to milk.

sekharu to plate, to mould.

sekhakeru to ornament.

Sekhat-Ḥeru a Cow-goddess.

Sekhāi to make to rise or appear, to crown.

Sekhiu the name of a double serpent god or fiend.

sekhu  to praise, glorify.

sekhu  praise.

sekhun 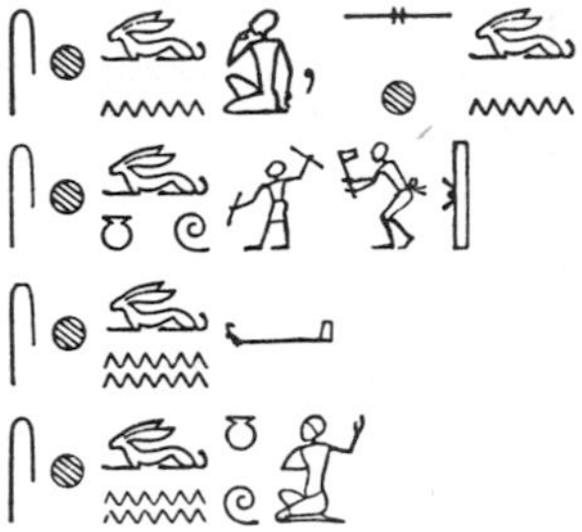 to revile, curse.

sekhuṭ  to fortify.

sekheb  see 

sekhep 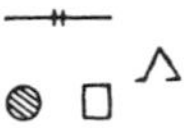 to make advance.

Sekhepti  a proper name.

sekheper 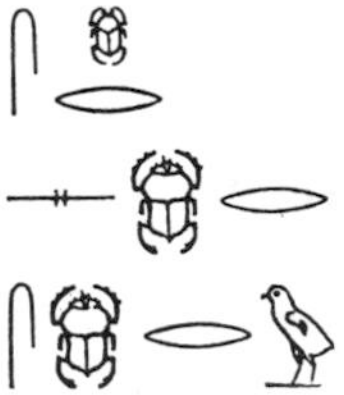 to make to become, to create, fashion, form.

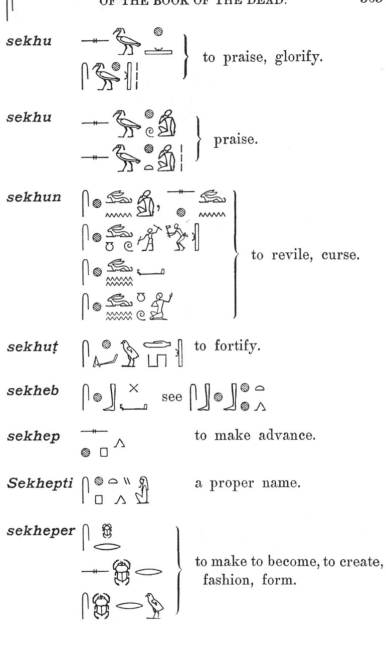

sekheperu 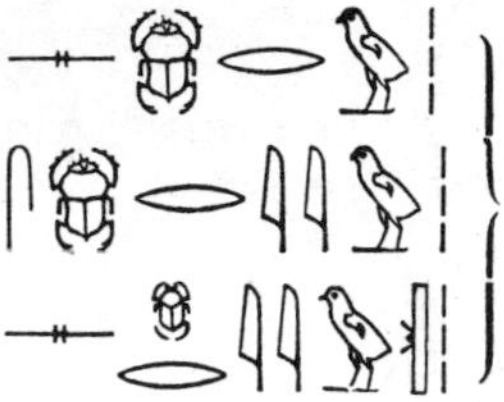 those who cause things to be.

sekhef  seven;  seventh.

sekhem 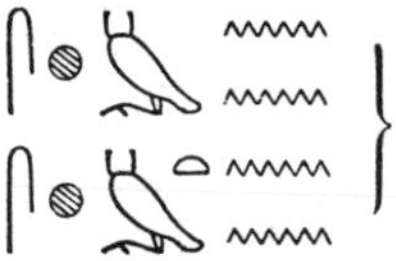 to forget, forgetfulness.

Sekhem 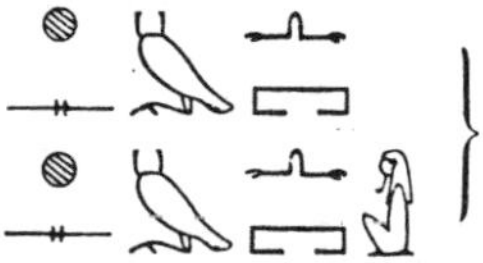 shrine, sanctuary.

 gods of the shrine.

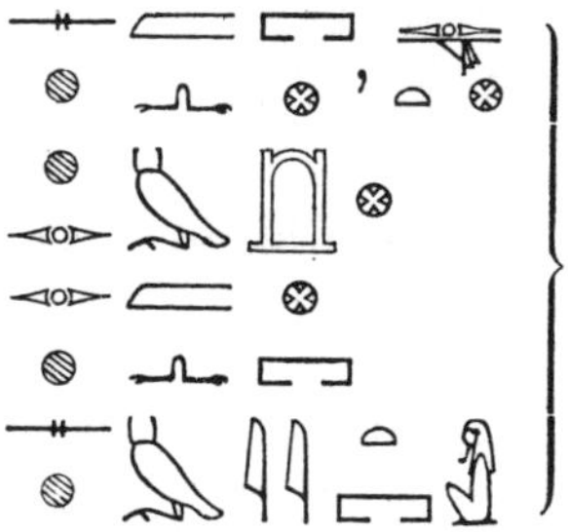 the city of Letopolis.

sekhem  to recite, to read.

sekhem — to be strong, mighty, to prevail over, to gain the mastery, show oneself strong, might, power.

bold man, victor.

brave in heart.

weak.

mighty one, strong.

Sekhem — the natural power, vital power of a man, any power spiritual or physical.

Sekhemu — the Powers; the Double Power.

Sekhem-ur — "great Power"; a proper name.

Sekhem-em-àb-f — "strong in his heart"; a proper name.

Sekhem-nefer "good Power"; a proper name.

Sekhmet-ren-s-em-ḥemut-s the name of a sacred cow.

Sekhmet (*Sekhet*) name of a goddess.

Sekhmet-Bast-Rā a solar triad.

sekhen to direct (?).

sekhen to embrace.

"great embracer"; a proper name.

sekhni to make to alight.

sekhenen to become rotten, to decay.

sekhensh to make to stink, to calumniate.

sekhent to make to advance.

sekhent pillars.

sekher to offend.

[***sekher*** plan, device, counsel, arrangement.]

plur. of preceding.

a plan of triumph, or blessedness.

celestial designs, ordinances of heaven.

sekher to overthrow.

fallen.

overthrow.

Sekher-āṭ the god of the Sixth Ārit.

Sekheriu the name of one of the Forty-two Judges in the Hall of Osiris.

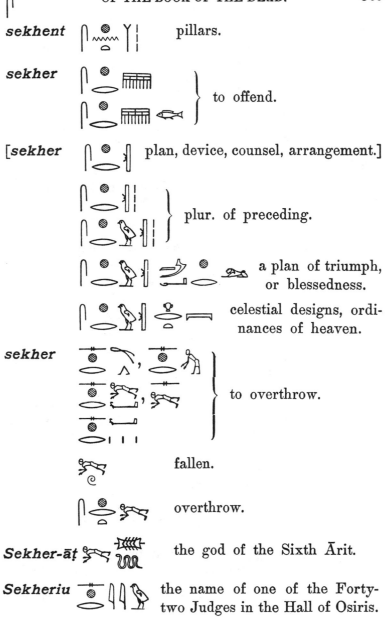

Sekher-remu a proper name.

sekhekh to straighten.

sekhes to run.

sekhes, ***sekhsekh*** to fasten, make firm.

sekhesef to meet with hostility, to repulse, to contradict, give evidence against.

sekhet to net, to snare, spread out a net.

sekhtu, ***sekhtiu*** snarers, hunters, fowlers, fishermen.

sekhet field, meadow; plur.

sekhtiu the divine field labourers.

"Great Field", *i. e.*, heaven.

Sekhet-Åanru (or ***Åaru***)  the "Field of reeds", *i. e.*, the Elysian Fields.

 a proper name?

Sekhet-neḥeḥ  "Field of Eternity".

Sekhet-neteru 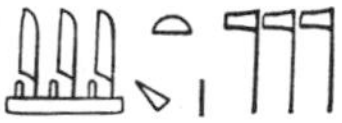 "Field of the gods".

Sekhet-Rā 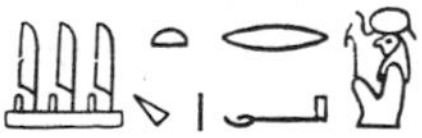 "Field of Rā".

Sekhet-ḥetep 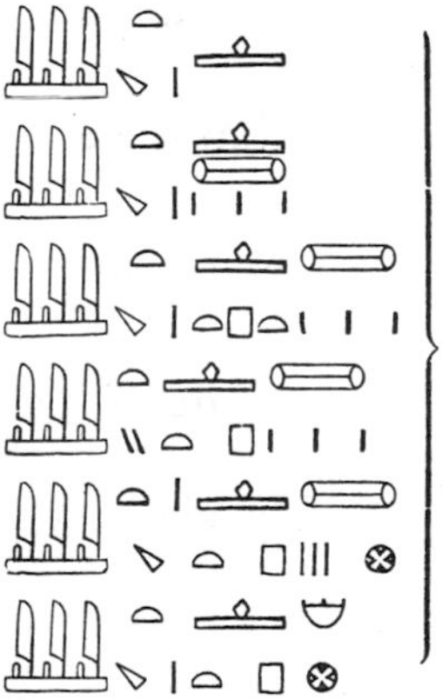 the "Field of Peace", or "Field of Offerings"; a name of the Elysian Fields.

Sekhti-ḥetep 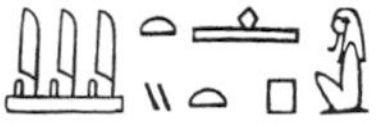 the god of the Field of Peace.

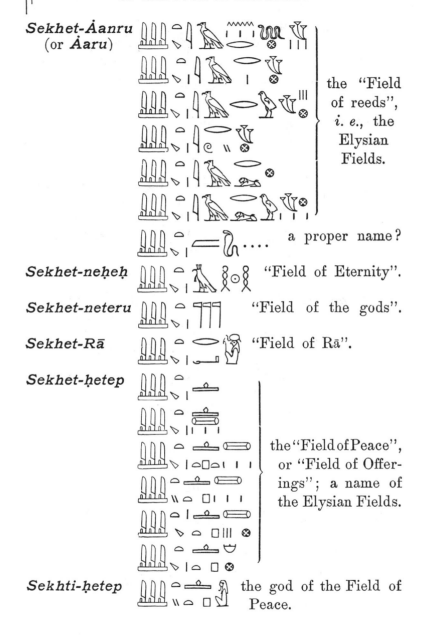

Sekhet-sanehemu "Field of the Grasshoppers".

Sekhet-Sȧsȧ "Field of Fire".

sekhettu plants.

sekhet

sekheṭ to turn upside down, invert, stand on the head;.

Sekheṭ-ḥer-āsh-ȧru "inverted face, of many forms"; the name of the porter of the First Ārit.

sekhṭu to hunger.

sesu times, days.

sesun to destroy.

sesunṭ to destroy.

seseb to slay.

sesen to snuff the air.

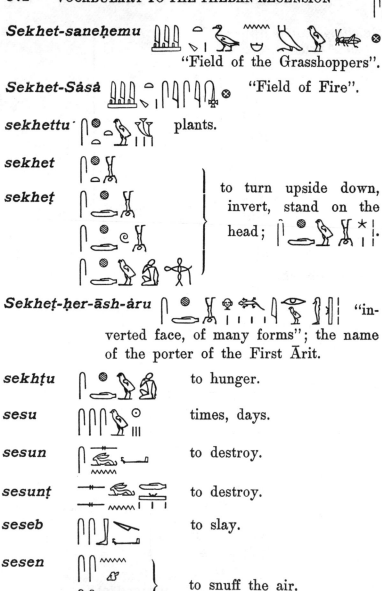

seska  body.

seset  legs.

seset  to burn up.

sesh 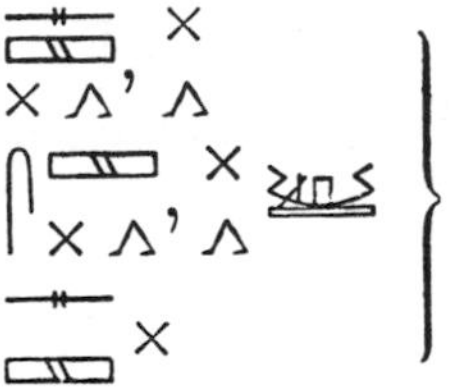 to pass, journey, travel.

 passage.

 impassable.

sesh 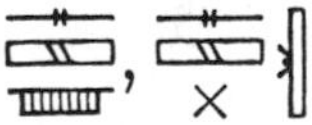 to open, unbolt.

sesh 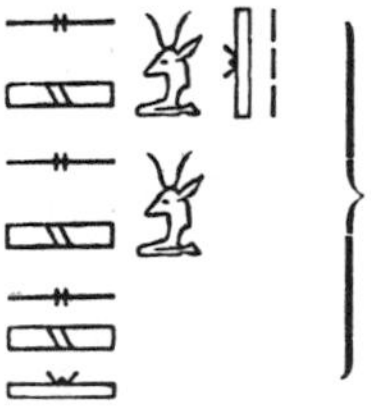 to be wise, skilful, knowledge.

sesh  nest; plur. .

 birth-place.

 two nests.

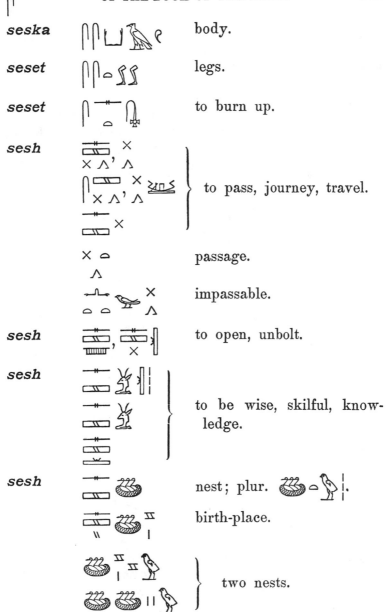

Seshet  name of a town and its god.

sesh 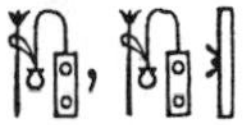 to write, draw, copy, make a plan.

seshu 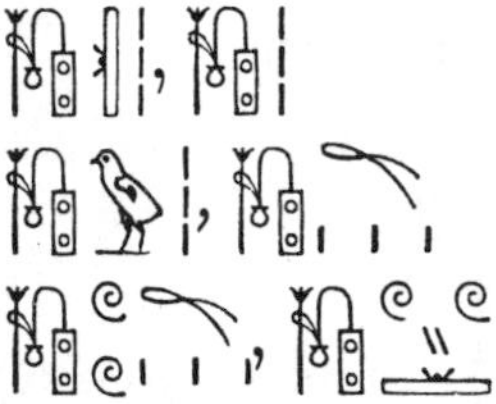 writings, decrees, documents, archives, books, copies of books, etc.

sesh 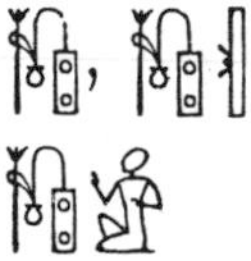 scribe, copyist.

 accomplished scribe.

 veritable scribe (as opposed to a titular scribe).

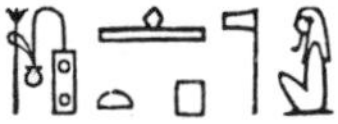 scribe of the temple property.

 scribe and draughtsman.

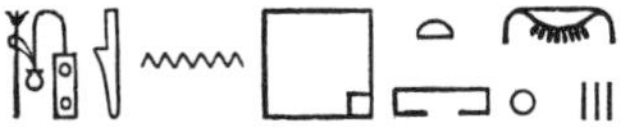 scribe and draughtsman of the house of gold.

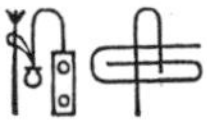 scribe and designer.

seshai  skilled, able, competent.

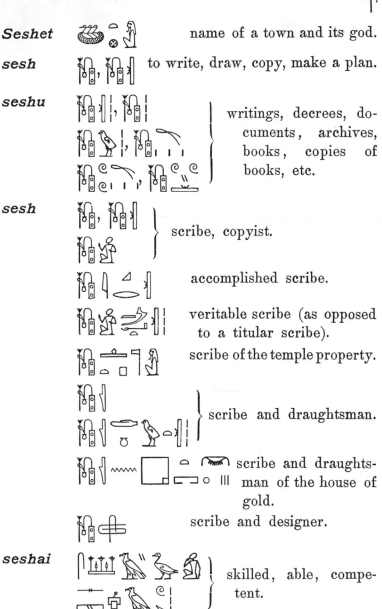

seshu  to be empty.

seshep  the measure of a palm.

seshepu 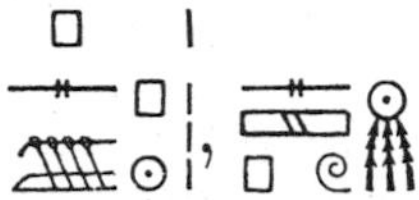 light, radiance; see SHESEP.

seshem  to lead, guide, conduct, guidance.

seshem  guide, leader.

 plur. of preceding.

seshmet  advance, guiding, guidance.

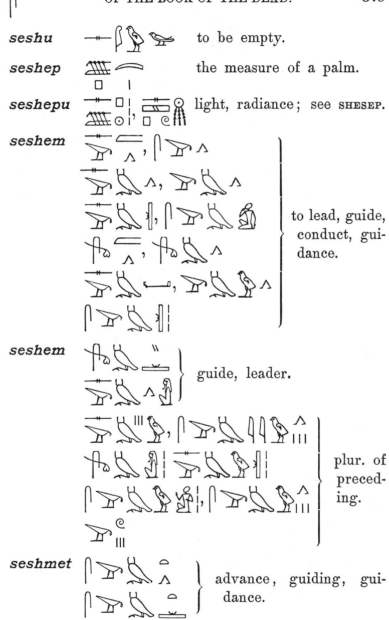

 gratification (?).

Seshemit  "conductress"; the name of a goddess.

Seshmu-ḥeḥ  "guide of eternity"; a proper name.

Seshmu-ta  "guide of the earth"; a proper name.

Seshmu-taui  "guide of the Two Lands"; a proper name.

Seshem  divine image, statue.

seshem  figure, design, image, form, similitude.

seshen 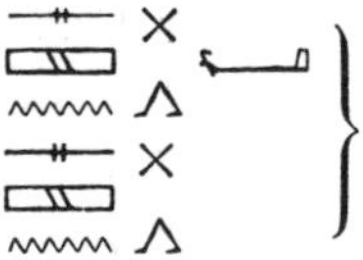 to scatter, destroy.

seshen  . . . . . .

seshen 

seshennu 

senshen 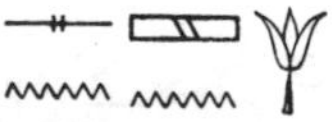

seshesh 

lily.

seshru  garments, apparel.

seshert 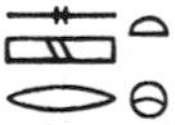 a cake, loaf.

seshet (?)  fire; plur. ; gods of fire .

Sesheta  the goddess of architecture.

sesheta  to be hidden, mysterious, incomprehensible.

sesheta  hidden things, mysteries, secrets.

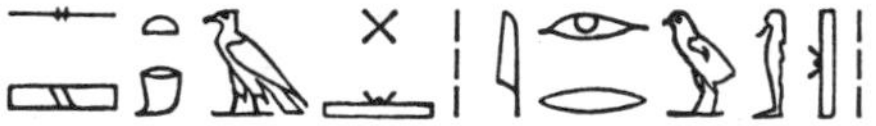 of invisible forms and shapes.

 hidden of name.

 very great mysteries indeed.

 great secrets of Ȧmenti.

seshetu  fiends (?).

seshet̥ 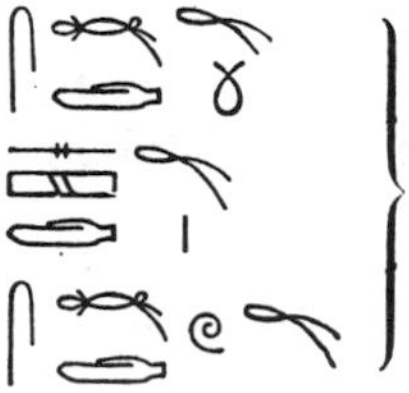 bandage, bandlet, tiara, girdle, fillet for the head.

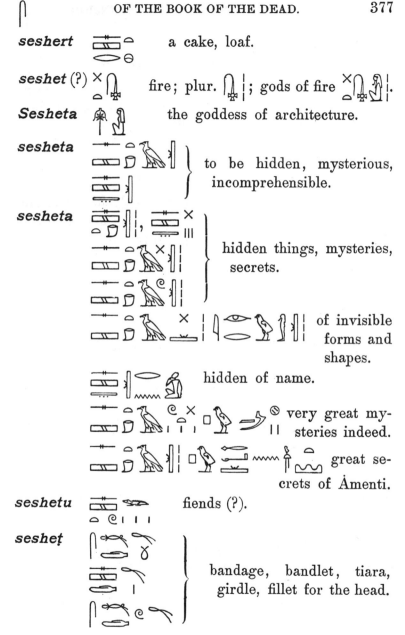

seshet-t 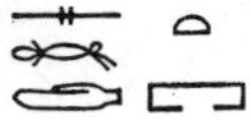 a chamber with a window or opening in it.

sek 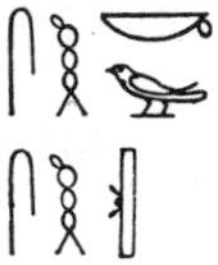 to decay, perish; 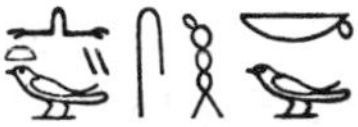 incorruptible.

sek 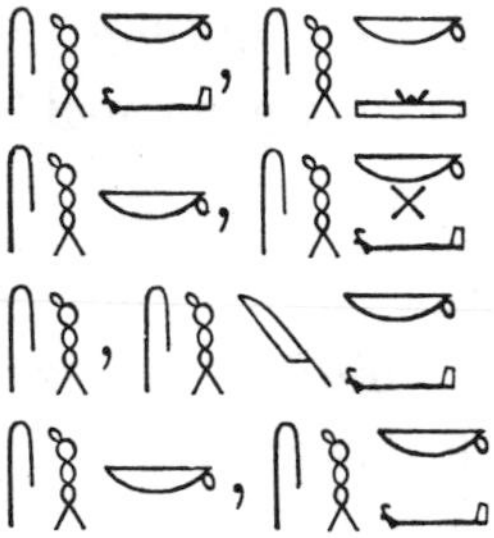 to break through, fight a way, to fight, destroy; to advance.

seksek

sek-re 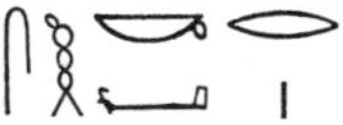 to direct.

Sek-ḥer 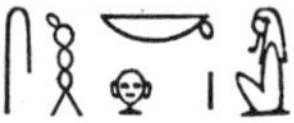 a proper name.

Seku  (with *åkhemu*) a class of gods.

seka  to plough.

sekemiu  grey or white hair.

Seker

Sekri 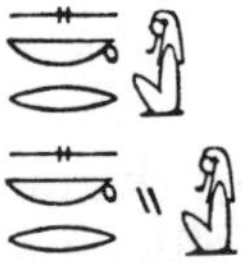 the ancient god of the Other World of Ṣaḳḳârah.

 Seker in his secret place.

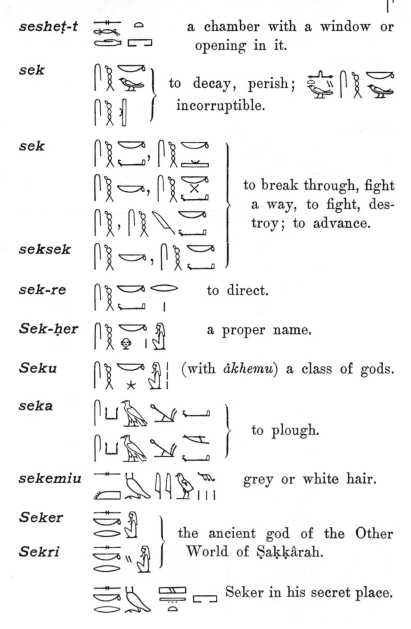

Seker, *Sekri*  the town of Seker.

Sekri 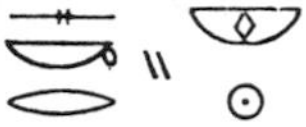 the festival of Seker.

Seker 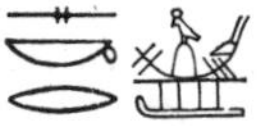 the sacred bark of Seker.

Seksek  the name of a fiend.

sektiu  to fetter.

Sektet 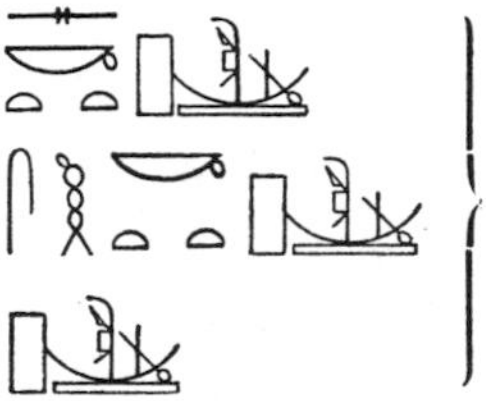 the boat in which the sun travelled from noon to midnight.

seq 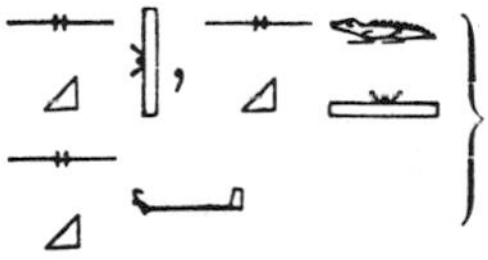 to collect, gather together.

seqa  to exalt, to lift up.

seqai  exalted one.

 plur. of preceding.

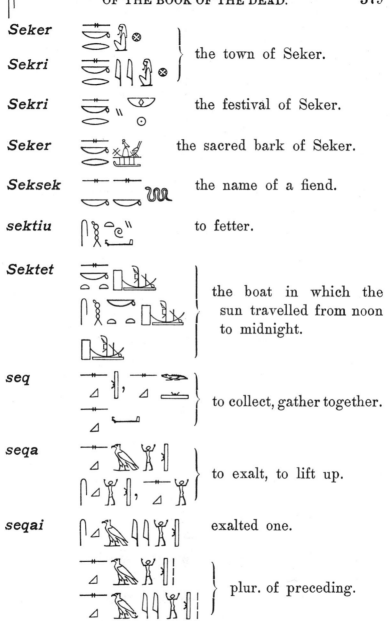

seqeb 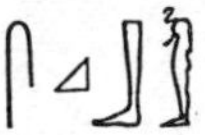 image (?).

seqebb 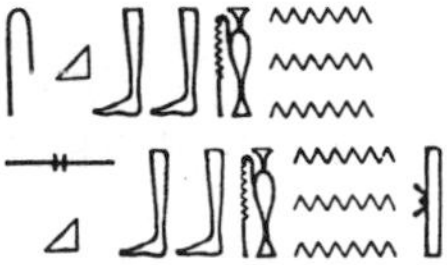 to cool, refresh oneself.

Seqebit  name of a goddess.

seqer  to smite, take prisoner.

 smiter.

seqeṭ 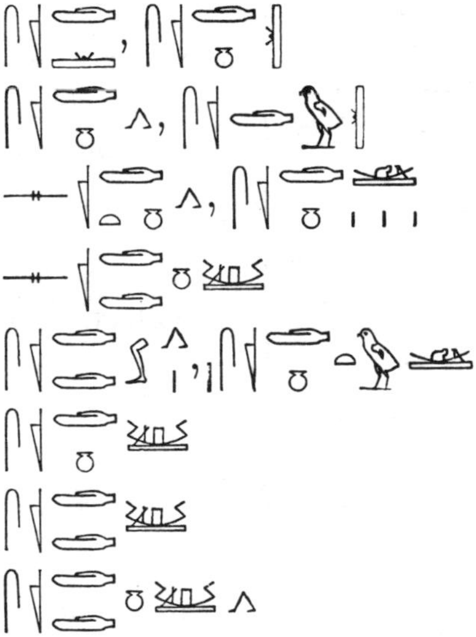 to sail in a boat, to journey, make a voyage;  encircled.

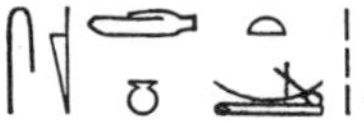 voyages, sailings.

 sailors, boatmen.

seqeṭ — dispositions.

Seqeṭ-ḥer — warder of the Second Ārit.

seḳenniu — helpless ones, weak.

seḳer — to put to silence, make quiet.

seḳert — silence.

set — she, it, its.

set — they, them, their.

set (?) — to break.

set — ground.

Set — the god of physical and moral evil; see SUTI.

set (*semt*) — mountain; plur.

set  to shoot arrows, to hurl stones.

set  to sow seed.

setit 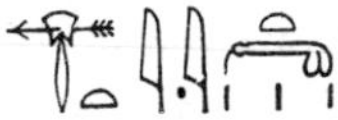 seed, progeny.

setut  arrows or beams of light, rays, radiance.

setau  to light a fire, to burn, flame.

seti 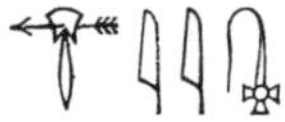 burning, burner.

setit  adversaries (?).

Sett  the name of a goddess of the First Cataract.

Sett  an Asiatic woman.

Set-ṭemui  a proper name (var.  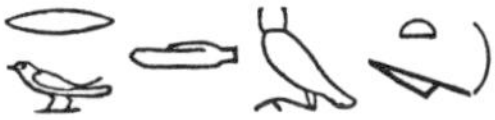).

Sta  a proper name.

sta, stat / *stau* 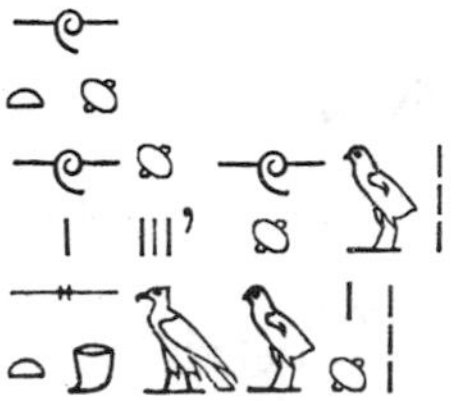 filth, dung.

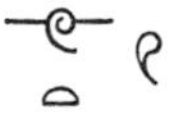 a portion of the body.

stat  filthy ones, fiends.

sta  to tow a boat, drag along, bring carry.

stau  those who tow, bearers, carriers.

stau 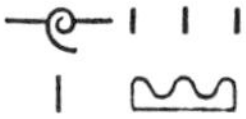 see 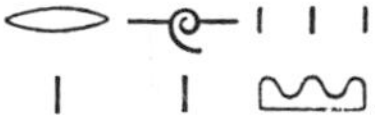 RE-STAU.

stat 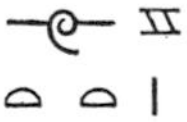 a measure of land.

sti  smell, odour.

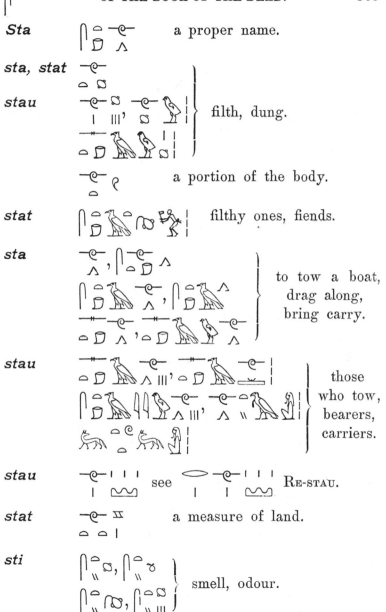

sti	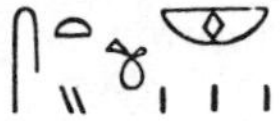	festal perfume.
Sti		"land of the bow"; a name of Nubia.
setua		to make or ascribe praise.
setut (or *sutet*)		to walk about.
setut		to symbolize, typify.
seteb		captives.
setep	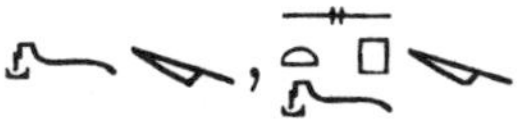	to cut.
setep		to chose, chosen.
setepu		choice cuts of meats.
setep sa	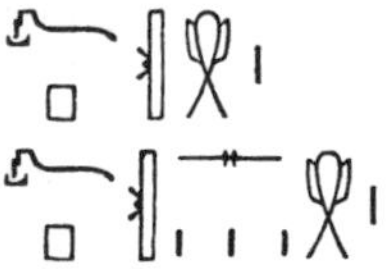	to work protection on behalf of someone.
setem		to hear; obey;  hearer.
		what is heard, listener.

setemiu  listeners.

Setem-ḥeri 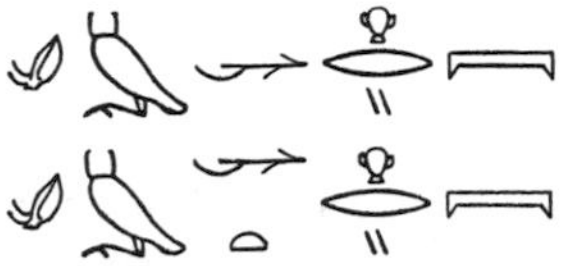 the name of the upper hinge.

Setem-kheri  the name of the lower hinge.

Setem-ȧnsi 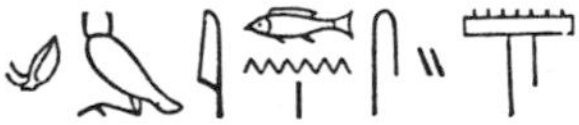 a proper name.

setennu  to be distinguished.

setentit 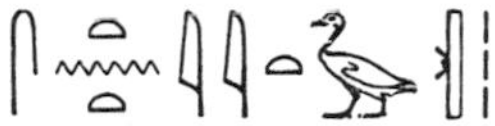 distinctions.

setenem 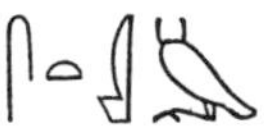 to make to walk.

seter  wooden tablet (?).

setḥu  to open.

set-ḥemt  woman, wife.

seteken 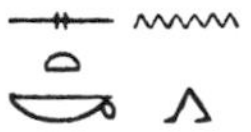 to make to enter.

 invaders, those who make to enter.

seṭ 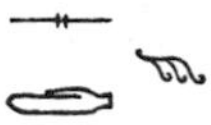 hair, foliage.

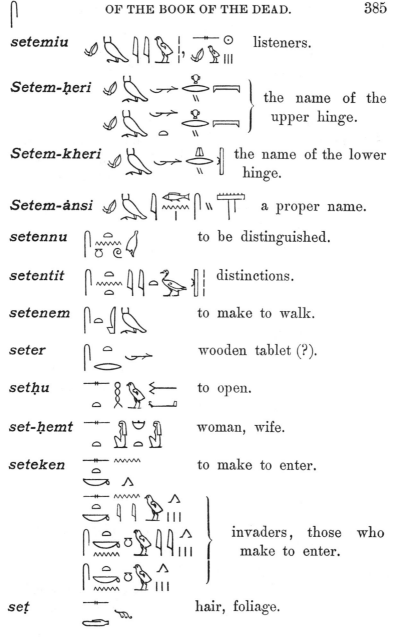

seṭ 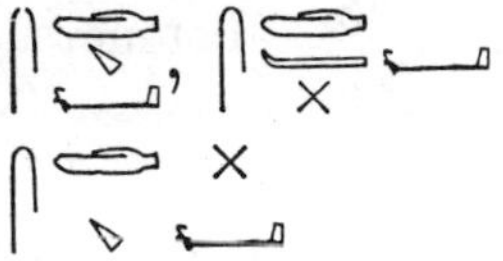 to break, split.

Seṭ-qesu (or, ***Seṭ-qersu***) 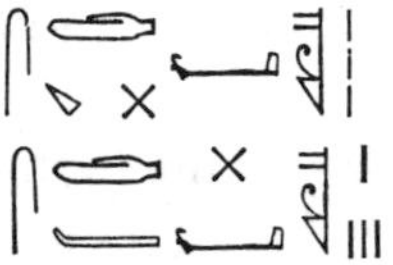 "bone-breaker"; the name of one of the Forty-two Judges in the Hall of Osiris.

seṭ 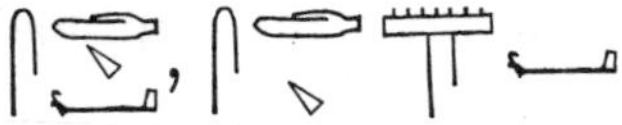 to clothe, to dress.

 a garment.

 those who clothe.

seṭa 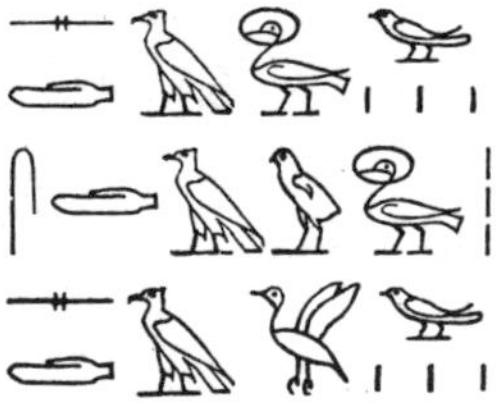 to tremble, quake, trembling, terror.

seṭui  to defame.

seṭu  . . . .

seṭeb 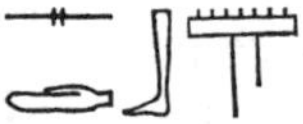 garment, hangings of a shrine.

seṭeb 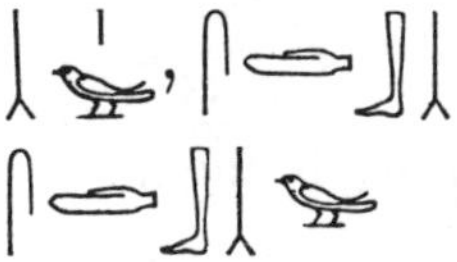 obstacle, disaster, calamity, misfortune.

		plur. of preceding.
seṭebḥ		to be ready, equipped.
seṭemu		edicts for slaughter.
seṭen		distinguished.
Seṭeḳ		a proper name.
seṭeḳa		to cover.
seṭeḳaut		sleep.
seṭet	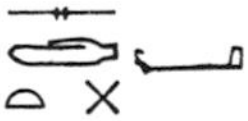	to break.
seṭeṭ	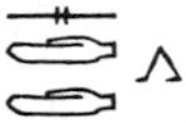	to travel.
seth	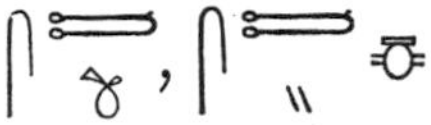	scent, unguent.
sethen		distinctions.
sethenem	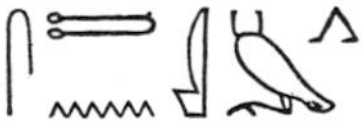	to make to walk.
sethes	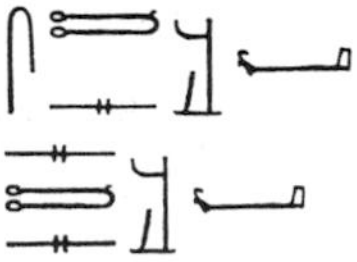	to raise up, lift up.

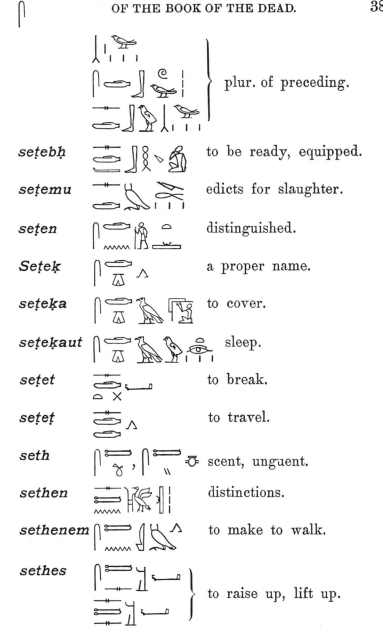

sethes 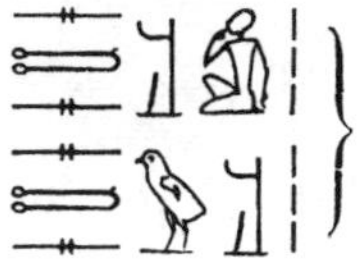 to praise, extol, "lift up", or "raise", a song or hymn, praisings.

sethesu  props, supports.

sethesu  supporters.

sethes Shu  what Shu raises up, *i. e.*, the sky.

sethesu Shu  the supports of Shu, *i. e.*, the four cardinal points.

sethes 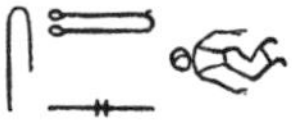 to be laid out.

sethes 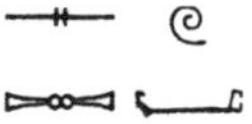 to knit together.

sethesu  libations.

setheken  to have sexual union.

setcha  to make to set out, travel.

setchami  to protect (?).

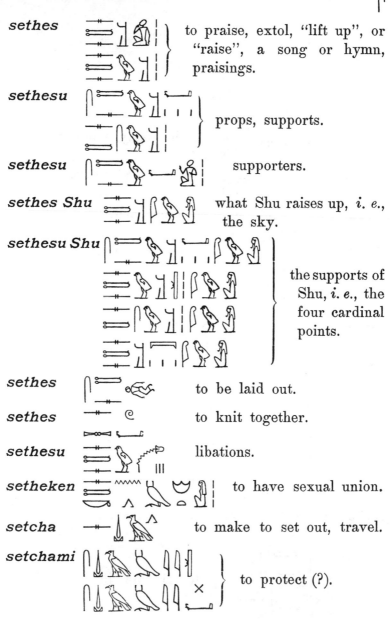

setchit  seeds of a plant (?).

setcheb  to oppose, be in the way of, obstruct.

setchefa  to feed with food celestial or terrestrial.

setcher 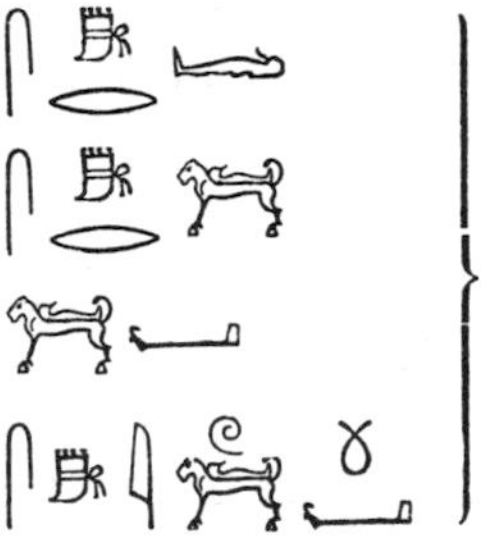 to lie down in sleep or death; dead, dead one;  the dead.

 bier.

setcheser 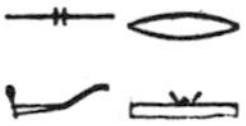 to sanctify.

setcheṭfu  to wound.

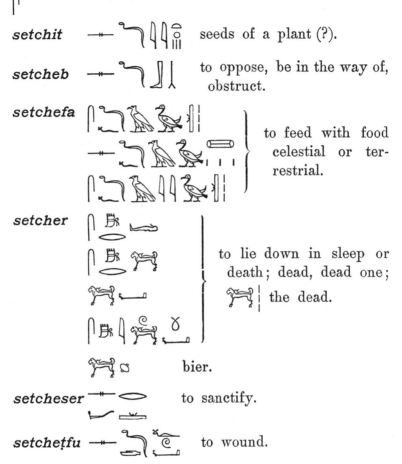

SH.

she pool, lake, laver; plur.

She asbiu Lake of flames.

She Aḳeb Lake of Aḳeb, *i. e.*, celestial ocean.

She Åqer Lake of Åqer, *i. e.*, the perfect lake (?).

She ur Great Lake.

She Maāti Lake of Maāti.

She em Māfket Lakes of Turquoise.

She Nu Lake of Nu.

She en Amu Lake of Fire.

She en Åsår Lake of Osiris.

She en Māat Lake of Māat.

She en Nesersert Lake of Fire.

	Lake of Fire.
She neter	Lake of the god, *i. e.*, Osiris.
She en Ḥeru	Lake of Horus.
She ḥeru	Lake of the celestial ones.
She ḥeḥ	Lake of Millions of years.
She en ḥesmen	Lake of Natron.
She Ḥetep	Lake of the god Ḥetep.
She ent ḥetch	Lake of Light.
She en khebentiu	Lake of the wicked.
She en kharu	Lake of the geese.
She en seḥetep	Lake of propitiation.
She en seshet	Lake of Fire.
Shet Ṭemui	Lake of the two knives.
She Tchesert	Lakes of the goddess Tchesert.
sha	field.

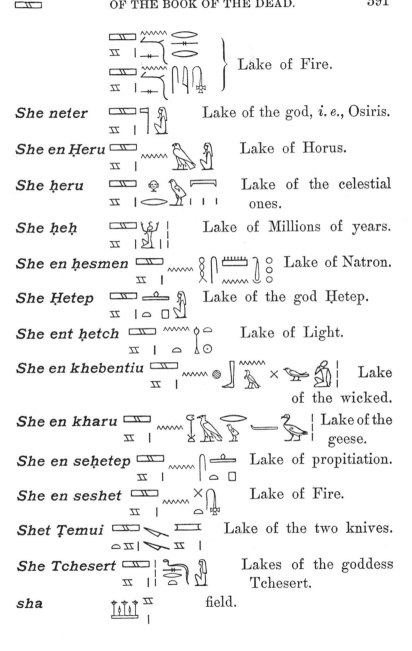

sha		bread-cakes, food.
sha		plants.
sha		to destine, predestine, foreordain.
shaȧ		pig.
shaȧs		to travel, journey, go forward.
shaā		one hundred.
shaā		to begin, beginning.
		unto, … unto all eternity.
Shau		the name of a city or town.
shauabti		the name of the figure inscribed with the VIth Chapter of the Book of the Dead.
shauā		book, writing.
Shai		the god of Luck or Destiny.
Shabu		the name of a god.
shabu		water plants.
shabti		See SHAUABTI.

shabu  cakes, food.

Shapuneterȧrka  name of an Utchat.

shamu  damned (?).

Sharshar... 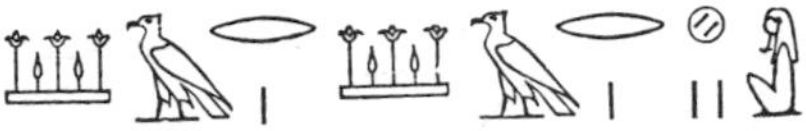 a proper name.

Sharsharkhet 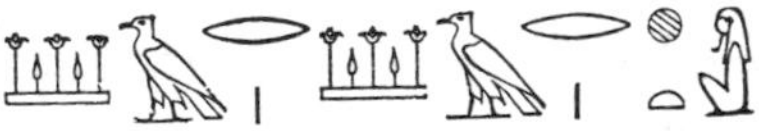 name of an Utchat.

Sharshatȧkatȧ  a proper name.

shaheb 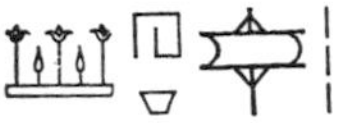 south wind.

shas  to journey, travel.

Shakanasa  a proper name.

Shaka  a name of Ȧmen.

shā 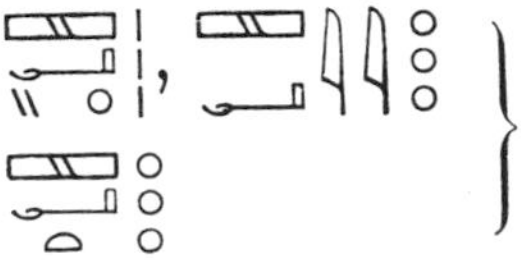 sand.

shā (?)

shāt 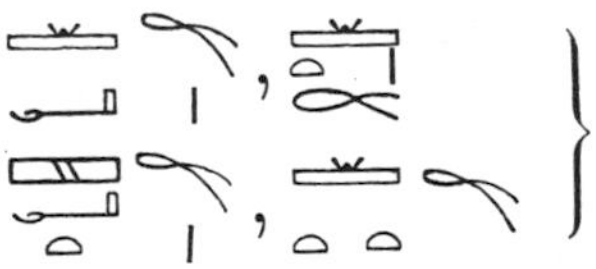 book, writing, document.

 Book of praise.

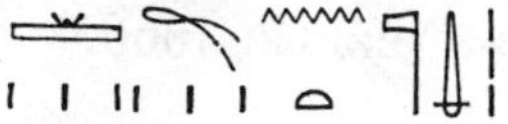 Books of holy words.

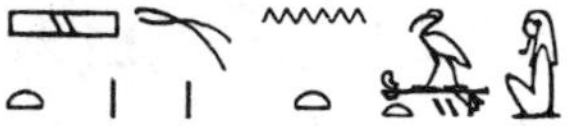 Book of Thoth.

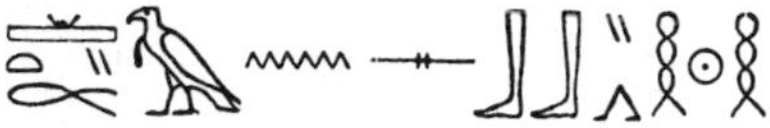 Book of traversing Eternity.

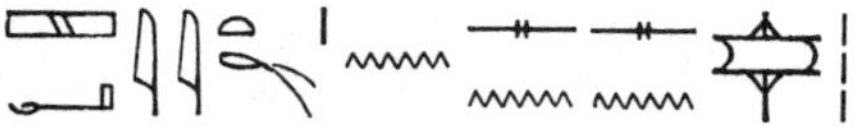 Book of Breathings.

shā  to cut, cut away, cut off.

shāit 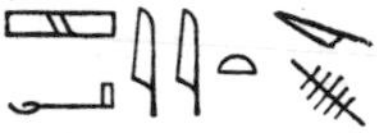 knife.

shāmu  decorated (?).

shāt  knife, knives.

shāṭ  to cut, to wound, hack off.

shāṭ
shāṭet 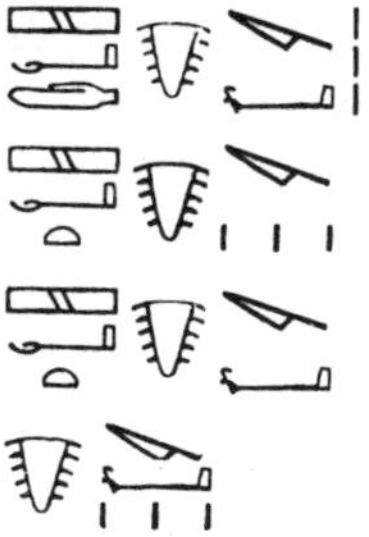 woundings, cuttings, slaughter, knives (?).

 slaughter-blocks (?).

shu  to be dry, hot.

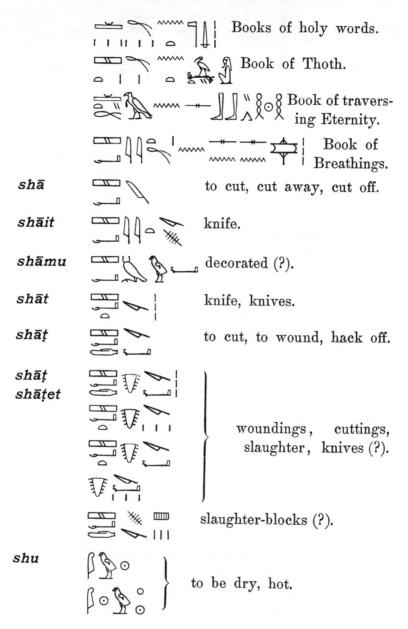

Shu  the god of the air, dryness, light, etc.; the counterpart of Tefnut.

Shut 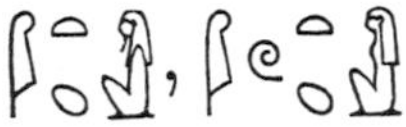 fem. of preceding.

Shuu 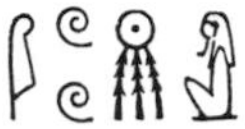 the Sun-god.

shuit  light.

shuit  the abode of light (?) sky (?).

shu  to lack, be needy, in want of.

shu  plants, papyrus.

shut  feather.

shuti 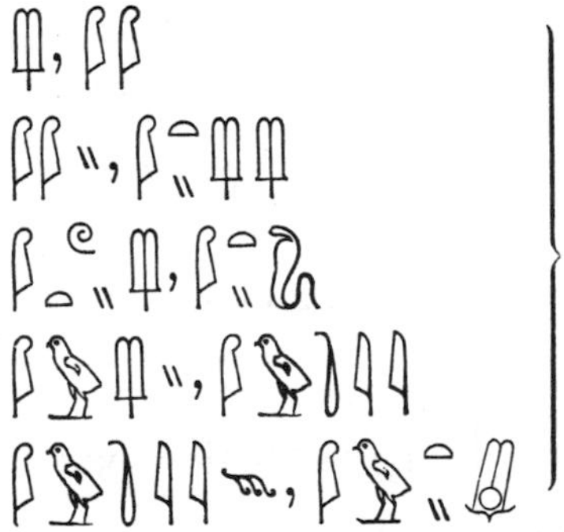 the two-feather crown, *e.g.*, that worn by Åmen.

shut  feathers, plumage.

shuti  merchant.

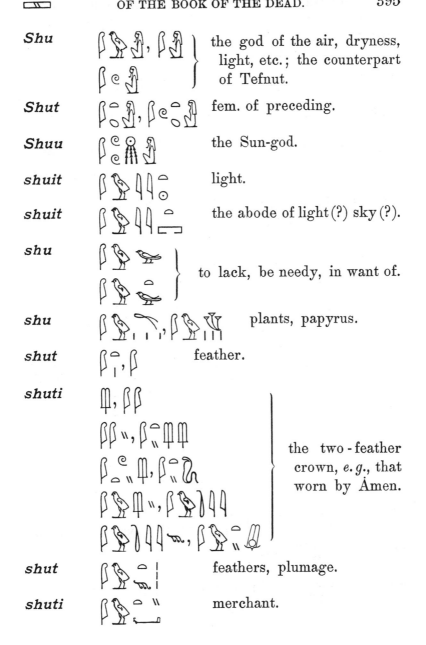

shutet  . . . .

shebu  cakes, food.

shebeb 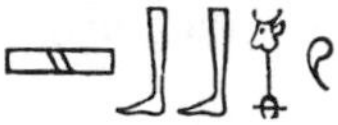 throat.

Shebeb en Ḳesti 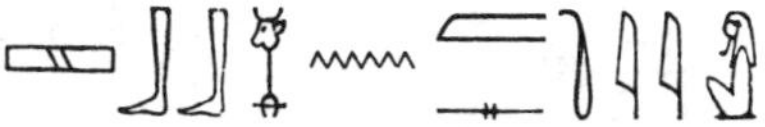 name of a part of a boat.

sheben 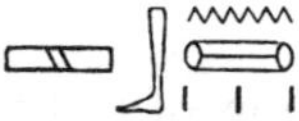 cakes, food.

shebenu  mixed.

shep 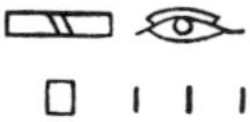 blind.

shepent 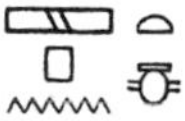 vessel.

sheps 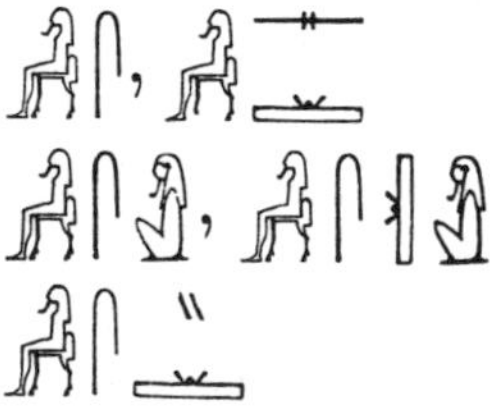 to be holy, venerable, sacred, worshipful, majestic, awesone.

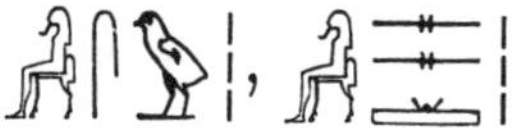 holy beings.

shept ȧb  shame of heart, loathing.

shefu 

shefut  boils, blains, insolence, arrogance.

sheft 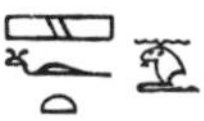 ram (?), strength, power, terror; plur. 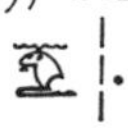.

terrible of face.

sheft, *shefit* — strength, power, terror.

Shefit, *Shefiti* — the Ram-god, symbol of strength.

Shefshefit — strength, power, might.

shem, *seshem* — to walk, go, travel.

to calumniate, set the mouth in motion against a man.

shemiu, *shemt* — journeys, goings about, travellers.

shemu — the season of summer.

shemem — to be hot.

shemmet — fire, flames.

shemmet — poison.

shemā		to sing, or play a musical instrument.
shemāit		a singer.
shemā		the south;  stones of the south.
Shemāit	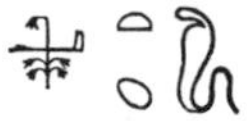	the goddess of the South, *i. e.*, Nekhebit.
shems		to follow, to accompany, be the member of a bodyguard.
shemsi	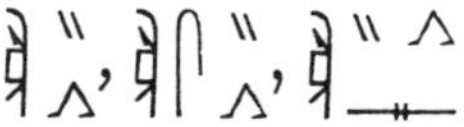	follower, body-servant.
		plur. of preceding.
		chief servants of Osiris.
		servants of His Majesty.
shen		to revolve.

shen, *shenit*, *shenu*, *shenn* — circuit, circle, orbit; circuit of the earth.

shen — hair.

shenȧ — hair.

Shenȧt-pet-utheset-neter — the name of a sacred cow.

Shenȧt-sheps-neteru — the name of a sacred cow.

shenā — granary.

shenā — breast, body.

shenā — to turn back, repulse.

shenā — repulse, violence (?).

shenāāu — wayfarers (?).

shenā  to turn back, repulse.

shenstet 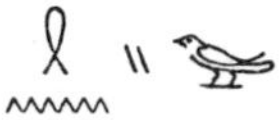 wickedness.

sheni  hair, locks.

shenit  storm.

sheniu  chamber.

shenit 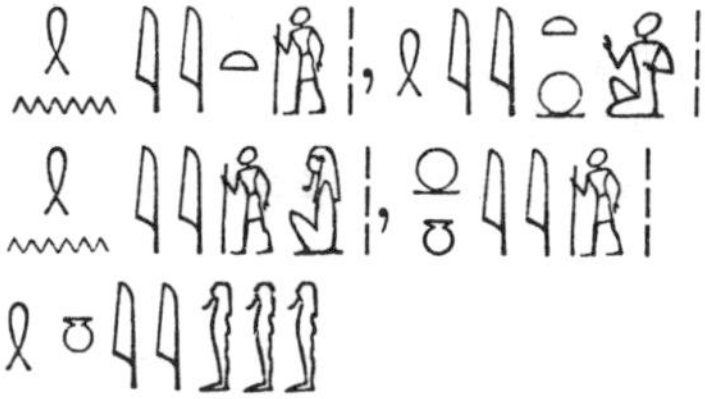 chiefs, princes.

shenbet 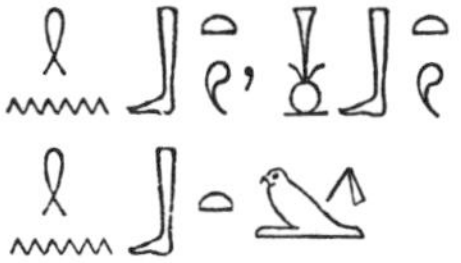 body.

shnemi 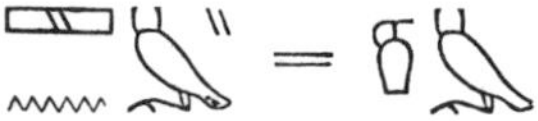

Shenmu  the name of a town.

shennu  a powder of some sort (?).

shennu snares (?).

shennu acacia trees.

Shennu the name of a town.

shens cakes, with shewbread.

shent flesh, skin (?).

shentu to curse, blaspheme.

shenti granary.

shenti heron.

shenti garment.

shentetu curse.

shenṭet a tree, the acacia.

shen-tȧ read .

Shentit the name of a goddess.

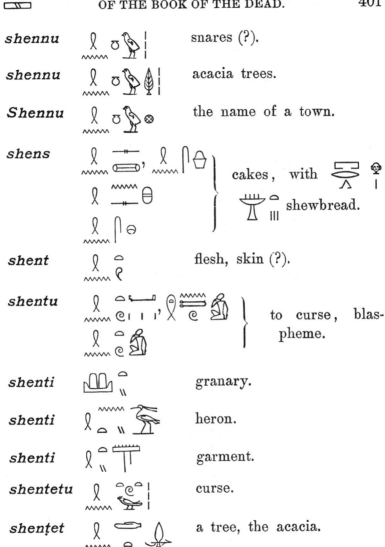

sher 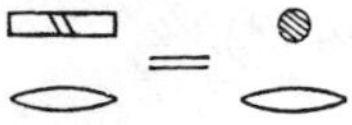 and .

[*sherr*  to be little.]

sherrȧu 
sherriu 
 — little ones, feeble men or gods.

sherȧt 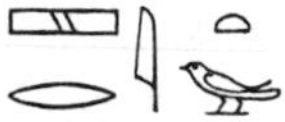
shert 
shertet  — little one or thing, something of no value.

Sherem  a proper name.

shersher 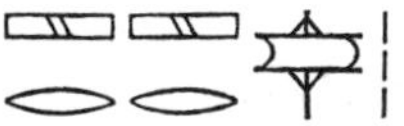 winds, breath.

shert 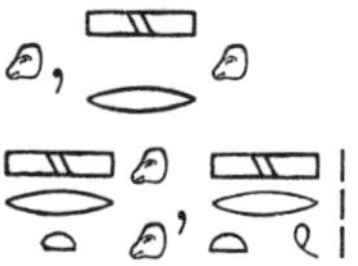 nose, nostrils.

shert  grain.

shert  cake, bread.

shes (?)  linen weavers (?).

shes 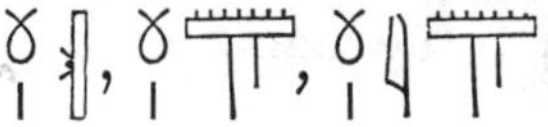 linen, a linen garment.

shes linen of the finest quality.

shes maāt "cord of law", *i. e.*, with unfailing correctness and regularity.

shes to be tied up, fettered.

shesui (?) the two eyes (?).

shesep palm, a measure.

shesep to take, undertake, accept, receive.

receivers.

heart's desire.

shesep to shine, be bright.

light. Note the forms and and SESHEP.

Shesep-temesu name of a fiend (?).

shesau skilled, able, intelligent, wise.

Shesmu  the headsman of Osiris.

Shes-khentet  a proper name.

sheta  tortoise.

sheta  to be hidden, secret, mysterious.

 hidden, hidden person or thing.

sheta  hidden thing, secret, mystery, something invisible and not understood.

 hidden places.

 hidden forms.

 hidden soul.

 hidden faces.

 hidden transformations.

 hidden things.

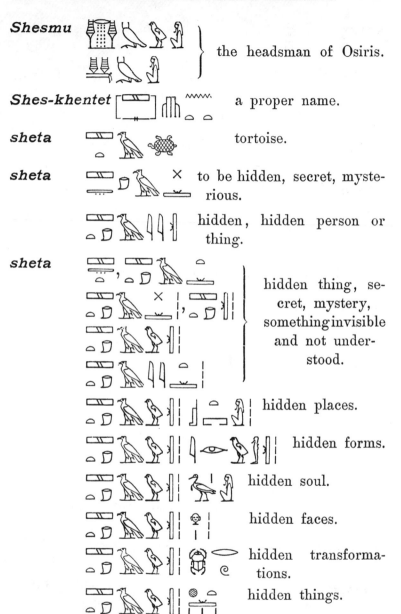

Shetait  ***Shetat*** — the "hidden place"; a name of the Other World of Seker at Ṣakkârah.

Sheta-ḥer  "hidden face"; a proper name.

Shetau-ā  "hidden of arm"; a proper name.

Shetet-pet  a proper name.

sheṭ 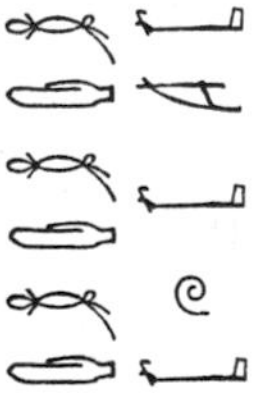 to break up the ground, dig out, tear open, to deliver, strengthen, tie, bind up. 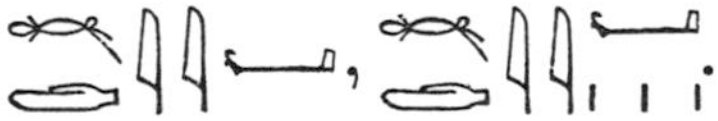

sheṭet 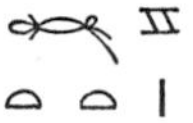 lake, pool; plur. 

sheṭit 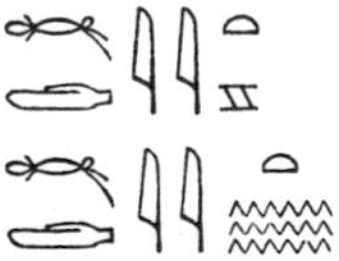 tank, cistern.

sheṭ  to read, recite a book or prayer.

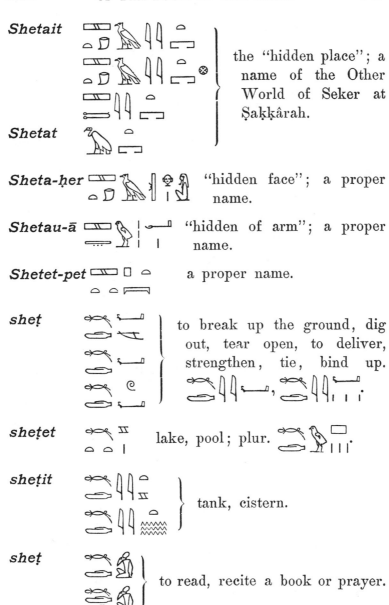

sheṭ 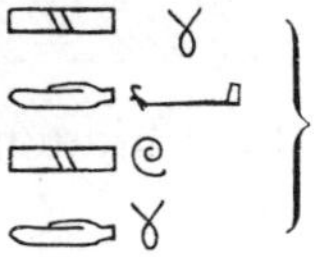 to swathe, to clothe.

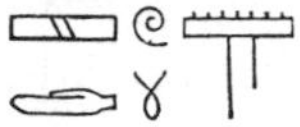 a garment.

 clothed, or covered, of arms.

sheṭu  leather straps.

sheṭḥu  crushed grapes (?).

Sheṭ-kheru 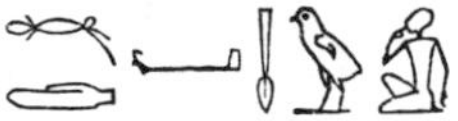 the name of one of the Forty-two Judges in the Hall of Osiris.

 K.

k  thee, thou, thy; with sign of the dual 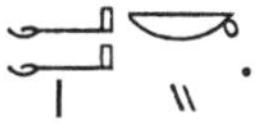.

ka  the double of a man or god, the personality of a man or god, self, the being of a man which is associated with the heart-soul , and is independent of the spirit-soul ; plur. .

Ka-ḥetep  a proper name.

kau 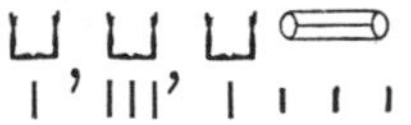 food.

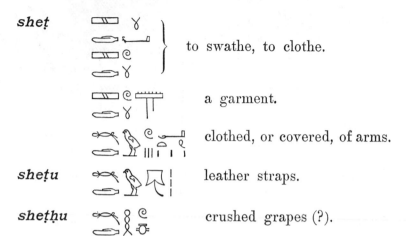

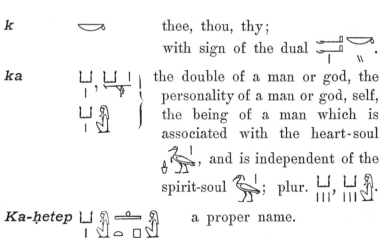

ka  bull.

 the divine bull.

Ka-Ȧmentet  "Bull of Amenti"; a name of Osiris.

Ka-ȧn-erṭā-nef-nebȧ-f 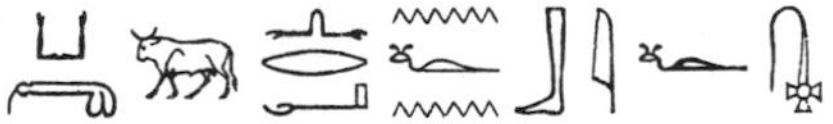 a proper name.

Ka-ur  "Great Bull".

Ka-ṭesher  "Red Bull".

Ka  "Bull husband of the cows".

kaut  cows.

ka  to think, to cry out.

 thought.

ka  verily, prithee.

Kaa  the name of a god.

kaiu  cries (?), criers (?).

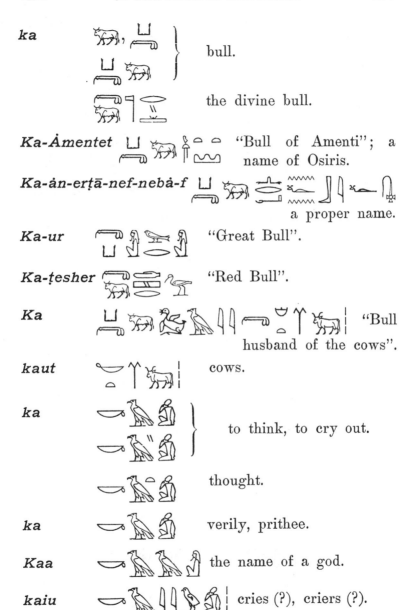

Ka-àri-k a proper name.

kaui a class of beings.

kabit lamentations.

karà shrine, chapel, sanctuary; , gods of the shrine.

Kaharsapusar-em-ka-ḥerremt a proper name.

Kasaika a proper name.

kat work, works, labours.

ki verily.

ki another. ... the one ... the other.

another man.

another chapter.

another person.

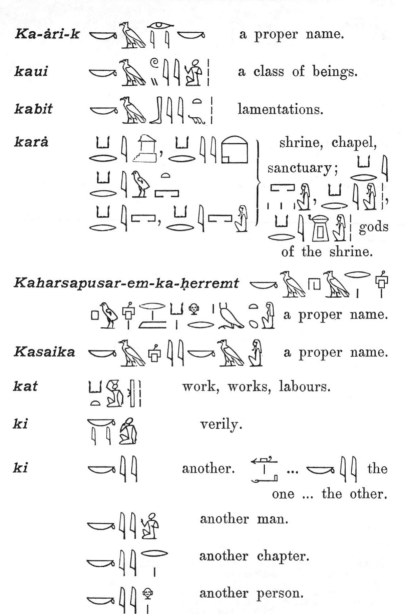

	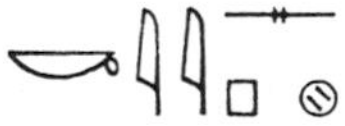	another time.
	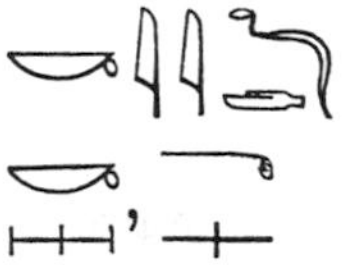	another reading, a variant.
kuȧ		I.
kep	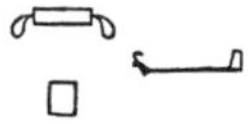	to hide.
		hidden place.
Kep-ḥer	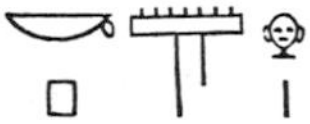	a proper name.
kefa	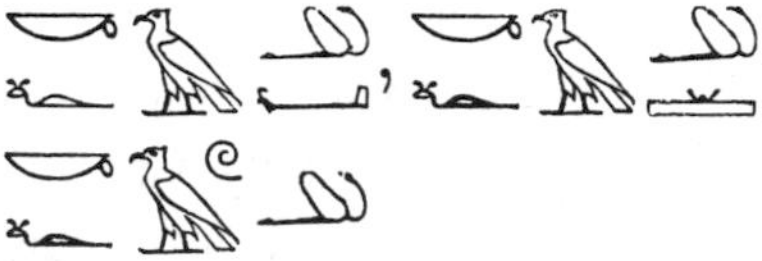	to act with violence, expel, drive away.
kefa	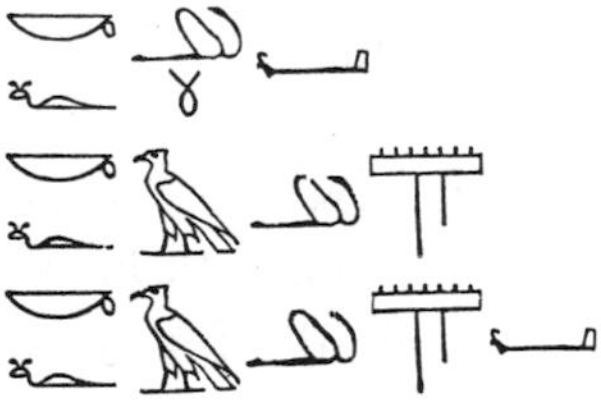	to remove the clothes, strip, undress.   uncover.
kem		to make an end of, to finish.
	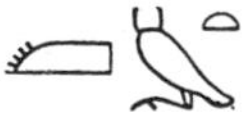	the end.
kem		black.
Kem-ur	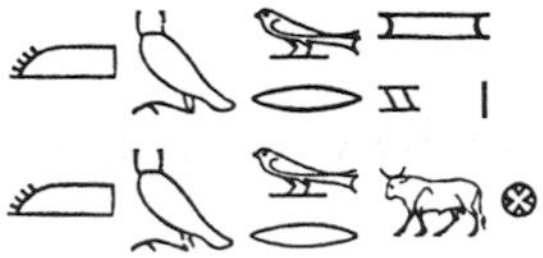	the name of a town and of a lake.

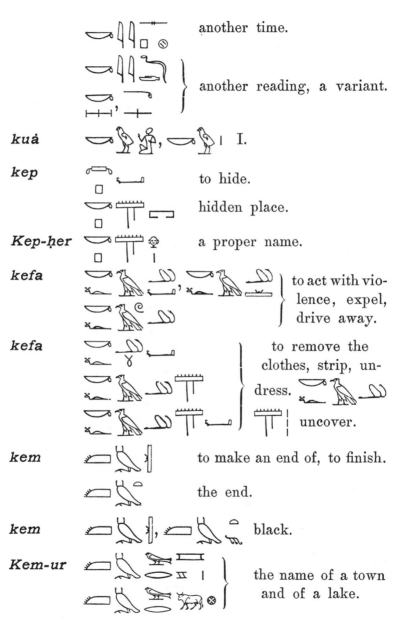

Kemt  the "black" land, *i. e.*, Egypt.

Kemkem  the name of a god.

kenȧ  to speak.

Kenemet  the name of a town.

kenemet  night, darkness.

Kenemti  the name of one of the Forty-two Judges in the Hall of Osiris.

kenḥu (?)  night.

Kenset  Nubia. The correct reading appears to be Sᴛɪ, *i. e.*, the "land of the bow".

Ker 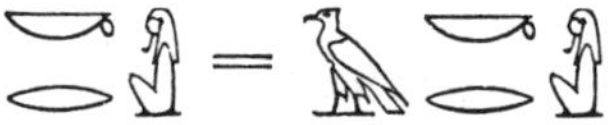 (?).

kerit 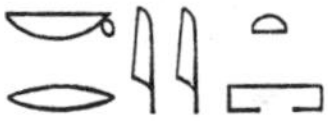 habitation, abode.

Keḥkeḥet  a proper name.

kes  to bow in homage.

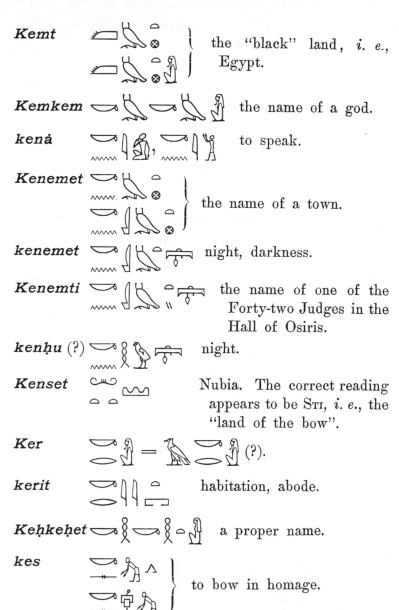

kesu  homage, bowings.

Kesemu-enent  a class of divine beings.

kek, kekui 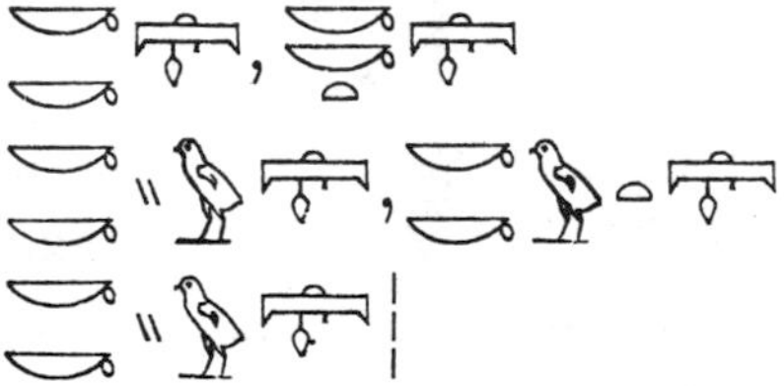 darkness, night.

ket  another.

ketuit 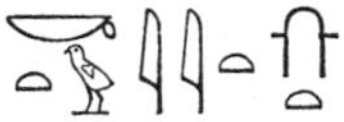 abode, habitation.

ketut  weapons, knives.

ket khu  other things.

ketet  little, bad.

⊿ Q.

qa  to be high, exalted, height.

 High God.

 Exalted one.

 doubly high, very high.

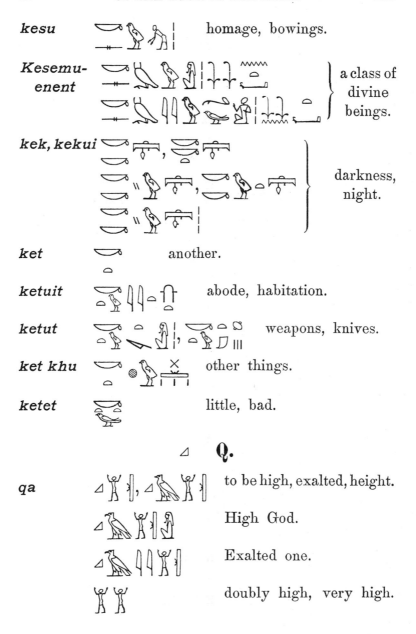

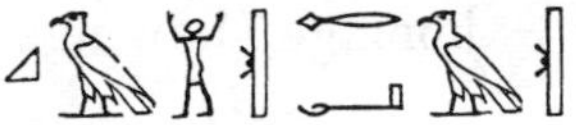 exceedingly high.

 height of heaven.

 high, *i. e.*, loud-voiced.

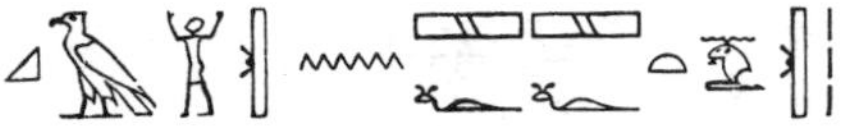 most terrible.

 high up on the standard.

 the god of the very high plumes.

Qa-ha-ḥetep  a proper name.

Qa-ḥer  a proper name.

qa  high ground, hill, staircase.

qa  to be rotten, putrefy.

qa  form.

qaat  bolts, fastenings.

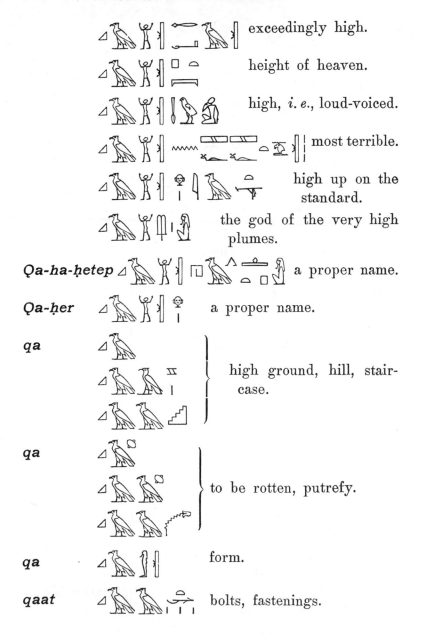

qaȧ  form, image.

Qai  the name of a god.

qab  the innermost part.

 the centre of Ȧmenti.

qabt  a part of the body.

Qabt-ent-Shu-erṭā-nef-em-sau-Ȧsȧr 
 a proper name.

qamȧi  incense, unguent.

qamemt  to weep (?).

qart  a part of the Other World.

qart  bolts, fastenings.

Qaḥu  a proper name.

qaḥit  fire (?).

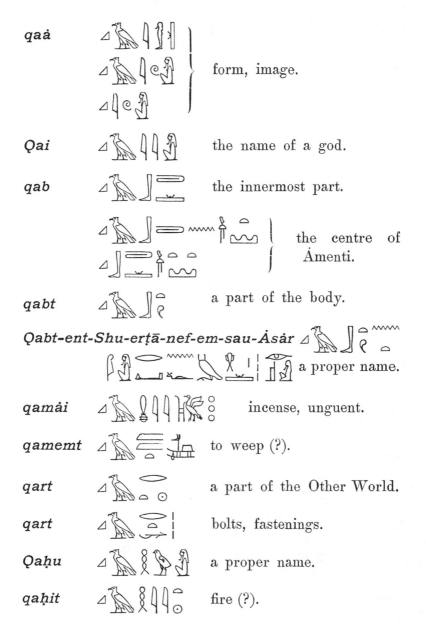

qasu  to tie, bind, fetter.

qass

 fetter.

 fetters.

qaqa  hill.

qā 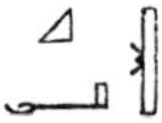 be provided with (?).

qāḥu  arm and shoulder; dual 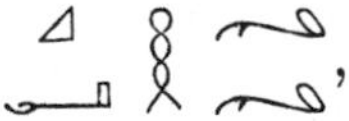, plur.  

qāḥ 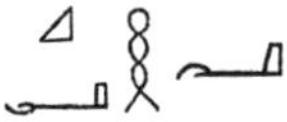 side of (?).

qu  limbs, flesh.

qeb 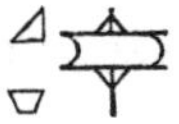 north wind.

qebbi 
qebti  shade, shadow.

qeb ,  see .

qebḥ 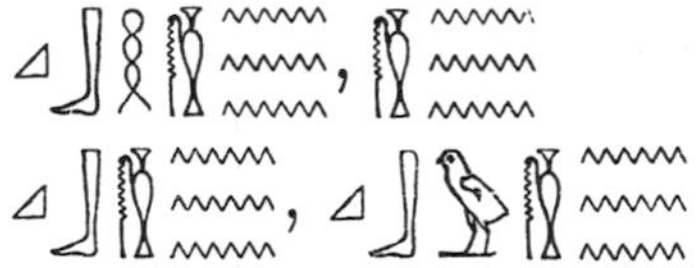 to cool, refresh, be cooled, refreshed.

 place of cooling, the bath (?).

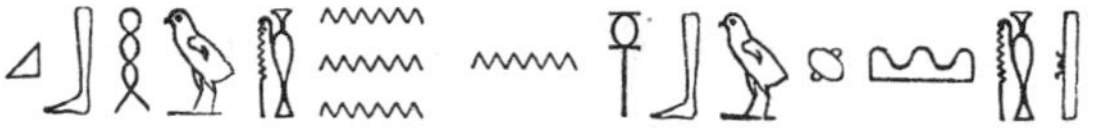 the cool water of the First Cataract.

Qebḥ  the marsh of water-fowl.

Qebḥ-senu-f  one of the four sons of Horus.

Qebti  Coptos.

qefen  baked cake.

Qefenu  the name of a town.

qefṭenu  ape.

qema  to create, to fashion, to form.

qemama 

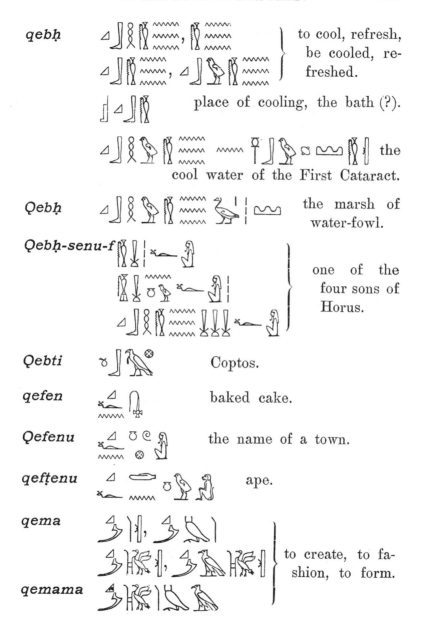

qemam	to create, to fashion, to form.
qemamu	to create, to fashion, to form.
	creatress.
	god of creation.
qemḥ	leaves of a tree.
qem-tu	to overturn.
qemṭu	to say, repeat.
Qen	a proper name (?).
qen	fat.
qen	to do evil, be evil.
qen	to be strong, bold, brave.
qenȧ	to embrace, embrace.
qenȧt	a kind of incense.

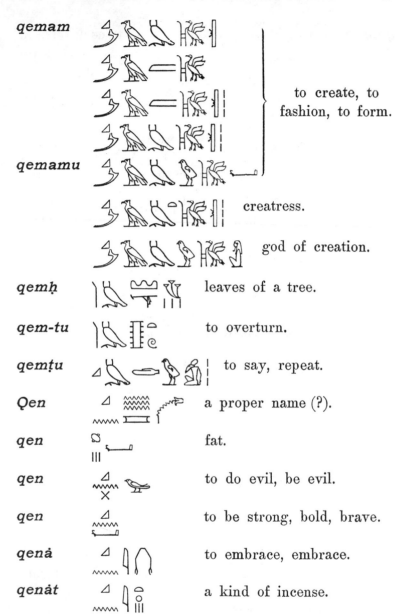

qeni		a kind of linen.
qenu		strong.
qenbet / *qenbit*		a class of officials, human or divine.
Qenna		a proper name.
qenert		grain (?) fruit (?).
qenqen		to beat, to strike.
qenqen		to feed, eat.
Qenqentet		the name of a lake in Sekhet-Åaru.
qer		the north wind.
qerȧ		storm, thunder, a proper name.
qerȧs		sepulture, burial.
qerfi	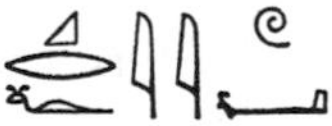	to tie, be tied.
Qernet		the name of a town.
qert, qerrt		cave, cavern.

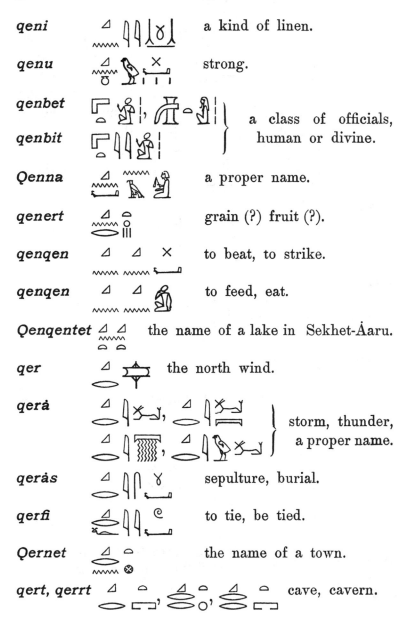

qerti  the name of the two caves near Philae wherein the Nile rose; the name of one of the Forty-two Judges in the Hall of Osiris.

qeres 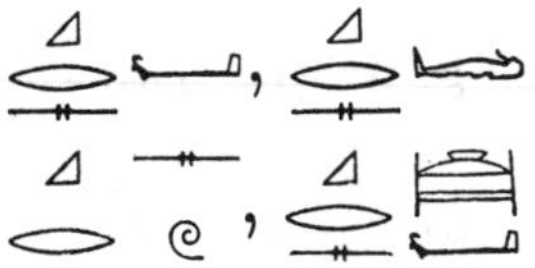 to bury; dead body.

qersu  coffin, sarcophagus.

qerset

qerset 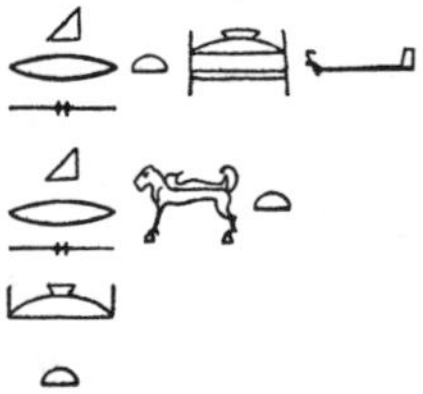 burial.

qerqer 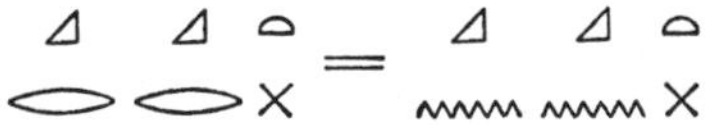

qert  bolt, fastening; .

qeḥḥtum (?)  castrated animals for sacrifice (?).

qes  burial (?).

qesu (for ***qersu***) 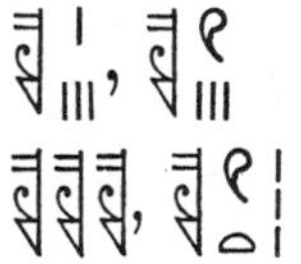 bones.

qesu (***qersu***)  preserves (of birds).

Qesi  Cusae, the capital of the XIVth nome of Upper Egypt.

qesen  to be evil, bad.

qeq  see Ȧm to eat.

Qetetbu  a proper name.

qeṭ 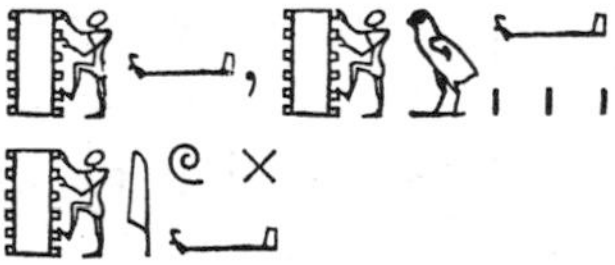 to build.

qeṭ 

qeṭu  to draw, sketch, make a plan or design; work of the artist.

qeṭu  sailors, mariners, crew of a boat.

Qeṭu  a fiend.

qeṭ  orbit, circle, like, similitude, character, dispositions.

 likewise, also, totality.

qeṭt 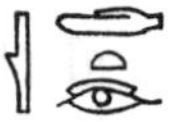 slumber.

 K.

ḳa  to besiege.

ḳa  filth, dung.

ḳa  to stink.

ḳaut
ḳau  calamity, calamities, misery, to suffer want, to lack something or anything.

ḳai  lake.

ḳau  a substance offered to the gods.

ḳauasha  to break.

ḳab  to depart (?).

ḳabti  the hair of some portion of the body.

ḳaf — ape; plur. .

ḳas — chamber.

ḳast (?) — . . . .

ḳat — claw, limb.

ḳatu — thoughts, meditations.

ḳuat — to besiege.

Ḳeb — = , (?)

ḳeb — the celestial ocean.

ḳeba — to suffer, be in misery.

ḳeba — to cast an evil glance (?).

ḳeba — some wooden object.

ḳem — to find, discover.

something found.

ḳemḳem	to discover, find out.
Ḳem-ḥeru	a class of divine beings.
ḳemut	weak, evil beings.
ḳemḥ	to see.
ḳemḥet	eye.
Ḳemḥu	the name of a god.
Ḳemḥusu	a proper name.
ḳemḥut	hair (?).
ḳen	weak, feeble, helpless.
ḳenn	weak, feeble, helpless.
ḳenu	cattle.
Ḳem-ur	a proper name.
Ḳen-ur	a proper name.
Ḳer-ur	a proper name.
ḳenut	deeds, documents, records.
Ḳenḳenur	the name of a god.

ḳent  slit.

ḳer  moreover.

ḳert 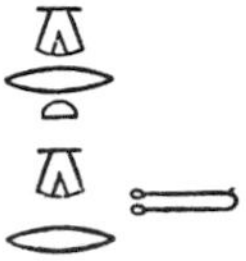 but.

ḳer  to be silent.

ḳerḥ 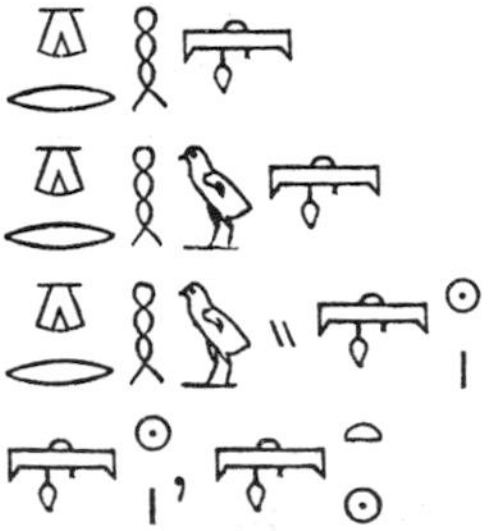 night, darkness.

Ḳersher  a proper name.

ḳer[ḳ]  to have, to hold, possess.

 possessor.

 possessions.

ḳer[ḳ]  lie, falsehood, deceit.

 lie, falsehood, deceit.

Ḳer[ḳ]et  the name of a town.

ḳeḥ  weak, helpless, wretched.

ḳes  one half.

ḳes  side; dual 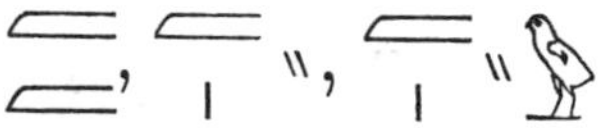 both sides; plur. .

 left side.

 right side.

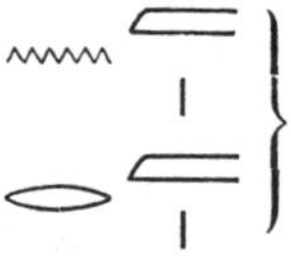 near, by the side of.

ḳesu  to anoint, ointment.

Ḳesui 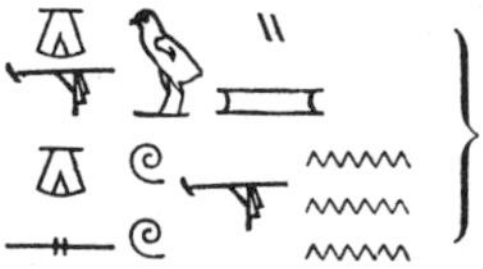 the name of a canal (?).

Ḳestȧ  one of the Four Sons of Horus.

ḳestȧ  scribe's palette.

ḳesh 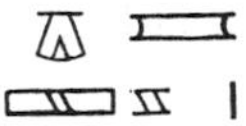 pool, lake.

T.

t 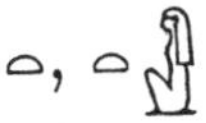 thy.

ta  the;  what is his, his.

ta  to be hot, to burn.

tau  flame, fire, hot, angry.

Ta-reṭ  the name of one of the Forty-two Judges in the Hall of Osiris.

ta 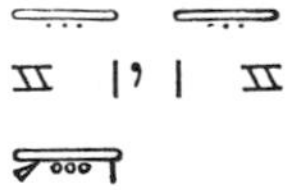 land, ground, country, the earth, the world.

taui  the "Two Lands", *i. e.*, Upper and Lower Egypt.

taiu — lands, countries, the world, all lands.

— the regions of the Other World.

— earth-gods.

Ta āb — "pure land", *i. e.*, the Other World.

Ta ānkhtet — "land of life", *i. e.*, the grave.

Ta ur — "great land"; a part of Abydos.

Ta en Manu — "land of Manu", *i. e.*, the West.

Ta en Maāt — "land of Law", *i. e.*, the Other World.

Ta en maākheru — "land of triumph", *i. e.*, the Other World.

Ta Merȧ — "land of Merȧ", *i. e.*, Upper and Lower Egypt.

Ta Meḥ — "land of the North", the Delta.

Ta mes tchetta — "land of eternity", *i. e.*, the Other World.

Ta Nefer — "beautiful land", *i. e.*, the grave.

Ta Nent 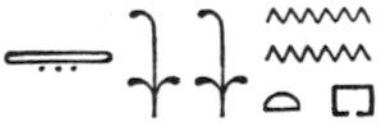 a portion of the Other World.

Ta neḥeḥ  "land of eternity", *i. e.*, the Other World.

Taiu nu neteru 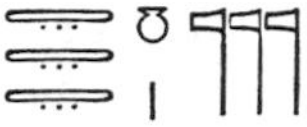 "lands of the gods", *i. e.*, heaven.

Ta remu  "land of fish".

Taui Rekhti 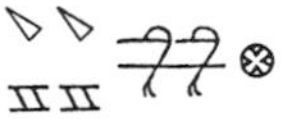

Taiu Rekhti  } "lands of the Rekhti", *i. e.*, Isis and Nephthys.

Ta kharu  "land of the *kharu* geese".

Ta Sekri 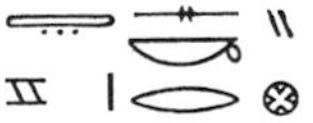 "land of Seker", *i. e.*, the Other World of Memphis.

Ta She  "land of the Lake", *i. e.*, the Fayyûm.

Ta shemā  "land of the South".

Ta sheta  "land of mystery", *i. e.*, the Other World.

Ta Sti 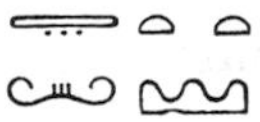 "land of the bow", *i. e.*, Nubia.

Ta qebḥ 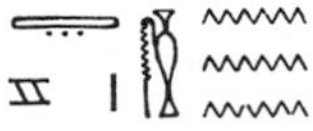 "land of cool water", *i. e.*, the Cataract region.

Ta Ṭuat 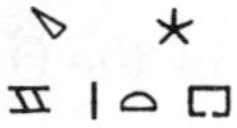 "land of the Ṭuat", *i. e.*, the Other World.

Ta Tchesert  "holy land", *i. e.*, the Other World.

Ta en tchetta  "land of eternity", *i. e.*, the Other World.

ta  bread, cakes.

 cakes made of fine flour.

 white bread.

 celestial bread.

 bread of Nenet (?).

 . . . . . .

Tait 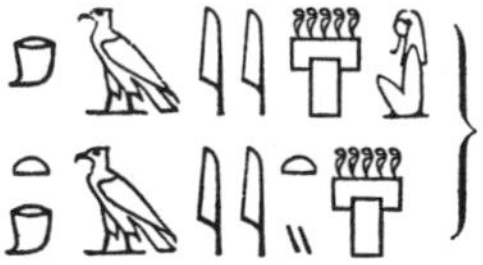 a proper name.

tait  sail.

Tait  the name of a goddess.

Tar  the name of a fiend.

taḥenen  to dip in water (?).

Ta-ḥer-sta-nef  a proper name.

Tatunen  the name of a god.

tȧt  emanation; plur. .

tiu  adorers.

tini 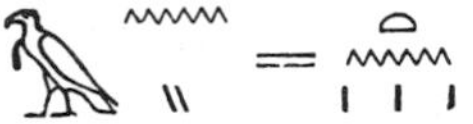 (?).

tu  a demonstrative particle.

tua  to adore.

tuȧ  I.

tui  a demonstrative particle.

tui  . . . . . .

tui  . . . . .

tuf  his.

tuni  . . . . . .

tur
turȧ 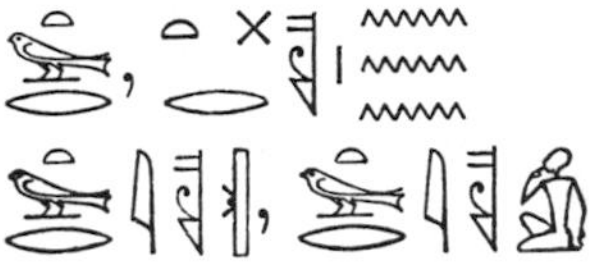 to cleanse, purify, be pure, clean.

tuk  thou.

tuḳ  apparel.

tut  to be like, similar.

tut  type, form, image, statue, portrait figure.

 as, like, similar.

tut  to arrange, group together.

tebu  to be shod, sandal (?).

teb  sandal.

tebi, tebt , 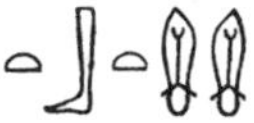 pair of sandals.

Tebu 
Tebti  } the name of a city.

tebteb  to walk.

tebtebti 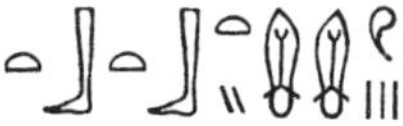 the soles of the feet (?).

tep  head, the tip, point, or top of anything.

tep  upon.

tepi 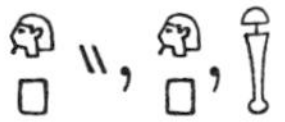 he who is on, the first, best, or finest of anything.

 the best of the offerings.

 the finest linen.

 the choicest flowers.

 the earliest hour of every day.

 the earliest dawn.

 the earliest twilight hour.

 the greatest happiness.

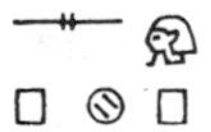 primeval time.

 New Year's Day.

 the best water in the lake.

 the original state of anything.

tep ā 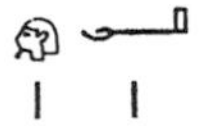 straightway.

tep ā  he of olden time, ancestor.

 she of olden time, ancestress. plur.  ancestors, forebears.

tep re 

tepi re

mouth, then what comes from the mouth, speech, voice, utterance; plur. .

tep reṭui  prescription, precept, command, chapter.

tep 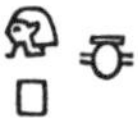 unguent of finest quality.

tep  a kind of goose.

tept  uraeus crown.

Tep-ṭu

Tep-ṭu-f 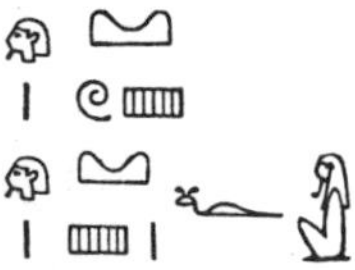 "he on the hill, or his hill"; a name of Anubis.

Tepa  the name of a cow.

tepȧ 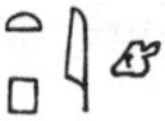 to snuff the air, breathe.

tepḥet 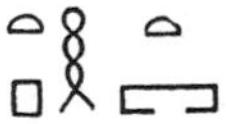 cavern, cave, den, hole in the ground; plur. .

tef  father.

tefa  that.

Tefnut 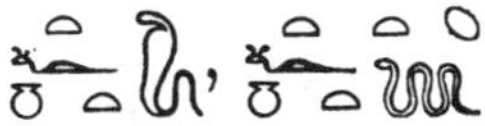 the name of a Water-goddess.

tem  to come to an end.

temt 
temtu 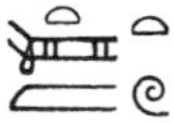
temti 
all, entirely;  wholly and entirely.

tem 
temem 
to be complete, whole, entire.

tem 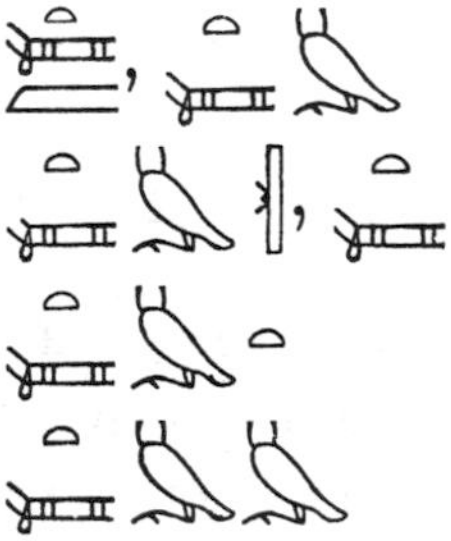 a particle of negation, no, not, without.

Tem		Tem, the "father of the gods".
Temu		
		Tem Harmakhis.
	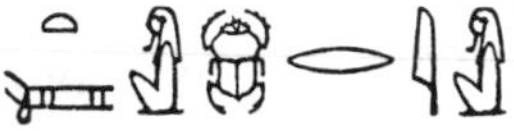	Tem Kheperȧ.
temam		basket (?).
temamu		stations (?).
temaāu(?)		winds.
temu		all people, mortals, mankind.
tememu	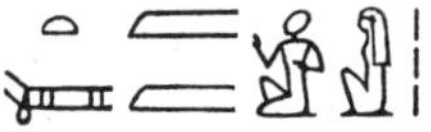	
temem		part of a sledge.
tememu		parts of a net.
Temem-re		a proper name.
Tem-sep		the name of one of the Forty-two Judges in the Hall of Osiris.

temt 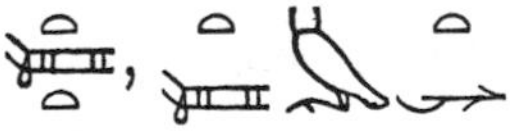 sledge.

ten  this.

ten 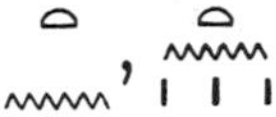 ye, you.

Teni  an ancient city near Abydos.

ten
teni
tenu 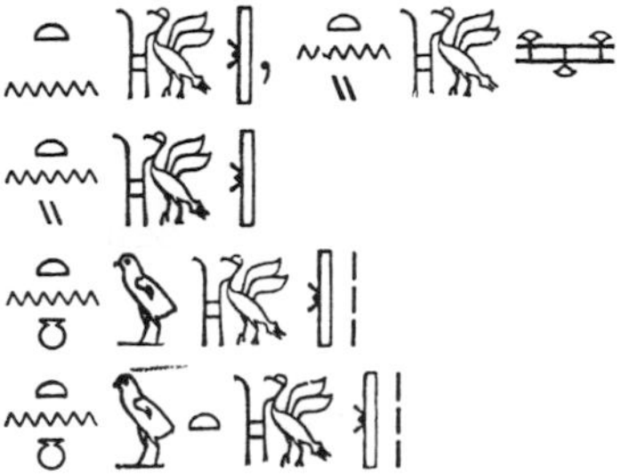 what kind of? what manner of? whence? where?

ten  to be or become great, great, distinguished.

tenait  light.

tenu  to divide, separate.

tenem  to turn back.

Tenemit  a proper name.

ter 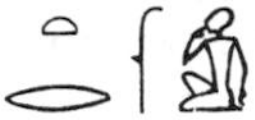 a particle, then, etc.

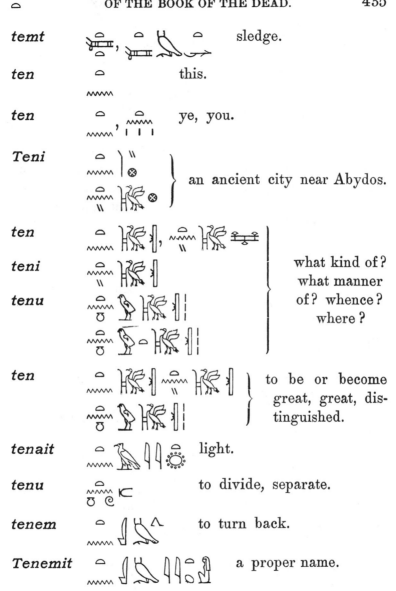

ter  time, season; plur. 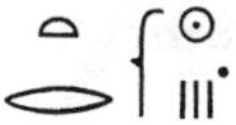.

terui  the two seasons, *i. e.*, morning and evening, or sunrise and sunset; .

teriti 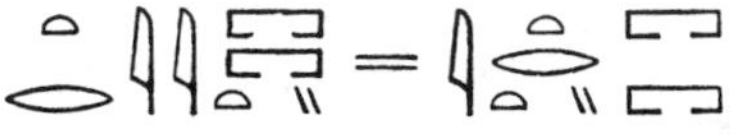 the northern and southern halves of the sky.

teru  stream.

teh 
teha  } to march against, attack.

tehami  strider.

tehenen  to appoint, raise up.

tiḥṭut  prayers, offerings.

tekh  the pointer or tongue of a balance;  "the pointer of the place of truth".

tekhni  hidden.

tekhtekh  to shake out the hair.

tesh 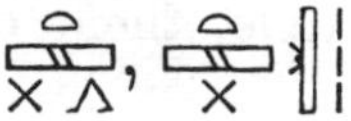 to depart, to go.

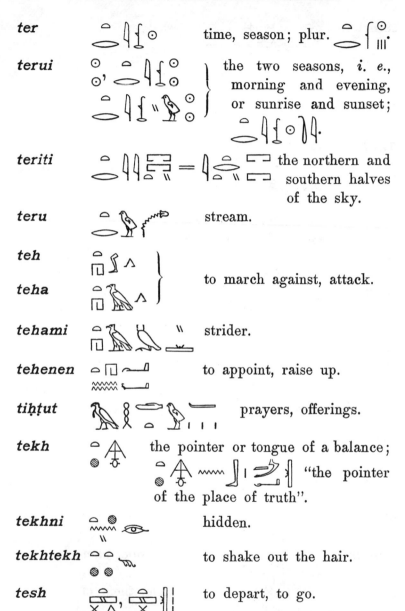

Teshtesh	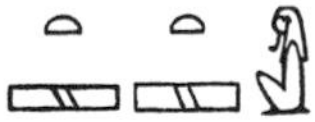	an image which was dressed up as Osiris.
teka		fire, flame, lamp.
tekau		fire, flame, lamp.
tekat		fire, flame, lamp.
Tekem		the name of a god.
tekem		to approach.
teken		to enter, go in.
		those who enter.
tektek		to pass, walk, go.
teḳa		to be hot, to kindle.
teḳas		to walk, march.
tetbu		to smear.

 Ṭ.

ṭa  to pass away.

ṭa  emission.

ṭaṭa  to pollute oneself.

ṭaȧu  the name of a garment.

ṭaȧr  restraint.

ṭā 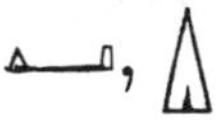
ṭāṭā 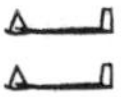
ṭāṭāu 
} to give, grant, set, place, ascribe.

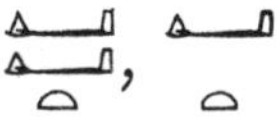 gift.

 giver, giving, placing.

 givers.

ṭāt ȧb 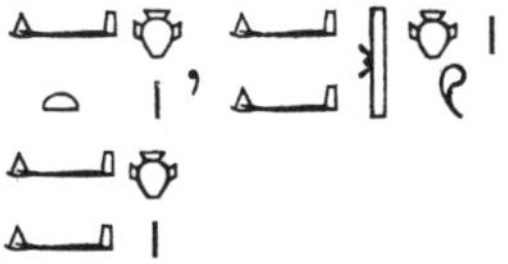 heart's desire.

ṭā  as auxiliary:

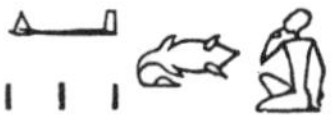 make to fear.

		cause to do.
		cause to be.
		cause to become, etc.
Ṭāṭāu		the city of Busiris or Mendes.
ṭit		gifts.
ṭu		evil, evil thing, sin, fault, wickedness, sinner.
ṭut		
		sin, evil.
		wickedness.
ṭuu		
Ṭut		
Ṭuṭu		the name of one of the Forty-two Judges in the Hall of Osiris.
Ṭuis (?)		the name of the rudder in the magic boat.
ṭuȧu		ale (?), drink.
ṭu		mountain; plur.

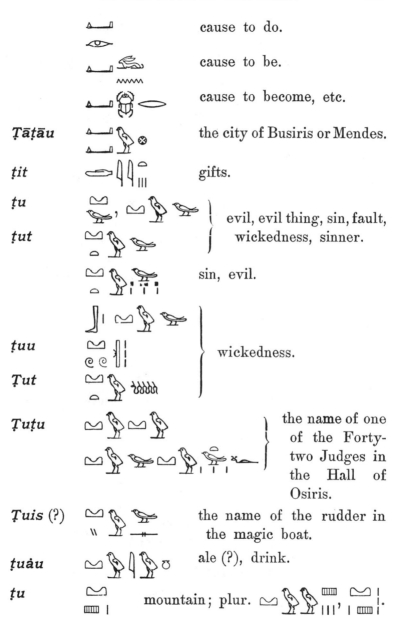

the two mountains.

two great high mountains.

Ṭu-en-Bakha Mount Bakha, the Mountain of Sunrise.

Ṭu-en-Neter-khert Mountain of the Other World.

Ṭut-f = (?).

Ṭu-menkh-rerek a proper name.

ṭu-ā to put forth the hand (?).

ṭua five; fifth.

ṭuau , to do something early in the day.

ṭuat dawn, daybreak, to-morrow.

ṭuait , dawn, daybreak, to-morrow.

ṭua , , , , , , to praise, worship, adore; praise.

praisers.

neter ṭua  to offer up thanksgiving.

Ṭuamutef  one of the Four Sons of Horus.

Ṭuat  The Other World.

 the everlasting Ṭuat.

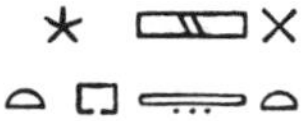 the hidden Ṭuat.

 the god of the Ṭuat.

 the beings of the Ṭuat.

ṭun  to lift up or stretch out the legs.

Ṭun-peḥti  the porter of the Second Ārit.

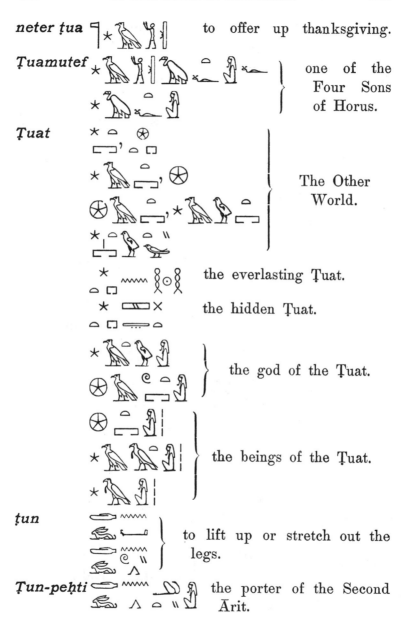

ṭur to be clean.

ṭurt . . . . . .

ṭeb horn; dual , .

ṭeb tomb (?).

ṭeb to be furnished or equipped.

ṭeb to wall up, to box in.

ṭebt , box, coffer, coffin, chest, tomb; plur. .

ṭebu , frame, framework of a net.

Ṭeb-ḥer-kehaat the herald of the Fifth Ārit.

ṭeben ,

ṭebenu to revolve.

ṭebḥ to pray, make supplication.

ṭebḥu (?) 
ṭebḥet  prayer, petition, supplication.

ṭebḥu 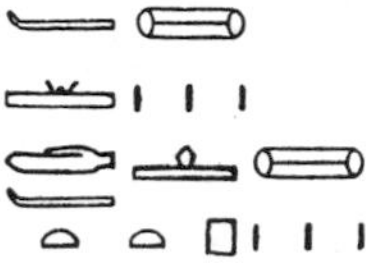 offerings, cakes, bread, etc.

ṭebḥu  funerary furniture.

ṭebḥ 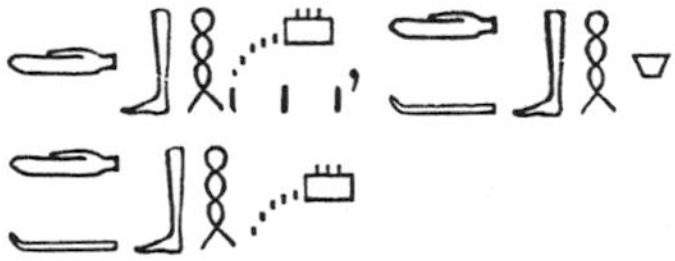 a grain measure.

ṭebt  block, slab, brick.

Ṭep 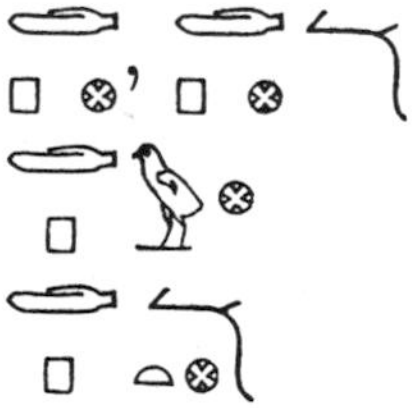 one half of the city of Buto,

ṭept 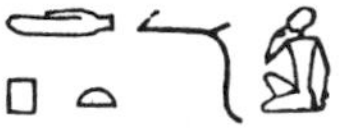 taste.

ṭepu 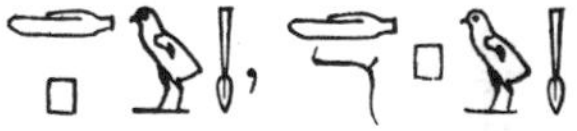 oar, paddle.

ṭept 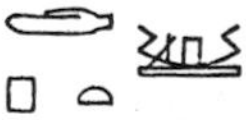 boat.

ṭem  to cut, stab.

 with  a piercing voice.

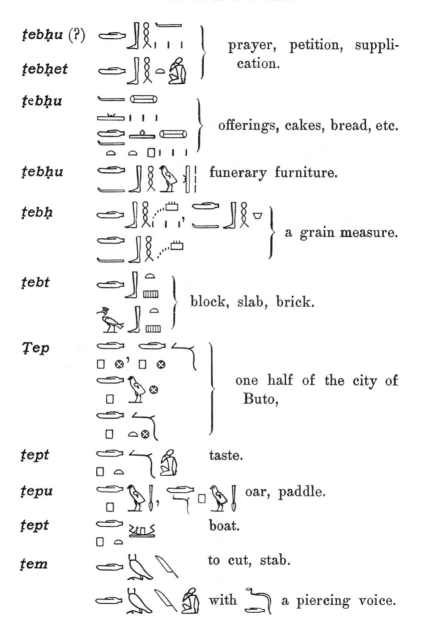

ṭem, *ṭemt* — knife, sword; plur.

two-edged knife, or sword (?).

Ṭem-r(?)*-khut-pet* . . . . . .

Ṭem-ur — a name of Osiris.

ṭemamt — a hairy covering, two locks.

ṭemam — to make an end of.

ṭemam (*sic*)

ṭemȧ, *ṭemȧi* — to unite, be united, touch, join.

ṭemȧ — city; plur.

ṭemi — shore, bank.

ṭemem — entire, totality.

ṭemṭ *ṭemtch*		to collect, gather together, unite, all, entire.
	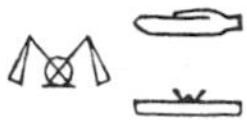	all, totality.
Ṭemṭiu		a class of divine beings.
ṭen	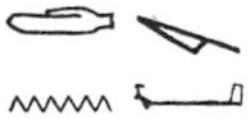	to cut off, or away.
ṭen		to place.
Ṭenȧ		the name of a god.
ṭenȧ		to separate.
ṭenȧt		bank of a canal, piece of land.
ṭenȧt	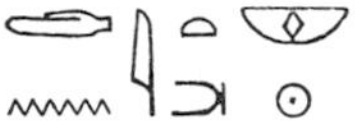	the weekly festival.
ṭenȧ		the name of a chamber.
ṭenȧ *ṭenȧt*	 	basket.
ṭenȧu		lot, share, division.
ṭeni		vessel.

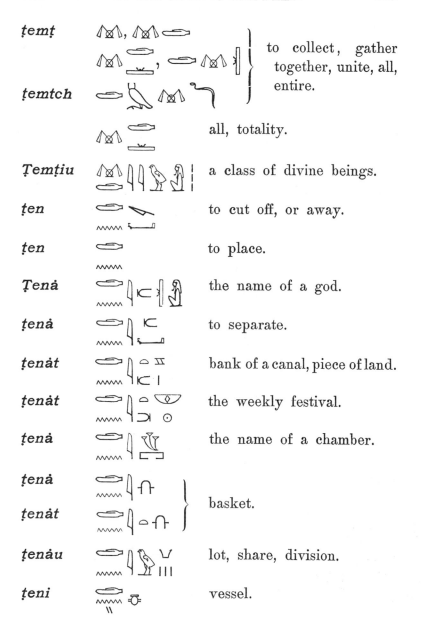

Ṭeni	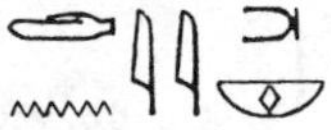	the name of one of the Forty-two Judges in the Hall of Osiris.
Ṭeniu		the god of old age.
ṭenu		to be distinguished.
ṭenb		to gnaw.
Ṭenpu		a proper name.
ṭenem		worms.
ṭenḥ		wing.
ṭenḥui		pair of wings.
ṭenḥṭenḥ		to fly.
ṭens		weights.
ṭent		abode.
ṭenṭ		slaughter.
ṭenṭen	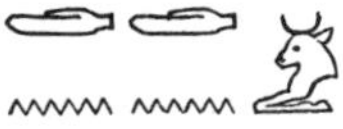	might, violence, valour.
ṭer	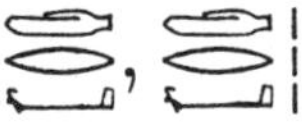	to destroy.

ṭerp		to offer.
ṭeref	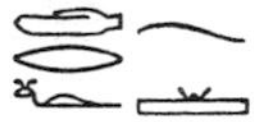	wisdom, skill, book of wisdom.
ṭehant		forehead.
ṭehen		to salute humbly.
ṭehen	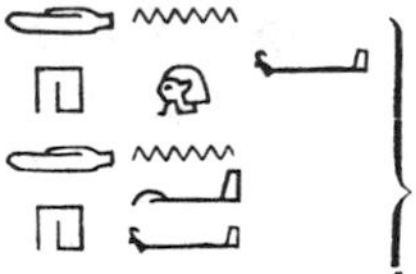	to place the forehead on the ground in token of homage.
ṭehen ta	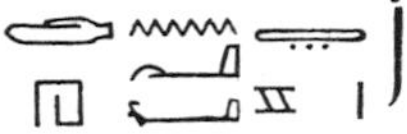	
Ṭehent		"brow of a hill"; a proper name.
Ṭeḥuti		the god Thoth, scribe of the gods, dweller in Khemenu 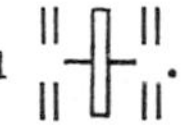.
Ṭeḥuti-Ḥāpi		Thoth-Ḥāpi.
Ṭeḥutit	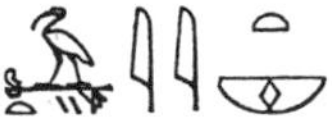	the Thoth festival.
ṭeḥer	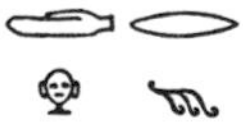	hair, feathers, foliage.
ṭeḥerȧu		injury, harmful person, sickness (?).
ṭes	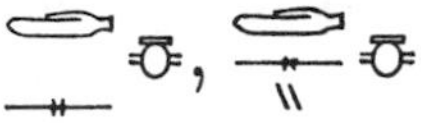	vase.

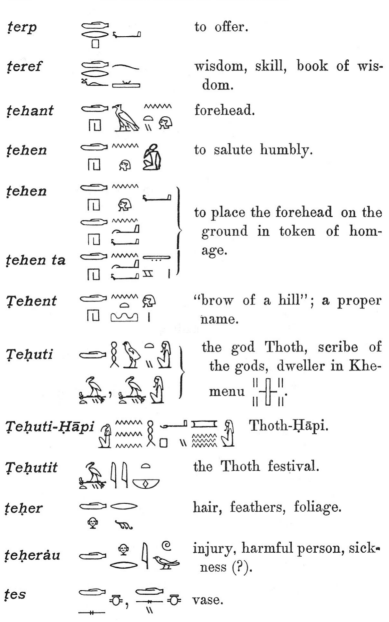

ṭes — to cut, smite.

ṭes — flint knife; plur. , .

ṭeser — sacred, holy.

Ṭesert-tep — a proper name.

Ṭesher — the name of a town and of its god.

ṭesher — to be red, become red, red, ruddy.

red ones, men or devils.

ṭesheru — gore, blood, redness (of clouds).

ṭesher — blood.

Ṭesher — the red land, *i. e.*, the desert.

ṭeshert — red flame.

ṭeshert — the Red Crown, *i. e.*, the Crown of Lower Egypt.

ṭeqer 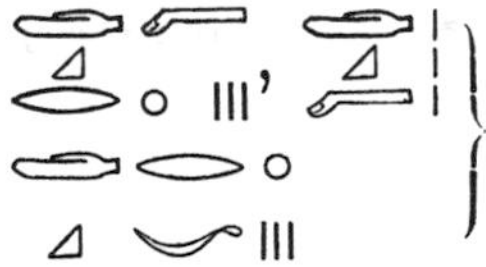 seeds, fruits.

ṭeḳa  to see.

 seeing.

 appearance.

ṭeḳaȧu  seeds, fruits (?).

ṭeḳ, ṭeḳeḳ  sight.

ṭeḳa  to hide.

ṭeḳa  plants.

ṭeḳas  to run, walk towards.

ṭetrit 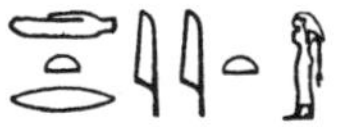 . . . . . Chap. XCIX, 12.

ṭet 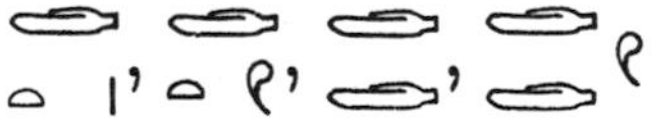 hand.

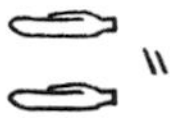 the two hands.

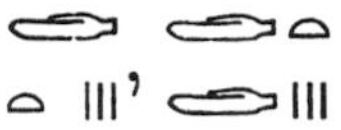 hands.

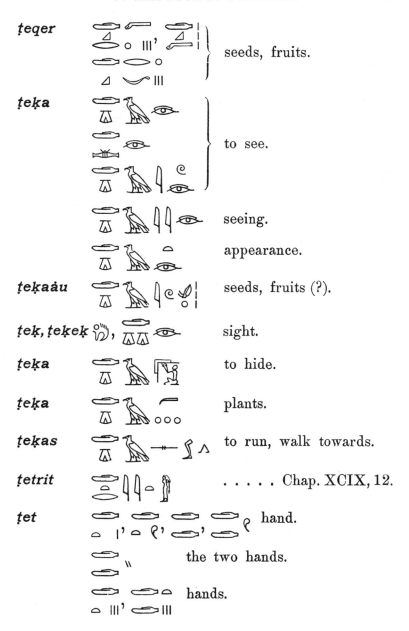

Ṭet-ent-Ȧst 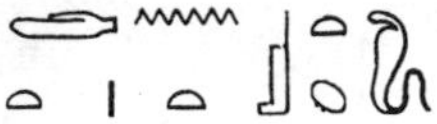 a proper name.

ṭeṭ / *ṭeṭṭeṭ* 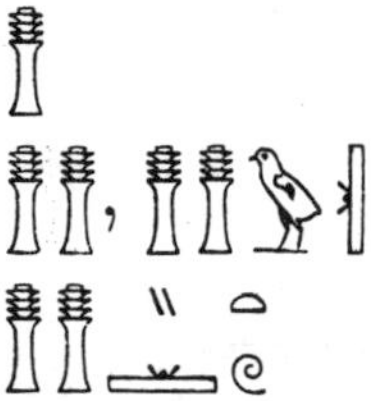 to stablish, be established, stable, permanent.

ṭeṭ  an amulet.

ṭeṭ 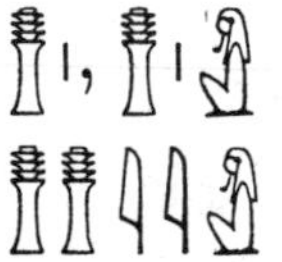 a figure, image, or tree trunk which was "set upright" during the festival of Osiris.

ṭeṭ  a building.

Ṭeṭu  the city of Busiris.

Ṭeṭt 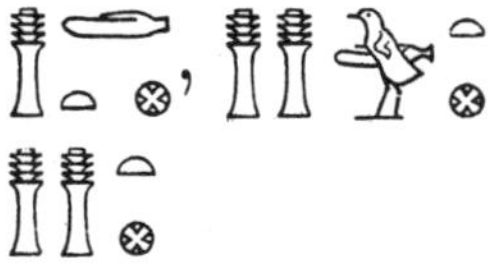 the city of Mendes.

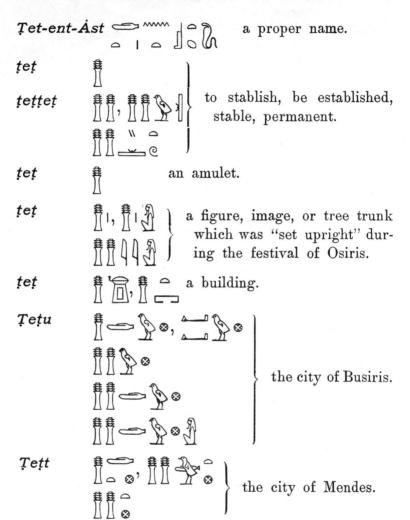

 TH.

th  thee, thou, thy,

thȧ (*tȧ*)  with verbs,  etc.

Thȧnasa (*Tȧnasa*)  a proper name.

thȧthȧ 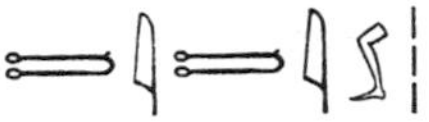 thighs.

thu  thou.

thut ȧs  behold!

thui  . . . .

theb (*teb*)  sandals.

Thefnut 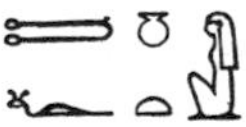 the name of a goddess.

thepḥet 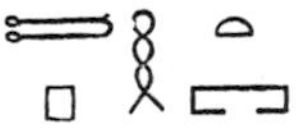 storehouse, cave, cavern, hole.

themes 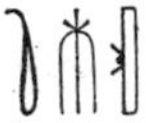 decree, writing.

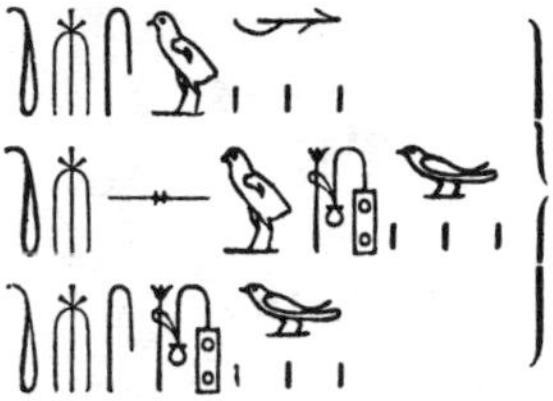 decrees.

then  this.

then 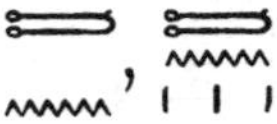 ye, you, your.

then  to be great, exalted, distinguished, worthy.

then  that.

Thena  a proper name.

Thenemi  the name of one of the Forty-two Judges in the Hall of Osiris.

Then-reṭ 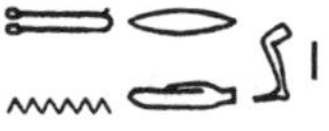 the name of one of the Forty-two Judges in the Hall of Osiris.

thentchat  throne chamber.

therem  to make to weep.

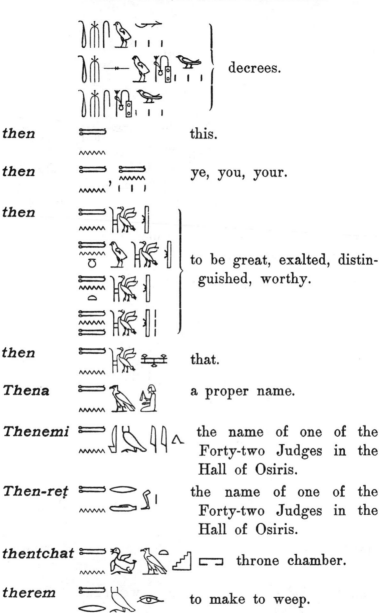

thert — a kind of tree.

theh — to attack.

theḥenu — unguent.

Theḥenu, *Teḥenu* — the name of a country, Libya.

theḥent — crystal (?), amber (?).

theḥen — to be yellow, or green (?); .

theḥeḥ — to cry out.

thes — to be strong, give orders.

thes — to support, lift up, raise; joy.

thesu, *thest* — supports, props.

thes	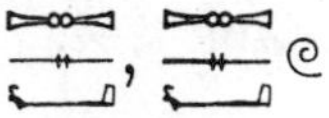	to tie in a knot, knot, fetter.
	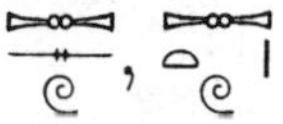	knot.
thes	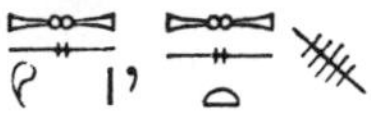	vertebra.
	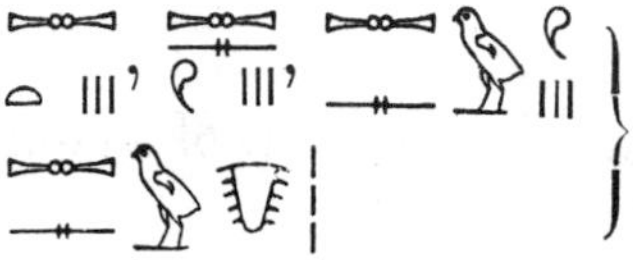	plur. of preceding.
thesu		word, speech, a saying, riddle.
		conversely.
thesȧu		to rule.
Thest-ur		a proper name.
thesem		dog, greyhound.
		plur. of preceding.
thesthes	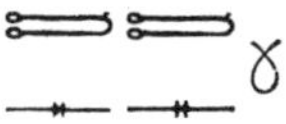	a garment.
Thekem		a proper name.

thet 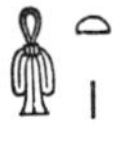 the name of a red stone, or faïence, amulet.

thet 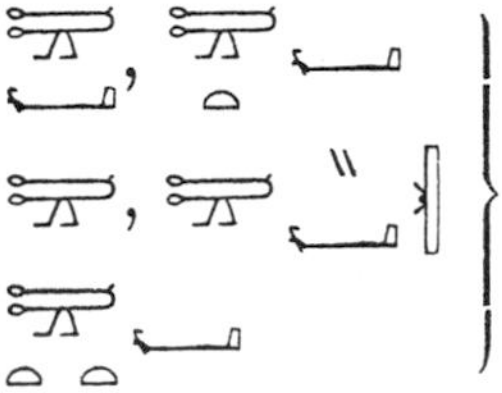 to take possession of, to seize, to carry off, conquer, acquire.

 seizers, robbers.

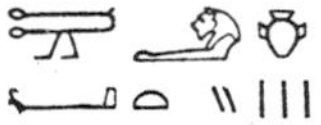 ravisher of hearts.

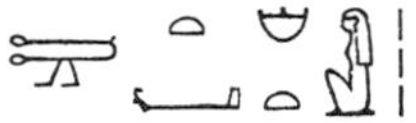 ravisher of women.

Thet-em-āua  the name of a plank or peg.

thetthet 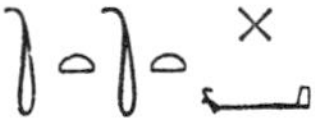 to destroy.

 TCH.

tcha  see .

tcha  safe, sound, in good case.

tcha  to split, to cut.

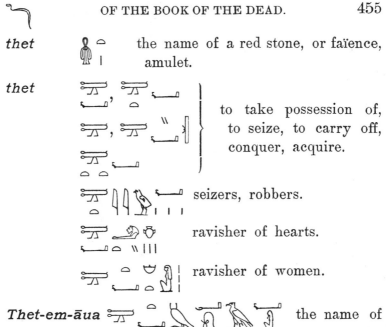

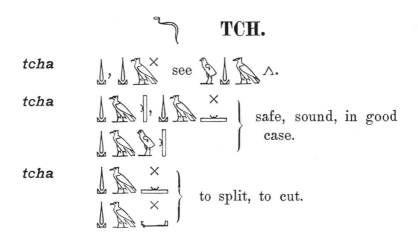

tcha abyss.

tcha to transport, to sail with something.

one who transports.

transport.

Great Boat.

tcha to set out, go forth.

tchaau hair.

tchau (?) birds.

tchat an official.

tcha to seize, grasp, rob, ravish.

robber.

plunder.

"wing-carrier", fan-bearer.

tcha male, husband, phallus.

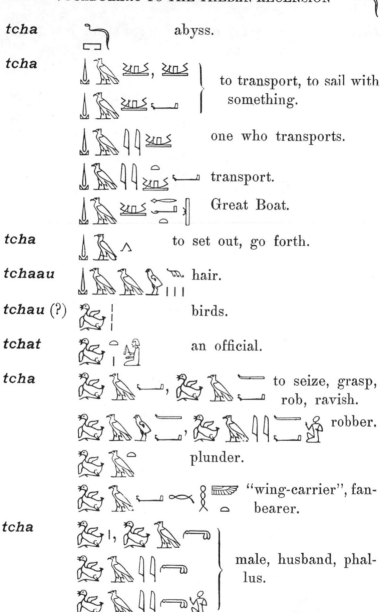

tchau  the west wind.

tchaui  Isis and Nephthys, the "two eagles".

tchaut  twenty;  twentieth.

tchafu  flames.

Tchafi  the souls of Horus and Rā.

tchai  fiend.

tchaitiu  slaughterers.

tcham  papyrus.

tchamet  coverings, garments.

tchart
tchat 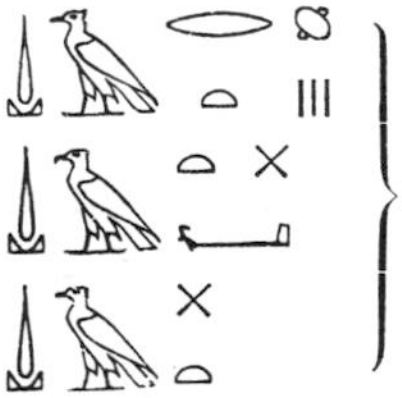 strength, strong.

tchat  measure.

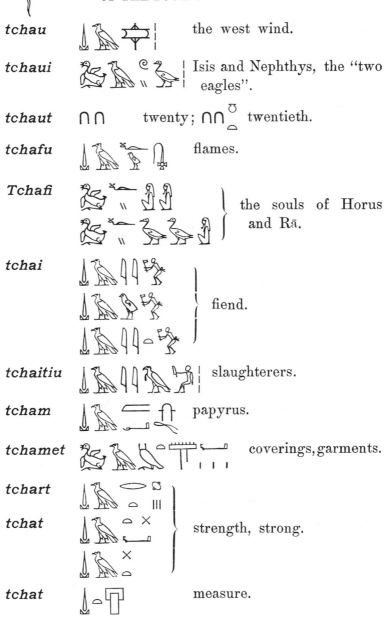

tchat 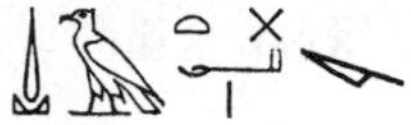 knife.

tchaut  foul things, filth.

tchaua 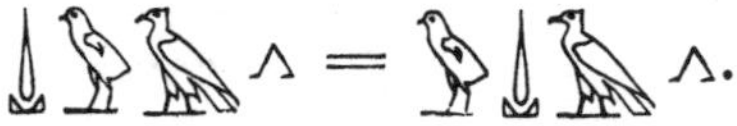

tchauu  amulet.

tchatcha  "head"; the name of the upper post.

tchatcha  head, top of anything, summit.

tchatchat 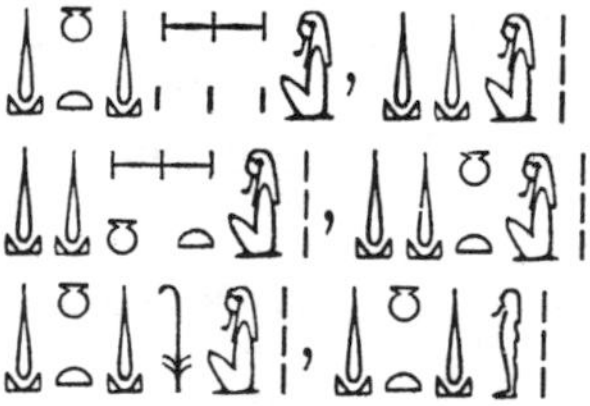 the "Heads", or "Chiefs", *i. e.*, the council of the gods in each great town of Egypt, and in the Other World. Every great god and goddess possessed a company or council of "Chiefs", *e. g.*, Osiris and Rā.

tchatchat  the domain of the cemetery in the hills; plur. 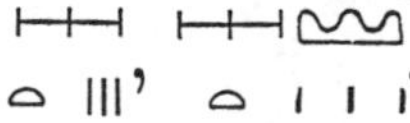

 the domain of eternity, *i. e.*, the grave.

 the holy domain, *i. e.*, the grave.

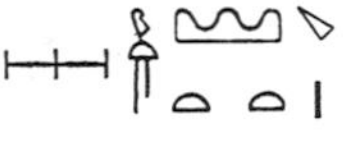 the domain of Ȧmenti, *i. e.*, the grave.

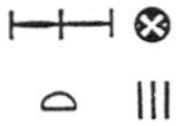 city boundaries.

tchāāu  staves.

tchābet  burning coals.

tchām  sceptre; plur. .

tchām  gold with a very large percentage of silver mixed with it, electrum.

tchār  to go about in search of, to pry into.

tchārȧ  fortress.

tchebā  to seal, make a reckoning (?).

tchebā  finger; plur. 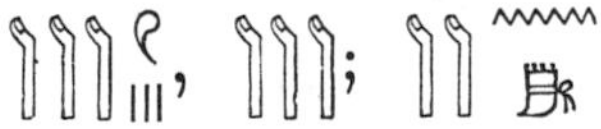  fingers which seize.

Tchebā-en-Sekri 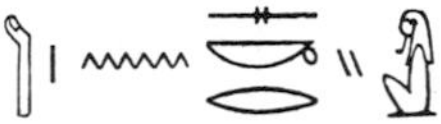  a proper name.

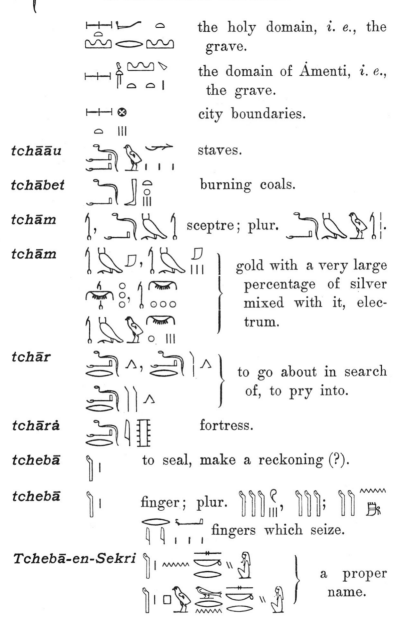

Tchebā-en-Shesmu a proper name.

Tchebāu-en-Ḥeru-semsu name of the paddles in the magic boat.

Tchebāui-en-tepu-ā-Rā a proper name.

tchefa the food of the dead, sepulchral offerings.

Tchefet, ***Tchefit*** a place and a goddess in the Elysian Fields.

tchefetch pupil of the eye.

pupil of the Utchat.

tchefetch to shed.

Tchen a proper name.

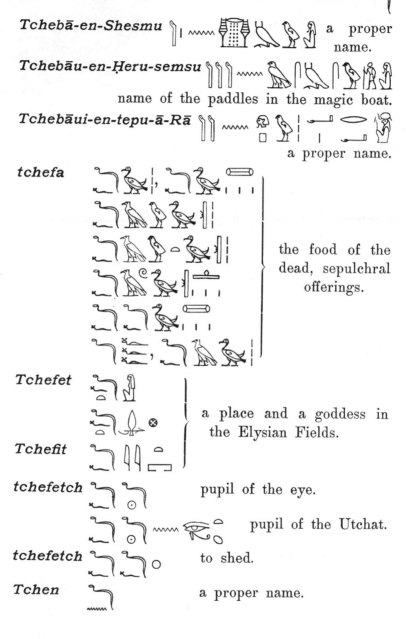

tchenḥu beams.

tchentchen to crush, break.

Tchentche[n] a proper name.

tcher to break.

tcher since, whilst, when.

tcher-ā straightway.

tcher-enti, *tcher-entet* since, because.

to the limit of, all, the whole.

tcher limit, boundary; plur. , boundless.

tcherȧu to constrain, fetter.

tcherȧ fort, stronghold.

tcherȧu heel, hoof.

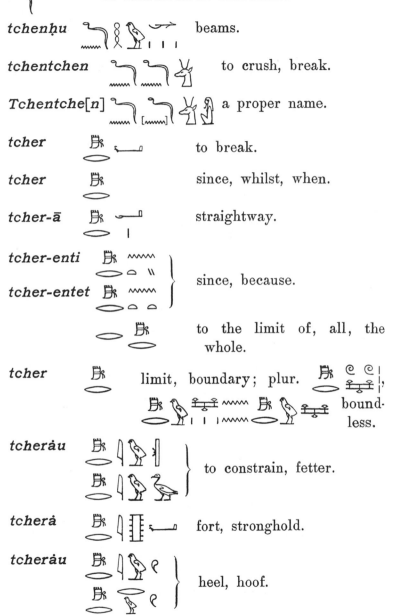

Tcheruu  the god of boundaries.

tcheru  a bird with a shrill voice.

tcheri 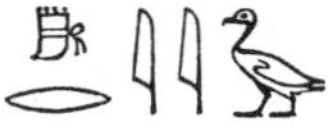

tcherit 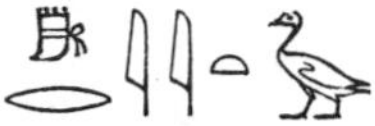 } a bird, the incarnation of Isis and Nephthys.

Tcherti  } Isis and Nephthys.

tcheres 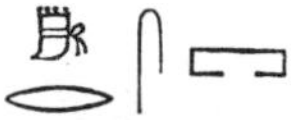 abode, chamber (?).

Tcheḥes  the name of a serpent.

tches  self; 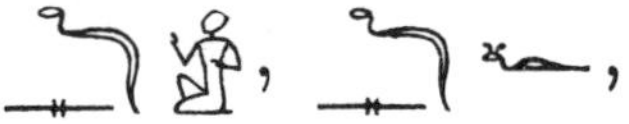 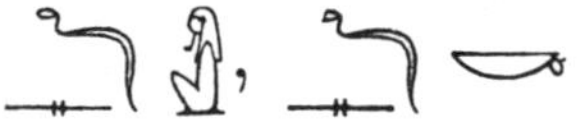 myself, himself. thyself,  themselves.

 with his own fingers.

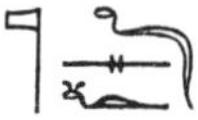 the god himself.

 with her own mouth.

tchesef  to snare.

 fowler.

tcheser 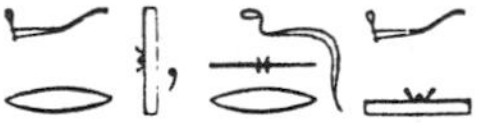 to make clear the ways, to put in good order, to be or make holy.

tcheseru  holy or beautiful things.

 glorious, splendid.

Tchesert  the beautiful mountain, *i. e.*, cemetery.

Tchesert  a proper name.

Tcheser-tep 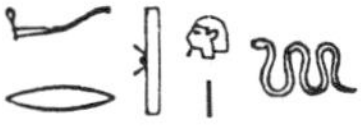 the name of one of the Forty-two Judges in the Hall of Osiris.

tchet 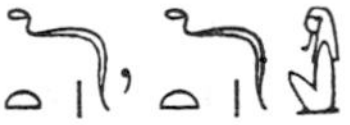 body, person;  my own self.

tchet  house, chamber; 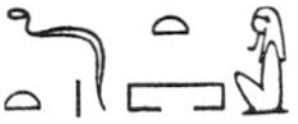 the Ṭuat(?).

tchetta  eternity, everlastingness.

 the god of eternity.

 eternity and everlastingness.

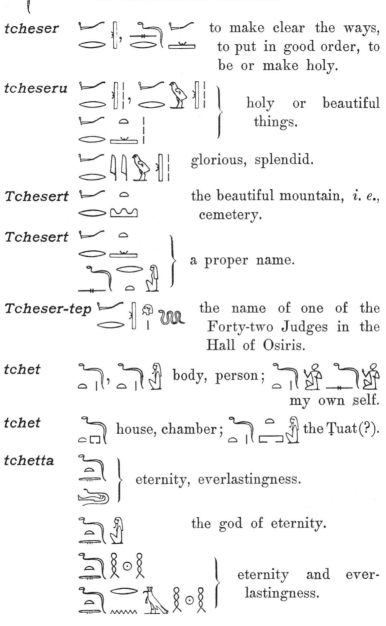

tcheṭ — to say, speak, declare, recite words, converse.

em tcheṭ — saying, introducing a quotation.

tcheṭu — to declare, speak, etc.

tcheṭ-t, *tcheṭu* — words, orders, things said.

tcheṭ meṭu — "shall be recited" [the following].

"another reading".

tcheṭ neḥes — negro speech, or language.

tcheṭfet — reptiles.

tcheṭḥu — a place of restraint.

tcheṭḥu — to shut in, imprison.

tchetch — an instrument or standard.

WORDS AND SIGNS OF UNCERTAIN READING.

 Chap. CXLV, IV, l. 16.

 Chap. CX, l. 5.

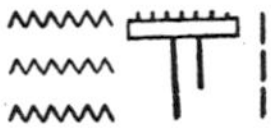 Chap. CX, l. 35.

 Chap. CXXXI, 5.

 Chap. XCIX, l. 38.

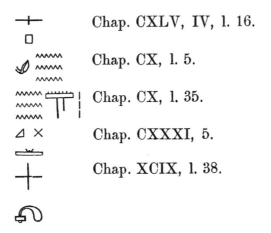

ENGLISH INDEX.

Testify 189.
Ṭeṭ, the 450.
Tet-Ṭemui 382.
Thanksgiving 225, 441.
That 206, 433, 452.
That which 42, 225.
The 139, 425.
Thebes 96.
Thee 406, 451.
Thefnut 451.
Theft 288.
Their 94, 351, 381.
Thekem, god 454.
Them 94, 225, 335, 337, 351, 381.
Themselves 462.
Then 235, 242, 435.
Thenemi 452.
Then-re 452.
There 32.
Therefore 235.
Therein 32.
These 28, 29, 30, 195, 209.
Thet amulet 455.
They 94, 225, 335, 351, 381.
Thigh 101, 149, 174, 292, 301, 313, 340, 451.
Thing, things 5, 300, 313, 320.
Things done 52.
Things said 464.
Think 51, 304, 407.
Thirst 21, 24.
Thirty 168.
This 141, 206, 209, 435, 452.
Those 192.
Thoth 9, 447; festival of 447; city of 105.
Thoth Ḥāpi 447.
Thou 219, 225, 406, 430, 451.
Thought 36, 407, 421.
Thousand 290.
Three 304.
Threshold 327.
Thrive 359.
Throat 57, 285, 290, 317, 396.
Throne 218, 319.
Throne-chamber 452.
Through 32.
Throughout 160.
Throw 290.
Thunder, thunder-storm 219, 417.
Thus 76.
Thy 219, 406, 425, 451.
Thyself 462.
Tiara 182, 209, 377.
Tidings 358.

THE BOOK OF BEASTS: Being a Translation from a Latin Bestiary of the Twelfth Century, T. H. White. Wonderful catalog real and fanciful beasts: manticore, griffin, phoenix, amphivius, jaculus, many more. White's witty erudite commentary on scientific, historical aspects. Fascinating glimpse of medieval mind. Illustrated. 296pp. 5⅜ × 8¼. (Available in U.S. only) 24609-4 Pa. $6.95

FRANK LLOYD WRIGHT: ARCHITECTURE AND NATURE With 160 Illustrations, Donald Hoffmann. Profusely illustrated study of influence of nature—especially prairie—on Wright's designs for Fallingwater, Robie House, Guggenheim Museum, other masterpieces. 96pp. 9¼ × 10¾. 25098-9 Pa. $7.95

FRANK LLOYD WRIGHT'S FALLINGWATER, Donald Hoffmann. Wright's famous waterfall house: planning and construction of organic idea. History of site, owners, Wright's personal involvement. Photographs of various stages of building. Preface by Edgar Kaufmann, Jr. 100 illustrations. 112pp. 9¼ × 10. 23671-4 Pa. $8.95

YEARS WITH FRANK LLOYD WRIGHT: Apprentice to Genius, Edgar Tafel. Insightful memoir by a former apprentice presents a revealing portrait of Wright the man, the inspired teacher, the greatest American architect. 372 black-and-white illustrations. Preface. Index. vi + 228pp. 8¼ × 11. 24801-1 Pa. $10.95

THE STORY OF KING ARTHUR AND HIS KNIGHTS, Howard Pyle. Enchanting version of King Arthur fable has delighted generations with imaginative narratives of exciting adventures and unforgettable illustrations by the author. 41 illustrations. xviii + 313pp. 6⅛ × 9¼. 21445-1 Pa. $6.95

THE GODS OF THE EGYPTIANS, E. A. Wallis Budge. Thorough coverage of numerous gods of ancient Egypt by foremost Egyptologist. Information on evolution of cults, rites and gods; the cult of Osiris; the Book of the Dead and its rites; the sacred animals and birds; Heaven and Hell; and more. 956pp. 6⅛ × 9¼. 22055-9, 22056-7 Pa., Two-vol. set $21.90

A THEOLOGICO-POLITICAL TREATISE, Benedict Spinoza. Also contains unfinished *Political Treatise*. Great classic on religious liberty, theory of government on common consent. R. Elwes translation. Total of 421pp. 5⅜ × 8½. 20249-6 Pa. $6.95

INCIDENTS OF TRAVEL IN CENTRAL AMERICA, CHIAPAS, AND YUCATAN, John L. Stephens. Almost single-handed discovery of Maya culture; exploration of ruined cities, monuments, temples; customs of Indians. 115 drawings. 892pp. 5⅜ × 8½. 22404-X, 22405-8 Pa., Two-vol. set $15.90

LOS CAPRICHOS, Francisco Goya. 80 plates of wild, grotesque monsters and caricatures. Prado manuscript included. 183pp. 6⅝ × 9⅝. 22384-1 Pa. $5.95

AUTOBIOGRAPHY: The Story of My Experiments with Truth, Mohandas K. Gandhi. Not hagiography, but Gandhi in his own words. Boyhood, legal studies, purification, the growth of the Satyagraha (nonviolent protest) movement. Critical, inspiring work of the man who freed India. 480pp. 5⅜ × 8½. (Available in U.S. only) 24593-4 Pa. $6.95

HOW TO WRITE, Gertrude Stein. Gertrude Stein claimed anyone could understand her unconventional writing—here are clues to help. Fascinating improvisations, language experiments, explanations illuminate Stein's craft and the art of writing. Total of 414pp. 4⅜ × 6⅜. 23144-5 Pa. $6.95

ADVENTURES AT SEA IN THE GREAT AGE OF SAIL: Five Firsthand Narratives, edited by Elliot Snow. Rare true accounts of exploration, whaling, shipwreck, fierce natives, trade, shipboard life, more. 33 illustrations. Introduction. 353pp. 5⅜ × 8½. 25177-2 Pa. $8.95

THE HERBAL OR GENERAL HISTORY OF PLANTS, John Gerard. Classic descriptions of about 2,850 plants—with over 2,700 illustrations—includes Latin and English names, physical descriptions, varieties, time and place of growth, more. 2,706 illustrations. xlv + 1,678pp. 8½ × 12¼. 23147-X Cloth. $75.00

DOROTHY AND THE WIZARD IN OZ, L. Frank Baum. Dorothy and the Wizard visit the center of the Earth, where people are vegetables, glass houses grow and Oz characters reappear. Classic sequel to *Wizard of Oz*. 256pp. 5⅜ × 8.
24714-7 Pa. $5.95

SONGS OF EXPERIENCE: Facsimile Reproduction with 26 Plates in Full Color, William Blake. This facsimile of Blake's original "Illuminated Book" reproduces 26 full-color plates from a rare 1826 edition. Includes "The Tyger," "London," "Holy Thursday," and other immortal poems. 26 color plates. Printed text of poems. 48pp. 5¼ × 7. 24636-1 Pa. $3.50

SONGS OF INNOCENCE, William Blake. The first and most popular of Blake's famous "Illuminated Books," in a facsimile edition reproducing all 31 brightly colored plates. Additional printed text of each poem. 64pp. 5¼ × 7.
22764-2 Pa. $3.50

PRECIOUS STONES, Max Bauer. Classic, thorough study of diamonds, rubies, emeralds, garnets, etc.: physical character, occurrence, properties, use, similar topics. 20 plates, 8 in color. 94 figures. 659pp. 6⅛ × 9¼.
21910-0, 21911-9 Pa., Two-vol. set $15.90

ENCYCLOPEDIA OF VICTORIAN NEEDLEWORK, S. F. A. Caulfeild and Blanche Saward. Full, precise descriptions of stitches, techniques for dozens of needlecrafts—most exhaustive reference of its kind. Over 800 figures. Total of 679pp. 8⅛ × 11. Two volumes. Vol. 1 22800-2 Pa. $11.95
Vol. 2 22801-0 Pa. $11.95

THE MARVELOUS LAND OF OZ, L. Frank Baum. Second Oz book, the Scarecrow and Tin Woodman are back with hero named Tip, Oz magic. 136 illustrations. 287pp. 5⅜ × 8½. 20692-0 Pa. $5.95

WILD FOWL DECOYS, Joel Barber. Basic book on the subject, by foremost authority and collector. Reveals history of decoy making and rigging, place in American culture, different kinds of decoys, how to make them, and how to use them. 140 plates. 156pp. 7⅞ × 10¾. 20011-6 Pa. $8.95

HISTORY OF LACE, Mrs. Bury Palliser. Definitive, profusely illustrated chronicle of lace from earliest times to late 19th century. Laces of Italy, Greece, England, France, Belgium, etc. Landmark of needlework scholarship. 266 illustrations. 672pp. 6⅛ × 9¼. 24742-2 Pa. $14.95

ILLUSTRATED GUIDE TO SHAKER FURNITURE, Robert Meader. All furniture and appurtenances, with much on unknown local styles. 235 photos. 146pp. 9 × 12. 22819-3 Pa. $8.95

WHALE SHIPS AND WHALING: A Pictorial Survey, George Francis Dow. Over 200 vintage engravings, drawings, photographs of barks, brigs, cutters, other vessels. Also harpoons, lances, whaling guns, many other artifacts. Comprehensive text by foremost authority. 207 black-and-white illustrations. 288pp. 6 × 9. 24808-9 Pa. $8.95

THE BERTRAMS, Anthony Trollope. Powerful portrayal of blind self-will and thwarted ambition includes one of Trollope's most heartrending love stories. 497pp. 5⅜ × 8½. 25119-5 Pa. $9.95

ADVENTURES WITH A HAND LENS, Richard Headstrom. Clearly written guide to observing and studying flowers and grasses, fish scales, moth and insect wings, egg cases, buds, feathers, seeds, leaf scars, moss, molds, ferns, common crystals, etc.—all with an ordinary, inexpensive magnifying glass. 209 exact line drawings aid in your discoveries. 220pp. 5⅜ × 8½. 23330-8 Pa. $4.95

RODIN ON ART AND ARTISTS, Auguste Rodin. Great sculptor's candid, wide-ranging comments on meaning of art; great artists; relation of sculpture to poetry, painting, music; philosophy of life, more. 76 superb black-and-white illustrations of Rodin's sculpture, drawings and prints. 119pp. 8⅜ × 11¼. 24487-3 Pa. $7.95

FIFTY CLASSIC FRENCH FILMS, 1912–1982: A Pictorial Record, Anthony Slide. Memorable stills from Grand Illusion, Beauty and the Beast, Hiroshima, Mon Amour, many more. Credits, plot synopses, reviews, etc. 160pp. 8¼ × 11. 25256-6 Pa. $11.95

THE PRINCIPLES OF PSYCHOLOGY, William James. Famous long course complete, unabridged. Stream of thought, time perception, memory, experimental methods; great work decades ahead of its time. 94 figures. 1,391pp. 5⅜ × 8½. 20381-6, 20382-4 Pa., Two-vol. set $23.90

BODIES IN A BOOKSHOP, R. T. Campbell. Challenging mystery of blackmail and murder with ingenious plot and superbly drawn characters. In the best tradition of British suspense fiction. 192pp. 5⅜ × 8½. 24720-1 Pa. $3.95

CALLAS: PORTRAIT OF A PRIMA DONNA, George Jellinek. Renowned commentator on the musical scene chronicles incredible career and life of the most controversial, fascinating, influential operatic personality of our time. 64 black-and-white photographs. 416pp. 5⅜ × 8¼. 25047-4 Pa. $8.95

GEOMETRY, RELATIVITY AND THE FOURTH DIMENSION, Rudolph Rucker. Exposition of fourth dimension, concepts of relativity as Flatland characters continue adventures. Popular, easily followed yet accurate, profound. 141 illustrations. 133pp. 5⅜ × 8½. 23400-2 Pa. $4.95

HOUSEHOLD STORIES BY THE BROTHERS GRIMM, with pictures by Walter Crane. 53 classic stories—Rumpelstiltskin, Rapunzel, Hansel and Gretel, the Fisherman and his Wife, Snow White, Tom Thumb, Sleeping Beauty, Cinderella, and so much more—lavishly illustrated with original 19th century drawings. 114 illustrations. x + 269pp. 5⅜ × 8½. 21080-4 Pa. $4.95

SUNDIALS, Albert Waugh. Far and away the best, most thorough coverage of ideas, mathematics concerned, types, construction, adjusting anywhere. Over 100 illustrations. 230pp. 5⅜ × 8½. 22947-5 Pa. $4.95

PICTURE HISTORY OF THE NORMANDIE: With 190 Illustrations, Frank O. Braynard. Full story of legendary French ocean liner: Art Deco interiors, design innovations, furnishings, celebrities, maiden voyage, tragic fire, much more. Extensive text. 144pp. 8⅞ × 11¾. 25257-4 Pa. $10.95

THE FIRST AMERICAN COOKBOOK: A Facsimile of "American Cookery," 1796, Amelia Simmons. Facsimile of the first American-written cookbook published in the United States contains authentic recipes for colonial favorites—pumpkin pudding, winter squash pudding, spruce beer, Indian slapjacks, and more. Introductory Essay and Glossary of colonial cooking terms. 80pp. 5⅜ × 8½. 24710-4 Pa. $3.50

101 PUZZLES IN THOUGHT AND LOGIC, C. R. Wylie, Jr. Solve murders and robberies, find out which fishermen are liars, how a blind man could possibly identify a color—purely by your own reasoning! 107pp. 5⅜ × 8½. 20367-0 Pa. $2.50

THE BOOK OF WORLD-FAMOUS MUSIC—CLASSICAL, POPULAR AND FOLK, James J. Fuld. Revised and enlarged republication of landmark work in musico-bibliography. Full information about nearly 1,000 songs and compositions including first lines of music and lyrics. New supplement. Index. 800pp. 5⅜ × 8¼. 24857-7 Pa. $15.95

ANTHROPOLOGY AND MODERN LIFE, Franz Boas. Great anthropologist's classic treatise on race and culture. Introduction by Ruth Bunzel. Only inexpensive paperback edition. 255pp. 5⅜ × 8½. 25245-0 Pa. $6.95

THE TALE OF PETER RABBIT, Beatrix Potter. The inimitable Peter's terrifying adventure in Mr. McGregor's garden, with all 27 wonderful, full-color Potter illustrations. 55pp. 4¼ × 5½. (Available in U.S. only) 22827-4 Pa. $1.75

THREE PROPHETIC SCIENCE FICTION NOVELS, H. G. Wells. *When the Sleeper Wakes, A Story of the Days to Come* and *The Time Machine* (full version). 335pp. 5⅜ × 8½. (Available in U.S. only) 20605-X Pa. $6.95

APICIUS COOKERY AND DINING IN IMPERIAL ROME, edited and translated by Joseph Dommers Vehling. Oldest known cookbook in existence offers readers a clear picture of what foods Romans ate, how they prepared them, etc. 49 illustrations. 301pp. 6⅛ × 9¼. 23563-7 Pa. $7.95

SHAKESPEARE LEXICON AND QUOTATION DICTIONARY, Alexander Schmidt. Full definitions, locations, shades of meaning of every word in plays and poems. More than 50,000 exact quotations. 1,485pp. 6½ × 9¼. 22726-X, 22727-8 Pa., Two-vol. set $29.90

THE WORLD'S GREAT SPEECHES, edited by Lewis Copeland and Lawrence W. Lamm. Vast collection of 278 speeches from Greeks to 1970. Powerful and effective models; unique look at history. 842pp. 5⅜ × 8½. 20468-5 Pa. $11.95

A CONCISE HISTORY OF PHOTOGRAPHY: Third Revised Edition, Helmut Gernsheim. Best one-volume history—camera obscura, photochemistry, daguerreotypes, evolution of cameras, film, more. Also artistic aspects—landscape, portraits, fine art, etc. 281 black-and-white photographs. 26 in color. 176pp. 8⅜ × 11¼. 25128-4 Pa. $13.95

THE DORÉ BIBLE ILLUSTRATIONS, Gustave Doré. 241 detailed plates from the Bible: the Creation scenes, Adam and Eve, Flood, Babylon, battle sequences, life of Jesus, etc. Each plate is accompanied by the verses from the King James version of the Bible. 241pp. 9 × 12. 23004-X Pa. $9.95

HUGGER-MUGGER IN THE LOUVRE, Elliot Paul. Second Homer Evans mystery-comedy. Theft at the Louvre involves sleuth in hilarious, madcap caper. "A knockout."—Books. 336pp. 5⅜ × 8½. 25185-3 Pa. $5.95

FLATLAND, E. A. Abbott. Intriguing and enormously popular science-fiction classic explores the complexities of trying to survive as a two-dimensional being in a three-dimensional world. Amusingly illustrated by the author. 16 illustrations. 103pp. 5⅜ × 8½. 20001-9 Pa. $2.50

THE HISTORY OF THE LEWIS AND CLARK EXPEDITION, Meriwether Lewis and William Clark, edited by Elliott Coues. Classic edition of Lewis and Clark's day-by-day journals that later became the basis for U.S. claims to Oregon and the West. Accurate and invaluable geographical, botanical, biological, meteorological and anthropological material. Total of 1,508pp. 5⅜ × 8½. 21268-8, 21269-6, 21270-X Pa. Three-vol. set $26.85

LANGUAGE, TRUTH AND LOGIC, Alfred J. Ayer. Famous, clear introduction to Vienna, Cambridge schools of Logical Positivism. Role of philosophy, elimination of metaphysics, nature of analysis, etc. 160pp. 5⅜ × 8½. (Available in U.S. and Canada only) 20010-8 Pa. $3.95

MATHEMATICS FOR THE NONMATHEMATICIAN, Morris Kline. Detailed, college-level treatment of mathematics in cultural and historical context, with numerous exercises. For liberal arts students. Preface. Recommended Reading Lists. Tables. Index. Numerous black-and-white figures. xvi + 641pp. 5⅜ × 8½. 24823-2 Pa. $11.95

HANDBOOK OF PICTORIAL SYMBOLS, Rudolph Modley. 3,250 signs and symbols, many systems in full; official or heavy commercial use. Arranged by subject. Most in Pictorial Archive series. 143pp. 8⅛ × 11. 23357-X Pa. $6.95

INCIDENTS OF TRAVEL IN YUCATAN, John L. Stephens. Classic (1843) exploration of jungles of Yucatan, looking for evidences of Maya civilization. Travel adventures, Mexican and Indian culture, etc. Total of 669pp. 5⅜ × 8½. 20926-1, 20927-X Pa., Two-vol. set $11.90

DEGAS: An Intimate Portrait, Ambroise Vollard. Charming, anecdotal memoir by famous art dealer of one of the greatest 19th-century French painters. 14 black-and-white illustrations. Introduction by Harold L. Van Doren. 96pp. 5⅜ × 8½.
25131-4 Pa. $4.95

PERSONAL NARRATIVE OF A PILGRIMAGE TO ALMANDINAH AND MECCAH, Richard Burton. Great travel classic by remarkably colorful personality. Burton, disguised as a Moroccan, visited sacred shrines of Islam, narrowly escaping death. 47 illustrations. 959pp. 5⅜ × 8½. 21217-3, 21218-1 Pa., Two-vol. set $19.90

PHRASE AND WORD ORIGINS, A. H. Holt. Entertaining, reliable, modern study of more than 1,200 colorful words, phrases, origins and histories. Much unexpected information. 254pp. 5⅜ × 8½. 20758-7 Pa. $5.95

THE RED THUMB MARK, R. Austin Freeman. In this first Dr. Thorndyke case, the great scientific detective draws fascinating conclusions from the nature of a single fingerprint. Exciting story, authentic science. 320pp. 5⅜ × 8½. (Available in U.S. only) 25210-8 Pa. $6.95

AN EGYPTIAN HIEROGLYPHIC DICTIONARY, E. A. Wallis Budge. Monumental work containing about 25,000 words or terms that occur in texts ranging from 3000 B.C. to 600 A.D. Each entry consists of a transliteration of the word, the word in hieroglyphs, and the meaning in English. 1,314pp. 6⅞ × 10.
23615-3, 23616-1 Pa., Two-vol. set $31.90

THE COMPLEAT STRATEGYST: Being a Primer on the Theory of Games of Strategy, J. D. Williams. Highly entertaining classic describes, with many illustrated examples, how to select best strategies in conflict situations. Prefaces. Appendices. xvi + 268pp. 5⅜ × 8½. 25101-2 Pa. $5.95

THE ROAD TO OZ, L. Frank Baum. Dorothy meets the Shaggy Man, little Button-Bright and the Rainbow's beautiful daughter in this delightful trip to the magical Land of Oz. 272pp. 5⅜ × 8. 25208-6 Pa. $5.95

POINT AND LINE TO PLANE, Wassily Kandinsky. Seminal exposition of role of point, line, other elements in non-objective painting. Essential to understanding 20th-century art. 127 illustrations. 192pp. 6½ × 9¼. 23808-3 Pa. $5.95

LADY ANNA, Anthony Trollope. Moving chronicle of Countess Lovel's bitter struggle to win for herself and daughter Anna their rightful rank and fortune—perhaps at cost of sanity itself. 384pp. 5⅜ × 8½. 24669-8 Pa. $8.95

EGYPTIAN MAGIC, E. A. Wallis Budge. Sums up all that is known about magic in Ancient Egypt: the role of magic in controlling the gods, powerful amulets that warded off evil spirits, scarabs of immortality, use of wax images, formulas and spells, the secret name, much more. 253pp. 5⅜ × 8½. 22681-6 Pa. $4.50

THE DANCE OF SIVA, Ananda Coomaraswamy. Preeminent authority unfolds the vast metaphysic of India: the revelation of her art, conception of the universe, social organization, etc. 27 reproductions of art masterpieces. 192pp. 5⅜ × 8½.
24817-8 Pa. $5.95

CHRISTMAS CUSTOMS AND TRADITIONS, Clement A. Miles. Origin, evolution, significance of religious, secular practices. Caroling, gifts, yule logs, much more. Full, scholarly yet fascinating; non-sectarian. 400pp. 5⅜ × 8½.
23354-5 Pa. $6.95

THE HUMAN FIGURE IN MOTION, Eadweard Muybridge. More than 4,500 stopped-action photos, in action series, showing undraped men, women, children jumping, lying down, throwing, sitting, wrestling, carrying, etc. 390pp. 7⅞ × 10⅝.
20204-6 Cloth. $21.95

THE MAN WHO WAS THURSDAY, Gilbert Keith Chesterton. Witty, fast-paced novel about a club of anarchists in turn-of-the-century London. Brilliant social, religious, philosophical speculations. 128pp. 5⅜ × 8½. 25121-7 Pa. $3.95

A CEZANNE SKETCHBOOK: Figures, Portraits, Landscapes and Still Lifes, Paul Cezanne. Great artist experiments with tonal effects, light, mass, other qualities in over 100 drawings. A revealing view of developing master painter, precursor of Cubism. 102 black-and-white illustrations. 144pp. 8¾ × 6⅜. 24790-2 Pa. $5.95

AN ENCYCLOPEDIA OF BATTLES: Accounts of Over 1,560 Battles from 1479 B.C. to the Present, David Eggenberger. Presents essential details of every major battle in recorded history, from the first battle of Megiddo in 1479 B.C. to Grenada in 1984. List of Battle Maps. New Appendix covering the years 1967–1984. Index. 99 illustrations. 544pp. 6½ × 9¼. 24913-1 Pa. $14.95

AN ETYMOLOGICAL DICTIONARY OF MODERN ENGLISH, Ernest Weekley. Richest, fullest work, by foremost British lexicographer. Detailed word histories. Inexhaustible. Total of 856pp. 6½ × 9¼.
21873-2, 21874-0 Pa., Two-vol. set $17.00

WEBSTER'S AMERICAN MILITARY BIOGRAPHIES, edited by Robert McHenry. Over 1,000 figures who shaped 3 centuries of American military history. Detailed biographies of Nathan Hale, Douglas MacArthur, Mary Hallaren, others. Chronologies of engagements, more. Introduction. Addenda. 1,033 entries in alphabetical order. xi + 548pp. 6½ × 9¼. (Available in U.S. only)
24758-9 Pa. $13.95

LIFE IN ANCIENT EGYPT, Adolf Erman. Detailed older account, with much not in more recent books: domestic life, religion, magic, medicine, commerce, and whatever else needed for complete picture. Many illustrations. 597pp. 5⅜ × 8½.
22632-8 Pa. $8.95

HISTORIC COSTUME IN PICTURES, Braun & Schneider. Over 1,450 costumed figures shown, covering a wide variety of peoples: kings, emperors, nobles, priests, servants, soldiers, scholars, townsfolk, peasants, merchants, courtiers, cavaliers, and more. 256pp. 8⅜ × 11¼. 23150-X Pa. $9.95

THE NOTEBOOKS OF LEONARDO DA VINCI, edited by J. P. Richter. Extracts from manuscripts reveal great genius; on painting, sculpture, anatomy, sciences, geography, etc. Both Italian and English. 186 ms. pages reproduced, plus 500 additional drawings, including studies for *Last Supper, Sforza* monument, etc. 860pp. 7⅞ × 10¾. (Available in U.S. only) 22572-0, 22573-9 Pa., Two-vol. set $31.90

CATALOG OF DOVER BOOKS

SIR HARRY HOTSPUR OF HUMBLETHWAITE, Anthony Trollope. Incisive, unconventional psychological study of a conflict between a wealthy baronet, his idealistic daughter, and their scapegrace cousin. The 1870 novel in its first inexpensive edition in years. 250pp. 5⅜ × 8½. 24953-0 Pa. $5.95

LASERS AND HOLOGRAPHY, Winston E. Kock. Sound introduction to burgeoning field, expanded (1981) for second edition. Wave patterns, coherence, lasers, diffraction, zone plates, properties of holograms, recent advances. 84 illustrations. 160pp. 5⅜ × 8¼. (Except in United Kingdom) 24041-X Pa. $3.95

INTRODUCTION TO ARTIFICIAL INTELLIGENCE: SECOND, ENLARGED EDITION, Philip C. Jackson, Jr. Comprehensive survey of artificial intelligence—the study of how machines (computers) can be made to act intelligently. Includes introductory and advanced material. Extensive notes updating the main text. 132 black-and-white illustrations. 512pp. 5⅜ × 8½. 24864-X Pa. $8.95

HISTORY OF INDIAN AND INDONESIAN ART, Ananda K. Coomaraswamy. Over 400 illustrations illuminate classic study of Indian art from earliest Harappa finds to early 20th century. Provides philosophical, religious and social insights. 304pp. 6⅝ × 9⅝. 25005-9 Pa. $9.95

THE GOLEM, Gustav Meyrink. Most famous supernatural novel in modern European literature, set in Ghetto of Old Prague around 1890. Compelling story of mystical experiences, strange transformations, profound terror. 13 black-and-white illustrations. 224pp. 5⅜ × 8½. (Available in U.S. only) 25025-3 Pa. $6.95

PICTORIAL ENCYCLOPEDIA OF HISTORIC ARCHITECTURAL PLANS, DETAILS AND ELEMENTS: With 1,880 Line Drawings of Arches, Domes, Doorways, Facades, Gables, Windows, etc., John Theodore Haneman. Sourcebook of inspiration for architects, designers, others. Bibliography. Captions. 141pp. 9 × 12. 24605-1 Pa. $7.95

BENCHLEY LOST AND FOUND, Robert Benchley. Finest humor from early 30's, about pet peeves, child psychologists, post office and others. Mostly unavailable elsewhere. 73 illustrations by Peter Arno and others. 183pp. 5⅜ × 8½. 22410-4 Pa. $4.95

ERTÉ GRAPHICS, Erté. Collection of striking color graphics: *Seasons, Alphabet, Numerals, Aces* and *Precious Stones.* 50 plates, including 4 on covers. 48pp. 9⅜ × 12¼. 23580-7 Pa. $7.95

THE JOURNAL OF HENRY D. THOREAU, edited by Bradford Torrey, F. H. Allen. Complete reprinting of 14 volumes, 1837–61, over two million words; the sourcebooks for *Walden,* etc. Definitive. All original sketches, plus 75 photographs. 1,804pp. 8½ × 12¼. 20312-3, 20313-1 Cloth., Two-vol. set $120.00

CASTLES: THEIR CONSTRUCTION AND HISTORY, Sidney Toy. Traces castle development from ancient roots. Nearly 200 photographs and drawings illustrate moats, keeps, baileys, many other features. Caernarvon, Dover Castles, Hadrian's Wall, Tower of London, dozens more. 256pp. 5⅜ × 8¼. 24898-4 Pa. $6.95